PERSPECTIVES
ON
CHRISTOLOGY

Paul King Jewett

Photo by David Pavol

Essays in Honor of Paul K. Jewett

Perspectives On Christology

Marguerite Shuster and Richard Muller, editors

ZondervanPublishingHouse
Academic and Professional Books
Grand Rapids, Michigan

A Division of HarperCollins*Publishers*

Perspectives on Christology: Essays in Honor of Paul K. Jewett
Copyright © 1991 by Marguerite Shuster and Richard A. Muller

Requests for information should be addressed to:
Zondervan Publishing House
Academic and Professional Books
1415 Lake Drive S.E.
Grand Rapids, Michigan 49506

Library of Congress Cataloging-in-Publication Data

Perspectives on Christology : essays in honor of Paul K. Jewett /
  edited by Marguerite Shuster and Richard A. Muller.
      p.   cm.
  Includes bibliographical references and indexes.
  ISBN 0-310-39731-6
  1. Jesus Christ—Person and offices.   2. Jesus Christ—History of
doctrines.   I. Jewett, Paul King.   II. Shuster, Marguerite.   III. Muller,
Richard A. (Richard Alfred), 1948-
  BT202.P435   1991
  232—dc20   90-48201
                                                                          CIP

Edited by L.G. Goss

Printed in the United States of America

91 92 93 94 95 96 97 98 / CH / 10 9 8 7 6 5 4 3 2 1

Table of Contents

Paul K. Jewett: A Personal Remembrance   vii
  Dolores Loeding

Paul K. Jewett: An Appreciation   xi
  Robert P. Meye

Biographical Note   xvii

Introduction   xxi

Scripture and Christology

The "Christ" of the Gospel: A Lesson from Mark's Christology   3
  Robert A. Guelich

Paul's Christology and Jewish Monotheism   19
  Donald A. Hagner

Scripture and Christology: A Protestant Look at the Work
  of the Pontifical Biblical Commission   39
  Colin Brown

The Person of Christ: Historical Perspectives

The Reformers and the Humanity of Christ   79
  Geoffrey W. Bromiley

Tradition and Innovation: The Use of Theodoret's *Eranistes*
  in Martin Chemnitz' *De Duabus Naturis in Christo*   105
  Robert A. Kelly

The All-Sufficient Jesus in Heinrich Müller's *Geistliche
  Erquickstunden* (*Moments of Spiritual Refreshment*)   127
  Gary R. Sattler

The Christological Problem as Addressed by Friedrich
  Schleiermacher: A Dogmatic Query   141
  Richard A. Muller

The Person of Christ: Contemporary and Literary Views

Psychological Evaluations of Jesus 165
Vernon Grounds

Jesus' Humanity and Ours in the Theology of Karl Barth 179
Elouise Renich Fraser

The Temptation, Sinlessness, and Sympathy of Jesus:
Another Look at the Dilemma of Hebrews 4:15 197
Marguerite Shuster

The Order of Temptations in *Paradise Regained*:
Implications for Christology 211
Anthony C. Yu

Ethics and Christology

The Sort of Friend We Have in Jesus 231
Lewis B. Smedes

Anselm and the Modern Mind 243
M. Eugene Osterhaven

Jesus and Political Authority 253
Richard J. Mouw

The Beatitudes of the Apocalypse: Eschatology and Ethics 269
Virgil P. Cruz

A Bibliography of Paul K. Jewett's Writings 285

Scripture Index 289

Subject Index 295

Paul K. Jewett: A Personal Remembrance

Dolores Loeding

Faculty Secretary
Fuller Theological Seminary

"But what is Dr. Jewett really like?"—away from the lectern and doctrines of election, imputation, transubstantiation—is a question often posed by curious, intimidated students, a question which a few personal remembrances and observations of an extended working relationship might elucidate but could never answer completely. The students may be at least half right in thinking there is something a bit enigmatic about him.

Long before computers and printers with microspace justification came on the scene, there was Professor Jewett, originator of justified margins in endlessly reworked double-column syllabi, revealing in his standards an unmistakable perfectionism and leaving a trail marked by gallons of correction fluid and frustrated, sometimes tearful (re)typists. As secretary to the dean of faculty, I became the reluctant liaison in a peacekeeping mission. Never accused of being a diplomat, I muddled early on into an uneasy truce that would progress into a treasured friendship.

It has been through the years a friendship stoked, and sometimes soothed, by a drawer regularly stocked with chocolate, shared with a secretary who must first pay her dues by helping to reduce the inventory of whole wheat fig bars and carob cookies, all supplied by a health-food addict with a Swiss chocolate addiction—an epicurean phenomenon not to be questioned, only enjoyed. The drawer rests on a one-of-a-kind, round, oak desk built by Jewett's father, measuring fourteen and a half feet in diameter and enclosing a center well to accommodate an office chair—a chair holding what must be a track record for going-in-circles mileage.

While I often included The Desk when giving students guided tours of the Fuller campus, I realize now that the sight of this imposing physical source of the dreaded multiple-choice exams did nothing to relieve the somewhat daunting image of their perpetrator. In any case, any building or room large enough to contain The Desk fell automatically under Jewett's jurisdiction. Destruction-construction ferment on campus demanded frequent relocations—from parlors of early Pasadena mansions with stained glass windows and inlaid floors, to the lower regions of Payton Hall, with overhead hot water pipes and concrete floor for monastic ambiance. All of this he endured, outwardly, in a triumph of grace.

This nomadic life-style has been made more tolerable by a notable scarcity of books among his possessions. His announced theory is that library buildings—and the offices of colleagues who readily succumb to book-buying binges—are places where collections belong. Provided, of course, that all are available for his use! My earlier employer, bibliophile Dr. Wilbur Smith, while aghast at what he considered an attitude bordering on sacrilege, nevertheless was a major participant in the "lending library" scheme. But the built-in bookcases soon filled with evidences of varied interests: old railroad schedules (Jewett is a steam engine buff); a sinister-looking wasp's nest; memorabilia from the Jewett family in America genealogy, dating back to 1633; odd rock formations; and hymn books of every description and ecclesiastical provenance. (All his classes begin with a hymn taken from his own popular bulletin, "Hymns with Annotations.")

His expertise in musicology surpasses his skill in handwriting and spelling, however. "If you cannot write legibly and spell, you will never be more in life than a ditch-digger": this pronouncement from a fifth-grade teacher comes to mind as I share with the word processing department a creative theological education received through guessing what Professor Jewett is supposed to be saying and making the handwriting, and then the spelling, conform. "If I learned to write, they would know I could not spell," he proclaims in mock self-defense. The finished product always reveals a vocabulary and style seldom surpassed in profundity and clarity.

Another aspect of a many-faceted character shows in his delight in annually "confiscating" persimmons, by light of moon and flashlight, from several trees on school property, from atop stacked-up benches and tables, with his own fruit plucker, aided and abetted by a not entirely averse secretary and one of the coeditors of this volume! Even a hovering police helicopter could not deter an operation carried out without benefit of faculty-trustee action.

Recently a reporter, commenting on the death of Bart Giamatti (ex-Yale president turned baseball commissioner), remarked on the unusual affinity of baseball and the intellectual. His theory was that while the academician lives in a world of abstracts, baseball is a refreshing yet technical game of absolutes—winners and losers. Dr. Jewett shares this penchant for and knowledge of the game with many colleagues, to the delight of a secretary who is privy to his arm-chair managing. An unforgettable experience was an afternoon at a Dodger game with Dr. Jewett and "Babe" Herman, an old-time Dodger great and a member of Dr. Jewett's Sunday school class. No second-guessing that day, as we listened to the vocal guru of the game—though it did not keep us from "reviewing" the expert later.

Other remembrances of this rather enigmatic personality include his wry, dry sense of humor, puncturing all pomposity—the product of a relentlessly active mind combined with a dose of deviltry. It incorporates an ability to laugh at his own eccentricities—and I hope it will extend to this "remembrance"! For making him an impeccable dresser (except when tending his rose garden), his wife Christine deserves the credit; but his own insistence upon suspenders long before they were in fashion is likely the sartorial statement of an independent spirit. He was, and is, in the office daily—a quaint behavior for professors generally—with door open (unless committee organizers are lurking about) to students who, after timid forays, find him a caring personal counselor and patient debater of matters theological. These traits and his influence on lives are confirmed by letters of appreciation from older and wiser alumni who as students were not always enchanted by precise study requirements and tough grading. So a statement such as, ". . . wish I could do it all over again," becomes an expression of true gratitude—possibly tempered by short memory?

Many members of the Seminary and church community have also seen evidences of a pastoral heart, having been recipients of a visit from Dr. Jewett while they were hospitalized. I personally recall waking from anesthetic stupor to hear him assuring me that I did not have to report for work the following day, and then, in true form, turning to the nurse to discuss the demerits of my pillow and the possibility of procuring another one. He has always wanted to make the world a little better, out of his commitment to Jesus Christ.

Paul K. Jewett: An Appreciation

Robert P. Meye

Dean
Fuller Theological Seminary

I am pleased to say that, even though I am a dean, some of my best friends are faculty members. What is more, some of those friends belong to the faculty I serve! I am grateful to God that one of those good friends has done his good theological work just around the corner from my own office for the last thirteen years. Of course I am speaking of Paul King Jewett, whom we wish to honor by means of this *Festschrift*, and whom I am delighted to honor as a former professor from my own seminary days at Fuller and then, in these latter years, as a faculty colleague and friend.

When I think of systematic theologians today, it is easy to think of Paul King Jewett as a preeminent person in that regard. Sadly, truly systematic theologians are a disappearing breed. Now everything is episodic, and "theology" is no longer "of the Word of God" but theology "of" a hundred and one other things. But Paul King Jewett is a theologian whose entire lifework is consciously and factually rooted in the Word of God. He seeks to state its meaning faithfully so that the Gospel is clearly interpreted and the church is well served.

Even though I am just a dean, not a systematic theologian, I dare to honor Paul because I have experienced him since the fifties, when I was privileged to be a student in his classes, as a truly disciplined craftsman-theologian. Paul's father was a craftsman with wood, a carpenter. This explains the wonderfully crafted, grand, circular desk in his office—a gift of love to him from his father and, some think, an object well qualified to be the eighth wonder of the world. Paul is a true son of his father in his own vocation as a systematic theologian. That grand and marvelously outfitted desk, with its special shelves and stands now stocked with all the theological tools of the trade— Bibles and lexicons and dictionaries and encyclopedias and major theological works—is a notable symbol of Paul Jewett's sturdy and substantial and far-ranging theological vocation.

Some years back several of us in the Chicago area set out to establish a consultation on divorce in Christian perspective—this at a time when divorce was suddenly rearing its unlovely head on the

Christian horizon with frightening frequency. Virtually without pause and in concert, each of us, though each had a background quite distinct from that of the others in the circle, agreed that Paul Jewett should be the conference theologian. It was the solidity and beauty and clarity of his work that had singularly impressed us all, whether we were former students or regular readers of Paul's work. Those who have hoped to see more of Paul's mature systematic reflections in print have not adequately counted the cost of the painstaking labor so characteristic of this theology. Its clarity and directness, sitting in a contemporary ocean of opacity and obfuscation, is purchased with much slow, careful, patient—and fruitful—effort.

It is a backhanded tribute to the very high regard in which Paul has been held that there was so much strife set in motion by his book *Man as Male and Female*. How many persons (if they had the gift to craft arguments as Paul does) could have stirred up the storm that was engendered by Paul's argument? I do not write lightly with respect to the now well-known "battle for the Bible," in which Paul was an object of attack. I write about it at all only because for me Paul's entire lifework clearly points to his relentless and single-minded commitment to Scripture as the Word of God. I have had other teachers in the same area (Carnell and Henry at Fuller and Barth at Basel) who have pointed in the same direction; Paul Jewett has contributed well to the kerygmatic harmony of a great quartet.

I leave to others more "systematic" reflections on the systematic theologian. I want simply to pass along some striking characteristics that, to my mind, must by all means be included in any tribute to Paul King Jewett, "systematic theologian." I begin with *clarity*, already noted above. I have not discussed this subject with Paul, but I have regularly noted his disdain of any lack of clarity and his quiet asser-tion that those committed to the proclamation of Christ's Gospel are surely bound, in such vocation, to be clear for the sake of the Gospel. If the rule of thumb for sales in real estate is "location, location, loca-tion," a corresponding rule in systematic theology as plied by Paul Jewett would be "clarity, clarity, clarity," as the medium for the truth of the Gospel. Although both Barth and Brunner were, like Paul Jewett, committed to theology as a handmaid of proclamation, and although Paul Jewett had opportunity to benefit greatly from both of these great teachers, it is Emil Brunner, whose theology provided the grist for the mill of Jewett's Harvard dissertation and first book (*Emil Brunner's Concept of Revelation*), who served as the model of clarity in the writing of systematic theology.

The second note I want to sound has to do with Paul's wide-ranging interests and his ability to turn these to meaningful reference points in the life of the Christian church and its dispersed commu-nity. The bibliography included in this *Festschrift* bears its own silent witness to these interests. Very early on in my always-interesting classes with Paul Jewett, I encountered his high interest in Christian hymnody and his gift for bringing Christian hymns into the service of Christian theology. I entered seminary on a musical high note, having come out of a "singing" church and having matured Christianly at university with an InterVarsity hymnal in hand. But Paul Jewett, more than all who had preceded him in my life taken together, put me in mind of what it is that the Christian hymnal really means for us and to us. How many thousands of Fuller Theological Seminary students have raised their voice in song in the systematic theology classrooms of Paul King Jewett! The hymns were never used as a mere devotional prologue or interlude, but as incorporating the great essentials of our faith. How much benefit has accrued to Fuller students and the churches they have served and will serve, through this linkage of the church singing its faith and the church pondering its faith. (Incidentally, during almost any lunch period you are apt to hear the sounds of a musical masterpiece, whether secular or sacred, emanating from Paul's office.)

I have always experienced Paul King Jewett as a "man with a cause." His great "cause," of course, has been the Gospel—and, along with it, faithful, and therefore meaningful, reflection on the Gospel. But that meaning has to be drawn out in life. As much as any other faculty colleague over the years, Paul has kept his hand at the causal plow, if I may so speak. These causes have ranged from the concern that justice be done in the case of a student or staff member or faculty colleague, to Paul's longtime espousal of the concerns of ethnic minorities and women. Paul was in Selma, Alabama, at a time when few evangelicals were marching. And Paul took up what he saw as the biblical mandate that justice be done in gender relationships and the ordination of women when he wrote *Man as Male and Female* and *The Ordination of Women*. His deep concerns have been felt on the campus and in the presbytery, in the classroom and in the ecclesia. And Paul's contributions are durable, pointing the church in the right direction and providing new personal and reflective undergirding to reach the right goals. The axis of evangelicalism has changed since mid-century, and Paul King Jewett has surely had a significant role in that movement toward justice. I thank God for his daring theological leadership!

The "activist" role just noted must be seen in juxtaposition to the disciplined and reflective posture characteristic of a good systematic theologian. Day after day over the thirteen-year period of my sojourn at Fuller Theological Seminary, I have had (literally) to walk by the slightly ajar (of this, more below!) door of Paul King Jewett as I have gone about my own business as dean of the School of Theology. There he sits at his massive desk, deeply engrossed in the theological task. He spends hour after hour, day after day, Saturdays included, unrelentingly noting items from all kinds of works, reviewing texts, taking note of the thought of (theological) friend and foe alike, arranging his own thoughts in his well-known scrawl (Paul has not succumbed to the modernity of the word processor!), and then writing out the latest monograph or section of his systematic theology. Paul is disciplined in his use of time, even as he is disciplined in the theological enterprise itself.

The result of Paul King Jewett's disciplined life is that what he writes is just plain good. Clear and crisp, yet grand, prose! How many tributes offered to others in this seminary have originated from the pen of Paul Jewett! How well crafted are the sentences and paragraphs and arguments that emerge from this disciplined work. And how persistently attentive he is to the text of Scripture. I remember a review of Paul's work on baptism in which the reviewer observed that Paul's was surely the best argument that could be made for his position—and that was precisely why the reviewer opposed the position!

I want to return to that door which is always ajar. That open door, has about it "the marks" of Paul King Jewett, systematic theologian par excellence. His is an open mind. All of us who have sat under his tutelage know that. But, thank God, that openness is an openness first of all to hear the Word of God in Scripture; then to the people of God in history, who have sought to hear the Word of God; and then to the world about him, to the movements and currents of the time in which people live out their lives. It is just because he has listened so well that his work will have an enduring meaning for us.

That open door of the office around the corner symbolizes another (delightful) quality of my friend. How many times I have walked the short distance from my office to his with the latest bit of humor in hand. My knowledge and certainty that this busy and disciplined man lives with an open door to the lighter side of life runs parallel to the experience of students and colleagues over the years. Paul Jewett's puckish sense of humor, manifest in the classroom and in social settings, is a constant reminder of his own recognition of the ambiguities of existence, but ambiguities that can be enjoyed rather than lamented, ambiguities that form the context for our theological work rather than block its way, ambiguities that establish the need for relationship, above all with God, rather than block out relationships. Perhaps that explains why I have always been blessed in those moments when Paul Jewett has led the community in prayer: something of the mystery of God always shines through, and something of our own finitude. Thank God for a colleague in theology who has devoted his lifelong effort to enlarging and clarifying our boundaries!

I think it right to close on a very personal and, in its own way, very painful note. In these latter years of Paul's career, he has had a serious bout with cancer—a most unwelcome diversion as he seeks to complete his systematic theology enterprise. We who have gathered about Paul know from him full well how all this slowed down his forward progress for a time; but we also know full well how he has stood fast, forged ahead, and now carries on his labors with the same exemplary discipline so characteristic of his entire career. I feel all this most keenly because a doctor told me in late summer of 1989 that I had a malignant carcinoma, and I have subsequently suffered together with Paul in my own healing process. It has been a blessing to me to walk around the corner to chat with this friend who has been a quiet but effective minister of grace in these days. We don't have to say much; we have just been there for each other.

"Being there for others" well characterizes the lifework of Paul King Jewett. The others are the people of God and the world for whom Christ died. The life-and-death, and global, dimensions of the Gospel have set the pace for Paul's endeavor; it has been nothing less than a lifelong struggle on behalf of the Gospel. Sometimes it is manifest in long, quiet hours at the great, circular desk; sometimes it has been manifest in the substantial offerings of the quintessential professor in the classroom; sometimes it has been an intense struggle within a presbytery or the larger setting of the ecclesia in history. No matter what the setting, the great Beginning, Midpoint, and End have been kept clearly in mind, and we are the beneficiaries of this lifelong labor of love for God and for us all.

Biographical Note

Paul King Jewett was born at home on October 6, 1919, in Johnson City, New York, the older of two children. His mother, a homemaker, had gone to normal school, training to be a teacher, and had a high view of education. His father had not gone beyond grade school but was nonetheless a skilled carpenter, who built not only the house in which Dr. Jewett was born, but also the others that he lived in during his growing-up years. While Dr. Jewett notes with satisfaction that his father's well-built houses (not to mention the famous desk) are still in use, he regrets that a freeway now runs where the old home town baseball diamond used to be. He had been a member of the "Knothole Gang": kids given free tickets to the bleachers in that old stadium. It was no doubt a good investment, for he is still a baseball fan.

Both parents were staunch Regular Baptists, and Dr. Jewett's sister and her husband are still Regular Baptist missionaries. He describes his ecclesiastical heritage as "a gospel church that majored in prophecy, especially Daniel and the Book of Revelation."[1] His academic pilgrimage no doubt contributed to the fact that, besides being a professor of theology, he is now an ordained minister in the Presbyterian Church (U.S.A.) and a reasonably staunch Calvinist.

Jewett attended grade school and high school in his home town and claims that while he worked hard and could never understand kids who brought no books home, he always hated school—which, considering his future endeavors, just goes to show that he must have been a glutton for punishment. He soon went off to Wheaton College, where he majored in philosophy (intending to prepare for ministry) and was influenced by Gordon H. Clark. After receiving his B.A. in 1941, he did some graduate work in New Testament Greek and then began formal theological studies at Westminster Theological Seminary in Philadelphia in 1942, graduating in 1945 with Th.B. and Th.M. degrees. The same year he married his wife Christine. Harvard came next, with thesis research done at the Universities of Berne, Zurich, and Basel. He attended lectures by both Brunner and Barth. His Ph.D. degree in Philosophy of Religion came in 1951. By this time his father was getting anxious, wondering if he would ever get a real job!

---

[1]*Theology, News and Notes* 34, no. 3 (November 1987): 17.

He had, however, begun teaching at Gordon Divinity School, now Gordon-Conwell, even before he finished his degree. He was called a professor of the philosophy of religion, but he was basically a utility person, lecturing in almost everything but dogmatics. During this period his two daughters were born, Fern in 1952 and Victoria in 1955. He taught at Gordon until 1955, when his longtime friend Edward John Carnell, recently become president of Fuller Seminary, encouraged him to come and teach systematic theology. He came and has taught theology at Fuller ever since—not only up until his formal retirement in the summer of 1990, but now as a part-time senior professor.

Shortly after Dr. Jewett came to Fuller, he was ordained as an American Baptist minister (1956), and he continues to believe strongly in believer baptism. However, in other respects he felt closer to the Reformed theological heritage of the Presbyterian Church and hence sought to transfer his credential. He was received by San Gabriel Presbytery in 1970, despite his views on baptism, on the grounds that, as a professor, he was not generally called upon to baptize! As a Presbyterian, he has sought to be a faithful presbyter, serving for many years on the Church and Society Committee and on the Ministerial Relations Committee. He taught a flourishing adult Sunday school class at the Glendale Presbyterian Church for more than twenty years and has taught series of classes for many other congregations.

Since Dr. Jewett is a systematic theologian by profession and a man of wide-ranging interests, it is not surprising that he pursued additional sabbatical studies at the Catholic Institute of Paris and the University of Paris, or that he has written books and articles relating to many and diverse issues in theology (see the bibliography at the end of this volume), or even that he had a major role in formulating Fuller's current Statement of Faith. It may surprise some, however, to learn that his commitment to promoting effective ministry to youth fostered his serving as dean of the Young Life Institute for twenty years, a responsibility that involved finding professors to provide a quality summer program of theological education for Young Life staff. His acquaintance with several of the contributors to this volume dates from those summer sessions in Colorado Springs.

Many might be even more surprised to hear that when asked to name books that have been especially influential in his life, Dr. Jewett named first not formal volumes in theology, but rather *The Autobiography of Malcolm X* and Betty Friedan's *The Feminine Mystique*.[2] Although a scholar's scholar, Paul King Jewett is also a man who hears what human beings who are in some significant way different

---

[2]Ibid.

from him say about their experience of life. He manifestly cares about the suffering of others and uses his gifts, his personal choices, and the tools of his own trade to work for justice. In 1965, when Fuller was almost lily-white, he drafted a statement for the seminary condemning racism. And in 1975, with his *Man as Male and Female*, he made a pioneer effort among American evangelical thinkers to state the case for the full equality and complementarity of the sexes (which sparked a debate on Scripture that led to his being mentioned in *Time* magazine, May 10, 1976).

At the time of the writing of this *Festschrift*, Dr. Jewett is working on the second volume of a multivolume systematic theology. His approach is characteristic of his long-term commitments. Besides seeking to expound on the traditional dogmatic loci, he is illustrating his treatment with the classic hymnody of the church, incorporating sermons to show that theology can be preached, and taking up many contemporary issues to which he believes theologians must strive to speak if they are truly to further the kingdom of Christ. Paul King Jewett is both a theologian and a minister of the Gospel; and he continues to believe that theology rightly done is theology that serves the church.

Introduction

At the very beginning of his year-long course of lectures in systematic theology, Paul Jewett has always been fond of making two points: the *function* of Christian theological reflection is not always to do away with mystery, but sometimes to preserve it; and the *end* of Christian theology is morality. Obviously, we would be presumptuous indeed to suppose that we human beings could comprehend almighty God in the limited sphere of our understanding. A properly humble faculty of reason will acknowledge its limits and will worship not itself but the God who created and transcends it. At the same time, however, reason governed by God's revelation of himself must not become esoteric, high-flown speculation that so revels in mystery that it never touches the ground on which we daily walk. If our thinking about God makes no difference in our behavior, then that is as good evidence as anyone should require that something is fundamentally wrong with our thinking.

Surely the doctrinal locus of Christology, in which we explore our understanding of the person and work of Jesus Christ, provides broad opportunities for illustrating both of these points. Conceiving of one who is wholly divine and wholly human, "without confusion, change, separation, or division," stretches mere logic and language to the breaking point. Acknowledging this one to be our Lord, our Prophet and Priest and King, means that who he is and what he asks of us must govern every aspect of our lives. The essays in this volume range from probing details of the mystery of the divine-human person to demanding a broadly ethical response to Christ's promises, and so provide a cross section of evangelical and Reformed thought touching on most key areas of Christological debate.

Not just any mystery is to be preserved, of course, and not just any morality is to be embraced, but only those mysteries and that morality which are made known to us in Holy Scripture. The conviction that theology must be governed by and subject to Scripture has been a touchstone of Dr. Jewett's theological career, in both his teaching and his writing. Indeed, he has always required memorization of Scripture in his basic courses in dogmatics. Thus, the first group of essays deal with key issues relating to Christology and Scripture.

What must be said, to begin with, about the fundamental content of the Gospel itself? Evangelicals have generally tended to proclaim, "Jesus didn't come to preach the Gospel, but in order that there might be a Gospel to preach." New Testament scholars, however, have in this century been struck by the seeming discrepancy between the Synoptics, in which Jesus proclaims the gospel of the kingdom; and Paul, who proclaims the gospel of Christ crucified. Have we two irreconcilable traditions contained within the New Testament itself? How can contemporary Christology be formulated both in recognition of this exegetical issue and in acknowledgment of the validity of the church's preaching of Jesus as the Christ? Robert Guelich takes up this question as he explores the Gospel of Mark, arguing that kingdom and Crucifixion are conjoined theologically in the Christology of Mark by a proper understanding of the Markan theme of the "Messianic Secret."

Another notable problem for the traditional Christology of the church, which has always insisted on the divinity of the Son, is the dearth of biblical statements that clearly, unequivocally, and incontrovertibly call Jesus "God." How shall we understand this lack if the church has indeed correctly understood Scripture to teach that Jesus is divine? Donald Hagner explores Paul's deep commitment to the monotheism so central to his Jewish heritage as a key to his reserved language about Christ. Hagner draws attention to the Pauline stress on the uniqueness of Jesus as the agent of redemption, noting the ultimacy of Jesus' agency and the intimate relation between the fundamentally functional character of New Testament Christology and the ontological questions that this ultimacy raises for the relationship between Jesus and God. Then Colin Brown takes the Roman Catholic Pontifical Biblical Commission's publication *Scripture and Christology* as an opportunity not only to review this significant statement, but in the course of doing so, to lay out and examine the broad array of contemporary Christological approaches that have been grounded in various approaches to Scripture. The way in which Roman Catholicism, with its powerful commitment to the normative value of the church's tradition, encounters and appropriates modern critical scholarship is significant for any effort to construct a biblically and exegetically grounded but also churchly Christology in our time. Here one may find a convenient summary of the main options, together with extensive references to literature expounding and evaluating each view.

Even more obvious, perhaps, than the several strands of biblical witness, is the diversity in the way Christ has been approached in different theological traditions. In the second division of this volume, the historical section, can be found not only summaries of the major Christological controversies that wrenched the ancient church, but also examples of Reformed, Lutheran, Pietist, and Liberal Protestant approaches to central Christological issues. In some respects, the tone and flavor of the essays themselves may reveal a little of the tone and flavor of the movements they represent, from the careful, detailed, logical formulations of the Reformed to the passionate, personal warmth of the Pietists.

Geoffrey Bromiley considers the fundamental Christological affirmation of the Reformed confessions of the sixteenth century, pointing toward the clarity of the Reformed affirmation of the true humanity and true divinity of Christ and to the differences—often the cause of bitter polemic—between the Reformed and the Lutheran affirmations concerning that central element of Christian confession. The Reformed were concerned to emphasize the integrity of the two natures in their union for the sake of underlining the importance of Jesus' humanity to the work of redemption. Accordingly, they leaned toward a view of the relationship of the natures similar to that associated with the Antiochene school of thought during the patristic period. In particular, they denied the Lutheran doctrine of a communication of divine attributes to the human nature of Christ, inasmuch as, they believed, such a doctrine would undermine the confession of the truth of Jesus' humanity. If, as Bromiley indicates, the Reformed and Lutheran theologians of the sixteenth century tended to accuse one another of violating the boundaries set by the early church's formulae and of teaching, respectively, Nestorianism and Eutychianism, both groups also had profound positive recourse to the patristic materials in the development of their doctrinal positions, as Robert Kelly's essay documents at length with reference to the theology of Martin Chemnitz. What Chemnitz was able to offer the orthodox Lutheran doctrine of Christ was a way of maintaining the affirmation of the genuineness of Christ's humanity and the concreteness of Christ's body in its own attributes while at the same time allowing a communication of the divine attributes in some manner to the human nature of Jesus. As its title indicates, the essay also raises the issue of "tradition and innovation" in the transmission and development of post-Reformation Protestantism.

The great difficulty faced by the theology of the late sixteenth and seventeenth centuries known as "Protestant Orthodoxy," can be described, in large part, in terms of continuities and discontinuities with the thought of the Patristic era, the Middle Ages, and the Reformation: how much of this new, specifically *Protestant* orthodoxy ought to draw on the tradition, how much ought to be innovation? How could a Protestant orthodoxy both remain Protestant and at the same time claim catholicity? These questions lie at the heart of Martin Chemnitz' use of patristic materials.

Gary Sattler's essay addresses this issue of developing Protestant doctrine from yet another vantage point. If Protestant orthodoxy addressed the problem of systematic formulation, it also raised the problem of emphasis on system and dogmatic formulae to the potential exclusion of the concerns of the heart. Sattler's choice of Heinrich Müller as an example of the Pietist approach to Christology highlights this point: Müller sought to present the religious aspect of Christology while at the same time remaining fully within the bounds of orthodox or confessional Protestantism. Nonetheless, his interest in the experiential side of the doctrine may also be seen as a bridge toward subsequent Christological concerns, as evidenced by the work of Friedrich Schleiermacher.

Richard Muller carries the discussion forward to the modern era with a meditation on Schleiermacher's identification of the difficulties inherent in traditional Christological language of "person" and "nature." Schleiermacher was able to argue most convincingly why the debates over patristic categories and dogmas typical of the era of Protestant orthodoxy sound so strange and distant to the modern ear—and why, consequently, some terminology other than the long-accepted patristic usages must be found. His work still stands as the most concerted effort to place Christology on a new foundation and to affirm in a different set of terms the centrality of Jesus Christ to the Christian religion and its theology.

In the third section, that containing contemporary and literary views of Christ, one will find essays whose theoretical analyses bear quite directly on current practical problems. Their authors take up Christological questions that relate not only to the niceties of doctrinal formulation, but that also have rather immediate application to the daily life of the average person. Some have raised the question of whether Jesus was simply psychotic, a man to be pitied rather than a model to follow or Savior to worship. Whether psychology has become more modest as it has matured and flourished as a discipline, or whether early writers pretty much exhausted the possibilities of discerning mental illness in Jesus, few are writing along these lines today. Vernon Grounds' essay, however, which details the judgment of the so-called pathographers (as well as illustrates the glowing counterverdict of superb mental health on Jesus' part given by a different set of analysts), provides a salutary lesson in what can happen when mystery is reduced to madness. One recalls, as a needed antidote to such presumption, the acerbic remark of John Newton:

> The gospel is not proposed to you to ask your opinion of it, that it may stand or fall according to your decision, but it peremptorily demands your submission. If you think yourselves qualified to judge and examine it by that imperfect and depraved light which you call your reason, you will probably find reasons enough to refuse your assent.[1]

---

[1]From his sermon, "The Small Success of the Gospel Ministry," in David Lyle Jeffrey, ed., *A Burning and a Shining Light: English Spirituality in the Age of Wesley* (Grand Rapids: Eerdmans, 1987), 398.

Elouise Fraser then tackles an issue that continues to divide certain segments of the Christian church, including its evangelical and Reformed component: the way women should understand their role and place. This is an issue that became salient for Dr. Jewett when he noticed to his surprise that his very few female students showed some significant tendency to outperform his male students (not surprising, perhaps, in a day when only the very gifted and dedicated woman pursued serious theological education; but surprising enough to one who had half-consciously assumed theology to be a male domain). His 1975 volume, *Man as Male and Female*—written well before feminist theology had an identity and before sensitivity to inclusive language made the first word of the title impossible— brought him a modest degree of fame and brought many Christian women with a heart for ministry a not-so-modest surge of hope. It drew some of its theological inspiration from Karl Barth's understanding of the divine image in terms of male and female together. Without discounting his positive contribution, Dr. Fraser argues here that Barth had a faulty and truncated view of the humanity of Jesus that bolstered his espousal of irreversible male priority in human relationships. Were we to think differently about Jesus, we would be helped to think differently about ourselves, and thence, one hopes, to *do* differently in the face of our human needs and hopes.

The final two essays in this section both deal with the subject of the temptation of Jesus. Temptation is surely a trial known to us all; but can we find any common ground between the temptation of the sinless Son of God and the struggles we ourselves undergo, or was Jesus' experience necessarily so utterly different in kind than our own that it really gives us no help or even instruction? Several nineteenth-century theologians raised the issue that not only was the temptation of Jesus genuine, but that the only way to affirm Jesus' identity as a human being was to argue the possibility of his failure in the face of temptation, even to the point of denying his sinlessness. Marguerite Shuster approaches the problem from a theological and pastoral perspective with reference to Heb 4:15 and an analysis of the *experience* of temptation, while Anthony Yu scrutinizes John Milton's use of the Gospel narratives in his *Paradise Regained* and the significance of Milton's choice of Luke's order as a vehicle for conveying his understanding of Jesus' conquest of temptation. Both treatments give food for thought as we face the seductive lures all around us. Both also raise, albeit from different vantage points, the central Christological point of the reality of Jesus' humanity.

The last section in this volume moves even more directly from the person of Christ to his work, and into the practical arena, with a series of explorations of ethics and Christology. Lewis Smedes examines the concept of friendship as understood when ordinary people speak of one another as friends and the significant differences we must take into account when we speak of Jesus as Friend on the basis of Jn 15:15 —"No longer do I call you servants, for the servant does not know what his master is doing; but I have called you friends, for all that I have heard from my Father, I have made known to you" (RSV). One who is not our equal cannot be our friend in the ordinary sense of the term. Smedes examines the ethical significance of this extraordinary "friendship" in the context of a juxtaposition of biblical and philosophical categories.

The remaining three essayists each focus on topics that relate more to the public than to the private arena and that illumine one of the aspects of what has traditionally been called Christ's threefold office— that of prophet, priest, and king. Using a nontraditional order, we begin with the office of priest. As Priest, Christ has been understood to bear the sins of his people (the Atonement) and to make intercession for their transgressions. He represents humankind before God. Eugene Osterhaven argues that a proper view of God as just and the Atonement as a propitiatory sacrifice on Jesus' part, fulfilling the divine demand for justice, has clear implications for the proper practice of punishment in the society at large. Merely rehabilitative views of punishment tend to remove it altogether from the realm of justice. Drawing on the insights of C. S. Lewis, Osterhaven examines the problem of guilt and the morality of punishment from a Christological vantage point that affirms the righteousness of God, the justice of punishment, and the free mercy that overcomes our punishment through the satisfaction of Christ.

When we speak of Christ as King, we not only think of him as our Lord, our absolute Sovereign, but also affirm that he will reign over all the nations and that of his kingdom there will be no end. He exercises dominion and, in so doing, restores the original dominion of humankind. Richard Mouw remarks, however, that it has been peculiarly difficult for the Christian politician—especially in a democratic society—to get the same kind of help and inspiration from the model of Jesus the King that the Christian medical doctor has gotten from the model of Jesus the Divine Physician. What does it mean for Christ to have his proper role in the shaping of our political life?

Then, taking last what is usually discussed first, we have Christ the Prophet, who reveals the will of God, teaches righteousness, and in general makes known what God requires of humankind. While the book of Revelation, with which the New Testament canon ends, clearly presents Christ in each of the three offices, Virgil Cruz elaborates his prophetic role in the so-called beatitudes of the Apocalypse. In these sayings, the blessings the risen Christ pronounces upon his people not only offer hope for the future, but come in the context of a clear ethical demand for righteous living in the present—a balance all Christians do well to keep in mind.

A few stanzas of Isaac Watts' classic hymn, "Join All the Glorious Names," provide a fitting close for this section and, indeed, for this introduction. In its combination of sincere piety with sound theology, it resonates with Dr. Jewett's career as a teacher and life as a Christian person. It also reminds us, by its inclusion here, of the central place given to worship in the theology of Paul Jewett, specifically to the prominent position given to the psalms and hymns of the church in his course on systematic theology and in his forthcoming theological system. The hymn, indeed, is one he loves well, and we present it here in the slightly modified version he includes in the annotated hymnal he prepared for use in his classes.

> Join all the glorious names,
> Of wisdom, love, and power
> That ever mortals knew
> That angels ever bore.
> All are too mean to speak his worth
> Too mean to set my Savior forth.
>
> Great Prophet of my God,
> My tongue would bless thy name;
> By Thee the joyful news
> Of our salvation came;
> Of hell subdued and peace with heaven
> The joyful news of sins forgiven.
>
> Jesus, my great high Priest,
> Offered his blood and died;
> My guilty conscience seeks
> No sacrifice beside;
> His powerful blood did once atone
> And now it pleads before the throne.
>
> Our dear Almighty Lord,
> Our Conqueror and our King,
> Thy scepter and thy sword
> Thy reigning grace we sing.
> Thine is the power; behold, we meet
> Thy willing bondmen at thy feet.

Marguerite Shuster
Richard Muller
Pasadena, California
1990

Scripture and Christology

The "Christ" of the Gospel:
A Lesson from Mark's Christology

Robert A. Guelich

Professor of New Testament
Fuller Theological Seminary

INTRODUCTION

Almost from the outset, the church has called Jesus "Christ"[1] and has confessed him to be the Messiah.[2] *Christ* is a proper name, as in Jesus Christ; *Messiah* is a title that designates Jesus to be God's promised King. Despite the apparent difference in these designations, few readers of this article need reminding that *Christ* represents a transliteration of the Greek word χριστός (="anointed") and *Messiah* a transliteration of the Hebrew מָשִׁיחַ (="anointed"), so that the two English words (*Christ, Messiah*) have the same root meaning ("Anointed One"). Nor does the reader need reminding that χριστός was first applied to Jesus in the early church as the Greek translation (="Anointed One") for מָשִׁיחַ (="Anointed One") to refer to Jesus as the Messiah, God's promised Anointed One of Israel.

The shift in χριστός from the title "Anointed One" to the name "Christ" represents more than simply a shift in language. It corresponds to an apparent difference in the nature of the Gospel itself. Jesus as Messiah corresponds more to the gospel of the kingdom. Jesus as Christ corresponds more to the gospel of Christ crucified. While not mutually exclusive, "Messiah" hardly connotes the Cross and "Christ" seldom connotes the kingdom of God.

This difference purportedly goes back to the New Testament itself, where we find Paul preaching Christ crucified as the gospel[3] and Jesus preaching the gospel of the kingdom.[4] The apparent difference has marked the discussion in New Testament studies of the modern period. Eschewing the doctrinally developed writings of Paul that

---

[1]Note the many such usages in Paul's letters. Scripture citations in this essay are translated directly from the Greek text.

[2]For example, Peter's confession in Mk 8:29 par.; John's statement of purpose in 20:31; and Paul's reference to the coming of the Messiah in Ro 9:5.

[3]E.g., Ro 3:21–26; 1Co 1:17–25; 1Co 15:1–5; Gal 3:1.

[4]E.g., Mk 1:14–15; Mt 4:23; Lk 4:18–21; cf. Jn 20:30–31.

underscore the benefits of the death of Christ, the nineteenth-century quest for the historical Jesus clearly saw Jesus' own message to be that of the kingdom.[5] How this gospel of the kingdom is to be understood or how it came to be supplanted in the history of the church by the gospel of the Cross became the dominant theme of New Testament theology for the last fifty years. During this period a doctrine of a post-poned kingdom in some evangelical circles and the emphasis on the gospel of the Cross almost at the exclusion of any mention of the gospel of the kingdom in most evangelical circles have not only perpetuated de facto the apparent distinction between the two gospels, but have also resulted in two Christologies, reflected in the distinction in English between Jesus *Messiah* (Jesus as *Messiah* of the kingdom) and Jesus *Christ* (Jesus as *Christ* crucified).

MARK'S CHRISTOLOGY

The Christology of the Gospel according to Mark illustrates how the gospel of the kingdom and the gospel of the Cross come together as one Gospel. That Christology stands out as a dominant theme in Mark becomes obvious from a simple reading of the Gospel. Jesus is the leading character as the protagonist in this narrative. And, except for the episode of the Baptist's death (6:17-29), he is involved in one way or another in every scene from 1:4–16:8.[6]

Yet Mark was not merely writing a dramatic story about a famous or heroic figure. He refers to his narrative as "the gospel concerning Jesus Messiah, Son of God" (1:1), who came "proclaiming the gospel from God, saying, 'The time has been fulfilled; the kingdom of God is at hand. Repent and believe the gospel'" (1:14b-15). The Christologically loaded opening statement, *Jesus Messiah, Son of God*, appears in

---

[5]Despite the agreement about the kingdom as the focus of Jesus' ministry, two very different understandings of Jesus' preaching of the kingdom emerged. On the one side, the kingdom was stripped of all eschatological nuances and understood ethically as a power, a religious blessing, an inner link with God, that works inwardly to help us get at the meaning of life through the affirming of the universal Fatherhood of God, the infinite value of the human soul, and a higher righteousness expressed through love (e.g., Adolf Harnack, *What is Christianity?* trans. Thomas B. Saunders [New York: Harper, 1957], 52-78). On the other side, Johannes Weiss argued that Jesus' gospel of the kingdom was strictly political and eschatological in terms of the apocalyptic expectation of his day (cf. *Jesus' Proclamation of the Kingdom of God*, trans. Richard H. Hiers and David L. Holland [Philadelphia: Fortress, 1971], 133). After his death, his disciples proclaimed him to be the imminently returning Messiah. Neither understanding of the gospel of the kingdom provided any connection with the gospel of the Cross.

[6]One can legitimately argue that the Evangelist even has Jesus in mind in 6:17-29, since the Baptist as the "forerunner" in Mark's portrait anticipates Jesus' own fate at the hands of the authorities. See Robert A. Guelich, *Mark 1–8:26*, Word Bible Commentary 34a (Waco: Word, 1989), 328-29.

the context of the "gospel of the kingdom" and intends to evoke from the reader a response of faith. It connotes a definite understanding of who Jesus was.

Jesus' identity as *Messiah, Son of God*, is explicitly given to the readers at the outset of the Gospel (1:1), confirmed by the voice from heaven at the Baptism (1:11) and the recognition of the demons (3:11; 5:7; cf. 1:24), repeated by Peter at Caesarea Philippi (8:29), and acknowledged by Jesus before the high priest at his trial (14:61-62a). Indeed, Jesus as *Messiah, Son of God*, proclaiming the gospel from God about the coming of the kingdom, forms the backdrop for the plot of Mark's story.[7]

In the story line of Mark's Gospel, however, Jesus' identity is much less apparent. The development of the story shows the meaning of *Messiah, Son of God*, to be quite complex. This complexity becomes evident in the underlying question about who Jesus is that runs throughout the narrative and involves the Roman authorities (15:2-15), the Jewish authorities (2:1–3:6; 8:11-12; 12:13-44; 14:60-64), Jesus' own family and neighbors (3:20-21, 31-35; 6:1-6), and even his disciples (4:40; 6:51-52; 8:14-21, 27-33). Except for Jesus and the demons, the full significance of his real identity escapes all the characters in the story until after the Crucifixion (15:32, 39). Therefore, at the heart of Mark's Gospel lies the question: Who was Jesus?

The Evangelist addresses this question in three ways. First, he addresses it by the designations used for and by Jesus. Second, he addresses it by his selection and arrangement of episodes involving Jesus' ministry, in other words, by his narrative structure. Third, he addresses the question of Jesus' identity by Jesus' response to the statements of others, the so-called messianic secret.

1. Designations Used for Jesus

Mark clearly intended to identify Jesus by the use of special designations. We see this at the outset (1:1) when he identifies Jesus as the *Messiah, Son of God*,[8] and continues to use designations of and by

---

[7]See Jack D. Kingsbury's *Conflict in Mark's Gospel* (Minneapolis: Fortress, 1989) for a good discussion of plot in Mark.

[8]While χριστοῦ can certainly be a proper name (so Vincent Taylor, *The Gospel According to St. Mark*, 2d ed. [London: Macmillan/New York: St. Martin, 1966], 152), as the Pauline corpus demonstrates (cf. Mk 9:41), Mk 8:29; 12:35; 13:21; 14:61; and 15:32 show it maintained its function as a title in Mark. "Jesus Christ" can hardly be interchangeable with "Jesus" in the Gospels, since Luke only uses "Jesus" (ca. 85x; "Jesus Christ," ca. 10x in Acts) and Matthew and Mark only use "Jesus Christ" at the beginning of their Gospels (cf. Mt 1:1, 18; Mk 1:1; Jn 1:17; cf. 17:3), in contrast to their frequent use of "Jesus" (Matthew—ca. 150x; Mark—ca. 80x; John—ca. 17x). Despite the absence of "Son of God" from some MSS (ℵ* θ 28 sy^pal), the internal evidence supports its reading here (cf. 1:11; 5:7; 9:7; 14:61; 15:39).

Jesus at crucial points in the story (e.g., 1:11 [the Baptism]; 8:27-33 [Caesarea Philippi]; 9:7 [the Transfiguration]; 14:61-62 [the trial]; 15:32, 39 [the death]). Occasionally Jesus is referred to as "Rabbi" by his disciples (9:5; 11:21; 14:45; cf. "Rabbouni," 10:51) and mistakenly as one of the prophets, Elijah or John the Baptist (6:14; 8:28), by others. For Mark, however, Jesus is more appropriately known as the *Messiah, the Son of God* (cf. "the Son" in 12:1-12 and 13:32) and the *Son of man*. But what do these designations connote in Mark?

1:1 Mark identifies Jesus in his heading as "Jesus *Messiah*, Son of God." Though *Messiah* and *Son of God* can be used separately,[9] they were meant by Mark to be taken as complementary.[10] The term *messiah* had various meanings in the social milieu of Jesus' day,[11] but when it appears alone in Mark, it consistently connotes a royal figure[12] whose eschatological character is amply attested by the Jewish writings of the centuries before and after Christ.[13] That Peter's confession in 8:29, "You are the *Messiah*," carried a similar connotation appears obvious from his incredulous response in 8:32 to Jesus' counter in 8:31.[14] Yet Mark never uses *Messiah* of Jesus without qualifying it in one way or another.

1:2 Most commonly the Evangelist qualifies Jesus as Messiah by using either "Son of God" (1:1; cf. 15:32, 39), "Son of man" (8:31), or both (14:61-62). *Son of God* represents the key designation for the Evangelist. Not only does he open his story with reference to Jesus as *Son of God* (1:1), but he uses the Roman centurion's acclamation of Jesus as the *Son of God* (15:39) in the climactic scene of Jesus' death, along with the voice from heaven at the Baptism, the initial scene in Jesus' ministry (1:11), to frame his story. Furthermore, the divine voice from heaven at the Baptism (1:11) and Transfiguration (9:7) calls Jesus "my Son," and the demons, who "knew who he was" (1:34), call him the *Son of God* (3:11; 5:7; cf. 1:24). Mark certainly expected the reader to understand the "beloved son" in the parable of the Wicked Vintners (12:1-12; cf. 1:11; 9:7), as well as the "Son" who

---

[9]E.g., "Son of God"—1:11; 3:11; 5:7; 9:7; "Messiah"—8:29; 13:21.

[10]E.g., 1:1; 14:61; 15:32 with 15:39; cf. 12:35.

[11]See Hank de Jonge, "The Use of the Word 'Anointed' in the Time of Jesus," *Novum Testamentum* 8 (1966): 132-48; Jacob Neusner, *Messiah in Context: Israel's History and Destiny in Formative Judaism* (Philadelphia: Fortress, 1984), ix-xviii, 227-31; Richard A. Horsley and John S. Hanson, *Bandits, Prophets, and Messiahs: Popular Movements at the Time of Jesus* (Minneapolis: Winston/San Francisco: Harper and Row, 1985), 88-134.

[12]Explicit in 12:35; 15:32, and implicit in 13:21-22; 8:29.

[13]E.g. PS 17:35-36; 2Ba 29:3; 30:1; 40:1; 72:2-6; 4Ezr 7:28-34; 12:31-34; 1En 48:10; 52:4; TReub 6:7-12; TSim 7:2; 1QS 9:10; CD 12:23; 14:9; 19:10. See Neusner, *Messiah in Context*.

[14]Similar understanding appears to underlie the question by James and John, the sons of Zebedee (Mk 10:37).

does not know "concerning that day or hour" of the consummation (13:32), to be Jesus' reference to himself.

In what sense, however, was Jesus the *Son of God* for Mark? The baptismal scene (1:9-11) provides the clue. As the opening scene for Jesus, it introduces him by depicting his calling and equipping for the ensuing ministry. After the coming of the Spirit, the divine voice from heaven identifies Jesus with a collage of Old Testament texts. "You are my son" echoes Ps 2:7 with its royal reference to kingship. "Beloved" may well echo Gen 22:2, 12, 16 with its reference to a unique filial relationship. "With whom I am pleased" echoes Isa 42:1 with reference to the servant of Yahweh.

All three aspects come into play in Mark's use of "Son of God." Since "Messiah" consistently has a royal connotation in Mark, that motif is certainly present when "Son of God"/"the Blessed" is combined with "Messiah" in 1:1 and 14:61 (cf. 12:35). It lies most likely implicit in the demons' recognition of Jesus' authority as the *Son of God* in 3:11 and 5:7 and possibly behind the divine pronouncement at the Transfiguration of the glorified Christ (9:7; cf. 9:1). The special filial motif appears in the parable of the Wicked Vintners (12:1-12) and in the logion contrasting the Father's and the Son's knowledge about the time of the consummation (13:32; cf. 14:36). Finally, the "servant of Yahweh" motif comes through both in the Spirit-empowered ministry of the Son anticipated by the coming of the Spirit on Jesus at his baptism (cf. Isa 42:1; 61:1) and by the Son's suffering the ignominious death of the servant of Yahweh in the parable of the Wicked Vintners (12:1-12), as well as on the occasion for the centurion's acclamation (15:33-39). Therefore, for Mark, *Son of God* designates Jesus to be the *Messiah*, a royal figure having a unique relationship to God, who comes equipped by God's Spirit to minister and suffer as the Servant of Yahweh. We have no evidence that "Son of God" ever connoted anything else in Mark or in his tradition.[15]

1:3 Son of man for Mark, by contrast, serves as Jesus' personal and public self-designation.[16] One hardly need review the debate over the background and meaning of this expression[17] nor the data showing

---

[15]Since Rudolf Bultmann (*Theology of the New Testament*, trans. Kendrick Grobel, 2 vols. [New York: Scribner and Sons, 1951], 1:131) "Son of God" has often been taken as Mark's use of a traditional expression of Jesus to be a "divine man" either positively, e.g., Sigfried Schulz, *Die Stunde der Botschaft: Einführung in die Theologie der vier Evangelisten* (Hamburg: Furche, 1967), 46, or negatively, e.g., Theodore Weeden, *Mark, Traditions in Conflict* (Philadelphia: Fortress, 1971), 154-55 (who argues that it reflects the Hellenistic *theios-aner* Christology of Mark's opponents).

[16]Jack D. Kingsbury, *The Christology of Mark* (Minneapolis: Fortress, 1989), 164-73.

[17]See the discussion of *Son of man* in Angus J. B. Higgins, *Jesus and the Son of Man*, (Philadelphia: Fortress, 1964); Heinz E. Tödt, *The Son of Man in the Synoptic Tradition*, trans. Dorthea M. Barton (Philadelphia: Westminster, 1965); Morna Hooker,

(1) that the underlying expression was Hebrew or Aramaic rather than Greek, (2) that it appears exclusively on the lips of Jesus, and (3) that a disproportionate number of occurrences[18] come in the second half of Mark's Gospel. The two references in the first half (2:10, 28) appear in controversy settings and involve the authority of the *Son of man* to forgive sins (2:6-10) and to overrule the Sabbath laws (2:28). Since the theme of Jesus' authority pervades all of the episodes in the first section of Mark's story (1:16–3:12), and since Jesus is identified as the *Son of man* in only two, we can conclude that Mark found these two occurrences in the tradition and that they function merely as a self-designation for Jesus.[19]

The majority of Mark's uses of "Son of man" has to do with the Passion.[20] Here too Jesus uses the designation to refer to himself, as Peter's response to the first of these usages at Caesarea Philippi indicates (8:31-33). Yet the fact that Mark uses "Son of man" three times more often with reference to Jesus' passion than to the Parousia does not mean that there was anything inherent in this expression that would lend itself particularly to this usage. This large number of occurrences comes partly from the use of an almost formulaic expression, "the *Son of man* is betrayed," (14:21, 41; cf. 9:31; 10:33) and partly from the repetition of the Passion sayings (8:31; cf. 9:12, 31; 10:33). This repeated teaching about the suffering of the *Son of man* does demonstrate, however, both by its frequency and by the direct and indirect references to Scripture,[21] just how integral the passion of the *Son of man* was to Jesus' identity for Mark.

Three times Mark uses *Son of man* with reference to the future Parousia—8:38; 13:26-27; 14:62. Yet in none of these does Jesus directly identify himself with the coming *Son of man*. In fact, he appears to

---

The Son of Man in Mark (Montreal: McGill Univ. Press, 1967); Norman Perrin, "The Creative Use of the Son of Man Tradition by Mark," *Union Seminary Quarterly Review* 23 (1968): 237-65 = *A Modern Pilgrimage in New Testament Christology* (Philadelphia: Fortress, 1974), 84-93; Geza Vermes, *Jesus the Jew* (New York: Macmillan, 1973); Barnabas Lindars, *Jesus Son of Man: A Fresh Examination of the Son of Man Sayings in the Gospels* (Grand Rapids: Eerdmans, 1983).

[18]Twelve as compared to only two in the first half.

[19]That each occurrence comes in a setting of mortal conflict, as seen in the capital charge of blasphemy (2:7, cf. 14:64) and the response of the Jewish authorities to his healing on the Sabbath (3:6), may explain why the Evangelist has these references to the Son of man here and nowhere else before Peter's confession at Caesarea Philippi. See Guelich, *Mark*, 93-94, 130; cf. Christopher Tuckett, "The Present Son of Man," *Journal for the Study of the New Testament* 14 (1982): 58-81.

[20]Nine of fourteen occurrences: 8:31; 9:9, 12, 31; 10:33, 45; 14:21 (2x), 41.

[21]Mk 9:12, ". . . how it was written about the Son of man"; 14:21, ". . . the Son of man goes just as was written"; cf. the possible allusion to Isaiah 53 underlying 8:31 and 10:45.

distinguish himself from the *Son of man* in 8:38.[22] At the level of Mark's text, however, the obvious identification of Jesus with the *Son of man* in 2:10, 28 and in the Passion sayings makes the lack of direct identification in these sayings moot. The high priest's response of tearing his robes and charging Jesus with blasphemy (14:63-64) when he answered affirmatively the question about being the Messiah, Son of the Blessed, and then referred to the coming of the *Son of man* implies that the high priest understood Jesus to have made the identification between himself and the coming *Son of man*.

This open, unqualified use of *Son of man* by Jesus with reference to his authoritative ministry, his suffering and death, and his future coming stands in stark contrast to Jesus' silencing of the demons and the disciples who correctly recognize him to be the Son of God and the Messiah respectively.[23] Where is Mark's so-called messianic secret if *Son of man* was clearly a Christological title? Why are we totally lacking a similar usage of *Messiah* by Jesus? And why does Mark have at most only a couple of oblique references by Jesus to himself as the Son (e.g., 12:1-12; 13:32)? Despite the tendency in some circles to discount the authenticity of the *Son of man* sayings,[24] the use of *Son of man* in Mark can only make sense if it was indeed understood to be used as a self-designation by Jesus which had no inherent messianic overtones in Mark's Gospel that needed any qualification.

1:4 In light of this review of the primary designations used in Mark for Jesus, in what way was Jesus the Messiah for Mark? Both the designation *Son of God* and the designation *Son of man* address that question. First, as the Messiah, *Son of God* (1:1), Mark affirmed that Jesus was the expected, divinely selected, royal Messiah (1:11 [Ps 2:7]; 12:35 [2Sa 7:14; Ps 110:1]; 14:61-62a; cf. 15:32). Second, at the same time the "Son," despite or because of his special relationship with the "Father" (12:1-12; cf. 14:36), would suffer death as the Messiah (15:39; cf. 15:32). This combination of *Messiah* and *Son of God* becomes strikingly clear in the last scenes of the Crucifixion. On the one hand, the Jewish authorities ("high priests" and "scribes," 15:31) mockingly refer to Jesus as the "Messiah, King of Israel" (15:32) whose current predicament on the cross appeared to invalidate the claim. On the other hand, when Jesus dies, the Roman centurion validates that

---

[22]For discussion see Reginald Fuller, *The Foundations of New Testament Christology* (New York: Scribner, 1965), 121-23, and Lindars, *Jesus Son of Man*, 48-58.

[23]Regarding the demons: 1:24-25, 34; 3:11-12; regarding the disciples: 8:30; 9:9; see below on the "Messianic Secret."

[24]E.g., Philipp Vielhaurer, "Jesus und der Menschensohn" in *Aufsätze zum Neuen Testament*, Theologische Bucherei 31 (Munich: Kaiser, 1965), 92-140 = *Zeitschrift für Theologie und Kirche* 60 (1963): 33-77; cf. Norman Perrin, who takes all Mark's uses of *Son of man* to be redactional in *Union Seminary Quarterly Review* 23 (1968): 237-65 = *A Modern Pilgrimage*, 84-93.

claim by asserting that "indeed, this man was the Son of God" (15:39). Therefore, as *Son of God*, Jesus was both the royal Messiah *and* the dying Messiah.

Like *Son of God*, *Son of man* also qualifies Jesus Messiah in terms of his death. First, in 8:29-31 Jesus does not reject Peter's confession, "You are the Messiah." The ensuing silence command (8:30) here as elsewhere implies that something real is not to be made known.[25] Rather, Jesus qualifies Peter's confession of him as the Messiah by speaking of the impending death and vindication of the Son of man, which clearly meant for Peter at least (8:32) that Jesus the Messiah was supposedly going to die. Second, to underscore the fact that Jesus Messiah would die, Mark repeats this suffering Son of man motif six times in the extended section of Jesus' instruction of his disciples (8:27–10:52) and returns to it in the privacy of the Last Supper (14:21) and at the time of the arrest (14:41) to show that the anticipated ("the Son of man is betrayed . . . ," 14:41, cf. 9:31; 10:33; 14:21) had come to pass. Like *Son of God*, therefore, *Son of man* points to a dying Messiah. *Son of man* simply makes the point quite explicitly.

Like *Son of God*, *Son of man* also qualifies Messiah in the light of its royal motif. In 14:61, the high priest asks Jesus if he is the Messiah, the Son of the Blessed, which clearly has royal implications. Jesus responds affirmatively in 14:62 and states that the high priest will see the Son of man as described with the help of Ps 110:1 ("seated on the right hand of Power") and Da 7:13 ("coming with the clouds of heaven"), obviously royal images. The difference, if any, between Mark's "royal" use of *Son of man* from the "royal" use of *Son of God* lies in the time frame. Whereas "Son of God" underscores the royal character of Jesus Messiah in the present (cf. "You *are* my Son," 1:11; "Son of God" applied directly to Jesus by the demons, 3:11; 5:7), "Son of man" underscores the royal character of Jesus Messiah in the future (cf. "you will see . . . ," 14:62). The "royal" uses of *Son of man* in 8:38 and 13:26 support this distinction. Yet the distinction is more apparent than real, since it results more from Mark's loyalty to his tradition rather than any attempt to distinguish between Jesus as Messiah, Son of God, and Jesus as Messiah, Son of man.[26]

---

[25]Cf. 1:34, 44; 3:12; 5:43; 7:36; 9:9

[26]Mark is hardly seeking to distinguish between the use of "Son of God" (e.g., "present" rule) and "Son of man" (e.g., "future" rule), since both support the royal character of Jesus as Messiah for the Evangelist. Lack of tradition prevents Mark from speaking about the Son of God's future role in the same way the Son of man tradition (e.g., 8:38; 13:26; 14:62) allows Mark to speak about the future role of the Son of man. Yet there is no reason to think that for Mark the royal Messiah, Son of God, will not be the same and thus have the same role in the future as the royal Messiah, Son of man, since Jesus Messiah is both the royal Son of God and the royal Son of man for Mark.

In short, both *Son of God* and *Son of man* show Jesus to be the royal Messiah whose way led through death. The Messiah of the kingdom is the Messiah (Christ) of the Cross.

2. Mark's Narrative

Does Mark's narrative about Jesus' ministry support this view of Jesus based on the designations? Does Mark portray Jesus to be the Messiah, Son of God, the divinely selected, Spirit-anointed, royal figure whose way would lead surprisingly through death and vindication, a way that was openly explicated by reference to the Son of man?

2:1 The answer begins in Mark's prologue. Despite the debate over the limits of the prologue,[27] the heading of 1:1-2a sets the parameters according to Isaiah's promise. Since "as written by" (1:2a) functions as a technical citation formula, and since the formula always connects a citation with something previous,[28] the heading must read: "The beginning of the gospel concerning Jesus Messiah, Son of God, as written by the prophet Isaiah." Consequently, the "gospel concerning Jesus Messiah, Son of God" has to refer to the entire story that follows, and "the beginning" has to refer to its "prologue," whose boundaries are set by what corresponds to Isaiah's promise.[29]

One can readily see that correspondence to Isaiah in the coming and ministry of John the Baptist (1:4-8), the "voice crying in the wilderness" to prepare the way (Isa 40:3). Jesus' baptism (1:9-11) also corresponds to Isaiah's promise—the "splitting of the heavens" (cf. Isa 64:1),[30] the coming of the Spirit (Isa 42:1; cf. Isa 61:1) and the divine voice that echoes the introduction of the servant (Isa 42:1). Though not as obvious, Jesus' experience in the wilderness (1:12-13) for forty days "with the wild animals" may suggest the coming of God's deliverance in the wilderness when harmony would be established anew in creation according to Isa 11:6-9 and 65:17-25. Finally, the summary of Jesus' proclamation of "the gospel of God, saying the time has been fulfilled, the kingdom of God is at hand, repent and believe the gospel" (1:14-15), set against the backdrop of the coming of the Spirit at the Baptism, reflects Isaiah's promise of the proclamation of the "gospel" summarized by the declaration, "Your God reigns" (Isa 52:7) and the "acceptable year of the Lord" (Isa 61:2, KJV).

Therefore, Mark "begins" his story (1:4-15) about Jesus identified as the Messiah, Son of God, by showing that he has come as

---

[27]See Guelich, *Mark*, 3-5.

[28]See Guelich, *Mark*, 10.

[29]See Robert A. Guelich, "'The Beginning of the Gospel,' Mark 1:1-15," *Biblical Research* 27 (1982): 5-15.

[30]Mark's language approximates that of Isa 64:1 in contrast to the more typical language of revelation found in Mt 3:16 and Lk 3:21-22.

God's selected, Spirit-equipped and anointed proclaimer of Isaiah's promised gospel of the coming of God's reign, the fulfillment of time. His coming was preceded by the Baptist, who came as Isaiah's "voice crying in the wilderness" to prepare the way of the Coming One. The congruence of all these events with Isaiah's promise is precisely what makes the following story in 1:16–16:8 about Jesus Messiah, Son of God, the "gospel," the promised "gospel" of salvation (1:1; cf. Isa 52:7; 61:1).

2:2 The story that follows from 1:16–16:8 sets forth this "gospel concerning Jesus Messiah, Son of God." Support for Jesus' identity as the Messiah, Son of God, sent to announce and effect the gospel of God concerning the coming of the kingdom and the fulfillment of time, comes first from Jesus' authoritative ministry. Within the first section of the Gospel (1:16–3:12) we see that Jesus authoritatively summons followers (1:16-20; 2:13-14); teaches (1:21-22); commands the demons (1:23-28, 34; 3:11-12); heals the sick (1:29-34; 2:1-12; 3:1-6, 7-10); cleanses a leper (1:40-45); forgives sins and sinners (2:6-10, 15-17); and counters the Sabbath laws (2:23-28; 3:1-6), purity laws (1:41; 2:15-17), and fasting regulations (2:18-20).

These and related themes continue to dominate the first half of Mark's Gospel from 3:13 to 8:26. Jesus calls twelve disciples (3:13-19), commissions them (6:7-13), teaches (4:1-34; 7:1-23), exorcises demons (5:1-20; 7:24-30; cf. 3:22-27), controls the forces of nature (4:35-41; 6:45-52), abundantly provides food for the hungry (6:32-44; 8:1-9), heals the sick (5:25-34; 7:31-37; 8:22-26), raises the dead (5:21-24, 35-43), suspends the purity laws (5:24-35, 41), ministers to Gentiles (7:23–8:9), annuls the food laws (7:1-23), and supersedes the divorce law (10:2-12).[31] And all these events come from units or collections of units of tradition that Mark has selected, arranged, and adapted to form his narrative.

2:3 Jesus stands squarely at the center of all this activity. But what is one to conclude from this regarding who he is? That appears to be the structural force of the question, "Who do the people say I am?" coming where it does at the pivot in Mark's narrative in 8:27.

The disciples' response indicates that Jesus was seen by the public, presumably based on Jesus' ministry as portrayed in Mark to that point, to be a special man of God, a prophet—either "John the Baptist, Elijah, or one of the prophets" (8:28; cf. 6:14-16). We have no hint in these terms of a cynic sage, a divine man, a magician, or merely a charismatic wanderer. All three answers echoed by the disciples

---

[31]Some of these motifs appear in the second half of Mark's Gospel, e.g., the exorcism of the mute spirit (9:17-27), the healing of blind Bartimaeus (10:46-52), the cursing of the fig tree (11:12-14, 20-21), and the cleansing of the temple (11:15-17), but they all serve the broader purpose of Jesus' authoritative teaching which predominates from 8:27–13:37.

belong to the same Jewish category of the "prophet" that suggests Jesus had a special calling to do and speak the will of God.[32]

Yet Jesus' follow-up in 8:29, "But who do you say that I am?" calls for a corrective answer. Peter responds, "You are the Messiah," an answer that correlates with Mark's opening statement in 1:1. In other words, the teaching and events of 1:16–8:26 do not reflect the work and words of a divinely commissioned prophet, not even of John the Baptist or Elijah, but of the *Messiah, Son of God,* whose ministry does more than announce; it actually effects the fulfillment of time and the coming of God's redemptive rule, the kingdom, in human history (1:14-15), as promised by Isaiah the prophet (1:2a).

2:4 From this point forward, however, the narrative shifts its thrust. While affirming Peter's confession with a silence command (8:30), Jesus qualifies Peter's confession by speaking "openly" about the coming passion of the Son of man (8:31-32). This theme dominates the second half of the Gospel. Underscored by the repetitive, though futile, attempts by Jesus in 8:27–10:52 to instruct his disciples about his death as the Son of man,[33] the mounting conflict with the authorities in 11:1–12:44 carries the story line inevitably to the fatal events of 14:1–15:39. This motif of conflict, however, that eventually leads to the execution of Jesus, had raised its head earlier in the story. The capital charge of blasphemy in 2:6-10 (cf. 14:64), the mention of the bridegroom's being taken away in 2:20, and the murderous council between the Pharisees and Herodians in 3:6 were harbingers of ominous things to come in the story, as was the story of the Baptist's death (6:17-29).

While the motif of conflict intensifies in 11:1–12:44 and results in arrest and death, Jesus' instruction about the death of the Son of man anticipates that conflict, according to Mark, by the specific allusions in 8:31 and 10:33 to the authorities with whom he is in conflict. At the same time, Jesus' instruction about the Passion introduces a corollary motif. The suffering and death of the Son of man does not result merely from a power struggle between Jesus and the authorities. It comes as God's plan (cf. 8:31—δεῖ) in accordance with the Scriptures (9:12; 14:21). Indeed, the Son of man has come to give his life as a ransom for many (10:45, cf. 14:24). This is also what it means to be the Messiah, though neither Peter and the disciples (cf. 8:32–16:8) nor the Jewish authorities (cf. 15:31-32) could comprehend this at the time.

It was Jesus' own affirmation that he was indeed the "Messiah, the Son of the Blessed" that incriminated him with the high priest

---

[32]Cf. Horsley and Hanson, *Bandits, Prophets, and Messiahs,* 135-89, for a discussion of first-century "prophets" and their social impact.

[33]E.g., 8:31; 9:9, 12, 31; 10:33-34, 45.

(14:62a; cf. 15:31-32). His indictment by the Romans, "The King of the Jews," was attached to the cross (15:26). The high priests and the scribes mockingly referred to him as the Messiah, the King of Israel, and challenged him to come down from the cross so that they might see and believe (15:32). Therefore, Mark's narrative, like the designations reviewed above, shows that the authoritative, redemptive way of Jesus Messiah, Son of God, also led inevitably, but according to God's plan, through the death and vindication of Jesus Son of man.

3. The Messianic Secret

We have seen how the use of the designations and the story line support each other and show that the identity of Jesus Messiah, Son of God, included as a critical part of that identity and ministry the way of the Cross. How does this relate to Mark's "messianic secret," which, since Wrede, has become an inevitable part in any discussion of Mark's Christology?[34] Here again we find a further parallel.

3:1 In Mark's Gospel, Jesus attempts to silence the demons, the healed, and the disciples. In 1:23-28, the first exorcism in Mark, Jesus silences the demon who has just identified him as the "Holy One from God" (1:24-25). Form-critically, the demon's use of the exorcist's name has been taken as an apotropaic device, a defensive maneuver, in the power struggle between the demon and the exorcist.[35] The exorcist's silence command, also a common feature of the exorcism story,[36] supposedly counters the demon's move to gain control in the power struggle. Mk 1:34 and 3:11-12, however, show that Jesus' silence command has a different function for the Evangelist. It prevents the demons, who know who Jesus is (1:34), from revealing Jesus' identity as the "Son of God" (3:11-12).[37]

---

[34]William Wrede, *The Messianic Secret*, trans. J. C. G. Greig (Edinburgh: T. & T. Clark/Greenwood, S.C.: Attic, 1971); Georges Minette de Tillesse, *Le secret messianique dans L'Evangile de Marc* (Paris: Cerf, 1968); Heiko Räisänen, *Das 'Messiasgeheimnis' im Markusevangelium* (Helsinki: Finnish Exegetical Society, 1976); Christopher Tuckett, *The Messianic Secret*, (London: SPCK/Philadelphia: Fortress, 1983).

[35]See Otto Bauernfeind, *Die Worte der Dämonen im Markusevangelium*, Beiträge zur Wissenschaft vom Alten und Neuen Testament 44 (Stuttgart: Kohlhammer, 1927): 3-10; cf. Dietrich A. Koch, *Die Bedeutung der Wundererzählungen für die Christologie des Markusevangeliums*, Beihefte zur Neutestamentliche Wissenschaft 42 (Berlin: DeGruyter, 1975): 57-61; K. Thraede, "Exorcismus," *Reallexikon für Antike und Christentum*, 14 vols. (Stuttgart: Anton Hiersemann, 1950-), 8:50-51, 59.

[36]See Thraede, "Exorcismus," 51.

[37]The silence command is missing in 5:7 despite the demon(s)' identification of Jesus as "Son of God," because no one else was present except the disciples to whom the demon(s) could have revealed Jesus' identity. In 9:25-26 the mute demon could not speak, which made the silence command redundant.

3:2 Jesus also issues a silence command in at least three healing stories (1:44; 5:43; 7:36; cf. 8:26[38]). In two of these instances (1:44-45 and 7:36), however, the command is immediately and deliberately broken.[39] Furthermore, Mark does not offer any explanation of these silence commands (cf. 1:34; 9:9), and the intention behind these commands appears to differ from those addressed to the demons.[40]

As with the exorcism stories, the silence command in the healings may have been originally a formal part of the stories. Two of the three healing stories contain what appears to have been at one point in the tradition a $\acute{\rho}\eta\sigma\iota\varsigma$ $\beta\alpha\rho\beta\alpha\rho\iota\kappa\acute{\eta}$, or a magical formula (cf. 5:41; 7:34). All four stories have a privacy motif. For example, the leper appears to be alone in 1:40-44; Jesus excludes the public mourners from the scene in 5:40; and he takes the two men of 7:31-37 and 8:22-26 aside to heal them. All this suggests a secrecy topos found in healing stories pertaining to the magical/healing rite itself.[41] This *topos*, however, is dropped by Mark, who translates the $\acute{\rho}\eta\sigma\iota\varsigma$ $\beta\alpha\rho\beta\alpha\rho\iota\kappa\acute{\eta}$ in each instance and shifts the presumably traditional silence command from referring to the means of healing to refer to the event as such. Why the shift?

The Evangelist uses the silence command in these stories as a literary device for crowd control. It sets the ensuing scene according to whether the command is kept or broken. In the two accounts where the silence command is not broken (5:43; 8:26), Jesus is able to slip away to another area (6:1; 8:27) without having to deal with large crowds. In the two instances where the command is broken, Jesus encounters large crowds (cf. 1:45; 8:1). Consequently, for Mark the silence command in the healing stories no longer functions as a secrecy motif either regarding the means of the healing or about the identity of the healer.

---

[38]Lacking an explicit silence command, the command to return home and avoid the village could be taken as such in this story.

[39]Consequently, Ulrich Luz ("The Secrecy Motif and Marcan Theology," trans. Robert Morgan, in *The Messianic Secret*, ed. Christopher Tuckett [London: SPCK/ Philadelphia: Fortress, 1983], 75-96) has distinguished between the "messianic secret" about Jesus' person and a "miracle secret" about his healings, with the former remaining intact until after Easter but the latter impossible to conceal. In fact, the whole point of the "miracle secret" was that it could not be concealed.

[40]First, Jesus frequently heals in public in Mark with no attempt at secrecy (e.g., 1:32-34; 2:1-12; 3:1-6, 7-12; 5:24-35; 6:53-56). There hardly seems to be anything distinctive about the healings of 1:40-45; 5:43; 7:31-37; and 8:22-26 that should call for a silence command. Second, in one story Jesus actually tells the Gerasene demoniac to go and announce what God had done for him (5:19-20). Third, the silence command is ineffective in two of the three examples (1:45; 7:36).

[41]Gerhard Theissen, *The Miracle Stories of the Early Christian Tradition*, trans. Francis McDonagh (Edinburgh: T. & T. Clark/Philadelphia: Fortress, 1983), 140-45.

3:3 Twice Mark has Jesus charge the disciples not to divulge information about him. In 8:30 Jesus responds to Peter's confession by commanding the disciples to "tell no one about him." The context makes clear that they are not to speak about Jesus as the Messiah. Similarly, in 9:9 after having experienced the Transfiguration, which would support Peter's confession of Jesus' messianic character in 8:29 (cf. 9:1), Jesus again orders the three disciples not to "relate what they had seen to anyone." Here we are on similar footing with Jesus' silence commands of the demons. Both the demons ("Son of God") and the disciples ("Messiah") recognized Jesus for who he was, but each was forbidden to reveal this information.

Mark 9:9 explains the silence command: "Coming down from the mountain he charged them that they should not tell anyone what they had seen until the Son of man was raised from the dead." Setting the limit of the silence command until after the Resurrection implies that, though accurate, it was inappropriate to speak publicly of Jesus as the Messiah or as the Son of God until after the Resurrection. As we have seen above, Mark's use of these designations and the narrative itself indicate that *Messiah* and its complement, *Son of God*, take on special meaning through the events of the Passion. Therefore, Mark's "messianic secret," his narrative development, and his designations used for Jesus all correspond in depicting the thrust of Mark's "gospel concerning Jesus Messiah, Son of God."

"THE GOSPEL CONCERNING JESUS MESSIAH, SON OF GOD"

We have seen that, for Mark, Jesus was the Messiah, Son of God, who came to announce the gospel from God about the fulfillment of time and the coming of God's reign (the kingdom) through his ministry (1:1, 14-15) in keeping with Isaiah's promise (1:1-2a). We have also seen that, for Mark, Jesus was the Messiah, Son of God, as God's Anointed One, through whose teaching and ministry God was acting in history to establish God's promised rule and kingdom (1:16–8:28). Yet we have also seen that, for Mark, Jesus could only be accurately seen as the Messiah, Son of God, in view of his death on the cross (8:27–16:8). Mark's use of the designations, the structure of his narrative, and the "messianic secret" show how integral the Cross was to a valid understanding of Jesus Messiah, Son of God. Jesus, Messiah, Son of God, came to announce and effect the coming of the kingdom as the gospel of God, which also meant to die in keeping with God's will as the Messiah, Son of God. The Christ of the Cross was the Messiah of the kingdom.

Setting Jesus Messiah, Son of God, in the light of the Cross qualified but did not eclipse Jesus' role as Messiah, Son of God. Therefore, for Mark a Christ of the Cross did not replace a Messiah of the kingdom, nor did a gospel of Christ crucified replace a gospel of the kingdom. Mark maintains Jesus' gospel of the kingdom (1:14-15) both by sustaining the royal motifs behind *Messiah, Son of God*, as noted above, as well as by holding to a future dimension of Jesus' message about the kingdom when God's reign will become apparent for all to see. This tension between the presence and the future of the kingdom, between the work of Jesus Messiah, Son of God, present and future, comes through above all in the parables of the kingdom of Mk 4:1-34, in the promise of 9:1 (cf. 8:38) and the proleptic experience of glory at the Transfiguration (9:2-9), in the promise of the Olivet Discourse, and in Jesus' response to the high priest in 14:62. This "already but not yet" of the gospel of the kingdom is the open-ended story of Mark's Gospel, which the Evangelist calls the "gospel concerning Jesus Messiah, Son of God" (1:1).[42]

The Pauline and Johannine Corpus, Hebrews, and 1 Peter develop the significance of the Cross and appear to do so with little reference to the kingdom of God. Yet their development of the significance of Christ's death is not done in contrast to a gospel of the kingdom but always "according to the Scriptures" to show that God was acting in and through Jesus as God's Anointed One to effect God's promise of shalom, salvation, indeed, God's reign. At the same time, each looks as well to a future manifestation of God's promised shalom, salvation, indeed, God's reign.

In reflecting today on the Christ of the Gospel, we need to remember that Jesus *Christ* is Jesus *Messiah* and that the gospel of the Cross belongs integrally to the gospel of the kingdom. Failing to do so can lead not only to a distorted Christology, it can lead to a distortion of the Gospel. For Mark and for us the gospel of Christ crucified belongs inherently to the gospel of the kingdom.

---

[42]Cf. Norman Petersen, "When is the End not the End?" *Interpretation* 34 (1980): 151-66.

Paul's Christology and Jewish Monotheism

Donald A. Hagner

Professor of New Testament
Fuller Theological Seminary

The apostle Paul describes himself as possessing the fullest Jewish pedigree (Php 3:4-6; cf. Ac 22:3) and regards his gospel as nothing less than the fulfillment of the hope of Israel as contained in the Old Testament Scriptures (cf. Ro 15:8). At the same time, as is well known, he was a diaspora Jew, deeply Hellenized, and a Roman citizen who was equally well at home in the Greco-Roman world of his day. Pauline scholarship has continued to debate whether Paul's theology is to be understood primarily in light of his Jewish or his Greek background.[1] Although it cannot be denied that both backgrounds are important and helpful in understanding Paul, to my mind Paul's Jewish background is by far the more determinative for his theology.[2]

Many Jewish scholars as well as radical-critical Christian scholars regard Paul as the virtual creator of Christianity. To the degree that his theology is thought to be incompatible with or disloyal to Judaism, these scholars appeal to the influence of pagan Greek ideas upon his thought.[3] This is especially the case with regard to Paul's "high" Christology. Is not that very Christology an insuperable argument against the fundamental Jewishness of Paul's theology? How can a Jew, particularly one who allegedly remained faithful to his Jewish convictions, have held the view of Jesus that he did? Is not Paul's Christology incompatible with the monotheism of his forefathers?

---

[1] The alternative is clearly posed by Leander E. Keck in *Paul and His Letters*, 2d ed. (Philadelphia: Fortress, 1988). Scripture citations in this essay are translated directly from the Greek text.

[2] This is a conclusion I cannot defend here. I find convincing the arguments of William D. Davies, *Paul and Rabbinic Judaism*, 4th ed. (Philadelphia: Fortress, 1980), and more recently, Johan C. Beker, *Paul the Apostle* (Philadelphia: Fortress, 1980).

[3] There is, however, a modern trend among Jewish scholars to reclaim even Paul for Judaism. I have documented this in "Paul in Modern Jewish Study" in *Pauline Studies: Essays Presented to F. F. Bruce*, Donald A. Hagner and Murray J. Harris, eds. (Grand Rapids: Eerdmans, 1980), 143-65.

To answer these questions it will be necessary to look in turn at the content of Paul's Christology, at Jewish monotheism, and at Paul's monotheistic texts, and finally to make some comments on the nature and complexity of Paul's Christology. The focus will be on what Paul himself has to say, with the goal of arriving at a better understanding of his Christology and thus of his theology as a whole. Because the problem in view is not Paul's alone, the discussion will broaden toward the end of the article to include the Christology of the New Testament writers generally.

I

That Paul's theology is Christocentric becomes readily apparent from the sheer mass of material that may be designated Christological.[4] It is of course impossible to give a complete survey of that material in an article of this length. Instead, we present a review of elements of Paul's Christology that are of key importance to the subject under discussion.

The elements of Paul's Christology, like that of the New Testament itself, can be analyzed as constituting a continuum. That continuum moves from, on the one hand, the view of Jesus as one sent by God— though even here he is never one among others whom God has sent, but a unique one who can be described as the supreme Agent of God—to one who, on the other hand, is to be put with God over against all else that exists, one who is somehow the very manifestation of God himself. Indeed, it is perhaps just because of the things that can be said of Jesus as God's Agent that the continuum extends as far as it does to include Jesus as God. Thus, although the two categories are hardly distinct and inevitably overlap, we will look first at Jesus as God's Agent and then at Jesus as God.

Jesus as God's Agent

For some scholars all of Paul's Christology can be categorized under this rubric.[5] It cannot be denied that most of Paul's Christology fits this classification, nor is the richness of this material to be doubted.

At the outset it is also worth emphasizing that the real and full humanity of Jesus was for Paul a given. It was a man who had been crucified and who had risen from the dead (cf. Ro 5:15-19; 1Co 15:21, 47; Php 2:7). This fact has its inevitable effect on Paul's Christological thinking and language.

---

[4]It is also true that there are distinctly theocentric aspects to Paul's thought. This merely serves to highlight the problem before us.

[5]James D. G. Dunn, for example, argues that Paul does not teach the preexistence, incarnation, or deity (at least in the traditional sense) of Jesus. *Christology in the Making* (Philadelphia: Westminster, 1980), 211-12.

We begin with the observation that Paul can at times use adoptionist-sounding language. Thus, in the well-known passage Ro 1:3-4, he refers to Jesus as "descended from David according to the flesh and designated Son of God in power according to the Spirit of holiness by his resurrection from the dead." The implied, simple, two-stage Christology would seem ideal for Jewish-Christians, including Paul, and it may well represent the most primitive Christology of the early Jerusalem church (cf. Ac 2:36; 3:22-26; cf. also the use of Ps 2:7 in Ac 13:33). Paul's language in this passage, however, probably does not reflect a strict two-stage adoptionist Christology. The beginning of v. 3 indicates that it is God's Son who was born of the seed of David. Thus the passage could represent only the second and third parts of what may in reality be a three-stage Christology. The three-stage Christology of the hymn in Php 2:5-11 can also sound adoptionist (see v. 9).[6]

Paul refers to Jesus as one *sent by God*. The two main passages here are Gal 4:4 and Ro 8:3, where in both instances it is God's Son who is sent forth. The sending language alone does not guarantee the pre-existence of the Son.[7] Despite Dunn's arguments to the contrary,[8] however, both passages probably assume a three-stage Christology. This is clearer in the Romans passage than it is in the Galatians passage, despite the words in the latter, "when the time had fully come." When Paul writes, "sending his own Son in the likeness of sinful flesh ($\dot{\epsilon}\nu$ $\dot{o}\mu o\iota\dot{\omega}\mu a\tau\iota$ $\sigma a\rho\kappa\dot{o}s$ $\dot{a}\mu a\rho\tau\dot{\iota}as$)," he probably reflects the perspective of a three-stage Christology, such as is contained in the hymn of Philippians 2 (cf. Php 2:7, "being born in the likeness of men" [$\dot{\epsilon}\nu$ $\dot{o}\mu o\iota\dot{\omega}\mu a\tau\iota$ $\dot{a}\nu\theta\rho\dot{\omega}\pi\omega\nu$ $\gamma\epsilon\nu\dot{o}\mu\epsilon\nu os$]).

One of the most striking of Paul's Christological passages, and one that clearly points to Christ as God's Agent, is that of 2Co 5:19, "in Christ God was reconciling the world to himself." The reconciliation that is the message of the Gospel is the work of God accomplished "in Christ ($\dot{\epsilon}\nu$ $X\rho\iota\sigma\tau\hat{\omega}$)" or "through Christ ($\delta\iota\dot{a}$ $X\rho\iota\sigma\tau o\hat{\upsilon}$)," as it is also put in v. 18. The first of these prepositional phrases occurs often in the Pauline letters in describing God's accomplishment of his saving purposes through the agency of Christ. By way of example, note "in Christ" in passages such as Ro 3:24-25; 6:23; 1Co 15:22; 2Co 2:14; [Eph 4:32][9], where God acts in Christ to accomplish something. The more obvious "through Christ" (or with the pronoun, "through him"),

---

[6]Dunn denies a three-stage Christology (i.e., including preexistence) in the Php 2 hymn, but his arguments have not persuaded many. What is interesting is that the argument can be made so effectively at all. *Christology in the Making*, 114-21.

[7]See Dunn, who refers to two groups sent forth by God: heavenly beings and human messengers. *Christology in the Making*, 38-39.

[8]Ibid., 38-46.

[9]Because some question the Pauline authorship of Ephesians, references to Ephesians in this article are placed in brackets.

with God as the assumed acting subject, occurs (in addition to 2Co 5:18) in Ro 2:16; 5:21; 1Co 8:6; 15:57; Col 1:16, 20; and 1Th 4:14 ("through Jesus"). The ubiquitous occurrence in the Pauline letters of "through Christ" in reference to what Christians are enabled to do or get is in reality only the obverse of this. That is, Christ is the means—and thus used by God—whereby humanity can appropriate the benefits of God's salvific work.

So indispensable is the agency of Christ in the accomplishment of God's work that the name of Jesus Christ becomes regularly and naturally associated with God. In the salutations of the letters we encounter regularly the formula, "Grace to you and peace from God our Father and the Lord Jesus Christ" (Ro 1:7; 1Co 1:3; 2Co 1:2; Gal 1:3; [Eph 1:2]; Php 1:2; 2Th 1:2; Phm 3). Even where the formula is lacking, the association can be present (cf. Col 1:3; 1Th 1:1). Often at the end of the letters the names occur together (e.g., Ro 16:27; 2Co 13:14; [Eph 6:23]), or there is simply reference to the grace of Jesus Christ (e.g., 1Co 16:23; Gal 6:18; Php 4:23; 1Th 5:28). There are places, moreover, where the names are closely associated in the body of the letters, beyond the constant reference involved specifically in agency (e.g., 1Th 3:11; 2Th 2:16).

The titles "Messiah" and "Son of God" occur most often in contexts where the unique agency of Jesus is in view. For Paul, of course, "Christ" is used almost exclusively as a proper name rather than as a title (for a probable exception, see Ro 9:5), although there are times when the titular aspect of the name may also be in Paul's mind (e.g., 1Co 1:23-24).[10] Paul's reference to Jesus as "the Son of God" is much less frequent and has primarily in view agency rather than the ontology of Jesus' person (Ro 5:10; 8:32; and the sending passages noted above, Ro 8:3 and Gal 4:4).[11]

In his role as the unique Agent of God, it is clear that Jesus functions on behalf of God, i.e., in God's place. We may conveniently summarize this under the words *creation* (1Co 8:6; Col 1:16), *redemption-salvation* (Ro 3:24; 5:9-10, 18; 1Co 1:30; Col. 1:14; 1Th 5:9; cf. Php 3:20), *judgment* (1Co 4:5; 11:32; 2Co 5:10; [Eph 6:8]), and *eschatological restoration* (1Th 1:10; 4:15-17; 1Co 15:22; Col. 3:4). All of these items are also associated directly with God, and such references are of

---

[10]Oscar Cullmann notes that the titular aspect may also be in Paul's mind when he reverses the usual order of the names and writes "Christ Jesus." *Christology of the New Testament*, trans. Shirley C. Guthrie and Charles A. M. Hall from the German original of 1957 (Philadelphia: Westminster, 1963), 134. See also Martin Hengel, "'Christos' in Paul," in his collection of essays *Between Jesus and Paul* (Philadelphia: Fortress, 1983), 65-77.

[11]Hengel, however, concludes that for Paul the "Son of God" title indicates that Christ "is identical with a divine being, before all time, mediator between God and his creatures." *The Son of God* (Philadelphia: Fortress, 1976), 15.

course more abundant. But one who is said to function as God in these and other ways, one who is thus like no other Agent ever used by God, one who is uniquely associated with God, can begin to be thought of as one who somehow manifests the very presence of God.

The "gospel of God" (Ro 1:1; 15:16; 1Th 2:2, 8-9) can at the same time be called the "gospel of Christ" (Ro 15:19; 1Co 9:12; Gal 1:7; Php 1:27; 1Th 3:2; 2Th 1:8). The "love of God" (Ro 5:5; 2Co 13:13) is also the "love of Christ" (Ro 8:35; 2Co 5:14; [Eph 3:19]). The "grace of God" (Ro 5:15; 1Co 3:10; 2Co 1:12; 6:1; 8:1; et al.) becomes also "the grace of our Lord Jesus Christ" (2Co 8:9, and often in the concluding benedictions in Paul's letters). There is of course more of this type of material than can be tabulated here.[12] The point to be made, however, is the ready application of the same language to God and to Jesus.

A further and important element in Paul's Christology is what C. F. D. Moule has called the "understanding and experience of Christ as corporate."[13] In view here are the remarkable ways Paul (and the Fourth Gospel) can speak of the believer's relation to Christ, particularly being "in Christ" (a favorite Pauline idiom), Christ's indwelling of believers, and the metaphor of the church as "the body of Christ." The Adam Christology of Ro 5:12-21 and 1Co 15:21-22, 45-49, with its corporate basis, also comes into view here.[14] That these things can be said with respect to an individual person who had recently appeared in history is astonishing. As Moule puts it, "A person who had recently been crucified, but is found to be alive, with 'absolute' life, the life of the age to come, and is found, moreover, to be an inclusive, all-embracing presence—such a person is beginning to be described in terms appropriate to nothing less than God."[15]

We turn now to Paul's belief in the preexistence of Christ,[16] which is discussed still under the heading of the Agent of God because

---

[12]Richard T. France points out similar correspondences between "the kingdom of God" (Col 4:11) and the "kingdom of his son" (Col 1:13), "the Spirit of God" and "the Spirit of Jesus Christ" (both in Ro 8:9), and "the churches of God" (1Co 11:16; 1Th 2:14) and "the churches of Christ" (Ro 16:16) ("The Worship of Jesus: A Neglected Factor in Christological Debate?" in *Christ the Lord: Studies in Christology Presented to Donald Guthrie*, Harold Hamlyn Rowdon, ed. [Leicester, England: Inter-Varsity Press, 1982], 31-32).

[13]*The Origin of Christology* (Cambridge: Cambridge Univ. Press, 1977), 47.

[14]Herman N. Ridderbos puts very great emphasis on the determinative importance of this view of Christ as the Second Adam for the formation of Paul's Christology. *Paul: An Outline of His Theology* (Grand Rapids: Eerdmans, 1975), esp. 77-78.

[15]*The Origin of Christology*, 53. We are driven, writes Moule, to ask, "Who is this, who can be understood in much the same terms as a theist understands God himself—as personal, indeed, but more than individual?" 87.

[16]See Robert G. Hamerton-Kelly, *Pre-Existence, Wisdom, and the Son of Man*, Society for New Testament Studies Monograph Series 21 (Cambridge: Cambridge Univ. Press, 1973), 103-96; Adolf von Harnack's appendix "On the Conception of

preexistence need not entail the conclusion that Jesus was actually God.[17] The rabbis spoke of several things as preexisting the world, that is, created before the world.[18] Far more significant for the Christology of Paul and that of other New Testament writers is the background of preexistent Wisdom. New Testament scholars increasingly appeal to Wisdom as one of the important factors, if not the most important, that enable New Testament Christology to become what it is. What is said of Wisdom in such passages as Pr 8:22-31, Sir 24, WS 6-9 is very similar to what Paul says about Christ. Although the conclusion has recently been challenged,[19] Paul almost certainly held a three-stage Christology—that is, one that included the preexistence of Christ. This seems clearest in the Christ-hymn of Php 2:5-11, in which v. 6a is most naturally read as referring to Christ's existence prior to his "being born in the likeness of men" (v. 7c).[20] Christ's role in the Creation, according to Paul, also points to his preexistence (Col 1:16; 1Co 8:6). As supportive of these clearer passages, we may mention Paul's statement concerning Christ, that unlike the first Adam, "the second man is from heaven" (1Co 15:47; further possibilities to be considered are 1Co 10:4; Ro 8:3; and Gal 4:4).[21]

The material surveyed thus far has its focus in Jesus as one who functions on behalf of God. But such is the uniqueness of this incomparably supreme Agent in the accomplishment of God's will and especially his saving purposes that it is no exaggeration to say that he functions as God. It is well known that most of the Christology of Paul, like that of the New Testament generally, is functional rather than ontological in character.[22] But function, especially the over-

---

Pre-Existence," *History of Dogma*, trans. Neil Buchanan, from 3d German ed., 7 vols. (New York: Dover, 1961), 1:318-31; Reginald H. Fuller, "Pre-Existence Christology: Can We Dispense With It?" *Word and World* 2, no. 1 (Winter 1982): 29-33.

[17]Anthony E. Harvey makes this point emphatically (*Jesus and the Constraints of History* [Philadelphia: Westminster, 1982], 177-78).

[18]"Seven things were created before the world was created, these they are: the Torah, repentance, the Garden of Eden, Gehenna, the Throne of Glory, the Temple and the name of the Messiah." BT Pesahim 54a. As Alan Segal points out, "the corner toward pre-existence of the messiah was turned by suggesting that God knew the messiah's name from creation" ("Pre-Existence and Incarnation: A Response to Dunn and Holladay," *Christology and Exegesis: New Approaches*, Robert Jewett, ed. *Semeia* 30 [Society of Biblical Literature, 1985]: 93).

[19]Dunn, *Christology in the Making*, 255.

[20]Cf. Ralph P. Martin's treatment of v. 6a under the heading, "The Pre-Existent Being," in *Carmen Christi* (Grand Rapids: Eerdmans, 1983 ed. of 1967 original), 99-133.

[21]Vincent Taylor, commenting on 1Co 15:47, writes: "Christ is not the Last Adam because He is divine: He is the Last Adam and therefore divine. Divinity is the inevitable attribute of His person and work" (*The Names of Jesus* [London: Macmillan, 1954], 155).

[22]In his masterly survey, Cullmann concluded that the New Testament generally

loaded kind in this instance, cannot help but imply ontology. What can be, what must be, said of an agent such as this? Does Paul's functional Christology ineluctably move to ontological assertions about the deity of Jesus?

Jesus as God

We may begin with a look at one of the most frequent titles Paul uses in referring to Jesus, one we have not yet mentioned. Whatever κύριος may be taken to mean at different points in the Gospels, as used by Paul it means "Lord," that is, it connotes deity. To confess Jesus as Lord (cf. Ro 10:9; 1Co 12:3) is to put him together with God as one who is sovereign and transcendent, to make him practically equal to God.[23] For Paul, Jesus is one no less than "the Lord of glory" (1Co 2:8), the one who can be described as "Lord both of the dead and of the living" (Ro 14:9), "a life-giving spirit" (1Co 15:45; cf. Ro 4:17). This exaltation of Jesus is not original with Paul, but marks the faith of the church from the beginning (cf. Ac 2:36). Paul's encounter with the risen Christ on the road to Damascus confirmed to Paul beyond any shadow of doubt that Jesus was the κύριος.

What is particularly revealing about the term κύριος is the fact that the Septuagint, the Greek translation of the Old Testament made by Jews and completed before the Christian era, used it to translate the tetragrammaton YHWH, Yahweh—the name of God introduced to Moses in Ex 3:13ff. This opened the door for the early church to identify Jesus with Yahweh where appropriate, and the writers of the New Testament were not slow to enter that door. Thus Paul can at the end of the Christ-hymn, which he probably borrowed from his predecessors in Christ, include the words: "Therefore God has highly exalted him and bestowed on him the name which is above every name, that at the name of Jesus every knee should bow, in heaven and on earth and under the earth, and every tongue confess that Jesus Christ is Lord, to the glory of God the Father" (Php 2:9-11). But in Isa 45:23, the passage alluded to here, it is Yahweh who is the speaker, who identifies himself as God (Isa 45:22), and to whom every knee shall bow and every tongue confess. Similarly, the Old Testament quotations in Ro 10:11 (Isa 28:16) and 10:13 (Joel 2:32) are applied to Jesus, whereas in

---

contains only functional Christology. *Christology of the New Testament*, 326. Strictly speaking this may be correct. But it is wrong to overlook the ontological implications of this functional Christology. Although Paul, for example, may not have been concerned with ontology per se, he may still have made statements or used terminology having ontological significance.

[23]With regard to the confession of Jesus as Lord, Taylor concludes: "Invocation is next door to prayer and confession to worship. Implicit in the recognition of the lordship of Jesus is the acknowledgment of His essential divinity" (*The Names of Jesus*, 51).

fact they speak of Yahweh (in the first instance of *Adonai Yahweh*, which the RSV translates "Lord God").[24]

Further to be considered for their ontological implications are Paul's descriptions of Jesus using such language as the following: "He is the image [εἰκὼν] of the invisible God" (Col 1:15), and "in him all the fullness of God was pleased to dwell" (Col 1:19), or even more strikingly, "in him the whole fullness of deity [πᾶν τὸ πλήρωμα τῆς θεότητος] dwells bodily [σωματικῶς]" (Col 2:9). As we have already noted, in the Christ-hymn Paul speaks of Christ as being "in the form [μορφῇ] of God" (Php 2:6). In the same passage he indicates that Christ possessed "equality with God" (ἴσα θεῷ). Elsewhere, Paul can speak of Christ as "the likeness [εἰκὼν] of God" (2Co 4:4)[25] and refer to "the light of the knowledge of the glory of God in the face of Christ" (2Co 4:6). He speaks too of Christ as "the Lord of glory" (1Co 2:8) and "Christ the power [δύναμιν] of God and the wisdom [σοφίαν] of God" (1Co 1:24).

Also significant for our discussion is the fact that Paul can pray to Jesus (cf. 1Co 16:22; 1Th 3:11; 2Th 2:16; 2Co 12:8). Passages such as Php 4:4, "Rejoice in the Lord always," and Col 3:15-17, as well as the Christological benedictions at the end of the letters (noted above) and the centrality of the Lord's Supper in the worship of the early church, together with the singing of Christological hymns (such as Php 2:6-11; Col 1:15-20; and others like them, of which we have abundant evidence in the New Testament besides in the Pauline letters), point to the place of Jesus in the worship of the Pauline churches. R. T. France concludes his discussion of the subject by noting that there is "convincing evidence that the attitude to Jesus which Paul and his churches shared could fairly be called 'worship.'"[26] In a recent and particularly helpful discussion of our subject, Larry W. Hurtado finds in the "religious devotion" of Christians to Christ the fundamental factor in determining the Christology of the early church in its distinctiveness over against Jewish monotheism.[27]

---

[24] D. R. de Lacey also calls attention to 2Th 1:8-10 (cf. also 2Th 2:8), where the Lord of v. 9 is Jesus, but the Old Testament texts alluded to refer to God: see his "'One Lord' in Pauline Christology," in *Christ the Lord*, Harold H. Rowdon, ed., 197-98. Cf. Denys E. H. Whiteley, *The Theology of St. Paul* (Philadelphia: Fortress, 1964), 106ff.

[25] According to Taylor, in referring to Jesus as the image of God, Paul "was attempting to say who Christ is; and his conviction is that he is not merely a reflection of God, but that in Him, so to speak, God comes to light and is expressed" (*The Names of Jesus*, 127).

[26] "The Worship of Jesus," 32.

[27] He mentions six factors in that early Christian devotion: "(1) hymnic practices, (2) prayer and related practices, (3) use of the name of Christ, (4) the Lord's Supper, (5) confession of faith in Jesus, and (6) prophetic pronouncements of the risen Christ"

But granted all this, does Paul in fact ever refer to Jesus explicitly as God? In light of what has been said above, it may seem surprising that this possibility emerges in only a very few instances, and even those are subject to differing interpretations.[28] The most important of these is Ro 9:5, where, to simplify the options, depending on how one punctuates, the doxological utterance refers to Christ as the one "who is God over all, blessed for ever," or begins a new sentence: "God who is over all be blessed for ever." Although the most natural rendering of the Greek favors the former translation,[29] it still remains true that the other is a possibility, and thus the conclusion cannot be beyond question.[30] The only other Pauline text that offers a possible reference to Jesus as God is even less likely. In a formulaic utterance in 2Th 1:12 the phrase, "our God and Lord Jesus Christ" is governed in the Greek by one definite article. Ordinarily this would indicate that one person is in view, but in this instance it is possible, and perhaps probable, that two (closely associated) individuals are in view. A third passage, Tit 2:13, is far less ambiguous, where Jesus Christ is referred to as "our great God and Savior."[31] This was probably not written by Paul himself, but as the work of a Pauline disciple it may be taken as fairly representative of Pauline thought.

Far from discouraging us in our quest, the meagerness of these direct references to Jesus as God is just what we might expect under the circumstances. That is, granted the strength of Paul's monotheism (see below) and the uniqueness of what Paul encountered in the person of Christ, it is not at all unusual that he should be slow in being able to refer to Christ as explicitly "God." The fact, however, that such an abundance of material exists that implicitly points to Christ as the unique manifestation of God, makes it possible, perhaps even probable, that Paul could have thought of Jesus as God, without yet being able comfortably to formulate the thought into the corresponding language. The further fact that the possible references that do occur are found in liturgical or formulaic contexts—just as much of the high Christological material considered above is found in hymns—suggests that the Christology of the early church was most naturally

---

(*One God, One Lord: Early Christian Devotion and Ancient Jewish Monotheism* [Philadelphia: Fortress, 1988], 100).

[28]See Raymond E. Brown, *Jesus: God and Man* (New York: Macmillan, 1967), 1-38, and A. E. Harvey, *Jesus and the Constraints of History*, 176ff.

[29]See especially Bruce M. Metzger, "The Punctuation of Rom. 9:5," in *Christ and Spirit in the New Testament, Studies in honour of C. F. D. Moule,* Barnabas Lindars and Stephen S. Smalley, eds. (Cambridge: Cambridge Univ. Press, 1973), 95-112.

[30]Among recent commentators who argue against the conclusion that Christ is referred to as God here are Käsemann, Robinson, Wilckens, Harrisville, and Dunn.

[31]See Murray J. Harris, "Titus 2:13 and the Deity of Christ," in *Pauline Studies*, 262-77.

expressed in its worship and with a focus on the function of Jesus Christ as God's Agent rather than on questions of ontology. Yet this emphasis inevitably implied certain ontological conclusions. But we must now turn to Paul's monotheism and the tenacity with which he continued to hold to it despite his very high Christology.

II

Paul, or Saul, as he was then called, was brought up as a strict monotheist. Through all of his adult life he said the *Shema*c twice daily in accordance with Jewish practice. The fundamental text of the *Shema*c was Dt 6:4-5, which begins, "Hear, O Israel: The LORD our God is one LORD." It would be hard to imagine a more fundamentally important Jewish text than this.[32] The pious Jew hoped to be able at the moment of death to utter this as a creedal statement of his loyalty to the God of Israel. For it was this belief especially that marked off the Jew from the surrounding pagan and idolatrous polytheism.[33]

The uncompromising monotheism of the Jews also characterized the early Jewish Christians[34] and had its predictable effect in the slowness and guardedness with which they articulated their Christology.[35] Despite his high Christology, Paul shows that same concern to protect monotheism. Several passages must be noted here, and as will be seen, they stand in some tension with Paul's Christology as outlined above.

The most striking of Paul's monotheistic texts is found in 1Co 8:4-6.[36] After an explicit citation of the beginning of the *Shema*c in v. 4, perhaps reflecting the statement of the Corinthians themselves, he writes in v. 6, contrasting the popular belief in many "gods" and "lords": "Yet for us there is one God, the Father, from whom are all things and for whom we exist, and one Lord, Jesus Christ, through whom are all things and through whom we exist" (cf. the related

---

[32]See the ninth excursus, on "the *Shema*c," in Hermann L. Strack and Paul Biller-beck, *Kommentar zum Neuen Testament aus Talmud und Midrasch*, 6 vols. (München: C. H. Beck, 1922-61), 4.1: 189-207.

[33]Cf. Arthur Marmorstein's essay on "The Unity of God in Rabbinic Literature" in his posthumous volume, *Studies in Jewish Theology* (London: Oxford Univ. Press, 1950), 72-105.

[34]In the New Testament, in addition to the Pauline passages about to be examined, the *Shema*c shows its influence in, among other passages, especially Mk 12:29, 32 and Jas 2:19.

[35]The primitive character of the Christology reflected in the early chapters of Acts underlines this point. For discussion, see S. S. Smalley, "The Christology of Acts Again," in *Christ and Spirit in the New Testament*, 79-93.

[36]These texts are carefully discussed by Charles H. Giblin in his article, "Three Monotheistic Texts in Paul," *Catholic Biblical Quarterly* 37 (1975): 527-47.

passage in 1Co 12:4-6). Here the words "God" and "Father,"[37] as well as the preposition ἐκ, "from," in the sense of source, are reserved for the one God of the Shema‵ (the allusion back to v. 4 is unmistakable). Paul refers to Jesus Christ, on the other hand, as "the one Lord," and employs the preposition διά, "through," in the sense of agency. The viewpoint is consonant with the agency of Christ in creation according to Col 1:16, which uses both ἐν αὐτῷ, "in (or by) him," as well as διά. In the latter passage, however, everything is said to be created εἰς αὐτόν, "unto him," a statement our passage makes of the Father rather than of Christ.

Paul leaves unclear what we are to make of the statement that there is one God and one Lord. Although, to be sure, as Giblin rightly points out, Paul is not concerned here with ontological questions,[38] for us his language cannot fail to raise the question of the relation between the two, especially since according to the Shema‵, God is the one Lord. It seems to me that the deity of Christ is an unavoidable conclusion from this passage and yet at the same time that this affirmation is to be maintained within the boundaries of monotheism.[39] If God is the Father (and by implication Jesus is the Son; cf. 1Co 1:9), and Jesus Christ is the Agent of God (as the preposition διά indicates), then clearly a subordination of economy is assumed—a point that will become clear in 1Co 15:28.

A second text where Paul refers to God as one is Gal 3:20, where Paul is pointing out the inferiority of the reception of the Law at Sinai "by the hand of a mediator" (Moses) compared with the fulfillment that has come in Jesus Christ. Although we cannot go into the considerable exegetical difficulties presented by this verse, the point seems to be that by contrast with Sinai, in Christ the encounter with God is direct rather than indirect. The effect of the verse is paradoxically to heighten the implied Christology by viewing Christ as directly representing deity. In view, according to Giblin, is "oneness in the sense of a unique, divinely personal *immediacy* of action entailing what may be called the '*im*mediatorship' of Christ."[40] A high agency

---

[37]The title "Father" is of course always reserved for God himself. The vast majority of Pauline references to God as Father occur in connection with mention of Jesus Christ, who by implication is indicated as the Son, with an implied economical subordination (as also in the present passage). This is obviously one important way in which Paul distinguishes between God and Jesus.

[38]Giblin shows that when seen in the larger context of 1Co 8, "Paul's monotheism is personalistic rather than ontological, functional rather than notionally abstract" ("Three Monotheistic Texts," 537).

[39]De Lacey comes to the same conclusion in his discussion of 1Co 8:6: "From within the security of Jewish monotheism, therefore, Paul was able to see a duality within the Godhead well expressed in the phrase 'one God . . . and one Lord'" ("'One Lord' in Pauline Christology," 202).

[40]"Three Monotheistic Texts," 538.

Christology is entailed—one that involves unavoidable ontological implications, which, however, Paul does not spell out. Again the emphasis is on function.

A third passage where Paul speaks of the oneness of God is Ro 3:30.[41] Here the affirmation is made in connection with God's salvific work on behalf of both Jew and Gentile. God, the only God, is the God of both Jew and Gentile (cf. v. 29). By implication, there are no other gods. Paul assumes, but does not mention, that Jesus Christ is the unique Agent in the accomplishment of the justification by faith of both Jew and Gentile that is in view here (cf. vv. 22, 24-25, 26).

Yet a fourth passage, which if it is a post-Pauline addition to the text at least represents Pauline tradition, refers to the oneness of God: "to the only wise God be glory for evermore through Jesus Christ" (Ro 16:27). In this instance the adjective μόνος rather than εἷς is used, and thus it is unlikely that we have here an allusion to the Shema᾿, as in the previous instances. Again, however, where the uniqueness of God is in view, so also Jesus Christ is closely associated with God, and the uniqueness of his agency is stressed. Two references in the deutero-Pauline 1 Timothy also employ μόνος in describing God.[42]

Related to these monotheistic texts are those passages that refer to the subordination of Christ to God. 1Co 15:28 is perhaps the most specific of these: "When all things are subjected to him, then the Son himself will also be subjected to him who put all things under him, that God may be everything to every one." This motif is already anticipated earlier in 1 Corinthians, when Paul says that "Christ is God's" (1Co 3:23) and that "the head of Christ is God" (1Co 11:3). It should be noted that these statements refer to the risen and exalted Christ and not simply to the earthly Jesus.

There can be little doubt but that the Pauline material just surveyed results from the continuing strong commitment of Paul to a mono-theistic perspective. But how are we to put this together with the very high Christology we have previously found in the Pauline letters? Failure to face the full range of the content of Paul's Christology and to maintain the tension within certain of its elements can lead to Arianism on the one hand or ditheism on the other. Quite clearly the Christology of Paul involves a complexity that does not lend itself to easy formulas. What finally may we say in analysis of this situation?

---

[41]See Nils A. Dahl, "The One God of Jews and Gentiles (Romans 3:29-30)" in his collected essays, *Studies in Paul: Theology for the Early Christian Mission* (Minneapolis: Augsburg, 1977), 178-91.

[42]1Ti 1:17 contains a doxology to "the King of the ages, immortal, invisible, the only God." A further doxology in 1Ti 6:15-16 refers to "the blessed and only Sovereign, the King of kings and Lord of lords, who alone has immortality and dwells in un-approachable light, whom no man has ever seen or can see."

What explains Paul's insistence upon what seem to us to be apparently contradictory elements in his Christology?

III

Before we attempt to say something in answer to the preceding questions, it is worth pointing out that the problems confronted in Paul's Christology are hardly unique in the New Testament. They are also found particularly in the Fourth Gospel, which, it is widely admitted, contains the highest Christology of the New Testament. Here we may see that our analysis of the Pauline data in all their complexity—and in particular that we have not created an artificial problem by overestimating the Pauline view of Christ—receives a degree of confirmation. There can be no question but that, in addition to the high Christology throughout the Gospel, the Evangelist can refer to Jesus as God quite explicitly (cf. Jn 1:1, 18 [reading μονογενής θεός, "the unique God"]; 20:28). At the same time, however, the Evangelist affirms a monotheistic viewpoint (cf. 5:44; 17:3; to which may be added 1:18, "no one has ever seen God," and 8:41, despite the fact that it is spoken by the Jewish opponents of Jesus). As in Paul, Jesus is the supreme Agent of God, but with far more emphasis on his being "sent" by the Father (e.g., 5:23-24, 37; 6:38-39; 12:45, 49; 20:21). Despite the unique relationship between the Father and the Son, which involves an unparalleled oneness of Jesus with God (e.g., 5:18; 10:30),[43] there are also distinct subordinationist notes, in addition to the distinction between the Father and the Son: the Son does only what the Father does (5:36; 10:37; 14:10); the Son speaks only what the Father speaks to him (7:16; 8:28); he came not to do his will, but only that of the One who sent him (6:38); and most strikingly, the statement of 14:28 that "the Father is greater than I." Here we encounter the same complex of elements we encountered in Paul's Christology, with perhaps an even more sharply posed problem. What is particularly interesting is the fact that a Christology that does not shy away from the explicit affirmation of the deity of Christ is at the same time able to put the greatest emphasis on the agency accomplished by the Son on behalf of the Father and to accept the clear subordination of the Son to the Father.

---

[43]In 10:33ff. the Evangelist comes close to addressing the problem before us. The Jews were about to stone Jesus "for blasphemy; because you, being a man, make yourself God." Jesus answers with the words, "Is it not written in your law, 'I said, you are gods'?" If the people of Israel can be called "gods" (ʾelohim, LXX: θεοί)—"sons of the Most High," as Ps 82:6 continues—it is not wrong that Jesus be called "the Son of God."

The divine claim, however, is hardly thereby turned away. The unique Son of God is also nothing less than God. Thus an apparent consciousness of the problem does not lead to any attempt at its solution.

In Paul's Christology, as in that of the Fourth Gospel, we are left with the quandary of an estimate of Jesus Christ that amounts to an affirmation of his deity, but yet with an unflinching commitment to Jewish monotheism that involves the subordination of Christ to God. It remains for us now to make some concluding remarks about this complexity of the Pauline Christology.

1. To begin with, the origin of Paul's Christology, like that of his predecessors in the Christian faith, is to be found in *the uniqueness of this Agent, Jesus the Christ.* Jesus Christ is the Agent of God, quite unlike all other agents of God in the history of salvation. He is, of course, on the one hand, quite like the rest of God's agents (angels excepted) in his full humanity (the confirmation—indeed, the purpose—of which is to be found in his death). Yet as they knew him during his ministry, he was more than a man. No one had spoken as he spoke; no one had done the deeds he did. And in particular, no one had proclaimed with such conviction and reality the dawning of the kingdom of God. Preeminently, however, it was his resurrection as the climactic sign of the establishment of a new order that served as the catalyst for Christological thinking. It was Paul's encounter with the risen Christ on the Damascus road that fundamentally altered his estimate of Jesus[44] and transformed him into the Apostle to the Gentiles. The uniqueness of Jesus Christ in God's salvific activity was unmistakable.

2. In the earliest Christology as also in the Christology of Paul (and indeed most of the New Testament), *the emphasis is on function rather than ontology.* Jesus is the incomparable Agent of God who is so closely associated with God that he acts as only God can act. By articulating the way Christ functions, Paul like his predecessors is virtually driven to affirm the deity of this person. That is, function implies an ontology, even if the ontological implications are not spelled out in so many words.[45] The ontological aspect is an inevitability, given the affirmations Paul makes concerning the work of Jesus, past, present, and future. Who is this concerning whom such astonishing statements are made? It is impossible to avoid putting him with God over against all else that exists.

3. A centrally important fact that accounts for the unresolved complexity we have encountered in Paul's Christology is to be found in

---

[44]For the extent to which Paul's Christology is dependent on his experience of the risen Christ, see especially Seyoon Kim, *The Origin of Paul's Gospel* (Tübingen: J. C. B. Mohr, 1981), 100-268.

[45]Whiteley's comment is helpful: "It might be said that he [Paul] came as near to asserting a metaphysical equality of community of natures as his non-metaphysical framework of thought permitted him to do" (*The Theology of St. Paul*, 123).

the constraint of monotheism.[46] The natural slowness and reluctance of Paul (and other New Testament writers) to refer to Jesus as God is surely the result of this constraint.[47] It is this, too, that prevents Paul from drawing ontological conclusions otherwise implied by his high Christology. In appealing to the force of this constraint, however, A. E. Harvey goes so far as to deny that the Christology of the New Testament (including that of the Fourth Gospel) can actually have contained the belief that Jesus Christ was "divine."[48] He accordingly attempts to press all the New Testament data into the category of Jesus as Agent. Harvey can show that practically all the Christological language of the New Testament is explainable in this way and need not be taken as indicating the actual deity of Christ.[49] It is tempting to take Harvey's solution to the complexity we have noted above, that is, to reduce all the language of high Christology to the category of unique Agent—especially since, as we have seen, this is the main way in which the New Testament writers conceived of Jesus. But given the full scope of the data of the New Testament, which we have only cursorily reviewed above, such a reductionism does not seem adequate.[50] The nagging question that remains after reading Harvey's discussion is whether the New Testament writers really adhered so closely to the sort of rigid monotheism he is so intent for them to preserve. And if so, why were they not more meticulous in their choice of language? To put the question in another way, if in Jesus Christ they had encountered the Agent of God whose uniqueness was of the staggering character we read of in the New Testament, was it impossible that they could have spoken as they did, i.e., to let

---

[46]A. E. Harvey devotes a chapter to the discussion of this constraint in his stimulating book *Jesus and the Constraints of History*, 140-41.

[47]Cf. Richard N. Longenecker, *The Christology of Early Jewish Christianity* (London: S. C. M. Press, 1970), 140-41.

[48]*Jesus and the Constraints of History*, 167.

[49]Harvey focuses on the Son of God title, concluding: "To call Jesus Son of God was therefore to accept the claim implied in his words and actions that he was totally obedient to the divine will, that he could give authoritative teaching about God, and that he was empowered to act as God's authorised representative and agent" (ibid., 164).

[50]Harvey essentially restricts his discussion to the Son of God title. If he had expanded his field of study to other Christological data, the problem would have emerged more sharply. An indication of this is already apparent when he attempts to apply his thesis to the confession of Thomas in Jn 20:28, "My Lord and my God!" Harvey at one point can write of the confession that "the presence of Jesus is acknowledged to amount to the presence of God himself" (ibid., 166), but then later he adds an "as if," which to my mind hardly does justice to the intent of the Evangelist: "[Thomas] is portrayed as acknowledging Jesus to be the fully accredited divine agent, to speak to whom was as if to speak to God himself" (ibid., 172).

function imply ontology, yet without compromising their basic monotheism?

It cannot be denied that the constraint of monotheism is a particularly important factor in accounting for the slowness of the earliest Christians in drawing out the ontological implications of their Christology. When one remembers the full humanity of Jesus—that he represents not a theophany, but an incarnation—the significance of this constraint becomes all the more apparent.

4. A key question in the whole discussion concerns *the nature of monotheism*. It is important to emphasize that no New Testament writer, however high his Christology, would want to be thought of as having given up monotheism. A number of scholars have thought it appropriate, however, to speak of a Christian modification of monotheism,[51] or as L. Hurtado puts it, a "mutation" of Jewish monotheism.[52] Certainly it is the case that monotheism has been defined by Judaism, and indeed from very early in the Christian era,[53] so as to exclude the Christology of Christianity. The result is that our monotheisms today are different. But was Christian monotheism really a *modification* of first-century Jewish monotheism?

Two important points support a negative answer to this question. First, the concept of oneness reflected in the ʾ*echad* ("one") of the *Shemaʿ*, rather than referring to a strict monism,[54] allowed a degree of self-expression or self-manifestation that made possible the Christology of the New Testament writers. As the Jewish scholar Pinchas

---

[51]See especially the essay by Gösta Lindeskog, with a focus on Jewish scholars: "Jüdischer und christlicher Monotheismus—ein dialogisches Problem," in *Der Herr ist Einer, unser gemeinsames Erbe*, Karl-Johan Illman and Jukka Thuren, eds. (Åbo, Finland: Åbo Akademi, 1979), 66-80. Lindeskog himself concludes, "Der Gottesbegriff des jüdischen Monotheismus ist ein anderer als der des Christentums" (ibid., 79). Hans J. Schoeps has put the Jewish objection in the strongest language: "Pauline Christology and soteriology is a dogmatic impossibility from the standpoint of strict Jewish transcendent monotheism." He attributes Paul's views to the "acute Hellenization of Christianity" (*Paul: The Theology of the Apostle in the Light of Jewish Religious History*, trans. Harold Knight from the German original of 1959 [Philadelphia: Westminster, 1961], 166-67).

[52]*One God, One Lord*, 95-124.

[53]A famous example from Exod. R. 39.5: "R. Abbahu said: An earthly king has a father, a brother or a son. With God it is not so. Because God says: 'I am the first, because I have no father. I am the last, because I have no brother, and there is no God besides me, because I have no son.'" For other references, see Marmorstein, *Studies in Jewish Theology*, 100ff.

[54]As articulated, for example, in the second (on the unity of God) of Maimonides' thirteen Articles of Faith (in his commentary on the Mishnah, introducing his discussion of Sanhedrin 10). Giblin correctly notes that, "Within the limited horizons of Paul's functional theology, the oneness of God remains at odds with a barren arithmetical soleness as well as with pagan pluralism" ("Three Monotheistic Texts," 546-47).

Lapide has put it, "The Oneness of God, which could be called Israel's only 'dogma,' is neither a mathematical nor a quantitative oneness in the sense of a rigid uniformity, but rather a living, dynamic Oneness out of whose inner essence the becoming-one of humanity in the reconciliation of the all-embracing Shalom comes forth."[55] Christian scholars have often pointed out that the Old Testament doctrine of God, rather than being a hindrance to the advance of Christology, provided a rich background against which the New Testament could move in the direction of trinitarianism.[56] There were, of course, still problems for the early Christians in coping with the uniqueness of Christ, but they were not insuperable.[57] The monotheism of the Old Testament was amenable to the data with which Paul and the apostles had been confronted. According to Reginald H. Fuller, a "modification of Jewish monotheism without its abandonment" had already occurred in Hellenistic Judaism by the New Testament period, wherein there was a movement from functional to ontological thinking and towards making "a distinction within the deity, between God as he is in himself and God going out of himself in revelatory an salvific activity."[58] Paul and his contemporary Christians were able to say the stupendous things about Jesus Christ they did without believing that they had infringed on the monotheism of the faith they now believed had found its fulfillment in that very person.

Second, in the context of our discussion it has been seldom appreciated enough that the purpose of monotheism was to protect against *false gods*. In Dt 6:14 the point of the *Shema*[c] is underlined with the command, "You shall not go after other gods, of the gods of the

---

[55]Pinchas Lapide and Jürgen Moltmann, *Jewish Monotheism and Christian Trinitarian Doctrine*, trans. Leonard Swidler from German original of 1979 (Philadelphia: Fortress, 1981), 29. Moltmann makes a similar point in his contribution to the dialogue, 45-50.

[56]On plurality within the unity of God, see, among others, George A. F. Knight, *A Biblical Approach to the Doctrine of the Trinity* (Edinburgh: Oliver and Boyd, 1953); Aubrey R. Johnson, *The One and the Many in the Israelite Conception of God*, 2d ed. (Cardiff: Univ. of Wales, 1961); and Arthur W. Wainwright, *The Trinity in the New Testament* (London: SPCK, 1962).

[57]Wainwright calls attention to the main one in these words: "The extension of the divine personality was not the main problem for the interpreters of the Christian doctrine of God. The doctrines of Wisdom and the Spirit were generally acceptable to Jews. Rigid monotheists did not find in them an insuperable obstacle to their faith. The problem which was presented by the Christian belief in Christ was of a different order. For Christ was no emanation from the Godhead. He was not a personified concept, an invisible idea which thought like a man or felt like a man. Christ did not resemble a man. He was a man" (ibid., 38). Cf. James D. G. Dunn, "Was Christianity a Monotheistic Faith from the Beginning?" *Scottish Journal of Theology* 35, no. 4 (August 1982): 330.

[58]"The Theology of Jesus or Christology? An Evaluation of the Recent Discussion," *Semeia* 30 (1985): 109.

peoples who are round about you." Now the thought furthest from Paul and from his contemporary Jewish Christians would have been that Jesus was a false god, a god somehow in competition with the true God.[59] Any debate about whether monotheism in this sense might be impugned by their high Christology could only have been met by scorn. It is thoroughly a feature of their Christology that Jesus is the Son who has come in obedience to the will of the Father. As we have seen above, the Son is constantly identified with the Father. Jesus is not a second god, nor does he himself in any sense exhaust what God is; he is rather the self-expression and Agent of the one true God. Jesus thus represents exactly the opposite of the threat monotheism is designed to counteract. If, furthermore, we look at the places in the Old Testament where the *Shema*ᶜ is alluded to, we can see how the New Testament writers could have believed that their proclamation of Jesus was consonant with the intent of the *Shema*ᶜ. The apocalyptic emphasis in Zec 14:9, "And the LORD will become king over all the earth; on that day the LORD will be one and his name one," would have been regarded as finding its fulfillment in Christ. The universalist perspective of Mal 2:10, "Have we not all one father? Has not one God created us?" also finds its fullest realization in the gospel of Christ (Paul indeed alludes to this very text in 1Co 8:6, see above; cf. Ro 3:29-30).[60]

That the highest Christology of the New Testament is no threat to monotheism is clear particularly from the subordination passages. Although the New Testament writers could not express themselves in these words, it remains true that their economical subordination of Christ to the Father allows the possibility of the affirmation of his full deity without at the same time necessitating a backing away from monotheism.

5. A final point to be emphasized again is that the Christology of the New Testament writers, including Paul, is not stated in abstract, theoretical, or discursive prose. It is articulated almost exclusively in hymnic or liturgical fragments, borrowed from the worshiping church. Paul's most revealing Christological passages appear to be borrowed in this way from those "in Christ" before him. This material is not any the less true because of not appearing in expository prose. Indeed, it may be the truer just because it reflects the living

---

[59]In a discussion of the problem of "Monotheism and High Christology in the Gospel of Matthew," B. Gerhardsson makes this point ("Monoteism och högkristologi i Matteusevangeliet," *Svensk Exegetisk Årsbok* 37-38 [1972-73]: 125-44). For Gerhardsson, Matthew's high Christology involves an enrichment of monotheism, not its betrayal.

[60]Cf. the stimulating essay of U. Mauser, "*Heis Theos* und *Monos Theos* in Biblischer Theologie," in *Einheit und Vielfalt Biblischer Theologie, Jahrbuch für Biblische Theologie*, Band 1 (Neukirchen-Vluyn: Neukirchener Verlag, 1986), 71-87.

experience and witness of the first-century church.[61] Perhaps it was easier for the earliest church to speak of its Christ in this way; its view of Jesus Christ could thus be left implicit.[62]

Paul and the other New Testament writers with him are confronted in Jesus Christ with a mystery that they are ill-equipped to understand and express. The difficulty is caused by their experience of one who was supremely the Agent of God, one who far exceeded all others God had sent and used, one who clearly belonged with God against all else, yet one who was fully human and who was put to death by the Romans as a criminal. They were, in short, confronted with a Christ *sui generis*; all parallels were only superficial.[63] It is not surprising that they were unable finally to resolve the inherent tensions between what they were forced to conclude about Jesus and the monotheism that was their second nature. If they lived with these tensions—how uncomfortably we do not know—a time was to come when the church would be forced to articulate its doctrine of Christ in a high degree of explicitness. The Christological councils of the fourth and fifth centuries attempted to do justice to the data of the New Testament. Faced with those data, they could—rightly, in my opinion—do nothing other than affirm the deity of Jesus Christ, while yet at the same time insisting that there is only one God.[64] If we

---

[61]Hurtado has recently called attention to this importance of early Christian experience for the development of Christology: "This innovation was first manifested in the devotional life of early Christian groups, in which the risen Christ came to share in some of the devotion and cultic attention normally reserved for God: the early Christian mutation in Jewish monotheism was a religious devotion with a certain binitarian shape. The earliest and key innovation in Christianity was not the use of certain honorific titles or other christological rhetoric. Rather, it was the nature of the religious praxis of early and influential groups" (*One God, One Lord*, 124). Cf. Wilhelm Bousset's comment that the early Christian community's faith "unconsciously has that mystery [of the deity of Christ] already in cult and praxis" (*Kyrios Christos*, trans. John E. Steely [Nashville: Abingdon, 1970], 210).

[62]In his valuable article on "Hymns and Christology," Hengel has expressed the point well: "The Spirit urged them on beyond the content of preaching, the exegesis of scripture and indeed the content of confessional formulae expressed in prose to express new, bolder, greater things in 'the new song' of the hymn to Christ, because earthbound language could not do justice to God." *Between Jesus and Paul*, 95.

[63]On the failure of *religionsgeschichtliche* parallels to explain New Testament Christology, see esp. Dunn, *Christology in the Making*. Cf. Frances Young, "Two Roots or a Tangled Mess?" in *The Myth of God Incarnate*, John Hick, ed. (Philadelphia: Westminster, 1977), 119.

[64]Dunn's conclusion is apposite: "The testimony of the first Christians and of the NT writers left them no choice. Because the man Jesus was from the first at the centre of Christianity, Christianity had to redefine its monotheism. But because it was the one God of Jewish faith whom those first Christians recognized in and through this Jesus it was a redefinition and not an abandoning of that monotheism. It is thus a fundamental insight and assertion of Christianity that the Christian doctrine of the

today find their language less than ideal and if we therefore find it necessary to reexpress the central mystery of our faith, we cannot sacrifice the truth they affirmed and also be faithful to the New Testament.

It is a pleasure to offer this modest essay in honor of my teacher, colleague, and friend, Paul K. Jewett, whom I admire and respect deeply. He will doubtless smile to learn that I have written my contribution to his *Festschrift* at the Young Life Summer Institute in Colorado Springs, over which he presided as dean for nearly a quarter of a century.

Trinity is but a restatement of Jewish monotheism" ("Was Christianity a Monotheistic Faith from the Beginning?" 335-36).

Scripture and Christology:
A Protestant Look at the Work of the
Pontifical Biblical Commission

Colin Brown

Associate Dean and Professor of Systematic Theology
Fuller Theological Seminary

To outsiders the Pontifical Biblical Commission has the appearance of being (if one may misappropriate a phrase of Rudolf Otto) a *mysterium tremendum et fascinans*. Its operations behind closed doors are something of a mystery, and its periodic pronouncements have inspired both awe and fascination. Conservatives, both Catholic and Protestant, applauded its early forthright judgments on critical questions. But more recently they have shaken their heads over the Commission's apparent backtracking on the same issues. While conservatives have begun to wonder whether Rome too was sliding down the slippery slope toward liberalism and skepticism, others have wondered about the seriousness of the Catholic Church's commitment to a historical approach to Scripture and doctrine.

The aim of the present article is to review the Commission's statement on *Scripture and Christology* (1984) against the background of the history of the Commission, and to offer some observations. *Scripture and Christology* is important in two respects. On the one hand, it provides an authoritative survey of Christology today. On the other hand, it opens up a window on the present state of Roman Catholic theology and biblical scholarship. My observations will take the form of a running commentary (which will be found in both my text and my footnotes), followed by some "Concluding Observations."

THE PONTIFICAL BIBLICAL COMMISSION

The Pontifical Biblical Commission has been in existence for all but two years of the twentieth century. Its creation in 1902 was part of the Catholic Church's response to Protestant biblical criticism and to the emergence within its own ranks of Modernism.[1] The Commission's

---

[1]The following account of the history of the Pontifical Biblical Commission is indebted to the following sources: Louis Pirot, "Commission Biblique," *Supplément au*

creator, Pope Leo XIII, had already commended the study of ancient languages and the use of sound criticism in his encyclical *Providentissimus Deus* (1893).[2] At the same time he insisted that the Vulgate was the "authentic" basic version of Scripture, and he sounded a warning against the harmful effects of what was "euphemistically called higher criticism [*criticae sublimioris*]." To combat these dangers, the pope laid down that the *analogia fidei* and Catholic teaching, as received from the authority of the Church, should be followed as the supreme norm. He cautioned that, "The sense of Holy Scripture can nowhere be found incorrupt outside the Church and cannot be expected to be found in writers who, being without true faith, only gnaw the bark of Sacred Scripture and never attain its pith."[3] Although copies of Sacred Scripture might contain copyists' errors, its inspiration and inerrancy extended to all its parts, excluding all error. For God, "the supreme Truth," cannot be the author of error.[4]

The Pontifical Biblical Commission (or Pontifica Commissio de Re Biblica, to give it its formal Latin title) was established nearly a decade later by Pope Leo XIII's Apostolic Letter *Vigilantiae*.[5] The Commission, which originally consisted of cardinals assisted by consultants, was given the double task of promoting biblical interpretation along the lines of *Providentissimus Deus* and of guarding against false

---

Dictionnaire de la Bible (Paris: Letouzey et Ané, 1934), 2:103-13; B. N. Wambacq, "Pontifical Biblical Commission," *New Catholic Encyclopedia*, 17 vols. (New York: McGraw Hill, 1967), 11:551-54; Thomas Aquinas Collins, O.P., and Raymond E. Brown, S.S., "Church Pronouncements," *The Jerome Biblical Commentary*, ed. Raymond E. Brown, S.S.; Joseph A. Fitzmyer, S.J.; and Roland E. Murphy, O.Carm. (Englewood Cliffs, N.J.: Prentice-Hall, 1968), 624-32; see also the 2d ed., *The New Jerome Biblical Commentary*, 1989, 1166-74; Joseph A. Fitzmyer, S.J., *A Christological Catechism: New Testament Answers* (New York/Ramsey: Paulist, 1982), 97-130. For collections of official documents pertaining to Scripture see *Enchiridion biblicum. Documenta ecclesiastica Sacram Scripturam spectantia auctoritate Pontificae Commissionis de re biblica edita*, 4th ed. (Naples: M. D'Auria; Rome: A. Arnodo, reprint 1965); *Rome and the Study of Scripture: A Collection of Papal Enactments on the Study of Holy Scripture Together with the Decisions of the Biblical Commission*, 7th ed. (St. Meinrad, Ind.: Abbey, 1964). On trends in American Catholicism and American responses to actions of the Commission see Gerald P. Fogarty, S.J., *American Catholic Biblical Scholarship: A History from the Early Republic to Vatican II* (San Francisco: Harper & Row, 1989).

[2] November 18, 1893 (*Acta apostolica sedis* 26 [1893-1894]: 269-92; *Enchiridion biblicum*, ##81-134; *Rome and the Study of Scripture*, 1-29).

[3] *Enchiridion biblicum*, #113; *Rome and the Study of Scripture*, 17.

[4] *Enchiridion biblicum*, #124; *Rome and the Study of Scripture*, 24.

[5] October 30, 1902 (*Acta apostolicae sedis* 35 [1902-1903]: 234-38; *Enchiridion biblicum*, ##137-48; *Rome and the Study of Scripture*, 30-35). In 1904, with a view to providing a supply of teachers committed to the integrity of Catholic doctrine, the Commission was given authority to award the degrees of master and doctor of Sacred Scripture. The baccalaureate in Scripture was created in 1942.

interpretation. As Fr. Fitzmyer remarks apropos the word *Vigilantiae* (Watchfulness, Vigilance) with which the Apostolic Letter began, the watchdog aspect of the Commission prevailed.[6] Under Pope Pius X the Commission fulfilled this task by answering a series of questions about critical issues.

Between 1905 and 1915 the Commission issued fourteen *responsa*[7] (commonly referred to as "decrees") on such matters as tacit quotations contained in Scripture; the historicity of biblical narratives; the Mosaic authorship of the Pentateuch; the authorship and historicity of the Fourth Gospel; the authorship of Isaiah; the historical character of the first three chapters of Genesis; the authorship and date of the Psalms; the authorship, date, and historical truth of the Gospel of Matthew; and likewise of Mark and Luke; the synoptic question; the authorship, date, and historical truth of Acts; the Pastoral Epistles; Hebrews; and the Second Coming in the Pauline Epistles. In each case the question was given a brief but thoroughly conservative answer. The answers were not invested with infallible authority. Nevertheless, Pope Pius X explained that "all are bound in conscience to submit to the judgments of the Pontifical Biblical Commission, which have been given in the past and which shall be given in the future, in the same way as to the Decrees which appertain to doctrine, issued by the Sacred Congregations and approved by the Sovereign Pontiff."[8]

In 1943 Pope Pius XII sought to mark the fiftieth anniversary of *Providentissimus Deus* by issuing a new encyclical, *Divino Afflante Spiritu*.[9] While ratifying the earlier encyclical, the new encyclical signaled a change of course. It recommended that Scripture should be explained from the original texts, which were also to serve as the basis of new translations. It stressed the importance of textual criticism; the literal sense of the text; and the historical character, background, and circumstances of the authors and of the different literary forms of Scripture. Biblical scholars were urged to make diligent use of the light supplied by recent discoveries. They were given the exhortation: "'Let them pray that they may understand'; let them

---

[6] *A Christological Catechism*, 97.

[7] *Enchiridion biblicum*, ##160, 161, 181-84, 187-89, 276-80, 324-31, 332-39, 383-89, 390-98, 399-400, 401-6, 407-10, 411-13, 414-16; Denzinger-Schönmetzer, ##3372, 3373, 3394-97, 3398-3400, 3505-9, 3512-19, 3521-28, 3561-67, 3568-78, 3581-90; 3591-93, 3628-30; *Rome and the Study of Scripture*, 117-37.

[8] Motu proprio *Praestantia Scripturae Sacrae*, November 18, 1907 (*Enchiridion biblicum*, [##268-98] 271; *Rome and the Study of Scripture*, [40-42] 41). The clarification was repeated with slight changes in the motu proprio *Illibatae* of June 29, 1910 (*Enchiridion biblicum*, [340-42] 341), and in a *responsum* of the Commission itself in 1934 (*Enchiridion biblicm*, [##515-19] 519; Fitzmyer, *A Christological Catechism*, 98).

[9] September 30, 1943, the Feast of S. Jerome (*Acta apostolicae sedis* 35 [1943]: 297-326; *Enchiridion biblicum*, ##538-69; *Rome and the Study of Scripture*, 80-107).

labor to penetrate ever more deeply into the secrets of the Sacred Pages; let them teach and preach, in order to open up to others also the treasure of the word of God."[10] The way was now open to a more historical, critical, but nevertheless devout, approach to Scripture. At the same time, the importance of Scripture in the life and faith of the church was given renewed emphasis.

The new mandate paved the way for a change of style in the pronouncements of the Commission. The *responsa* began to give way to "letters" and "instructions,"[11] and the status of the earlier "decrees" was redefined in a carefully worded semiofficial explanation.[12] A distinction was drawn between "decrees" that touched on faith and morals and those that dealt with historical and critical matters. The former were regarded as still valid, while the latter were time-conditioned and belonged to a context that no longer existed. Since most of the early "decrees" belonged to the latter category, it could be assumed that Catholic scholars were free to pursue their research, provided that they defer to the supreme teaching authority of the Church.

In the years that followed, the watchdog aspect of the Commission has receded further into the background. A *monitum* was issued in 1961,[13] warning against the dangers of questioning "the genuine [Lat. *germanum*] historical and objective truth" of Scripture with regard not only to the Old Testament, but also to the words and actions of Jesus Christ. However, it came not from the Biblical Commission, but

---

[10] *Enchiridion biblicum*, #107; *Rome and the Study of Scripture*, 107; citation from Augustine, *De doctrina christiana*, 3.56.

[11] Fitzmyer, *A Christological Catechism*, 98-99, who sees tangible evidence of the change in the nuanced answer given in January 1948 to the question of Cardinal Suhard of Paris about the character of Genesis 1–11 (*Acta apostolicae sedis* 40 [1948]: 45-48; *Enchiridion biblicum* ##577-81; *Rome and the Study of Scripture*, 150-53). The Commission had already given an instruction on the use of versions of Scripture in the vernacular (August 22, 1943 [*Enchiridion biblicum*, ##535-37; *Rome and the Study of Scripture*, 148-49]).

[12] In 1951 the Commission dropped from the list of examination topics required for ecclesiastical biblical decrees its own previously required "decrees." In 1955 the secretary and subsecretary of the Commission used identical wording about the "decrees" in articles reviewing a new edition of the *Enchiridion biblicum* (Athanasius Miller, O.S.B., "Das neue biblische Handbuch," *Benediktinische Monatsschrift* 31 [1955]: 49-50 [excerpt in *Rome and the Study of Scripture*, 175-76]; Arduin Kleinhans, O.F.M., "De nova Enchiridii biblici editione," *Antonianum* 30 [1955]: 53-65). Despite some protest to the articles, no official repudiation was made, and there can be little doubt that the articles represent the official view (Jacques Dupont, O.S.B., "À propos du nouvel *Enchiridion biblicum*," *Revue Biblique* 62 [1955]: 414-16; E. F. Siegman, C.PP.S., "The Decrees of the Pontifical Biblical Commission: A Recent Clarification," *Catholic Biblical Quarterly* 18 [1956]: 23-29; Fitzmyer, *A Christological Catechism*, 99-100; Fogarty, *American Catholic Biblical Scholarship*, 261-64).

[13] *Acta apostolicae sedis* 53 (1961): 507; *Rome and the Study of Scripture*, 174; Latin text and Fitzmyer's translation in *A Christological Catechism*, 101-2.

from the Holy Office, with the consent of the cardinals of the Biblical Commission.

In the 1960s membership of the Biblical Commission was enlarged to include outstanding scholars who were also less rigidly conservative. In 1964 the Commission issued *An Instruction about the Historical Truth of the Gospels*[14] which identified three stages in the gospel tradition: "the *ipsissima verba Iesu*," apostolic preaching, and finally the writing of the Evangelists, which followed the "method suited to the peculiar purpose which each [author] set for himself." The Commission's position won endorsement from the fathers of the Second Vatican Council in the Apostolic Constitution on Divine Revelation *Dei Verbum*, #19.[15]

In 1971 Pope Paul VI reconstituted the Pontifical Biblical Commission, making it a counterpart to the International Theological Commission. Both Commissions were associated more closely with the Congregation of the Doctrine of the Faith (formerly the Holy Office). The Pontifical Biblical Commission was no longer staffed by cardinals aided by consultants, but (in the laconic words of Fr. Fitzmyer) by "twenty members of international background—many of them biblical scholars of recognized importance."[16]

SCRIPTURE AND CHRISTOLOGY

In 1984 the Pontifical Biblical Commission published what may turn out to be the most significant document in its history to date, its statement on *Scripture and Christology*. It is significant both for its subject-matter and for its manner of treatment. In its original form the statement was published in Paris under the title of *Bible et Christologie*.[17] The book contains the official text in Latin and the working

---

[14]*Instructio de historica evangeliorum veritate: Sancta Mater Ecclesia* in *Acta apostolicae sedis* 56 (1964): 712-18; H. Denzinger and A. Schönmetzer, *Enchiridion symbolorum*, 33d ed. (Freiburg: Herder, 1965) ##3999-99e; commentary and trans. in Fitzmyer, *A Christological Catechism*, 104-40.

[15]*Acta apostolicae sedis* 58 (1966): 826-27; trans. in Fitzmyer, *A Christological Catechism*, 141-42. The passage occurs in the context of the chapter dealing with the New Testament. For a translation of the full text see Austin Flannery, O.P., ed., *Vatican Council II: The Conciliar and Post Conciliar Documents* (Northport, N.Y.: Costello, 1975), 750-65.

[16]*A Christological Catechism*, 103.

[17]*Bible et Christologie* (Paris: Les Éditions du Cerf, 1984). Membership of the Commission is identified by Fitzmyer, *Scripture and Christology* (see n. 19, below), 54: José Alonso Díaz, S.J. (Spain); Jean Dominique Barthélemy, O.P. (France/Switzerland); Pierre Benoit, O.P. (France/Israel); Henri Cazelles, S.S. (France); Guy Couturier, C.S.C (Canada); Alfons Deissler (Germany); Bishop Albert Descamps (Belgium); Jacques Dupont, O.S.B. (Belgium); Joachim Gnilka (Germany); John Greehy (Ireland); Pierre Grelot (France); Augustyn Jankowski, O.S.B. (Portugal);

text in French on facing pages, accompanied by nine "Commentaires" written in French. The latter are not so much commentaries on the text as essays by members of the Commission on themes, relating to what Part II of the statement calls "The Global Testimony of Sacred Scripture about Christ."[18] In what follows we shall focus attention on the main text, which has been translated by Fr. Fitzmyer under the title of *Scripture and Christology: A Statement of the Biblical Commission with a Commentary*.[19]

Unlike the *Instruction* of 1964, which carried the approval of Pope Paul VI, the new statement appeared without papal approval. In this respect it was like the Biblical Commission's own earlier text *Fede e cultura alla luce della Bibbia*,[20] and the statement of the International Theological Commission *Select Questions on Christology*.[21] This fact

---

Carlo Maria Martini, S.J. (Italy); Antonio Moreno Casamitjana (Chile); Laurent Naré (Upper Volta); Angelo Penna (Italy); Ignace de la Potterie, S.J. (Belgium/Italy); Jerome D. Quinn (U.S.A.); Matthew Vellanickal (India); Benjamin Wambacq, O. Praem. (Belgium).

[18]P. Grelot, "Pour une étude scripturaire de la christologie: Note méthodologique" (113-52); A. Moreno Casamitjana, "De l'Exode au «nouvel Exode» du Deutéro-Isaïe" (153-60); A. Deissler, "La composante sociale dans le message messianique de l'Ancient Testament" (161-72); J. Greehy and M. Vellanickal, "Le caractère unique et singulier de Jésus comme Fils de Dieu" (173-96); J. Gnilka, "Réflexions d'un crétien sur l'image de Jésus tracée par un contemporain juif" (197-218); J. Dupont, "Le point de départ de l'affirmation christologique dans les discours des Actes des Apôtres" (219-36); A. Jankowski, "Connaître Jésus-Christ aujourd'hui «dans l'Esprit Saint»" (237-52); P. Benoit, "L'Aspect physique et cosmique du salut dans les écrits pauliniens" (253-69); I. de la Potterie, "Christologie et pneumatologie dans S. Jean" (271-87). In a preface, Henri Cazelles, S.S., Professor of Old Testament at the Institut Catholique, and subsequently named secretary of the Commission, describes the essays as "not . . . properly exegetical studies, but rather theological syntheses or biblical methodologies bearing on disputed topics in Christology" (*Scripture and Christology*, viii).

[19]New York/Mahwah: Paulist, 1986. Translation revised from Fitzmyer, "The Biblical Commission and Christology," *Theological Studies* 46 (1985): 407-79. Fitzmyer's translation generally follows the official Latin text, noting where appropriate variations from the French working text. He omits the "commentaries." In the following account I have preserved the italics of the original Latin and French texts, and of the English translation. I wish to acknowledge the kindness of the Paulist Press in granting permission to quote from this translation. Fr. Fitzmyer himself was not a member of the Commission when it produced the statement but has been subsequently named a member.

[20]*Atti della sessione plenaria 1979 della Pontifica Comissione Biblica*, ed. D. Barthélemy (Turin: Elle di Ci, 1981).

[21]Eng. trans. from the French text (Washington, D.C.: United States Catholic Conference, 1980). The International Theological Commission was established in 1969 as an adjunct to the Sacred Congregation for the Doctrine of Faith, in order to provide the Holy See and the Congregation with the consultative and advisory service of theologians, scriptural and liturgical experts of various schools of thought. Members of the International Theological Commission that produced *Select Questions on*

may, in itself, be an indication of the provisional character accorded to such an exercise of thinking aloud about guidelines for dealing with difficult questions. At any rate it contrasts starkly with the authoritarian, dogmatic character of the Commission's early *responsa*, and it matches the exploratory tone of the Commission's present statement.

The preface disavows certain roles that might have been assumed. It is not the function of the Commission to engage in exegetical work. Its mandate is to "promote biblical studies in a correct and proper way and to provide worthwhile assistance to the Church's magisterium." The Commission had been asked about biblical teaching concerning "the Christ-Messiah." (It is not stated who asked it, though the question is all the more tantalizing in view of the fact that the International Theological Commission had already given its own answer.) In reply the Biblical Commission did not produce a document directed at scholars. Rather, it has sought to promote an understanding of the Bible and to aid pastors in their mission by assuming a twofold task:

1. To carry out a careful examination of present-day studies in biblical Christology in order to reflect their diverse orientations and different methodologies and not neglect the risks that the exclusive use of some one methodology runs vis-à-vis a comprehensive understanding of the biblical testimony and of the gift of God given in Christ.

Christology included Barnabas Ahern, C.P.; Juan Alfaro, S.J.; Catalino Arevalo, S.J.; Hans Urs von Balthasar; Walter Burghardt, S.J.; Carlo Caffarra; Raniero Cantalamessa, O.F.M.; Yves Congar, O.P.; Wilhelm Ernst; Olegario Gonzaléz D. de Cardedal; Edouard Hamel, S.J.; Monsignor Bouslaw Inlender; Bonaventura Kloppenburg, O.F.M.; Marie Joseph Le Guillou, O.P.; Karl Lehmann; Joseph F. Lescrauwaet, M.S.C.; John Mahoney, S.J.; Gustave Martelet, S.J.; Jorge Medina Estévez; Vincent Mulago; Cardinal Joseph Ratzinger; Bishop Georges Saber; Heinz Schürmann; Otto P. Semmelroth, S.J.; Anton Strlè; Jean-Marie Tillard, O.P.; Cipriano Vagaggini, O.S.B.; and Jan Walgrave, O.P. A brief account is given by Gerald O'Collins, S.J., *What Are They Saying about Jesus?* 2d ed. (New York/Ramsey: Paulist, 1983), 64-74.

The text of *Select Questions on Christology* has been reprinted with minor changes in Michael Sharkey, ed., *International Theological Commission: Texts and Documents, 1969-1985*, with a foreword by Joseph Cardinal Ratzinger (San Francisco: Ignatius Press, 1989), 185-205. This volume also contains other documents relevant to Christology: "Christological Theses on the Sacrament of Marriage" (1977), 175-83; "Theology, Christology, Anthropology" (1981), 207-23; "The Consciousness of Christ Concerning Himself and His Mission" (1985), 305-16. To explore these documents would require separate study. However, Cardinal Ratzinger's view of the International Theological Commission is worth noting: "The special contribution of the Commission is to gain a hearing for the common voice of theology amid all the diversities that exist. . . . The wider dialogue of theologians with the bishops, as well as between bishops and the Petrine office in the Church, has found a voice. It is precisely for this reason that the Theological Commission represents an authentic continuation of the great experience of the [Vatican] Council and a clarification of its true bearing" (viii).

2. To present a summary of what the Bible affirms: a. in the Prior or Old Testament about God's promises, the gifts he has already bestowed, and the hope of God's people about a future Messiah; b. in the New Testament about the faith-understanding that Christian communities finally arrived at concerning the words and deeds of Jesus of Nazareth, understood in the light of those texts which Jewish communities had already come to acknowledge as of divine authority.[22]

The text of the statement is divided into two main parts, corresponding to the two parts of the task. It is further subdivided into numbered chapters and sections. Fitzmyer's personal commentary, which takes up almost half the pages of *Scripture and Christology*, supplies detailed documentation that is lacking in the official text[23] and offers numerous incisive comments. We shall look at the two parts in turn.

PART I. SURVEY OF METHODOLOGIES

Part I consists of "A Survey of Methodologies Used Today in Christology." Chapter 1 outlines eleven "methodologies"[24] or distinctive approaches. Chapter 2 notes sundry "risks and limits" that attach to them. It generously allows that each of the approaches "has its strong points, is based on biblical texts, and also possesses advantages and stimulative qualities." But it goes on to warn that a number of them, "if used alone, run the risk of not explaining fully the biblical message or even of proposing a watered-down picture of Jesus Christ."[25] In effect, chapter 2 does in its own mild-mannered way what the *responsa* did in earlier times, though with a significant difference. It permits itself to deal critically with earlier pronouncements, including conciliar decisions. Chapter 3 asks briefly how the risks, limitations, and ambiguities attached to the methodologies may be averted. We shall now look in turn at the eleven different methodologies under the headings assigned to them by the Commission. To

---

[22]*Scripture and Christology*, vii, quoted from the preface by the secretary of the Commission, Henri Cazelles, P.S.S.

[23]For details of works of scholars mentioned in the text of the statement and in the following discussion, readers should consult Fr. Fitzmyer's commentary in *Scripture and Christology*, 54–96.

[24]The term "methodology" is used to translate the Latin *methodus* and the French *approche*. As such, it may suggest more than what is intended in some cases. For the eleven sections do not always deal with distinctive methodologies. Sometimes they include more than one approach. In several cases the approach described is predicated on methods described in other sections. In some cases what is discussed is more a distinctive emphasis than a statement of method. The text (p. 3) indicates that no claim is made to logical or chronological order.

[25]*Scripture and Christology*, 19.

avoid repetition, we shall take together under each heading the description of the methodology, the Commission's response, and the comments of Fr. Fitzmyer.

1. The "Classical" or Traditional Approach[26]

The statement begins by noting the approach used in dogmatic theology that presents a Christology worked out systematically from conciliar definitions and patristic writings. Such an approach may be elaborated by drawing on biblical criticism (as in the work of J. Galot), salvation history, or by developing the medieval approach of Jesus' knowledge (as Jacques Maritain has done).

The Commission does not note what advantages might accrue from this traditional approach, but in its response it sees two hazards.[27] On the one hand, formulation of doctrine in this approach depends more on *"the language of the theologians of the patristic period and the Middle Ages* than on the language of the New Testament itself, as if this ultimate source of the revelation (about him) were less accurate and less suited to setting forth a doctrine in well-defined terms."* On the other hand, preoccupation with establishing classical orthodoxy runs the risk of not being open to critical exegetical questions.

In his commentary, Fr. Fitzmyer is even more specific.[28] He sees the great Chalcedonian formula with its vocabulary of *physis* ("nature"), *prosopon* ("person"), *hypostasis* ("subsistent being") as taking the New Testament data and casting them "into a philosophical construct or setting that they did not have in the New Testament itself." This enterprise runs the risk of appealing to Scripture merely to bolster up the traditional formulation. In such cases the Commission "is pointing its critical finger at Catholic fundamentalism." A case in point is the use of John 10:30 ("I and the Father are one") to establish the divinity of Christ.[29]

---

[26]Ibid., 4.

[27]Ibid., 19-20.

[28]Ibid., 58-60.

[29]Ibid., 60, where Fitzmyer cites as examples of this dubious exegesis A. C. Cotter, *Theologia fundamentalis*, 2d ed. (Weston, Mass.: Weston College, 1947), 217-25, esp. 223-24; J. Galot, *Who Is Christ: A Theology of the Incarnation* (Chicago: Franciscan Herald, 1980), 99; Galot, *La conscience de Jésus* (Gembloux: Duculot, 1971), 159. A more balanced approach is given by R. E. Brown, *The Gospel According to John (i-xii)*, Anchor Bible (Garden City, N.Y.: Doubleday, 1960), 403, 407; T. E. Pollard, "The Exegesis of John x. 30 in the Early Trinitarian Controversies," *New Testament Studies* 3 (1956-57): 334-49.

2. Speculative Approaches of a Critical Type[30]

The Commission's guarded attitude toward the language of the classical conciliar definitions becomes even more pronounced in the next section. Here note is taken of "speculative theologians" who think that the critical methods applied to the study of Scripture should be extended to the works of the Fathers and medieval theologians and even to the definitions of the Councils. The statement acknowledges that the definitions have to be interpreted in the light of their *historical and cultural context* and that the *object* of a definition (like that of Chalcedon) might be distinguished from the *formula* used to express it. Hence, when the cultural context changes, the formula could lose its force. Such formulas, therefore, have to be compared with "the basic sources of revelation," especially the New Testament.

As an instance of the kind of speculative approach that the Commission has in mind here, the statement notes the preference of the controversial Dutch scholar, Piet Schoonenberg, for speaking about the "human person" of Christ.[31] The Commissioners' own preference is to speak of his "human personality," in the sense in which the scholastics spoke of his "individual" and "singular human nature."[32]

---

[30]*Scripture and Christology*, 4-5.

[31]Piet J. A. M. Schoonenberg, S.J., was for many years professor of systematic theology at the Catholic University of Nijmegen. A leader of Dutch Catholic theology, he sought to renew traditional scholastic and neo-Thomist theology by taking into account contemporary biblical scholarship. In 1969 he published a volume on Christology entitled *Hij is een God van Mensen* (lit. *He is a God of Men*). The work had been destined for the series *Mysterium Salutis* but was rejected on account of its unorthodox tendencies. Schoonenberg was criticized by J. Galot in *Vers une nouvelle christologie* (Paris: Gambier, 1971). In 1972 the Congregation for the Doctrine of the Faith published a *Declaration to Preserve the Faith in the Incarnation and Trinity from Recent Errors* (*Acta apostolicae sedis* 64 [1972]: 237-41), which criticized the error that God "was present only in the highest degree in the human person of Jesus" (#3). Although Schoonenberg was not named in the *Declaration*, it is thought that his teaching was a target. He subsequently reformulated his position in "God's Presence in Jesus: An Exchange of Viewpoints," *Theology Digest* 19 (1971): 29-38. A sample of reactions appears in the anonymous article "Is Jesus 'Man plus God'?" *Theology Digest* 23 (1975): 59-70.

In his commentary (p. 60), Fitzmyer elucidates the issue and notes the following works by Schoonenberg: *Hij is een God van Mensen: Twee theologische Studies* ('s-Hertogenbosch: Malmberg, 1969), 66-88; Eng. trans. by Della Couling, *The Christ: A Study of the God–Man Relationship in the Whole Creation and in Jesus Christ* (New York: Herder and Herder, 1971); "Denken über Chalkedon," *Theologische Quartalschrift* 160 (1980): 103-7; "Alternativen der heutigen Christologie," *Theologisch-Praktische Quartalschrift* 128 (1980): 349-57; "Arianische Christologie? Antwort an J. Galot," *Theologie der Gegenwart* 23 (1980): 50-56.

Schoonenberg has set out his views on dogma in "De Interpretatie van het dogma," *Tijdschrift voor Theologie* 8 (1968): 243-347; German trans. Schoonenberg, ed., *Die Interpretation des Dogmas* (Düsseldorf: Patmos–Verlag, 1969). He has further

In its response,[33] the Commission tacitly passes over discussion of Schoonenberg and turns instead to further evaluation of the language of the creeds and classical theology. It acknowledges that, "The attempt at theological speculation that proceeds from a *critique of the language employed by theologians and councils* is basically correct." But it goes on to say that the critique must be tempered by two conditions, lest the testimony of Scripture be distorted. On the one hand, the "auxiliary" languages of the Church, while not enjoying the same authority as the "referential language" of the inspired authors of Scripture, are nevertheless means through which "*the absolute value of revelation*" may be grasped. The "express affirmations of Scripture" cannot be done away with. On the other hand, absolute value should not be ascribed to modes of thinking and speaking proper to our own age, especially if they were to call in question the understanding of Christ that flows from the Gospels.

---

developed his views in Schoonenberg, "Notes of a Systematic Theologian," *Concilium* 70, *Theology, Exegesis, and Proclamation*, ed. Roland Murphy (1971): 90-97; Schoonenberg, "Trinity—The Consummated Covenant: Theses on the Doctrine of the Trinitarian God," *Studies in Religion* 5 (1975–76): 111-16; Schoonenberg, "Process or History in God?" *Theology Digest* 23 (1975): 38-44; Schoonenberg, "Spirit Christology and Word Christology," *Bejdragen* 38 (1977): 350-75; Schoonenberg, "A Sapiental Reading of John's Prologue: Some Reflections on Views of Reginald Fuller and James Dunn," *Theology Digest* 33 (1986): 403-21.

Schoonenberg is critical of patristic and scholastic notions of the term *person* and of their applicability to the biblical view of God. He questions the warrantability of using the term *person* in connection with the Trinity prior to the Incarnation. In contrast to the patristic Christology which spoke of the *enhypostasia* of Jesus in the "person" of the divine Logos or Word, Schoonenberg proposed the *enhypostasia* of the Word in the "human person" of Jesus. The Logos becomes a person over against the Father only through incarnation in Jesus.

[32]*Scripture and Christology*, 5. Neither the Commission nor Fr. Fitzmyer enters into discussion with Schoonenberg. However, the Commission's suggestion is not simply a modification of phraseology; it is in effect an alternative compromise proposal that sidesteps the question of how to conceive of the ontological Trinity. Fitzmyer (p. 61) draws attention to the fact that the Commission's value judgment about Schoonenberg is placed in the descriptive part of the statement rather than in the response. It might also be asked why the Commission chose to remark on Schoonenberg here rather than in #7 on "Christology and Anthropology," which deals critically with other Catholic theologians, including de Chardin, Rahner, Küng, and Schillebeeckx. Such treatment would have been appropriate in view of Schoonenberg's affinities with at least the latter, and also in view of the fact that his own approach could properly be described as anthropological on account of its concern with personhood. The reason might be put down to a lapse in the Commissioners' thinking. Alternatively, it might be ascribed to a wish to dissociate themselves from the strongly negative criticism of Schoonenberg. By not bracketing him with Küng and Schillebeeckx, and by treating him in the way that it has done, the Commission has given tacit approval to Schoonenberg's questions without giving formal approval to his answers.

[33]*Scripture and Christology*, 20-21.

3. Christology and Historical Research[34]

In this section the statement sketches (though not quite accurately[35]) the course taken by historical research. While commending the essential rightness of the historical, critical approach, the statement dwells on the negative conclusions and impasses that it detects in it. On the Catholic side, M.-J. Lagrange emerges as the hero, though the French text of the statement appears to be saying slightly less than the English of Fitzmyer's translation, which records that Lagrange "firmly established 'the historical critical method' in the study of the Gospels."[36]

---

[34]Ibid., 5-7.

[35]It is incorrect to claim that this methodology had already proved its worth in the study of ancient texts and was therefore suitably applied to the texts of the New Testament. Critical study of sacred and profane history proceeded concurrently. A secularized approach to history was inspired by antisupernatural philosophy, as in the case of Spinoza and the English Deists, who initiated the so-called quest of the historical Jesus. In his comments Fitzmyer (p. 62) wrongly attributes the beginning of the quest to H. S. Reimarus, who has now been shown to be deeply indebted to the English Deists. Fitzmyer's observation, that the study of history as the attempt to show (in Ranke's memorable words) "how it really was [*wie es eigentlich gewesen*]" was anticipated by Reimarus, illustrates the weakness of the claim that the critical approach to biblical history was adopted from secular historians. Reimarus had been dead for over half a century when Ranke made his celebrated remark about his aim in writing history. (See Colin Brown, *Jesus in European Protestant Thought, 1778–1860* [reprint, Grand Rapids: Baker, 1988]; Brown, *Miracles and the Critical Mind* [Grand Rapids: Eerdmans, 1984]; Brown, *History and Faith: A Personal Exploration*, Grand Rapids: Zondervan, 1987).

It is also inaccurate to suggest that inquiry into the historical Jesus led to such conflicting results that it finally came to be regarded as an unsuccessful undertaking (Albert Schweitzer, *Geschichte der Leben-Jesu Forschung*, 2d ed. [Tübingen: J. C. B. Mohr, 1913]; Eng. trans. by W. Montgomery, *The Quest of the Historical Jesus: A Critical Study of its Progress from Reimarus to Wrede*, Introduction by James M. Robinson [New York: Macmillan, 1968], based on the first German ed. of 1906). Schweitzer himself believed that he had recovered the historical Jesus in his account of Jesus and his eschatological message of the kingdom. A steady stream of work on the historical Jesus continued to be produced (James M. Robinson, *A New Quest of the Historical Jesus and Other Essays* [Philadelphia: Fortress, 1983], 9-10). Nor is it correct to say that Bultmann's approach found its starting point in the impasse that the life of Jesus research had reached. In many ways Bultmann's work was a continuation of earlier critical work, developed in the context of the history of religions, as indeed the statement later acknowledges in its discussion of Bultmann (*Scripture and Christology*, 13; cf. also Colin Brown, "Bultmann Revisited" *The Churchman* 88 [1974]: 167-87).

[36]". . . ait fermement posé le principe de la «méthode historique» pour l'étude des Évangiles" (*Bible et christologie*, 21; with reference to Lagrange, *La méthode historique*, Études Bibliques Édition augmentée, [Paris: Lecoffre, 1904]; *Historical Criticism and the Old Testament* [London: Catholic Truth Society, 1905]). Fitzmyer (pp. 64-65) notes examples of Catholic scholarship that sought to avoid being reactionary, but was nevertheless hindered by the negative character of the Commis-

The Commission welcomes the ways in which the "historical method" has advanced beyond the earlier negative, "positivistic" view of history. Historical objectivity is now recognized to be not the same as that in the natural sciences. History has to do with *human experiences* that must somehow be understood "from within" and yet that occurred in a past which can never be fully reconstructed. Historical work necessarily involves an element of *human subjectivity*. The *subjectivity of the historian himself* is mingled with the historian's work at every step. There are also the factors of the "preconceived view [German: *Vorverständnis*]" that is brought to the work and of the interaction that takes place between the historian's understanding and the object of study.[37] In short, the historical study of Jesus *is never neutral*. Jesus' impact on human life and his significance go far beyond historical research. "Nevertheless, *this sort of historical investigation is quite necessary* that two dangers may be avoided, viz. that Jesus not be regarded as a mere mythological hero, or that the recognition of him as Messiah and Son of God not be reduced to some irrational fideism."[38]

4. Christology and the History of Religions[39]

Since the beginning of the nineteenth century the comparative study of religions has undergone considerable development. Impetus was given by the recovery of the literature of the ancient Near East through the deciphering of Egyptian and cuneiform inscriptions and through ethnological investigation. The History of Religions School sought to explain the religion of ancient Israel in terms of its historical, religious background. This led to Rudolf Bultmann's attempt to explain Christian origins in terms of a syncretistic fusion of Hellenistic and Gnostic elements.

The Commission's response seeks to preserve the uniqueness of Jesus, while recognizing the importance of the history of religions.

---

sion's early *responsa*, which "cast a dark cloud of fear over Catholic biblical studies in the first part of this century and induced a mentality of suspicion about any kind of critical or historical study of the Gospels and the New Testament—a mentality that still persists among many pastors, teachers, and faithful in the Church today."

[37]Fitzmyer (p. 66) draws attention to Hans-Georg Gadamer, *Truth and Method* (New York: Seabury, 1975), 235-67, 460-91 [a 2d rev. ed. with revisions by R. G. Marshall and J. C. Weinsheimer and further material by the author, was published in 1989]; Xavier Léon-Dufour, *The Gospels and the Jesus of History* (New York/ Tournai: Desclée, 1968), 28-30.

[38]*Scripture and Christology*, 7. The response (p. 21) underlines the importance of historical investigation, which must take into account the faith of the early church and the *profound unity* of Christology in its development in the New Testament.

[39]Ibid., 7-8.

Two risks are noted.[40] One is the *preconceived view* that Christ is to be explained by a *fusion* or *syncretism* of elements from his social and religious milieu. The other is that of attributing to the primitive Christian communities "a creative force deprived of all check," which turned Jesus into a "hero," like a figure in a mystery cult, and so creating the Christian myth. As in the study of other religions, the task of investigation is to discover the *specific character of the religion of Christ* and thus open a way to Christology.

5. The Approach to Jesus from Judaism[41]

From the broad context of the history of religions in general, the Commission turns to the specific context of Judaism. Two areas of scholarly interest are noted. One is what used to be called the Jewish background of Jesus. Throughout the twentieth century scholars have shown a growing interest in Jewish writings, especially after World War II in the Qumran literature and the Palestinian targum of the Pentateuch, for the light that they shed on the New Testament. More recently this interest has shifted from concern with the historical value of the Gospel texts to recognition of the Jewish roots of Christianity.

However, the statement pays more attention to the other area of interest—the attitude of Jewish scholars to Jesus. Here, too, shifts are noted. In the period after World War I, scholars like Joseph Klausner, Martin Buber, and J. C. G. Montefiore sought to break with the old religious animosity (which both Christians and Jews had indulged in) and began to study Jesus and Christian origins. Attention came to be focused on *the Jewishness of Jesus*. More recent Jewish scholars, like David Flusser, see Jesus as a religious teacher like the Pharisees of old.[42] Geza Vermes depicts Jesus as a Galilean charismatic miracle-

---

[40]Ibid., 22-23. Fitzmyer's comment (66-69) significantly enhances the discussion by filling in details.

[41]Ibid., 8-10. The statement mentions the following Christian scholars: H. L. Strack, P. Billerbeck, J. Bonsirven, R. Le Déaut, and M. MacNamara. The following Jewish scholars are named: J. Klausner, M. Buber, J. C. G. Montefiore, P. Lapide, Y. Yadin, S. ben Chorin, D. Flusser, G. Vermes, S. Sandmel, and the agnostic J. M. Allegro. Fitzmyer (pp. 69-70) supplies brief bibliographical annotation.

More recent discussions of Jesus within the context of Judaism include E. P. Sanders, *Jesus and Judaism* (Philadelphia: Fortress, 1985); Marcus J. Borg, *Jesus, A New Vision: Spirit, Culture, and the Life of Discipleship* (San Francisco: Harper & Row, 1988); James H. Charlesworth, *Jesus within Judaism: New Light from Exciting Archaeological Discoveries* (New York: Doubleday, 1988); Sean Freyne, *Galilee, Jesus and the Gospels: Literary Approaches and Historical Investigations* (Philadelphia: Fortress, 1988); Irving M. Zeitlin, *Jesus and the Judaism of his Time* (Oxford: Blackwell, 1988).

[42]Fitzmyer (p. 70) cites D. Flusser, *Jesus in Selbstzeugnissen und Bilddokumenten* (Reinek bei Hamburg: Rohwalt, 1968); Eng. trans. by Ronald Walls, *Jesus* (New York: Herder and Herder, 1969); Flusser, *Die rabbinischen Gleichnisse und der Gleichnis-*

worker, like Honi the Circle-Drawer and Hanina ben Dosa.[43] Martin Buber has compared the passion of Jesus with the sufferings of the servant of the Lord in Isaiah.[44] On the other hand, writers like Samuel Sandmel[45] treat Jesus' divine sonship as the creation of the apostle Paul.

While commending *the diligent study of Judaism* as "of the utmost importance for the correct understanding of the person of Jesus, as well as of the early Church and its specific faith," the statement sounds two notes of caution.[46] On the one hand, studies conducted *only* on these lines reduce Jesus to being just another teacher, prophet, wonder-worker, or political instigator. On the other hand, such studies tend to overlook the distinctiveness of Jesus. The statement reminds its readers that the vitality of the Christian movement and the new understanding that Jesus' gospel of the kingdom brought to human relationships with God and to "the fulfilment of Scripture," set Jesus apart from his Jewish contemporaries.

6. Christology and Salvation History[47]

In the nineteenth century "salvation history [*Heilsgeschichte*]" was championed by the Lutheran theologian, J. C. K. von Hofmann, as an attempt to ground faith in God's saving acts in history.[48] As such, it offered an alternative to narrow biblicism, critical liberalism, and speculative idealism. The Commission sees similarities with the patristic and medieval idea of the *oikonomia* of salvation.[49] In the

---

erzähler, Judaica et Christiana 4 (Bern: P. Lang, 1981). For further discussion and other literature see Donald A. Hagner, *The Jewish Reclamation of Jesus: An Analysis and Critique of Modern Jewish Study of Jesus* (Grand Rapids: Zondervan, 1984), 227-71, 313-21.

[43]G. Vermes, *Jesus the Jew: A Historian's Reading of the Gospels* (London: Collins, 1973); Vermes, *Jesus and the World of Judaism* (Philadelphia: Fortress, 1983); Vermes, "Hanina ben Dosa," *Post-Biblical Jewish Studies*, Studies in Judaism and in Late Antiquity 8 (Leiden: E. J. Brill, 1975): 178-214. For discussion see Colin Brown, "Synoptic Miracle Stories: A Jewish Religious and Social Setting," *Foundations and Facets Forum* 2 (1986): 55-76.

[44]Fitzmyer (p. 70) notes Buber's *Two Types of Faith* (London: Routledge & Kegan Paul), 102-13. For discussion of other views of the Suffering Servant see Hagner, *The Jewish Reclamation of Jesus*, 205-7.

[45]S. Sandmel, *We Jews and Jesus* (New York: Oxford Univ. Press, 1965); see Hagner, *The Jewish Reclamation of Jesus*, passim.

[46]*Scripture and Christology*, 23.

[47]Ibid., 10-11.

[48]For an account and literature see Colin Brown, *Jesus in European Protestant Thought, 1778–1860*, 244-48, 339-41.

[49]Fitzmyer (p. 73) traces the idea to Eph 1:10; 3:9, and draws attention to Ignatius, *Ephesians* 18.2; 20.1; Clement of Alexandria, *Stromateis* 1.19 #94.1; Origen, *De principiis* 3.1.14; Irenaeus, *Adversus haereses* 1.10.3.

twentieth century this type of approach has taken various forms. Some scholars, like Ferdinand Hahn, Vincent Taylor, and Leopold Sabourin, have approached Christology through the titles ascribed to Jesus in the New Testament. Among New Testament scholars, the most notable attempt to approach "salvation history" on these lines is that of Oscar Cullmann.[50] Cullmann's "functional" Christology is based on his consideration of the titles and actions of Jesus, and excludes all metaphysical and ontological considerations.

Among contemporary systematic theologians the Commission sees "salvation history" further developed in the work of Wolfhart Pannenberg[51] and Jürgen Moltmann.[52] Whereas Cullmann focused attention on biblical history, Pannenberg attempts to see salvation history in the context of universal history. The resurrection of Jesus is the anticipation of the end of history, and as such provides the key to understanding history. Moreover, Pannenberg sees the resurrection of Jesus as a historical event, accessible to the historian following generally accepted methods of procedure. As such, Pannenberg appears to treat Jesus' resurrection as *Historie*. However, Pannenberg goes on to introduce a theological element into history, when he claims that the Resurrection confirms Jesus' mission and illuminates his identity as God and man. Moltmann's eschatological perspective views human history as turned toward promise and hope. God is not an immutable, impassible being, remote from the human condition; God enters into human suffering and even death. God's action in Christ is thus the basis of social action.

---

[50]O. Cullmann, *Christ and Time*, rev. ed. (Philadelphia: Westminster, 1964); Cullmann, *The Christology of the New Testament* (Philadelphia: Westminster, 1963); Cullmann, *Salvation in History* (New York: Harper & Row, 1967).

[51]W. Pannenberg, *Jesus—God and Man*, 2d ed. (Philadelphia: Westminster, 1968, 1977); Pannenberg et al., *Revelation as History* (New York: Macmillan, 1968). For appraisals and literature see Carl E. Braaten and Philip Clayton, eds., *The Theology of Wolfhart Pannenberg: Twelve American Critiques, with an Autobiographical Essay and Response* (Minneapolis: Augsburg, 1988); Timothy Bradshaw, "God's Relationship to History in Pannenberg," in Nigel M. de S. Cameron, ed., *Issues in Faith and History* (Edinburgh: Rutherford House Books, 1989), 48-67.

[52]Fitzmyer (p. 72) notes Moltmann, *Theology of Hope: On the Ground and the Implications of Christian Eschatology* (New York: Harper & Row, 1967), 95-229; Moltmann, *The Crucified God: The Cross of Christ as the Foundation of Christian Theology* (New York: Harper & Row, 1974). In addition one may note Moltmann, *The Trinity and the Kingdom: The Doctrine of God* (San Francisco: Harper & Row, 1981); Moltmann, *Der Weg Jesu Christ. Christologie in messianischen Dimensionen* (Munich: Chr. Kaiser, 1989). For critiques see Richard Bauckham, *Moltmann: Messianic Theology in the Making* (Basingstoke: Marshall Pickering, 1987); Wayne R. Herman, "Moltmann's Christology," *Studia Biblica et Theologica* 17 (1989): 3-31; Stephen N. Williams, "On Giving Hope in a Suffering World," in Cameron, ed., *Issues in Faith and History*, 3-19.

In its response to "salvation history,"[53] the Commission sees important advantages in its approach, though it questions the vagueness of the term and notes that different practitioners raise different questions. The Commission draws a distinction between two approaches to history connoted by the German terms for "history": *Historie* and *Geschichte*. The former indicates a historical understanding based on empirical facts, gained from a study of documents. However, this attempt at detachment is significantly different from the kind of understanding associated with *Geschichte* in relation to *Heilsgeschichte*. The latter embraces common experience and "presupposes a certain *understanding* to which one has access only by the intelligence that comes with faith." The Commission implicitly distances itself from Pannenberg and some traditional positions when it insists that *the resurrection of Christ* "cannot be proved in an empirical way." For by it Jesus was introduced into "the world to come" which transcends empirical observation. Although the appearances of Christ were corroborated by the empty tomb, the Resurrection itself cannot be proved by scientific observation as a fact accessible to any observer whatsoever.[54]

With regard to the titles of Jesus, the Commission deems it insufficient to distinguish between titles that Jesus used during his earthly life and those that were given him in the apostolic age. It is more important to distinguish between the *functional titles* (defining his salvific activity) and the *relational titles* (which pertain to his relation to God as both Word and Son). However, it is not enough to focus solely on titles, for habits, deeds, and conduct "reveal what is most profound about a person."

Finally, the statement insists that a Christology "true to its colors" ought to explain more fully the meaning of eschatology and what it entails. Did Jesus announce the end of the world in his generation? Or did he introduce a new way of thinking about the course of history? "Was it not rather a question of the last stage of the *oikonomia* of salvation, inaugurated by the message of the gospel of the

---

[53] *Scripture and Christology*, 23-25.

[54] The Commission seems here to be leaning toward a fideistic position and at the same time not fully appreciating Pannenberg's approach. Pannenberg insists that the historian must use the method of analogy in assessing the credibility of an alleged event. But where evidence and testimony warrant positing the actuality of the event which nevertheless bursts analogies with our common, uniform experience, it is appropriate to accept it. Pannenberg does not deny that the Resurrection transcends ordinary experience. He insists that it can only be spoken about through the medium of this-worldly language. See Pannenberg, *Jesus—God and Man*, 53-114; Pannenberg, "Redemptive Event and History," *Basic Questions in Theology*, trans. G. H. Kehm (London: S.C.M. Press, 1970), 1:15-80; Colin Brown, *History, Criticism and Faith: A Personal Exploration* (Grand Rapids: Zondervan, 1987), 44-45, 66-70.

kingdom, but not yet consummated, which extends through the entire span of church history?"

7. Christology and Anthropology[55]

Under this heading the Commission considers four different approaches. What they have in common is that they belong to leading Catholic theologians who are perceived to take different aspects of human experience or anthropology as their starting point. As such, they reopen nineteenth- and early twentieth-century questions about "signs of credibility" that lead to faith.

Teilhard de Chardin's[56] Christology is set in the context of an evolutionary process that is moving toward increasingly higher levels of complexity and consciousness. Jesus Christ, as the incarnate Son of God, is seen as *the unifying principle of all human history and of the whole universe* from its beginning. By his birth and resurrection the meaning of the "human phenomenon" is disclosed to believers.

For Karl Rahner[57] the starting point of Christological reflection is the "transcendental" aspect of human existence: knowledge, love, and freedom. These aspects of human existence find their perfection in the person of Jesus. By his resurrection, his life in the church, and the gift of the Spirit to believers, Christ makes possible the realization of the perfect image and the goal of humanity.

---

[55] *Scripture and Christology,* 11-13.

[56] In his more detailed account of Teilhard de Chardin, Fitzmyer (p. 76) notes de Chardin's *The Phenomenon of Man* (New York: Harper, 1959); *Man's Place in Nature: The Human Zoological Group* (London: Collins, 1966); *The Divine Milieu* (New York: Harper, 1960); C. F. Mooney, *Teilhard de Chardin and the Mystery of Christ* (New York: Harper & Row, 1966); R. L. Faricy, "Teilhard de Chardin's Theology of Redemption," *Theological Studies* 27 (1966): 553-79; T. M. King, "The Milieux Teilhard Left Behind," *America* 152 (1985): 249-53. Fitzmyer draws attention to the Commission's silence concerning de Chardin's notion of the three natures of Christ, the third being neither human nor divine, but cosmic (de Chardin, *The Heart of Matter* [London: Collins, 1978], 93; de Chardin, *Toward the Future* (London: Collins, 1975), 198; cf. H. de Lubac, *Teilhard de Chardin: The Man and His Meaning* [New York: Hawthorne Books, 1965], 40; King, "The Milieux," 250).

[57] Fitzmyer (p. 77) notes Karl Rahner, *Foundations of Christian Faith: An Introduction to the Idea of Christianity,* trans. W. V. Dych (New York: Seabury, 1978); "Current Problems in Christology," *Theological Investigations* (London: Darton, Longman and Todd), 1:149-200; "On the Theology of the Incarnation," *Theological Investigations* 4 (1966): 105-20; "The Position of Christology in the Church between Exegesis and Dogmatics," *Theological Investigations* 11 (1974): 185-214; "Christology in the Setting of Modern Man's Understanding of Himself and of His World," *Theological Investigations* 1 (1974): 215-29; "The Death of Jesus and the Closure of Revelation," *Theological Investigations* 18 (1983): 132-42; "What Does it Mean Today to Believe in Jesus Christ," *Theological Investigations* 18 (1983): 143-56; "Jesus Christ: IV History of Dogma and Theology," *Sacramentum Mundi,* 6 vols. (New York: Herder and Herder, 1968-70), 3:192-209; and the German original of Karl Rahner and

The Commission gives the appearance of treating Hans Küng[58] as a scholar whose views merit attention and not as a deposed theologian of the Church.[59] In any case, Küng's tensions with the hierarchy centered on his attitude to the authority of the Church rather than on his Christology, though even here alarm bells have been sounded.[60] The Commission's interest in Küng at this point lies in his focus on the historical existence of the Jew that was Jesus. In his book *On Being a Christian* Küng faults various current views: the Christ of piety, the Christ of dogma, the Christ of the enthusiasts, and the Christ of literature. He desires a Christology that takes historical research into account, and poses the question: "Can we have less of a Christology in the classical manner, speculatively or dogmatically 'from above,' but

---

Wilhelm Thüsing, *A New Christology*, trans. D. Smith and V. Green (New York: Seabury, 1980).

For accounts of Rahner's Christology in wider context see Rahner, *The Trinity*, trans. Joseph Donceel (New York: Crossroad, 1974); Paul Imhof and Hubert Biallowons, *Karl Rahner in Dialogue: Conversations and Interviews, 1965–1982* (New York: Crossroad, 1986); Herbert Vorgrimler, *Understanding Karl Rahner: An Introduction to His Life and Thought* (New York: Crossroad, 1986).

[58]Attention is focused chiefly on Küng's views of Christ in *On Being a Christian*, trans. Edward Quinn (Garden City, N.Y.: Doubleday, 1976), 119-74.

The statement omits discussion of Küng's massive study *The Incarnation of God: An Introduction to Hegel's Theological Thought as Prolegomena to a Future Christology*, trans. J. R. Stephenson (Edinburgh: T. & T. Clark; New York: Crossroad, 1987 [German original 1970]). For discussion of this see Walter Kern, "A Theological View of Hegel," in Hermann Häring and Karl-Joseph Kuschel, eds., *Hans Küng: His Work and His Way*, trans. Robert Nowell (New York: Doubleday, 1980), 105-14. For Küng's somewhat Barthian Christological approach to the afterlife, which is also omitted from consideration, see Küng, *Eternal Life? Life after Death as a Medical, Philosophical, and Theological Problem*, trans. Edward Quinn (Garden City, N.Y.: Doubleday, 1984).

[59]On December 18, 1979, the Vatican announced that Küng, who taught in the Catholic Faculty at Tübingen, could no longer be considered a Catholic theologian. The German Bishops' Conference simultaneously announced its agreement. See John Jay Hughes, "Hans Küng and the Magisterium," *Theological Studies* 41 (1980): 368-89; Leonard Swidler, ed., *Küng in Conflict* (New York: Doubleday, 1981). For appraisals of Küng's earlier work see Häring and Kuschel, eds., *Hans Küng*.

[60]In 1977 Küng was accused by the German Bishops' Conference of denying the Nicene Creed and holding that Jesus Christ was "only an exemplary human being" and "merely God's spokesman and advocate." Küng flatly denied the charges, insisting that they were "an incomprehensible misrepresentation of his ideas." He complained of the "apparently unteachable teaching office of the church." However, he preferred a "functional Christology" to "essence Christology" and wanted to construe the Nicene Creed as meaning simply "God in Jesus Christ." See Hans Küng, *Does God Exist?: An Answer for Today*, trans. Edward Quinn (Garden City, N.Y.: Doubleday, 1978 [German original 1978]), 677-96, 792; Walter Jens, ed., *Um nichts als die Wahrheit. Deutsche Bischofskonferenz contra Hans Küng. Ein Dokumentation* (Munich: R. Piper, 1978); Klaas Runia, *The Present-Day Christological Debate* (Downers Grove, Ill.: InterVarsity Press, 1984), 58-65; Swidler, *Küng in Conflict*, 455-66.

—without disputing the legitimacy of the older Christology—more of a historical Christology 'from below,' in the light of the concrete Jesus, more suited to modern man?"[61] For Küng, Jesus was a man who took upon himself God's cause, which as such is also the cause of humanity. He is *"in person the living, archetypal embodiment of his cause."*[62] This cause is continued in the church through the Holy Spirit, and thus Christian conduct is a "radical humanism" that gives human beings true freedom.[63]

Finally, the Commission notes the thought of Edward Schillebeeckx, the former professor of the Catholic University of Nijmegen in the Netherlands, who has found himself in repeated conflict with the Congregation of the Doctrine of the Faith.[64] In his book on *Jesus,* Schillebeeckx tried to reconstruct the growth of faith among the disciples from the beginning of Jesus' ministry. The sequel on *Christ* reviews the church's experience of grace and salvation and its meaning for humanity. The Commission sees Schillebeeckx as trying to build a bridge between Jesus' experience and common human experience. His death as an "eschatological prophet" did not put an end to his followers' faith. The resurrection of Jesus is understood as divine ratification of his life. It is an experience of reality, in which Jesus is manifested as overcoming death and pledging salvation for all who follow him in his church.

The Commission's response[65] to these *anthropological approaches* to Christology recognizes that they embrace a whole gamut of differ-

---

[61]*On Being a Christian,* 133.

[62]Ibid., 545. Küng has earlier explained how he understands Jesus Christ to be "True God and true man." He repudiates the "mythological" idea of bitheism and also the heresies of monarchianism. Küng suggests the following formula: "the *true man* Jesus of Nazareth is for faith the real *revelation* of the one *true God*." Küng explains: "The man Jesus shows, manifests, reveals this human visage [of God] in his whole being, speech, action and suffering. He might almost be called the *visage* or *face of God* or—as in the New Testament itself—the *image* or *likeness of God*. The same thing is expressed also in other terms: when Jesus is called the *Word of God* or even the *Son of God*" (ibid., 444).

[63]Ibid., 554-602.

[64]Fitzmyer's commentary (pp. 80-81) focuses on Schillebeeckx's monumental companion volumes *Jesus: An Experiment in Christology,* trans. Hubert Hoskins (New York: Seabury, 1979), and *Christ: The Experience of Jesus as Lord,* trans. John Bowden (New York: Crossroad, 1981). In addition, mention may be made of Schillebeeckx, *Interim Report on the Books Jesus & Christ* (New York: Crossroad, 1981); Robert J. Schreiter, ed., *The Schillebeeckx Reader* (New York: Crossroad, 1984); Robert J. Schreiter and Mary Catherine Hilkert, eds., *The Praxis of Christian Experience: An Introduction to the Theology of Edward Schillebeeckx* (San Francisco: Harper & Row, 1989); O'Collins, *What Are They Saying about Jesus?,* 57-63; Runia, *The Present-Day Christological Debate,* 53-58. On Schillebeeckx's ecclesiastical difficulties see Ted Schoof, ed., *The Schillebeeckx Case* (Mahwah, N.J.: Paulist, 1984).

[65]*Scripture and Christology,* 25-27.

ent modes of reflection. Nevertheless, it detects a common tendency to downplay certain components that constitute human personhood in existence and history. This downplaying inevitably leads to defective Christology. The response makes no mention of names, but the nature of the comments and the matching paragraph numbers leave little room for guessing as to whom the Commission has in mind. The comments fall short of open censure, but they leave no doubt about the Commission's view of the selective and defective character of the work under review.

Evidently with an eye on the work of Teilhard de Chardin, the Commission wonders whether the evolutionary approach has paid enough attention to history and to the "Jewish milieu" of Jesus and the church. It also wonders whether evolutionary optimism deals adequately with evil and Jesus' redemptive death.

With Rahner in view, the Commission notes the risk of rejection by those who do not share the same philosophical analysis of human existence, and wonders whether enough attention has been paid to the multiplicity of New Testament Christologies.

The Commission acknowledges the legitimacy of beginning *a historical investigation about Jesus considering him as true human being*. This includes "his life as a Jew." But the Commission detects dangers lurking behind Küng's approach. The risk with Küng's Christology is seen to lie in his over-reliance on critical hypotheses that are "as restrictive as possible." Küng tends to treat as trustworthy only certain "older" texts, assuming that later ones have changed the "original" data concerning "the historical Jesus." In a manner reminiscent of C. F. D. Moule's *The Origin of Christology*,[66] the Commission asks whether the later texts did not aim at making explicit what was present implicitly from the beginning. The kind of selective treatment that Küng engages in may result in an "erroneous" interpretation of the New Testament.[67]

With regard to Schillebeeckx, the Commission recognizes the legitimacy of attempting *to establish continuity between Jesus' experience and that of Christians*. But it must be established without reliance on overly minimal hypotheses about how and in what sense Jesus, "the

---

[66]In *The Origin of Christology* (Cambridge: Cambridge Univ. Press, 1977) C. F. D. Moule rejects the idea of an evolutionary process in the New Testament, whereby Jesus was transformed from one species into another, in favor of a developmental understanding of Christology, in which later writings make explicit what was implicit in earlier ones.

[67]The Commission's main point about development is well taken. But the response to Küng raises the question of whether the statement has addressed the issues that he has raised. The complaint about selectivity leading to erroneous interpretation might well prompt Küng to complain that he too is the victim of erroneous interpretation based on a selective account of his Christology.

eschatological prophet," came to be acknowledged as "the Son of God." The Commission finds ambiguity in the way that Schillebeeckx handles this and other crucial questions.

8. The "Existentialist" Interpretation of Jesus Christ[68]

This section is remarkable in a number of ways. It is the only section to be devoted almost exclusively to the thought of one scholar. The scholar is the Protestant Rudolf Bultmann, who is treated at much greater length than any Catholic theologian. It is a little puzzling why Bultmann is treated at this point, in view of the fact that a number of the positions described earlier were taken up either in positive response or in reaction to him. Bultmann's approach could well have been described in sections 2 or 3. For his demythologizing, existentialist program was based on critical work which extended the methods of the History of Religions School and Form Criticism. Moreover, it is not quite accurate to describe Bultmann's Christology as "existentialist." Although Bultmann drew on Heidegger's existentialism for categories in which to express the Gospel for the modern world, Bultmann's thought involved much more than existentialism, as the statement itself recognizes.

Rudolf Bultmann[69] is seen as an "exegete and theologian" who picked up the negative results of the liberal lives of Jesus and agreed with the "History of Religions School" about the syncretistic origins of Christianity. As a consequence, "the 'Jesus of history' is separated as far as possible from the 'Christ of faith' (according to the principle proposed by M. Kähler at the end of the nineteenth century)."[70] In order to preserve the kerygma (albeit in a reduced form), Bultmann identified the message of the Cross and Easter with God's word of forgiveness to sinners which called for a decision of faith. Construed in existentialist terms, such decision (which has no doctrinal content) alone offers human beings the possibility of "authentic" existence. The mythological language of the New Testament has to be "demythologized," so as to permit the *existential interpretation* to emerge.

---

[68] *Scripture and Christology*, 13-14.

[69] Fitzmyer (p. 82) notes Bultmann, *Primitive Christianity in its Contemporary Setting*, trans. R. H. Fuller (London: Thames & Hudson, 1956); *Theology of the New Testament*, trans. Kendrick Grobel, 2 vols. (London: S.C.M. Press; New York: Scribner, 1952–55); *Jesus and the Word*, trans. L. P. Smith and E. H. Lantero (New York: Scribner, 1935); *Faith and Understanding*, trans. L. P. Smith (New York: Harper & Row, 1969); *Jesus Christ and Mythology* (New York: Scribner, 1958); Hans-Werner Bartsch et al., *Kerygma und Mythos*, 6 vols. (Hamburg/Volksdorf: H. Reich, 1948-75), Eng. trans. by R. H. Fuller of vols. 1 and 2 in combined volume *Kerygma and Myth: A Theological Debate* (London: SPCK, 1972).

Other works relevant to Bultmann's Christology include Bultmann, *The History of the Synoptic Tradition*, trans. John Marsh, rev. ed. (Oxford: Blackwell, 1972); *Essays Philosophical and Theological*, trans. J. C. G. Greig (New York: Macmillan, 1955);

The Commission closes its account of Bultmann's work by noting
that in this regard Bultmann's reasoning depends heavily on the
philosophical principles set out by Martin Heidegger in *Sein und
Zeit*.[71] Note is taken of Bultmann's exegetical work, where "no differently from his contemporaries" Martin Dibelius and K. L. Schmidt,
Bultmann pressed beyond classical literary criticism into form criticism which was more interested in the use of Jesus-material in the
primitive church than in its historicity. Finally, note is taken of the
need that Bultmann's students have sensed to situate Jesus "at the
outset and origin of Christology."[72]

History and Eschatology: The Presence of Eternity, Gifford Lectures 1955 (Edinburgh:
Edinburgh Univ. Press; New York: Harper & Row, 1957); *The Gospel of John: A Com-
mentary*, trans. G. R. Beasley-Murray (Philadelphia: Westminster, 1971); *New
Testament and Mythology and Other Basic Writings*, ed. Schubert M. Ogden
(Philadelphia: Fortress, 1984); *Interpreting Faith for the Modern Era*, ed. Roger
Johnson (London: Collins, 1987); Charles W. Kegley, ed., *The Theology of Rudolf
Bultmann* (New York: Harper & Row, 1966 [containing Bultmann's "Autobiographical
Reflections," xix–xxv]); Walter Schmithals, *An Introduction to the Theology of
Rudolf Bultmann* (London: S.C.M. Press, 1968); Roger A. Johnson, *The Origins of
Demythologizing: Philosophy and Historiography in the Theology of Rudolf Bult-
mann*, Studies in the History of Religions (Supplements to *Numen*) 28 (Leiden: E. J.
Brill, 1974); Erich Dinkler, ed., *Zeit und Geschichte. Dankesgabe an Rudolf Bultmann
zum 80. Geburtstag* (Tübingen: J. C. B. Mohr [Paul Siebeck], 1964), partial English
version, *The Future of our Religious Past: Essays in Honor of Rudolf Bultmann*, ed.
James M. Robinson (London: S.C.M. Press, 1971); Berndt Jaspert, ed., *Rudolf Bultmanns
Werk und Wirkung* (Darmstadt: Wissenschaftliche Buchgesellschaft, 1984). For
other literature see Brown (n. 35).

[70]*Scripture and Christology*, 13. Here the Commission seems to have misunderstood Kähler's intention, for Kähler was highly critical of the liberal quest to find a
"historical Jesus" who was different from *the historic biblical Christ of faith* (see
Martin Kähler, *The So-Called Historical Jesus and the Historic Biblical Christ*,
trans. and ed. with an intro. by Carl E. Braaten, Fortress Texts in Modern Theology
[Philadelphia: Fortress, 1988]).

[71]An English translation of *Sein und Zeit* (1927) has been made by John Macquarrie
and Edward Robinson, *Being and Time* (New York: Harper & Row, 1962).

[72]Here the name of Ernst Käsemann is noted in allusion to the so-called "new
quest" of the historical Jesus, conducted by members of the Bultmann school on the
basis of a Bultmannian understanding of the kerygma. The discussion was opened in
1953 when Käsemann presented an address to a meeting of "old Marburgers" on "The
Problem of the Historical Jesus" (Eng. trans., from 2d German ed., by W. J. Montague in
Käsemann, *Essays on New Testament Themes*, Studies in Biblical Theology 41
[London: S.C.M. Press, 1964], 15–47). The discussion was carried forward by Ernst
Fuchs, Gerhard Ebeling, Günther Bornkamm, Hans Conzelmann, and others.

The emphasis of the post-Bultmannian "new quest" of the historical Jesus fell on
positing a historical Jesus behind the Bultmannian understanding of the kerygma of
the Cross and Resurrection. As such, it was confined to members of the Bultmann
school who accepted Bultmann's basic approach. Bultmann himself responded with a
qualified affirmation in a lecture to the Heidelberg Academy of Sciences ("The Primitive Christian Kerygma and the Historical Jesus," [1960], Eng. trans. in Carl E.
Braaten and Roy A. Harrisville, eds., *The Historical Jesus and the Kerygmatic*

In response,[73] the Commission expresses appreciation for the way in which the existentialist approach seeks to relate exegesis to living faith and to show how texts function in the life of the church past and present. However, the approach tends to minimize the importance for faith of both Jesus and the Old Testament. Its treatment of mythological language runs the risk of reducing Christology to anthropology. Bultmann and his followers tend to equate the *symbolic language* of the New Testament with "mythological" language. If Christ's resurrection and exaltation are merely "mythological transformations" of the Easter message, it is incomprehensible how the Christian faith could have been "born of the Cross." Likewise, if Jesus is not the Son of God in a unique sense, it is not evident why we should follow Bultmann in regarding him as God's "last word" to us through the medium of the Cross. Moreover, the existentialist emphasis on the *decision of faith* is apt to exclude the *social aspects of faith*, and the vaguely defined "morality of love" seems to be opposed to the "morality of law" and the positive demands of justice. The limitations of Bultmann's position are seen to be underscored by the desire of Bultmann's disciples to restore Jesus to *the origins of Christology* in what has been called the "new quest" of the historical Jesus.

9. Christology and Social Concerns[74]

Bultmann and his followers formed a fairly closely knit school of thought, linked chiefly by their shared skepticism as to what may be known about the Jesus of history and an existential interpretation of

---

Christ: Essays on the New Quest of the Historical Jesus [New York, Nashville: Abingdon, 1964], 15-42). For an account and apologia see James M. Robinson, *A New Quest of the Historical Jesus and Other Essays* (Philadelphia: Fortress, 1983).

[73]*Scripture and Christology*, 27-28. The reservations expressed by the Commission are shared by many others, including the present writer (see n. 35). Fitzmyer (p. 85) notes that his own work on the term *Son of God* calls in question the Bultmannian account of its Hellenistic provenance (J. A. Fitzmyer, "The Contribution of Qumran Aramaic to the Study of the New Testament," in *A Wandering Aramean: Collected Aramaic Essays*, Society of Biblical Literature Monograph Series 24 [Missoula, Montana, 1979], 85-113, esp. 90-94).

However, it must also be observed that the representation of Bultmann primarily as an existentialist may be misleading. Bultmann's critical work was based on his massive form-critical and literary studies, which from the outset were deeply influenced by the "history of religions school" of which Bultmann could be said to be a representative. His understanding of the world in relation to the transcendent was formed under the influence of Neo-Kantianism and Enlightenment historiography. It was only at a relatively late stage in his career that Bultmann turned to Heidegger's existential categories in order to express his understanding of the meaning of the Gospel for the modern world. In other words, the existentialist aspect of Bultmann represents a hermeneutic that is grounded on critical and philosophical positions derived from elsewhere.

[74]*Scripture and Christology*, 14-16.

faith. The writers considered in the following section represent a variety of viewpoints (both Christian and atheistic). They share a common confidence that they know something of the historical Jesus and that something shows him to have been a social reformer.

In the nineteenth century Socialist Utopians studied the social principles of the Gospel. Even Karl Marx was influenced by a biblical messianism, despite his well-known denunciation of religion as the opium of the people. However, the Commission's main concern lies with diverse contemporary trends.

The Commission notes the landmark work of S. G. F. Brandon, who linked Jesus with the Zealots engaged in a political resistance movement against the Roman Empire.[75] However, Liberation Theology has gone beyond mere academic interest in trying to discover what Jesus actually thought and did; in its picture of "Christ the liberator" it has sought a foundation for hope and *praxis*. "To bring a social and political freedom to human beings ... did not Jesus *espouse the cause of the poor* and rise up against the abuses of authorities who were oppressing the people in economic, political, ideological, and even religious matters?"[76] In particular, two of the many different types of Liberation Theology are noted. On the one hand, theologians like G. Gutiérrez (who is widely credited with coining the term *liberation theology*) and his disciple and friend, Leonardo Boff, see liberation as embracing all human affairs, including the basic relationship of humans to God. On the other hand, theologians like Jon Sobrino concentrate mainly on social relations.[77]

---

[75]S. G. F. Brandon, *The Fall of Jerusalem and the Christian Church: A Study of the Effects of the Overthrow of A.D. 70 on Christianity* (London: SPCK, 1951); Brandon, *Jesus and the Zealots: A Study of the Political Factor in Primitive Christianity* (Manchester: Manchester Univ. Press; New York: Scribner, 1967). Brandon claimed that Jesus sympathized with the ideals and aims of the Zealot movement, though this was obscured by Mark and even more so by Matthew and the pacifist Luke.

Numerous studies have thrown light on the issue and have questioned Brandon's thesis. See Alan Richardson, *The Political Christ* (London: S.C.M. Press, 1973); Martin Hengel, *Victory over Violence: Jesus and the Revolutionists* (Philadelphia: Fortress, 1973); *Christ and Power* (Philadelphia: Fortress, 1974); *The Zealots: Investigations into the Jewish Freedom Movement in the Period from Herod I until 70 A.D.* (Edinburgh: T. & T. Clark, 1989, based on 2d German ed. of 1976); Gerd Theissen, *Sociology of Early Palestinian Christianity* (Philadelphia: Fortress, 1978); Ernst Bammel and C. F. D. Moule, eds., *Jesus and the Politics of His Day* (Cambridge: Cambridge Univ. Press, 1984); Marcus J. Borg, *Conflict, Holiness and Politics in the Teachings of Jesus* (New York, Toronto: Edwin Mellen, 1984); Richard A. Horsley and John S. Hanson, *Bandits, Prophets, and Messiahs: Popular Movements at the Time of Jesus* (Minneapolis: Winston, 1985); Richard A. Horsley, *Jesus and the Spiral of Violence: Popular Jewish Resistance in Roman Palestine* (San Francisco: Harper & Row, 1987); Horsley, *Sociology and the Jesus Movement* (New York: Crossroad, 1989).

[76]*Scripture and Christology*, 15.

[77]Fitzmyer (p. 86) notes G. Gutiérrez, *A Theology of Liberation: History, Politics*

The statement then turns to Marxists, whom it carefully distinguishes from Liberation Theologians. (In fact, the statement studiously avoids the identification of Liberation Theology with Marxist teaching and ideology, even though some of its proponents have been so influenced.) It notes Ernst Bloch's "principle of hope," Milan Machoveč's appeal to the *praxis* of Jesus, and Fernando Belo's materialist reading of the Gospel, and their influence on Christian thought.[78] It ruefully observes that in such readings of the Gospels,

---

and Salvation, trans. and ed. C. Inda and J. Eagelson (Maryknoll, N.Y.: Orbis, 1973 [Spanish original 1971]); Leonardo Boff, *Jesus Christ Liberator: A Critical Christology for Our Time,* trans. Patrick Hughes (Maryknoll, N.Y.: Orbis, 1978 [Spanish original 1972]); Jon Sobrino, *Christology at the Crossroads: A Latin American Approach,* trans. John Drury (Maryknoll, N.Y.: Orbis, 1978 [Spanish original 1976]). More recently Sobrino has published *Jesus in Latin America,* trans. R. K. Barr (Maryknoll, N.Y., 1982 [Spanish original 1982]).

The statement omits mentioning the extensive work of Juan Luis Segundo, *Jesus of Nazareth Yesterday and Today, 1. Faith and Ideologies, 2. The Historical Jesus of the Synoptics, 3. The Humanist Christology of Paul, 4. The Christ of the Ignatian Exercises, 5. An Evolutionary Approach to Jesus of Nazareth,* trans. and ed. J. Drury (Maryknoll, N.Y.: Orbis, 1984–88 [Spanish original 1982]). In *The Liberation of Theology,* trans. J. Drury (Maryknoll, N.Y.: Orbis, 1976 [Spanish original 1975]), 8, Segundo developed the theme that Liberation Theology is based on "the hermeneutic circle" in which present-day social reality and the reality of the text mutually interpret each other. His process methodology leads to an evolutionary Christology like that of Teilhard de Chardin.

Since the appearance of *Scripture and Christology,* Leonardo Boff has published *Trinity and Society* (Maryknoll: Orbis, 1988 [Portuguese original 1986]). In 1985 Boff received official notice from Cardinal Joseph Ratzinger, Prefect of the Sacred Congregation for the Doctrine of the Faith, that he was to begin immediately to observe an "obedient silence" for an unspecified period of time. It was lifted ten months later, shortly before the Vatican issued the "Instruction on Christian Freedom and Liberation." A journalistic account of the affair has been given by Harvey Cox, *The Silencing of Leonardo Boff: The Vatican and the Future of World Christianity* (Oak Park, Ill.: Meyerstone Books, 1988).

Secondary literature includes J. Andrew Kirk, *Liberation Theology: An Evangelical View from the Third World* (Atlanta: John Knox, 1979); Kirk, *Theology Encounters Revolution* (Downers Grove, Ill.: InterVarsity Press, 1980); Deane William Ferm, *Third World Liberation Theologies: An Introductory Survey* (Maryknoll, N.Y.: Orbis, 1986); Ferm, *Third World Liberation Theologies: A Reader* (Maryknoll, N.Y.: Orbis, 1986); Ronald Nash, ed., *Liberation Theology* (Milford, Mich.: Mott Media, 1984).

[78]Sources include Ernst Bloch, *Das Prinzip der Hoffnung,* 5 parts (Frankfurt am Main: Suhrkamp Verlag, 1959), Eng. trans. *The Principle of Hope,* 3 vols. (Cambridge, Mass.: MIT Press; Oxford: Blackwell, 1986); Bloch, *Man on His Own: Essays in the Philosophy of Religion,* trans. E. B. Ashton (New York: Herder and Herder, 1970); Bloch, *Atheism in Christianity: The Religion of the Exodus and the Kingdom,* trans. J. T. Swann (New York: Herder and Herder, 1972); Milan Machoveč, *A Marxist Looks at Jesus* (Philadelphia: Fortress, 1976); Machoveč, *Marxmismus und dialektische Theologie. Barth, Bonhoeffer und Hromádka in atheistischkommunistischer Sicht* (Zürich: EVZ-Verlag, 1965); Fernando Belo, *A Materialist Reading of the Gospel of Mark,* trans. M. J. O'Connell (Maryknoll, N.Y.: Orbis, 1981).

the interpretation of Jesus as the liberator takes the traditional place of the doctrine of redemption and social ethics.[79]

In response to these views,[80] the Commission acknowledges that proponents of Liberation Theology are right to recall that the salvation brought by Christ is not solely "spiritual." Salvation is concerned with liberation from every tyranny that oppresses human beings. But dangers arise if teaching on redemption is not linked with a system of ethics consonant with the precepts of the New Testament. Moreover, Marxist analysis is tied to an economic and political philosophy, whose theoretical basis includes atheism. Uncritical adoption of such an approach and *praxis* runs the risk of falsifying the nature of God, Christ, and humanity itself. There is the further danger among some (unnamed) Liberation Theologians of separating "the Jesus of history" from "the Christ of faith." A particular view of the former serves as the basis for *praxis*, while the latter is deemed to be a mere "ideological" or even "mythological" interpretation of his historical person. Thus, Jesus becomes no more than a "model" from the past. Where all this is divorced from an understanding of the role of the church and of the Holy Spirit within the church, alternative approaches to *praxis* ostensibly better suited to our times may be sought. Thus, Christology runs the risk of being "completely *reduced to anthropology.*"

10. Systematic Theologies of a New Sort[81]

Under this heading the Commission considers two "syntheses" in which "*Christo*-logy is understood as a *theo*-logical revelation of God

---

Secondary literature includes Carl Heinz Ratschow, *Atheismus im Christentum. Eine Auseinandersetzung mit Ernst Bloch* (Gütersloh: Gütersloher Verlagshaus Gerd Mohn, 1970); Felix Gradl, *Ein Atheist liest die Bibel: Ernst Bloch und das Alte Testament* (Frankfurt am Main: Lang, 1979); Wayne Hudson, *The Marxist Philosophy of Ernst Bloch* (New York: St. Martin's Press, 1982). Bloch's influence on Moltmann is discussed by M. Douglas Meeks, *Origins of the Theology of Hope*, Foreword by Jürgen Moltmann (Philadelphia: Fortress, 1974), 15-19, 80-88, 108-17.

[79]The section concludes with a reference to studies "from a notably different point of view" (like those of Johannes-Baptist Metz), that are aimed at *practical theology*. Through the Cross God has made himself an intimate member of humanity to bring about liberation. Fitzmyer (p. 87) notes that Metz's work differs considerably from those Christologies that are more Marxist-oriented (cf. J. B. Metz, *Faith in History and Society: Toward a Practical Fundamental Theology*, trans. David Smith [New York: Seabury, 1980]; Metz, *The Emergent Church: the Future of Christianity in a Postbourgeois World*, trans. Peter Mann [New York: Crossroad, 1981]; J. B. Metz, K. Rahner, and M. Machoveč, *Can a Christian Be a Marxist?* [Chicago: Argus, 1969]). Metz has edited several issues of *Concilium*, including as co-editor with E. Schillebeeckx, *Jesus, Son of God? Concilium* 153 (Edinburgh: T. & T. Clark; New York: Seabury, 1982).

[80]*Scripture and Christology*, 28-29.

[81]Ibid., 16-17.

Himself." One is the work of the Swiss Protestant, Karl Barth, and the other is that of the Swiss Catholic and former Jesuit, Hans Urs von Balthasar. The two theologians have other things in common. Both have written down their thoughts at overwhelming length in the form of multivolume works, subdivided into huge part-volumes. Balthasar, whose thought has been influenced by Barth, is the author of a major discussion of Barth's theology. In one respect, however, Balthasar has a unique distinction. He is the only member of the International Theological Commission, which produced the report *Select Questions on Christology*, to merit consideration in the present statement, even though the Biblical Commission is somewhat ambivalent in its response.

In the case of Barth, the word "new" in the section heading is a relative term, for the aspect of Barth's teaching that is considered is at least half a century old and thus predates much of what is discussed elsewhere in the statement. The Commission focuses on Barth's understanding of *the self-revelation of God* in Christ, whose "entire existence takes on meaning only from the fact that he is the supreme *Word* of the Father. In communicating this Word through His Spirit in His Church, God opened the way to an ethic that demands of those who believe an involvement in the affairs *of this world*, even in those of a political nature."[82]

---

[82]The primary source for Barth's teaching on revelation is his *Church Dogmatics,* ed. G. W. Bromiley and T. F. Torrance, 4 vols. (Edinburgh: T. & T. Clark, 1932–75), 1/1, rev. Eng. trans. by G. W. Bromiley 1975; 1/2 Eng. trans. by G. T. Thomson and H. Knight 1956. The statement does not take into account the development of Barth's Christology in the remaining volumes and part-volumes of the *Church Dogmatics.* Barth went on to see Jesus Christ as God's incarnate Word to humankind, in whom God had indissolubly bound himself to humankind. Barth saw the union of God and man in the person of Jesus Christ as the *covenant* between God and humankind in general, which forms the ground and basis of all God's gracious dealings with humanity. The *covenant* as such is the key to understanding the attributes of God. It is the ground and goal of creation. Because of their common humanity with Christ, the head of all humanity, human beings are already "in Christ." Through Jesus Christ's atoning death all are reconciled to God, whether they know it or not, or indeed whether they have responded in faith and obedience. Barth's position pushed him to the brink of a form of universalism, though he repeatedly disowned Origen's form of universalism. For a critical account of Barth's Christological approach to dogmatics, and bibliography, see Colin Brown, *Karl Barth and the Christian Message* (London: Tyndale, 1967).

Catholic studies of Barth include J. Hamer, *Karl Barth* (Westminster, Md.: Newman, 1962); Hans Urs von Balthasar, *Karl Barth. Darstellung und Deutung seiner Theologie* (Olten: Summa-Verlag, 1951); partial Eng. trans. of 2d ed. (1962) by J. Drury, *The Theology of Karl Barth* (New York: Holt, Rinehart and Winston, 1971); Henri Bouillard, *Karl Barth,* 3 vols. (Paris: Aubier, 1957); Hans Küng, *Justification: The Doctrine of Karl Barth and a Catholic Reflection* (London: Burns & Oates, 1964); Philip J. Rosato, S.J., *The Spirit as Lord: The Pneumatology of Karl Barth* (Edinburgh: T. & T. Clark, 1981).

In some respects, Balthasar is a Catholic counterpart to Barth. The Commission draws attention to the way in which Balthasar reflects on the *kenosis* (emptying, cf. Php 2:7) of Christ, which is manifested in his absolute obedience to the Father, even to his death on the cross. This revelation of the essential divine life of the Trinity in history (which Balthasar terms "Theo-Drama [German: *Theodramatik*]" also brings about the salvation of humankind, as Christ experiences death on its behalf. Another way of looking at revelation is to see it as theological aesthetics, concerned with the contemplation of divine glory (German: *Herrlichkeit*) through rational reflection, historical investigation, and involvement coalescing in the mystery of Easter. The Commission sees in this approach a *theology of history* which avoids the restricted conclusions of Idealists and Materialists.[83]

The Commission's brief response to Barth and Balthasar[84] acknowledges that such approaches are not without reason in their refusal to depend on *critical hypotheses* that are always subject to revision. However, "excessive concern to make a synthesis" leads to the obscuring of *the variety of New Testament Christologies* and to the neglect and even dismissal of the Old Testament. The statement remarks on the desirability that "exegetical studies find a more precise and well-defined place in the study of revelation." Fr. Fitzmyer puts the point more bluntly when he observes that Barth and Balthasar "tend to

---

Studies of Barth's Christology include John Thompson, *Christ in Perspective: Christological Perspectives in the Theology of Karl Barth* (Grand Rapids: Eerdmans, 1978); Charles T. Waldrop, *Karl Barth's Christology: Its Basic Alexandrian Character* (Berlin, New York, Amsterdam: Mouton, 1984). Other studies include Eberhard Busch, *Karl Barth: His Life from Letters and Autobiographical Texts* (London: S.C.M. Press; Philadelphia: Fortress, 1976); Geoffrey W. Bromiley, *Introduction to Karl Barth* (Grand Rapids: Eerdmans, 1979); Eberhard Jüngel, *Karl Barth: A Theological Legacy* (Philadelphia: Westminster, 1976); S. W. Sykes, ed., *Karl Barth: Studies in His Theological Method* (Oxford: Clarendon, 1979); Sykes, ed., *Karl Barth: Centenary Essays* (Cambridge: Cambridge Univ. Press, 1989).

[83]Fitzmyer (p. 89) notes Balthasar's treatment of *kenosis* in his *Theodramatik*, 2/2, "Christi Sendung und Person" (Einsiedeln: Johannes-Verlag, 1978), 136-238, esp. 206-9. The discussion bears marked similarities to that of Barth's treatment of divine condescension, Jesus Christ the Lord as Servant, and Jesus Christ the Servant as Lord (on Barth's views see W. Pannenberg, *Jesus—God and Man*, 312-15). On the idea of *kenosis* in nineteenth-century thought and the suggestion that it reveals the inner life of God, see Brown, *Jesus in European Protestant Thought, 1778–1860*, 248-54.

Balthasar's *Theodramatik*, 2 vols. in 3 parts (Einsiedeln: Johannes-Verlag, 1973-78), is being published as *Theo-Drama* (San Francisco: Ignatius Press, 1988–). Balthasar's *Herrlichkeit*, 3 vols. in 5 parts (Einsiedeln: Johannes-Verlag, 1961–69), is being published as *The Glory of the Lord: A Theological Aesthetics*, trans. E. Leiva-Merikakis, ed. J. Fessio and J. Riches, 8 vols. (Einburgh: T. & T. Clark, 1982–). *The von Balthasar Reader*, ed. Medard Kehl, S.J. and Werner Löser, S.J. (New York: Crossroad, 1982) contains an extensive introduction by Medard Kehl (pp. 1-54) which discusses the influence of Barth and others on Balthasar.

[84]*Scripture and Christology*, 29.

sacrifice the variety of New Testament Christologies to their ideally conceived syntheses" and "quote Scripture for their purposes."[85]

11. Christologies "From Above" and Christologies "From Below"[86]

One might have expected in this final section a discussion of the approach advocated by Wolfhart Pannenberg[87] and others.[88] However, neither here nor in the section where Pannenberg has already been discussed[89] does the Commission engage in a comparative critique of the two approaches. It contents itself with noting (without saying which) that various Christologies discussed earlier fall into one or the other category and with commending various attempts by Protestant and Catholic scholars to combine both.[90]

Despite their diversity, these attempts have two points in common. On the one hand, they recognize that one must distinguish between the way Jesus appeared to his contemporaries in his earthly life and the way in which Jesus was understood *after the manifestations of him as one raised from the dead.* Between these two periods there was an *advance* that is "a constitutive element of Christology itself." "This Christology, if it has to take into account the limits of the

---

[85]Ibid., 89.

[86]Ibid., 17-19.

[87]In *Jesus–God and Man*, 21-37, Pannenberg argues the need to show from history what are the grounds for the church's faith. He characterizes traditional approaches, from the ancient church to Barth, as Christologies "from above," in that they begin with the divinity of Christ and treat the concept of the Incarnation as their center. "A Christology 'from below,' rising from the historical man Jesus to the recognition of his divinity, is concerned first of all with Jesus' message and fate and arrives only at the end at the concept of the incarnation" (p. 33). To Pannenberg, Christology "from above" presupposes the divinity of Christ and ignores the most important task of Christology—the presentation of reasons for confessing his divinity. To take the divinity of Christ as the starting point tends to devalue the real historical person of Jesus and his relationship with Palestinian Judaism. Moreover, the believer stands in history; one would have to stand in the position of God in order to follow the way of God's Son into the world.

Pannenberg's approach appears to be a form of phenomenology that deliberately suppresses judgment about the transcendent and metaphysical, including the activity of God in Jesus, prior to the Resurrection, at which point an approach "from above" is allowed to take over. There appears to be something arbitrary about Pannenberg's approach, for nothing can be apprehended from a point of absolute neutrality. Judgments about Jesus did not begin with the Resurrection. (See Brown, *Miracles and the Critical Mind*, 289; for responses to Pannenberg see Stanley J. Grenz, "The Appraisal of Pannenberg: A Survey of the Literature," in Braaten and Clayton, eds., *The Theology of Wolfhart Pannenberg*, 19-52, esp. 36-45.)

[88]On Hans Küng, see above, #7.

[89]#6, "Christology and Salvation History."

[90]The names of L. Bouyer, R. H. Fuller, C. F. D. Moule, I. H. Marshall, B. Rey, Chr. Duquoc, W. Kasper, M. Hengel, and J. D. G. Dunn are given as examples. Fitzmyer (p. 90) gives a brief bibliography.

humanity of 'Jesus of Nazareth,' has to acknowledge in him at the same time 'the Christ of faith,' fully revealed by his resurrection in the light of the Holy Spirit." On the other hand, they give recognition to the fact that there are different ways of understanding the mystery of Christ, which appear already in the New Testament books themselves.[91]

The section concludes with three observations about how exegetes and theologians approach *the individual personality of Jesus.* The observations are stated as facts, but they have something of a mildly imperative mood about them. First, they bear in mind the fact that, while Jesus received a Jewish education in a Jewish culture, he was also endowed with a *quite singular consciousness of himself* in relation to God and his mission. Some Gospel texts (e.g., Lk 2:40, 52) indicate *growth* in this consciousness. Second, exegetes and theologians refuse to speculate about the "psychology" of Jesus, both because of problems presented by the texts in this regard and because of the inherent dangers attending to this kind of speculation. Third, scholars agree that *Christology should in no way be separate from soteriology,* for as Scripture attests (Jn 1:14), his mediating role is inseparable from his person. Inevitably, this gives rise to questions about Christ's knowledge and preexistence, but they are seen to belong to a later stage of Christology.

The Commission's response[92] to all this is to underscore the need for continued historical and critical study, while recognizing Christ as the Savior of the world, the Wisdom and Word of God, the author and exemplar of creation, and the governor of human history, who continues to act in the world. Further biblical study is needed of the relations between the church, as the body of Christ guided by the Holy Spirit, and the societies that it develops. "Given such a consideration,

---

[91]The Commission instances the use of the Old Testament ways of speaking and the idea of fulfillment, as when Scripture is said to have been *fulfilled* in Jesus. The Commission understands such fulfillment, not in the simplistic sense of the church Fathers and later apologists who regarded fulfillment as prediction come true, but in the sense of *amplification of meaning.* Such amplification should not be seen as secondary speculation, for it had its origin in the person of Jesus himself.

It may be noted that the Christian use of the Old Testament played a significant part in the quest of the historical Jesus, in that skeptics claimed that the application to Jesus of prophecy and Old Testament concepts was thoroughly unhistorical. The Deist Anthony Collins complained of the misuse of prophecy, claiming that Christian orthodoxy could be sustained only by means of allegorical interpretation. D. F. Strauss argued that the appropriation to Jesus of Old Testament concepts was essentially mythological. See Brown, *Jesus in European Protestant Thought, 1778–1860,* 38-40, 183-204. The issue has been one of continuing concern for Catholic biblical scholars (Fogarty, *American Catholic Biblical Scholarship,* 267).

[92]*Scripture and Christology,* 30.

ecclesiology becomes *an essential aspect of Christology*, and precisely at the moment when it is confronted by the studies of sociologists."

The "Survey of Methodologies" concludes with a brief chapter that asks how risks, limitations, and ambiguities are to be avoided.[93] By way of answer, readers are directed back to the study *of the Bible as a whole*, as the *norm* for Christian faith and life. The literary development of the Bible is itself a reflection of the gift of God that has brought revelation and salvation. The apex of this gift is the Son of God, true man "born of the Virgin Mary." The unity in the Scriptures is seen in the fulfillment of promise and expectation through the coming of Christ. The Commission emphasizes that faith and historical study are not mutually exclusive. Indeed, they are mutually necessary. But it warns against the deceptive superficiality of so-called theological ways of reading Scripture that seek to dispense with scholarly study. Facile solutions "can in no way provide the solid basis needed for studies in biblical theology, even when engaged in with full faith." Though many problems remain obscure, the Commission judges that biblical studies have made "sufficient progress that *any believer can find in their results a solid basis for his/her study about Jesus Christ*."

PART II. THE GLOBAL TESTIMONY OF SCRIPTURE

Part II of *Scripture and Christology* is devoted to "The Global Testimony of Sacred Scripture about Christ."[94] Its two chapters deal with the Old and New Testaments respectively. It is a document to be studied, rather than to be summarized. We shall, therefore, confine comment to features of the text, omitting the many biblical references that it contains.

The Commissioners approach the Old Testament under the heading, "God's Salvific Deeds and the Messianic Hope in Israel." While the people of the ancient Near East where "groping for" God, God manifested himself to Israel as One who was seeking out human beings. God called Abraham and promised universal blessing through him. The Creator of the universe manifested himself as Lord and Governor of history. As such he is King of Israel, who has established his covenant and promises of deliverance with Israel and ultimately with humankind. In so doing, God makes use of different forms of mediation.

The statement draws attention to the role of king, priest, and prophet, which have also figured prominently in Protestant accounts

---

[93]Ibid., 31-32.
[94]Ibid., 32-53.

of Christology and soteriology.[95] However, the Old Testament ampli-
fies its notion of mediation through the King-Messiah who will bring
everlasting peace and justice, the Servant of the Lord who will bear
the weight of sin in order to bring many to righteousness, and the
Danielic Son of Man who will receive universal dominion. God's
activity is also depicted by means of *certain figurative powers*: the
Spirit of God, the Word of God, and the divine creative Wisdom.
Israel was characterized by expectation and hope, which took various
forms. The Pharisees looked for a Davidic messiah, and the Essenes a
priestly messiah. John the Baptist announced the imminent coming
of the kingdom, which would be inaugurated by one mightier than
himself.

Chapter 2 approaches Christology under the heading, "The Fulfilment of the Promises of Salvation in Christ Jesus." It begins by examining the Gospel testimony which sees the fulfillment in Christ of
Old Testament expectations. This fulfillment is not to be seen as similar to other contemporary ways of reading Scripture. The New
Testament writings are to be viewed as the testimony of Christians
who were guided by the Holy Spirit in the apostolic community to
reflect on the words and deeds of Jesus *in an ever richer and more
developed way*.

Jesus' own attitude was shaped by the relationship that he enjoyed
with God, viz., "that of a son toward his father." This relationship
affected the way that Jesus regarded the law and also the titles ascribed
to mediators of salvation in Scripture. He accepted titles like Master,
Prophet, and Son of David. However, he rejected the title of king, as
understood in an earthly sense, and forbade public ascription to himself of the term *Messiah* or *Christ*. Jesus used the title Son of Man as a
self-designation. In the Book of Daniel it denotes a mediator of salvation, but Jesus was reluctant to reveal the "secret—or rather the
mystery—of his person" to people who were not yet able to understand it.

The Commission sees links between the Son of Man and the
Suffering Servant, in that Jesus came not to be served but to give his
life as a ransom for many, and also in Jesus' words at the Last Supper.
It also notes allusions to the Word, Spirit, and Wisdom of God. Jesus

---

[95]Luther and others had spoken of the kingship and priesthood of Christ, as
Calvin had also done in his commentaries. However, Andreas Osiander referred to
the threefold offices of Christ in his written statement at the Diet of Augsburg
(1530). Calvin used the idea in the Geneva Confession (1536) and gave his fullest
account of it in the final Latin version of his *Institutes* (1559), 2.15. Thereafter, it was
widely adopted in Reformed and Lutheran theology (Pannenberg, *Jesus—God and
Man*, 212-25). It is even found in a somewhat attenuated form in Schleiermacher,
The Christian Faith, secs. 102-6 (see Brown, *Jesus in European Protestant Thought,
1778-1660*, 122-23).

spoke the Word of God with the authority of the Father, and in the Fourth Gospel he is actually called the Word. Elsewhere, he claims to speak and act by the Spirit of God. There are also hints that in Jesus the Wisdom of God is present and active. In the manifestation of God's Word, Spirit, and Wisdom in Jesus, the Commission sees the elements of a Christology "from above." In the picture of Jesus as a King of justice and peace, the lowly Suffering Servant, and the mysterious Son of Man, the Commission sees an approach "from below." They present two ways to Christology: God's communication of himself and the appearance of the new Adam with the primordial call to be adoptive children of God.

The ultimate explanation "or rather the mystery" of Jesus lies in his *filial relation to God*, which finds expression in the way Jesus addressed God as "Abba" and is the basis of his obedience as God's Son. On account of this, "all the titles, all the roles and mediatory modes related to salvation in Scripture have been assumed and united in the person of Jesus." In the light of Easter, the meaning of Jesus' previously obscure sayings and deeds begins to become clearer. Through Pentecost the Spirit is outpoured.

The *gospel traditions* were gathered and gradually committed to writing in the light of Easter, eventually finding "a fixed form in four booklets." Referring to its own earlier *Instruction* of 1964,[96] the Commission reminds its readers that the Gospels are not bare accounts of what Jesus said and did, but present "theological interpretations of such things." One must therefore look for *the Christology of each evangelist*. This is especially true of John, who in the patristic age was given the title "Theologian." Similarly, one must look for the distinctive Christologies of Paul, the Epistle to the Hebrews, the Book of Revelation, and other writings. It is not a case of determining which of these Christologies are more historically accurate or theologically correct. Rather "*all these testimonies must be accepted in their totality* in order that Christology, as a form of knowledge about Christ rooted and based in faith, may thrive as true and authentic among believing Christians."[97] No text should be rejected on the grounds that, being a "secondary development," it did not express "the *true* image of Christ," or because it bears traces of a bygone cultural context it is no longer important. Serious attention must be paid to the modes of expression employed by the New Testament writers.

The statement closes on a doxological note. Christ, as the mediator of salvation, is present in his church, whose function it is to recognize authentically his presence and activity through the Holy Spirit. The "total Christ" is the goal of all things. The church is called and

---

[96]*Scripture and Christology*, 48; see above, n. 14.
[97]Ibid., 49.

sent on his mission in the world until the final consummation of all things to his praise and glory.

CONCLUDING OBSERVATIONS

By any reckoning *Scripture and Christology* is a remarkable document. It is remarkable not least as an expression of the changes that have taken place in Roman Catholicism during the twentieth century. When the Pontifical Biblical Commission was created, Modernism was seen as a deadly danger, and the *responsa* delivered by the Commission were uniformly conservative, authoritarian, and uncompromising. *Scripture and Christology* carries on the Commission's original mandate to guard against false interpretation. But it discharges this obligation by engaging in dialogue, offering comment, and suggesting guidelines for pursuing Christology. The reader can certainly find "responses" to a whole range of questions and approaches, but they take the form of thinking aloud about how to approach issues, rather than that of specific, definitive answers to specific questions.

In the process several notable changes have quietly taken place. The Commission embarks on public dialogue with a wide variety of individual scholars. Protestant, Jewish, and even atheistic scholars are brought into the discussion as partners in the dialogue. Merit is seen even in the contribution of those whose work is perceived to be one-sided and defective. The harshest criticism seems to be reserved for Catholic scholars who fall into this category, for conservative traditionalists who desire to work out their Christology in terms of conciliar pronouncements embellished by scriptural references, and for those who erect theological systems likewise garnished by texts.

The Commission permits itself to comment on the methodological shortcomings of different approaches, but it does not offer its own methodology. It commends the variety of approaches, and recommends the need for balance and a devout, historical approach. The primary antidote to the sundry ills that the Commission sees is to insist upon the need to address the global testimony of Scripture. As an indication of what it has in mind, the Commission sketches its own approach in Part II of the statement. A hostile critic might complain of a sudden switch of moods and treatment. Whereas Part I has examined a variety of approaches at a high level of sophistication, Part II appears at first glance to plunge headlong into uncritical proof-texting. Every point that is made is supplied with biblical references, and little attempt is made (especially in chapter 1) to differentiate sources and strata of tradition. An alternative way of looking at Part II is to see it as an attempt to identify the "testimony" of Scripture and present it as guidelines for thinking about Christology. As such it is unashamedly a statement of Christology from the standpoint of salvation history. Although the Commissioners do not expressly say so, they have implicitly identified themselves with the general approach which they discussed in Part I, #6. In so doing, they have done what the preface to *Scripture and Christology* disavows: they have in fact engaged in a disguised form of exegesis, for the very act of selecting and highlighting certain passages of Scripture in this way involves exegesis.

Moreover, exegesis is involved not only in what is put in, but also in what has been left out. The Christology that is commended approaches the person of Jesus from the standpoint of the history of salvation. Although the statement makes repeated references to salvation, the classic approach to Christology via soteriology has been quietly modified. Classic statements of this approach, like Athanasius' *De incarnatione*, Anselm's *Cur deus homo*, and Luther's *Bondage of the Will*, stressed sin and human inability to attain salvation. Jesus had to be both God and a human being: God in order to be our Savior, and a human being in order to be our representative. The Commission has quietly avoided such an exercise in Christology "from above" and has chosen instead to focus more positively on biblical statements. At the same time it has laid itself open to the criticism of having attempted to lay the foundations for a biblical approach to Christology without dealing seriously with the question of atonement.

In this respect, the Biblical Commission's statement on Christology stands in marked contrast to the International Theological Commission's statement. The latter statement devoted almost half of its text to "Christology and Soteriology."[98] *Scripture and Christology* also differs from the International Theological Commission's statement in one other major respect. Whereas the latter reviewed the teaching of the early councils, stressing their continued relevance,[99] *Scripture and Christology* is more concerned with the development of Christology from Scripture in the face of contemporary thought. In a century that has witnessed numerous reaffirmations of conciliar Christology,[100] the Biblical Commission has sought to address the question of method and to redirect Christology to its biblical roots.

---

[98] *Select Questions on Christology*, 12-19. Five main elements are identified: "(1) The Christ gives himself. (2) He takes our place in the mystery of salvation. (3) He frees us 'from the wrath to come' and from all evil powers. (4) In so doing, he fulfills the salvific will of the Father. (5) He wants to insert us into the life of the Trinity through participation in the grace of the Holy Spirit" (p. 17).

[99] *Select Questions on Christology*, 4-12.

[100] The most notable of the encyclicals is *Sempiternus Rex Christus* (1951), commemorating the fifteenth hundredth anniversary of Chalcedon (Eng. trans. in *Christ our Lord: Official Catholic Teachings*, ed. Amanda G. Watlington [Wilmington,

In doing so, the Commission has engaged in its own tacit form of systematic theology. It has not only expressed its doubts about the continued relevance of Christology oriented to the conciliar definitions. It has also engaged in dialogue with contemporary Catholic and Protestant systematic theologians and criticized their work. It has gone on to identify norms, material, and methods for engaging in constructive Christology for today. In this respect the scholars of the Biblical Commission have done what their Protestant counterparts have also frequently done. They have gone beyond the strict realm of biblical studies and produced their own form of systematic theology. The lesson to be learned from this is not that biblical scholars should be barred from engaging in systematic theology, but that it is impossible to engage in any kind of constructive theology for today without doing systematic theology. It shows the need for biblical scholars and systematic theologians not only to talk to each other, but also to be actively involved in each others' disciplines.

As it is, Part II of *Scripture and Christology* functions like a new form of the *Quicunque Vult*. Admittedly, it does not insist on belief in its teaching as a prerequisite for salvation. It has substituted a biblical account of Christology for a conciliar account of the Trinity. But like the *Quicunque Vult*, what it gives is intended to be a statement of the Catholic Faith. It is a statement which offers a summary of biblical testimony, as the basis for Christology in the light of today's questions. The statement quietly bypasses the earlier judgments of the Biblical Commission on matters of biblical authorship, and it makes

---

N.C.: Consortium Books, 1978], 243-60). See also Aloys Grillmeier, S.J., and Heinrich Bacht, S.J., *Das Konzil von Chalkedon*, 3 vols. (Würzburg: Echter Verlag, 1951–54); Grillmeier, *Christ in Christian Tradition*, 1, *From the Apostolic Age to Chalcedon (451)*, 2d rev. ed. (London: Mowbrays, 1975). On the trend away from the strict Chalcedonian approach to Christology see Brian O. McDermott, S.J., "Roman Catholic Christology: Two Recurring Themes," *Theological Studies* 41 (1980): 339-67.

A conservative defense of a more traditional Catholic theology has been made by Walter Kasper in *Jesus the Christ*, trans. V. Green (New York: Search Press, 1977 [German original 1974]). Kasper criticizes the purely functionalist approach "from below" on the grounds that philosophical questions cannot be avoided, because Christianity is a living faith. Its claims demand that it be presented in the light of ongoing questions. The shift from functional to ontological categories should not be regarded as a distortion but as a necessary application of the meaning of Jesus the Christ. To Kasper "the Christological dogma of the Council of Chalcedon constitutes, in the language and in the context of the problem at that time, an extremely precise version of what, according to the New Testament, we encounter in Jesus' history and what befell him: namely in Jesus Christ, God himself has entered into a human history, and meets us there in a fully and completely human way. The dogmatic profession of faith that Jesus Christ in one person is true God and true man, must therefore be regarded as a valid and permanently binding interpretation of Scripture" (p. 238). As such, the dogma of Chalcedon represents a "contraction" of the Christological witness of Scripture.

no attempt to harmonize the Gospels and the diverse Christologies of the New Testament. Instead, it presents a kind of canon summarizing the faith of the Church expressed in Scripture, inviting Christian believers to rethink and live out their faith on the basis of the testimony of Scripture.

In the early church there was no question that was more crucial than Christology. In today's church and world the shape of the question has changed, but the issue is as vital as ever. As a review of approaches to Christology, the statement makes no claims to completeness. In the nature of the case, it is inevitably far less comprehensive than the accounts of Karl J. Kuschel,[101] Werner Georg Kümmel,[102] Arland J. Hultgren,[103] and the authors of *Theologische Berichte*.[104] Nevertheless, *Scripture and Christology* provides a valuable introduction to the state of the question today. It does not say the last word on the Christology. But it says many things that deserve to be heard—by Catholics and Protestants alike.

---

[101]K.-J. Kuschel, *Jesus in der deutschsprachigen Gegenwartsliteratur*, paperback ed. (Munich and Zurich: Piper, 1987).

[102]W. G. Kümmel, "Jesusforschung seit 1950. 1 Das methodische Problem der Frage nach dem historischen Jesus," *Theologische Rundschau* 31 (1965–66): 15-46; "Jesusforschung seit 1950. 2. Gesamtdarstellungen Jesu," *Theologische Rundschau* 31 (1965-66): 289-315; "Ein Jahrzehnt Jesusforschung (1965–1975). 1. Forschungsberichte, Ausserevangelische Quellen, Methodenfrage," *Theologische Rundschau* 40 (1975): 289-336; "Einjahrzehnt Jesusforschung (1965–1975), 2. Nicht-wissenschaftliche und wissenschaftliche Gesamtdarstellungen," *Theologische Rundschau* 41 (1976): 197-258; "Ein Jahrzehnt Jesusforschung (1965–1975). 3. Die Lehre Jesu (einschliesslich der Arbeiten über Einzeltexte," *Theologische Rundschau* 41 (1976): 295-363; "Jesusforschung seit 1965. 4. Bergpredigt—Gleichnisse—Wunderberichte (mit Nachträgen)," *Theologische Rundschau* 43 (1978): 105-61, 233-65; "Jesusforschung seit 1965. 5. Der persönliche Anspruch Jesu," *Theologische Rundschau* 45 (1980): 40-84; "Jesusforschung seit 1965. 6. Der Prozess und der Kreuzestod Jesu," *Theologische Rundschau* 45 (1980): 293-337; "Jesusforschung seit 1965: Nachträge 1975–1980," *Theologische Rundschau* 46 (1981): 317-63; "Jesusforschung seit 1965: Nachträge 1975–1980," *Theologische Rundschau* 47 (1982): 136-65, 348-83; the foregoing reprinted with a postcript in Kümmel, *Dreissig Jahre Jesusforschung (1950–1980)*, ed. Helmut Merklein, Bonner Biblische Beiträge 60 (Königstein: P. Hanstein, 1985); Kümmel, "Jesusforschung seit 1981. 1. Forschungsgeschichte, Methodenfragen," *Theologische Rundschau* 53 (1988): 229-49; "Jesusforschung seit 1981. 2. Gesamtdarstellungen," *Theologische Rundschau* 54 (1989): 1-53.

[103]A. J. Hultgren compiler, G. E. Gorman, advisory editor, *New Testament Christology: A Critical Assessment and Annotated Bibliography* (New York: Greenwood, 1988).

[104]*Theologische Berichte VII: Zugänge zu Jesus* (Zürich, Einsiedeln, Cologne: Benzinger Verlag, 1978) contains the following: Dietrich Wiederkehr, "Christologie in Kontext," 11-62; Walter Kern, "Jesus—marxistisch und tiefenpsychologisch," 63-100; Josef Pfammatter, "Katholische Jesusforschung im deutschen Sprachraum. 200 Jahre nach Reimarus," 101-48; Clemens Thoma, "Jüdische Zugänge zu Jesus Christus," 149-76; Karl H. Neufeld, "Leben mit Jesus. Versuche des Zugangs in neueren Jesus-Bewegungen," 177-204.

The Person of Christ:

Historical Perspectives

The Reformers and the Humanity of Christ

Geoffrey W. Bromiley

Senior Professor of Church History and Historical Theology
Fuller Theological Seminary

TRINITARIAN AND CHRISTOLOGICAL ORTHODOXY

In principle the Reformers relativized the rulings of church councils. The Scots Confession includes the typically challenging statement: "Without just examination dare we not receive whatsoever is obtruded unto men under the name of general councils." Even the milder Anglican Articles allow that when councils "be gathered together (forasmuch as they be an assembly of men, whereof all be not governed with the Spirit and the Word of God) they may err, and sometimes have erred, even in things pertaining unto God." Hence the Second Helvetic Confession concludes: "we suffer not ourselves, in controversies about religion or matters of faith, to be pressed with the bare testimonies of fathers or decrees of councils."[1]

The relativizing of creeds and councils is by Holy Scripture, which the Reformers plainly established as the norm of faith and practice. The First Helvetic Confession, for example, applauds the holy fathers and ancient doctors who explained and expounded Scripture according to the rule of faith and love. The Gallican will accept no authority, whether of "proclamations, or edicts, or decrees," that is opposed to Holy Scripture. The Belgic argues that councils, decrees, and statutes must all be compared with "the truth of God," which it equates with Scripture and describes as "most perfect and complete in all respects." The Scots concedes: "So far then as the council proves the determination and commandment that it gives to be the plain Word of God, so soon do we reverence and embrace the same." The Second Helvetic, too, gives final judgment to Scripture: "In controversies of religion or matters of faith, we cannot admit any other judge than God himself, pronouncing by the Holy Scriptures what is true, what is false."[2]

---

[1] Scots Confession, 20; Thirty-nine Articles, 21; Second Helvetic Confession, 2. Unless otherwise noted, the text of the confessions is cited from Philip Schaff, *The Creeds of Christendom*, 3 vols. (repr., Grand Rapids: Baker, 1985), vol. 3.

[2] First Helvetic Confession, 3; Gallican Confession, 5; Belgic Confession, 7; Scots Confession, 20; Second Helvetic Confession, 2.4; cf. Westminster Confession, 1.10.

As regards the Trinitarian and Christological decisions of the early church, the Reformers believed unanimously that these were, in fact, in accordance with Scripture. They thus readily endorsed the three historic creeds (Apostles', Nicene, and Athanasian). The Augsburg Confession says at the outset that "the churches ... teach that the decree of the Nicene Synod ... is true." The later Formula of Concord refers to the "primitive church symbols" and adds: "We publicly profess that we embrace them," though only as "witnesses," not as "the rule and norm" of doctrine.[3] On the Reformed side the Gallican Confession accepts "the three creeds ... because they are in accordance with the Word of God." The Belgic states that in the matter of the Trinity "we do willingly receive the three creeds." The Anglican in a special article claims that the creeds "ought thoroughly to be received and believed: for they may be proved by most certain warrants of Holy Scripture." The Second Helvetic accepts "the Apostles' Creed, because it delivers unto us the true faith," and it later consents to "whatsoever things are defined out of the Holy Scriptures, and comprehended in the creeds ... touching the mystery of the incarnation of our Lord Jesus Christ."[4]

Endorsing the early creeds, the Reformers also followed conciliar rulings on the Trinity and Christology. Calvin in the *Institutes* certainly finds problems in the use of nonbiblical terms like "essence" and "person," but he clearly adheres to Nicene and Chalcedonian orthodoxy in his treatment of both the Trinity and Christ.[5] Regarding the divine triunity, the Gallican Confession accepts "that which hath been established by the ancient councils," and regarding Christology it stays close to Chalcedon: "We believe that in one person ... the two natures are actually and inseparably joined and united, and yet each remains in its proper character" (*propriété distincte*). The Belgic acknowledges that the biblical doctrine of the Trinity "hath always been defended and maintained by the true church," and in its account of Christology it, too, is very close to Chalcedon: "Two natures united in one single person."[6]

No less expressly orthodox on these two points are the Scots and the Second Helvetic. As regards Christology the latter specifically commends "the decrees of those first four and most excellent councils —held at Nicaea, Constantinople, Ephesus, and Chalcedon," and insists that "we retain the Christian, sound, and Catholic faith, whole and inviolable," there being nothing in the creeds "which is not

---

[3] Augsburg Confession, 1.1; Formula of Concord, Epitome, Comprehensive Rule, 1-3.

[4] Gallican Confession, 5; Belgic Confession, 9; Thirty-nine Articles, 8; Second Helvetic Confession, 3.4; 11.18; cf. Irish Articles, 7.

[5] John Calvin, *Institutes of the Christian Religion*, ed. J. T. McNeill, 2 vols. (Philadelphia: Westminster, 1960), 1.8.1ff.; 2.14.1ff.

[6] Gallican Confession, 6; 15; Belgic Confession, 9; 19.

agreeable to the Word of God, and makes wholly for the sincere declaration of the faith."[7] The Anglican statements that "in the unity of this Godhead there be three persons, of one substance," and that in Christ "two whole and perfect natures . . . were joined together in one person," also echo Nicaea and Chalcedon, as do the corresponding definitions in the Irish Articles and Westminster.[8] An interesting point is that while espousing Chalcedonian orthodoxy, the confessions do not use the phrase "in two natures" which those who favored "of two natures" had earlier found so objectionable. They speak of two natures being "actually and inseparably joined and united" in one person,[9] or "two perfect natures united, and joined in one person."[10] As Calvin puts it, the union of deity and humanity is such that "each retains its distinctive nature unimpaired, and yet these two natures constitute one Christ."[11]

Accepting early conciliar rulings, the Reformers flatly rejected all Trinitarian and Christological heresies. Augsburg condemns the Valentinians, Arians, Eunomians, and "Samosatenes, old and new." The Formula of Concord opposes "all heresies and all dogmas" not in keeping with the creeds.[12] Calvin says that by holding fast to what is shown from Scripture, "the gate will be closed not only to Arius and Sabellius but to other ancient authors of errors," along with "Servetus and his like" in his own day. In the field of Christology he specifically mentions Nestorius, Eutyches, and the "no less deadly monster . . . Michael Servetus."[13] More generally the Gallican Confession detests "all sects and heresies which were rejected by the holy doctors, such as St. Hilary, St. Athanasius, St. Ambrose, and St. Cyril," also "all the heresies that have of old troubled the Church, and especially the diabolical conceits of Servetus." The Scots refers to "the damnable and pestilent heresies of Arius, Marcion, Eutyches, Nestorius and such others, as either did deny the eternity of his Godhead, or the verity of his human nature, or confounded them, or else divided them." The Second Helvetic condemns a whole list of Trinitarian heretics and then in Christology singles out the docetic errors of Valentinus and Marcion, the thesis of partial humanity held by Apollinaris and Eunomius, the teaching of Nestorius, "the madness of Eutyches and of the Monthelites and Monophysites, who

---

[7]Second Helvetic Confession, 11.18, 19; cf. Scots Confession, 1; 6.

[8]Thirty-nine Articles, 1; 2; Irish Articles, 8ff. and 29; Westminster Confession, 2.3 and 8.2.

[9]Gallican Confession, 15.

[10]Scots Confession, 6; cf. Thirty-nine Articles, 2, and Westminster Confession, 8.2.

[11]*Institutes*, 2.14.1.

[12]Augsburg Confession, 1.1; Formula of Concord, Epitome, Compendious Rule, 2.

[13]*Institutes*, 1.13.22; 2.14.4-5.

overthrow the propriety of the human nature," and "the blasphemies of Michael Servetus, the Spaniard, and of his complices."[14]

The Reformers did not pretend, then, to advance any new insights in these areas. Going back to Scripture, they were satisfied that the early church, even though using alien terms, had retained the substance of the biblical teaching. Their own task was to reaffirm the orthodox doctrine, to trace its implications, and to make the application to their own day. In fulfilling this task Christology would necessarily claim particular attention. But it would be a biblical and historic Christology. The idea of a historical Jesus behind the biblical records and detached from the incarnate Word would have made no sense to them. Such a Jesus would have been a phantom, a figment of the imagination, with no objective reality. The Jesus of history was for them the Jesus of biblical testimony, whom the disciples confessed as the Son of the living God even though they knew him in his true humanity as the Word made flesh. Apart from this Jesus we can know no other. He alone is Jesus.

STRESS ON THE HUMANITY OF CHRIST

Fully committed to Chalcedon and the biblical teaching it enshrines, the Reformers contended firmly for the true deity of Christ. They defended terms like *homoousios* as necessary in efforts "to rout the enemies of pure and wholesome doctrine."[15] We know Christ in his true reality only when we know him also in his glory. Yet the Reformers contended equally firmly for Christ's full and true humanity. As Calvin says, "it has been of the greatest importance for us that he who was to be our Mediator is both true God and true man."[16] Indeed, Hooper observes that if anything, Scripture, numerically at least, makes more of the humanity than it does of the deity: "As many places of the New Testament proveth Christ's humanity, as proveth his deity, and more."[17]

As is well known, Luther laid very strong emphasis on the humanity of Christ. In a famous comment, he says that the deeper we go into the flesh of Christ, the better it is.[18] The flesh means the "total humanity, body and soul." Mary was a "normal natural mother" and

---

[14]Gallican Confession, 6; 14; Scots Confession, 6; Second Helvetic Confession, 3; 11.7; 11.3.

[15]Calvin, *Institutes*, 1.13.4; cf. 1.13.7ff.; and note John Jewel, *Works*, ed. J. Ayre, Parker Society Publications 23-26, 4 vols. (Cambridge: Cambridge Univ. Press, 1845-1850), 1:533.

[16]*Institutes*, 2.12.1.

[17]John Hooper, *Early Writings of John Hooper*, ed. Samuel Carr, Parker Society Publications 20 (Cambridge: Cambridge Univ. Press, 1843), 113.

[18]Martin Luther, *Dr. Martin Luthers sämmtliche Werke*, 2d ed. (Erlangen, 1832-85), 6:155 (Sermon on Lk 2:22ff.). (Hereinafter this edition is cited as EA.)

Christ a "normal natural son." We have to let Christ be a "natural human being, in every respect exactly as we are," though with a pure nature. God shows his goodness to us by "stepping down so deep into flesh and blood."[19] John in the Gospel speaks of God's almighty and eternal Word only in terms of the flesh and blood that walked on earth.[20] True knowledge of God in faith is knowledge that God was born of the Virgin, sucked her milk, and ate at her hands, for only in grace and love could God have taken upon himself poor, wretched human nature. That he became human as we are is a cause, not of doubt, but of wondering joy. In Christ's humanity, in which the eternal Father's Son became the temporal Virgin's Son, we see that God and we are not farther apart than heaven and earth but closer than two brothers.[21]

Zwingli, too, made much of the reality of Christ and his human experiences. In his *Exposition of the Faith* he says of Christ that "according to his human nature he is in every way man, having all the properties which belong to the true and proper nature of man, save only the propensity of sin."[22] Christ received this human nature when he was born of the Virgin, and according to it "he increased and grew both in wisdom and stature," and "suffered hunger and thirst and cold and heat and all other infirmities, sin only excepted." In it he "suffered, being nailed to the cross under Pilate the governor." As Zwingli sees it, there is "no humiliation which he has not experienced and borne."[23]

Calvin dealt no less thoroughly with Christ's humanity than with his deity. Beginning with the need for the Incarnation, he takes pains to stress the authenticity of the human nature, to explain the relation of the humanity to the deity, and to expound the statements of the Creed regarding the Crucifixion, the Descent, the Resurrection, and the Ascension and Session.[24] Assertion of the true humanity of Christ was especially urgent and important for Calvin and the other Reformers because of the divergent view of some radicals, including Menno Simons, that the Word did not assume our earthly flesh but a new and heavenly flesh. As Calvin saw it, the incarnational passage

---

[19]Martin Luther, *Works*, ed. J. Pelikan and H. T. Lehmann (St. Louis: Concordia/Philadelphia: Fortress, 1955–86), 52:80-81, 11-12. (Hereinafter this edition is cited as LW.)

[20]Martin Luther, *D. Martin Luthers Werke: Kritische Gesamtausgabe* (Weimar: Bohlau, 1883ff.), 10/1:1, 202 (Sermon on Jn 1:1ff.). (Hereinafter this edition is cited as WA.)

[21]Luther, EA, 6:40, 42 (Sermon on Isa 9:1ff.).

[22]Huldreich Zwingli, *Exposition of the Faith,* in *Zwingli and Bullinger,* ed. G. W. Bromiley, Library of Christian Classics 24 (Philadelphia: Westminster, 1953), 251.

[23]Ibid., 252; cf. Zwingli, *On the Lord's Supper,* in ibid., 212.

[24]*Institutes,* 2.12-16.

Php 2:5ff. shows that Christ allowed his deity to be "hidden by a 'veil' of flesh, emptying himself in a nature truly human" and manifesting "only human likeness" in his "lowly and abased condition." This biblical testimony to a true humanity disposes of the docetism of Marcion, the Manichean idea of a body of heavenly essence, and the "subtleties" of their "modern disciples." As for Menno's argument that women play only a receptive part in procreation, Calvin saw here an overturning of the principles of nature. Against an appeal to the genealogies, he exclaimed, "must we then say that women are nothing? Why, even children know that women are included under the term 'men'!" Engendered of the seed of Mary, Christ is true Son of David and true Son of Adam, "the common father of us all."[25] In England Hutchinson found in Menno's view a threat to the whole truth of the Atonement: Christ partook of Mary's "substance and nature," he claimed, because "it was needful that the same flesh should be punished on the tree, which offended in eating of the fruit of the tree."[26]

Did this mean that Christ took sinful flesh? The Reformers did not deal specifically with this question which Barth raised in his *Church Dogmatics*. Barth himself believed that in spite of Christ's sinlessness, full humanity means sinful humanity. In a historical survey he found the statements of the Reformers ambivalent on the issue. Calvin, for example, could say that Christ in grace "joins himself to base and ignoble men," but Calvin and other Reformers shrank from stating boldly that Christ took "the concrete form of human nature marked by Adam's fall," as Barth thought we have to do, and as Menno also believed we must do unless we find in Christ the heavenly flesh that he did not take from Mary.[27] Hutchinson probably expressed the common Reformation view when he found in Christ an assuming, not of sinful flesh itself, but of all its infirmities: "Albeit he were not born in sinful flesh, yet, because he was born in the likeness of this sinful flesh, he was born a babe" and "took both this and all other human infirmities . . . upon him."[28]

Barth himself, of course, had to allow that there is difference as well as likeness. The Son of God is the same as we are "in quite a different way from us." Living where we are, he sinlessly bears the burden that we should bear as sinners.[29] Calvin, perhaps, had some-

---

[25]*Institutes*, 2.13.3.

[26]Roger Hutchinson, *Works*, ed. J. Bruce, Parker Society Publications 22 (Cambridge: Cambridge Univ. Press, 1842), 145.

[27]Karl Barth, *Church Dogmatics*, trans. and ed. G. W. Bromiley and T. F. Torrance, 4 vols. (Edinburgh: T. and T. Clark, 1956–75), 1/2:151 (hereinafter cited as CD); cf. Calvin, *Institutes*, 2.13.2, 4.

[28]Hutchinson, *Works*, 150.

[29]CD, 1/2:155-56.

thing similar in view when he traced Christ's sinlessness to the sanctifying of the Spirit and emphasized that his purity calls for notice in the Bible precisely because it is the purity of his true human nature. Like the Fathers, however, Calvin gave the sinlessness a broader reach when he acutely pointed out that since human nature is intrinsically good as created, and only accidentally vicious, it is no wonder that he "through whom integrity was to be restored, was exempted from common corruption."[30] If Barth was sharply critical of this view in CD 1/2, arguing that created human nature cannot be the same as corrupted human nature, he later seemed to come close to accepting it when in his theological anthropology he presented Christ as him in whom alone we see *real* humanity, as distinct from the falsified humanity that we find in ourselves.[31] The humanity that Christ assumed is the true humanity that is sinful in us.

The confessions shared with Luther, Zwingli, Calvin, and the Anglicans a concern to stress the reality of Christ's humanity, i.e., that "not fantastically," but "truly and unfeignedly he appeared very man in the flesh," as Becon puts it.[32] The First Helvetic has a long article on Christ's incarnation and his saving work in the flesh, which is like ours in all things but sin. The Gallican stresses that "we so consider him in his divinity that we do not despoil him of his humanity." The Belgic adduces various texts of Scripture to prove that Christ took flesh of the Virgin and insists that in the hypostatic union the humanity "has . . . not lost its properties."[33] The Scots expounds the Creed to show that the union of natures in one person made it possible for the "infirmity" of the one to suffer death for us and "the infinite and invincible power of the other" to "purchase to us life, liberty, and perpetual victory." The Anglican singles out the Passion ("who truly suffered") in a way that draws attention to the real humanity. The Second Helvetic, with Apollinarianism in view, states that the Incarnation involved both "a soul with its reason, and flesh with its senses, by which senses he felt true griefs in the time of his passion."[34]

The Reformers made no effort to work out all the possible ramifications of the humanity, as some modern theologians try to do. They saw no reason to try to go behind the New Testament in reconstruction of a supposed historical Jesus whom the biblical records have

---

[30]Calvin, *Institutes*, 2.13.4; cf. Hutchinson, *Works*, 147.

[31]Cf. CD 3/2.

[32]Thomas Becon, *The Governance of Virtue*, in *The Early Works of Thomas Becon*, ed J. Ayre, Parker Society Publications 2 (Cambridge: Cambridge Univ. Press, 1843), 318.

[33]First Helvetic Confession, 11; Gallican Confession, 15; Belgic Confession, 18; 19.

[34]Scots Confession, 8, cf. 9-11; Thirty-nine Articles, 2; Second Helvetic Confession, 11.5.

overlaid. They did not ask about possible temptations, illnesses, habits, emotions, or problems in human relations. They recognized the speculative and therefore the futile nature of such inquiries. They made statements about Christ's humanity only on the basis of the information available: the temptations that Jesus did in fact suffer, the pains he did in fact undergo, the habits and customs he is known to have observed, the relations he had, and the experiences of life to which he was exposed, e.g., dependence as an infant, and then later in life, hunger, thirst, weariness, sorrow, and pain.[35] Beyond that they saw that we have only a blank page. The imagination might suggest that this or that belongs also to true humanity, but there are no objective facts with which to fill the page, and hence the Reformers viewed it as illegitimate and unprofitable to try to fill it. Not presuming to say what is or is not necessary to true and full humanity, they knew enough to be sure that Jesus was fully human, even though there was much about his humanity that they did not know and were content not to know if the human authors (and the divine Author!) of the New Testament did not think it important to tell them.

Taught by Scripture, the Reformers attached great significance to the humanity of Christ because it relates so plainly and categorically to his mediatorial work. In this regard they followed the classical line of patristic and medieval theology. Answering the question: *Cur Deus homo*? they linked the Incarnation to the Atonement. Luther, as already noted, believed that Christ took our humanity in order that God might be close and not distant. Zwingli, insisting that Christ was weak and suffered according to his humanity, pointed out that "to make atonement for our sins he suffered the most ignominious form of execution," which he could not do in his impassible divine nature.[36] Calvin wrote a whole chapter on why "Christ had to become man in order to fulfill the office of Mediator."[37] The necessity, he shows, is not absolute. It is that of a heavenly decree on which salvation depends. No human intermediary could bridge the gulf between us and God. If God decides to bridge it, God must do it, but God in human nature, for "otherwise the nearness would not have been near enough . . . for us to hope that God might dwell with us." God "used a most appropriate remedy," setting "the Son of God familiarly among us as one of ourselves" to offer satisfaction for us.[38] Hutchinson, too, underlines the appropriateness: "As through a natural man we were banished out of paradise, so it pleased the almighty Trinity, by a natural man, to restore us again, and make us

[35]Becon, *Early Works*, 416.

[36]Zwingli, *Exposition of the Faith*, 252.

[37]Calvin, *Institutes*, 2.12.

[38]Ibid., 12.1; cf. 12.3.

heirs of salvation." "He is wisdom; wherefore he took the most wisest way."[39]

The actual relation between Incarnation and Atonement made it unnecessary, the Reformers thought, to ask whether Christ would have become man had there been no Fall. When Osiander suggested that he might have done so in order to give us assurance of God's love, Calvin dismissed this as vague speculation and unlawful inquiry. Reformation theology did not deal with possibility, but with biblical reality. The Spirit has declared that Incarnation and redemption are conjoined "by God's eternal decree." The further argument that Adam was patterned on the future Messiah "whom the Father had already determined to clothe with flesh" had no cogency, for Christ was already God's image, and we are to seek the image in the marks of excellence with which God distinguished Adam.[40] The idea that Christ could be King only as man also had no merit, for the eternal Son, even if not "endued with human flesh," could still have gathered unfallen humanity "into the fellowship of his heavenly glory." In Calvin's view speculation breeds "trivialities." The "sober truth" of Gal 4:4-5 "is more than enough to nourish perfectly the children of God."[41]

The confessions and catechisms, too, saw a close relation between the need for redemption and the need for incarnation. In the words of Augsburg, "Christ, true God and true man . . . was born of the virgin . . . that he . . . might be a sacrifice, not only for original guilt, but also for all actual sins." The First Helvetic states that Christ assumed human nature so that as our Brother he might give us life again and make us coheirs of God. The Heidelberg Catechism, asking what manner of Mediator and Redeemer we must seek, offers the reply: "One who is a true and sinless man, and yet more powerful than all creatures." God's justice "requires that the same human nature which has sinned should make satisfaction for sin," but no sinner can do this, only Christ, "who is at the same time true God and a true, sinless man."[42] The Scots Confession echoes Calvin: the "most wondrous conjunction betwixt the Godhead and the manhead in Christ Jesus, did proceed from the eternal and immutable decree of God, from which all our salvation springs and depends." According to the Gallican, Christ became man like us so as to be "capable of suffering in body and soul." The Belgic claims that "our salvation and resurrection also depend on the reality of his body." Westminster

---

[39]Hutchinson, *Works*, 143, 154.

[40]Calvin, *Institutes*, 2.12.5, 6.

[41]Ibid., 2.12.7.

[42]Augsburg Confession, 1.3; First Helvetic Confession, 11; Heidelberg Catechism, qq. 15, 16, 18.

argues that in virtue of the human nature united to the divine, the Lord Jesus was "thoroughly furnished to execute the office of a mediator and surety."[43] Clearly, if the real humanity of Christ were in any way to be doubted, minimized, or disparaged, the Gospel itself would be overthrown, and all Reformation theology would fall to the ground.

HUMANITY AND REVELATION

One aspect of the humanity of Christ is that in and by it God reveals himself both fully and understandably. This was not a primary thesis for the Reformers, as it would be in our own century for Barth. They did not develop it in detail nor look too deeply into its implications. Nevertheless, it certainly played a part in their view of Christ and his incarnation and mission.

Luther stated the matter with his usual verve and vividness. We can know God, he said in a letter to Spalatin (2.12.1519),[44] only if we begin with the humanity of Christ. Even if we were to hunt and poke around in heaven, as he quaintly puts it, we would find only Christ in the crib and on the Virgin's lap, and end up breaking our necks. We must start here below, not up above.[45] There is no bare knowledge of God. To know and grasp God properly and savingly, we must not try to know him in himself but seek him only in Christ and his work in him. The only God we can truly know is God in Christ.[46] In Jacob's dream, the first movement is that of ascent, from Christ's human nature to knowledge of God. It is in Christ that we know the Father's will. Christ is the mirror of the Father's heart.[47] As creatures, and especially as sinners, we cannot know God directly, only indirectly through masks. We cannot see or feel but move as it were across an abyss, wrapped in a cloak, with Christ as our guide. Whereas we want to mount up to heaven, God comes down to earth. In Christ he is ready to lie in the cradle and hang on the cross. It is here that we know God.[48]

Calvin in the *Institutes* adopted an order that follows the Creed. It might well suggest that a knowledge of God the Creator precedes the fuller knowledge of God the Redeemer. Calvin states expressly, however, that "the whole knowledge of God the Creator . . . would be useless unless faith also followed, setting forth for us God our Father in

---

[43]Scots Confession, 7; Gallican Confession, 14; Belgic Confession, 19; Westminster Confession, 8.3.

[44]Luther, WA, *Briefwechsel*, 1:328-29.

[45]Luther, WA, 9:406.

[46]Luther, Sermon on Jn 17:3, WA 28:100-101.

[47]Luther, WA 40/1:98; 30/1:192.

[48]Luther, WA 47:33-34; 28:135-36.

Christ." A true knowledge of God must be saving knowledge, and "unless God confronts us in Christ, we cannot come to know that we are saved." Calvin can thus approvingly cite Irenaeus. The infinite Father has become finite in the Son, accommodating himself "to our little measure lest our minds be overwhelmed by the immensity of his glory." We ourselves, being finite and sinful, would be terrified were God to come in his majesty. Graciously heeding our weakness, he has concealed his glory lest it overthrow us. He is comprehended in Christ alone.[49]

Calvin makes this point very clearly in the commentaries. On Jn 1:14 he says of Christ that "having been clothed with our flesh"—which here denotes mortality rather than corrupt nature—"he showed himself openly to the world." The Incarnation involved both a hiding and a disclosing. The majesty of God was "concealed," "but so as to cause its splendour to be seen." The comment on Jn 1:18 drives home the point. "It is by Christ alone that God makes himself known to us." Formerly concealed in his secret glory, he "may now be said to have made himself visible." God is "openly beheld in the face of Christ."[50] On Col 2:3 Calvin insists again that "the Father has manifested himself wholly in him" (Christ). He has done so, "fully and perfectly in Christ" (on 2:9).[51] On Heb 1:3 Calvin notes that "we are blind to the light of God, until in Christ it beams on us."[52]

Of other Reformers who make occasional mention of this aspect of Christ's humanity we may refer to Zwingli, who says that "God clothed his only son with flesh to reveal . . . to the whole earth salvation and renewal."[53] Among the Anglicans Becon lists it as the second purpose of Christ's coming "that men may learn to know the true God."[54] Hutchinson describes the humanity as "the mean whereby we must obtain all things; the way by which we must climb up to heaven; the ladder that Jacob saw."[55]

The confessions, too, found a place for the role of the incarnate Christ in revelation, but they tended in the main to focus on the revelation of the character or will of God rather than of God himself. The Gallican, for example, maintains that in sending the Son, God "intended to show his love and inestimable goodness." The Belgic

---

[49]Calvin, *Institutes*, 2.6.1, 4; citing Irenaeus, *Adversus haereses*, 4.4.2 (MPG 7, 982).

[50]John Calvin, *Commentary on John*, trans. W. Pringle, 2 vols. (Grand Rapids: Eerdmans, 1949), 1:45.

[51]John Calvin, *Commentary on Philippians, Colossians, and First and Second Thessalonians*, trans. and ed. J. Pringle (Grand Rapids: Eerdmans, 1948), 182.

[52]John Calvin, *Commentary on Hebrews*, trans. and ed. J. Owen (Grand Rapids: Eerdmans, 1948), 36.

[53]Zwingli, *Exposition of the Faith*, 249-50.

[54]Becon, *The News Out of Heaven*, in *Early Works*, 50-51.

[55]Hutchinson, *Works*, 35.

sees in the incarnate Son a manifestation of divine justice and mercy. The Second Helvetic makes the point that our sinful understanding is darkened, but in such a way as to mislead the will and thus to produce wicked acts. Hence the problem that Christ's coming deals with is primarily disobedience rather than ignorance, although the two are intertwined. Along these lines the Westminster Shorter Catechism relates the revealing ministry of Christ to his prophetic ministry. In the prophetic office Christ teaches us the truth about God and in so doing he shows us "the will of God for our salvation."[56]

Where the Reformers stressed the revelation of God's very self in Christ, and not merely of his will or his goodness, they had a keen sense of the veiling as well as the unveiling that the Incarnation involves.[57] Calvin, for example, recognizes that God made himself visible in Christ, but he also sees that by taking the image of a servant Christ "allowed his divinity to be hidden by a 'veil' of flesh . . . [so that] for a time the divine glory did not shine."[58] Philip, then, "had God present in Christ, and yet he did not behold him."[59] To penetrate the veil, to see Christ as he truly is, the Spirit must give us the knowledge of faith and lead us to Christ. Only in heaven is there "no longer any veil intervening, but God appears to us openly."[60]

The confessions point out that there can be no authentic knowledge of Christ without the Holy Spirit, although usually with more stress on what Christ has done than on who he is. Thus Augsburg, with reference to justification, throws us back on the Spirit, "who worketh faith, where and when it pleaseth God." Similarly in the Heidelberg Catechism it is the Spirit who "makes me by a true faith partaker of Christ and all his benefits." Along the same lines the Gallican Confession says that we are "enlightened in faith by the secret power of the Holy Spirit," the Scots describes faith as "the inspiration of the Holy Ghost," the Second Helvetic speaks of illumination by the Spirit so that we may "understand both the mysteries and the will of God," and the Westminster sees a need for an enlightening of the mind, "spiritually and savingly, to understand the things of God." Knowing God in the man Jesus undoubtedly has an important place in this illumination, although predominantly with a view to the reconciliation that God accomplished in him.[61]

---

[56]Gallican Confession, 16; Belgic Confession, 20; Second Helvetic Confession, 9.2; Westminster Shorter Catechism, q. 24.

[57]CD, 1/1:174ff.

[58]Calvin, Institutes, 13.2; cf. 2.9.1.

[59]Calvin, Commentary on Jn 14:8-9 (p. 97).

[60]Cf. Institutes, 3.2.33ff. with the Commentary on Heb 7:25 (p. 175).

[61]Augsburg Confession, 1.5; Heidelberg Catechism, q. 53; Gallican Confession, 21; Scots Confession, 12; Second Helvetic Confession, 9.7; Westminster Confession, 10.1.

HUMANITY AND RECONCILIATION

The Reformers plainly regarded the humanity of Christ as integral to reconciliation. They approached this fact from different angles, but the fact itself remained constant. The human race has fallen from God and cannot restore itself. It has incurred a guilt that it cannot expiate. A penalty lies upon it which means its ruin unless vicariously suffered. The work of restoration, expiation, and penalty-bearing must obviously be done by a representative of humanity. Yet God alone can do it. If God is to do it, he must do it as man. The Son of God, therefore, becomes man and does it for us.

Zwingli offers a bold statement of the role of Christ's humanity in reconciliation when he points out that since God's justice demands expiation and his mercy forgiveness, "the Son of the Most High King, clothed therefore with flesh, for according to his divine nature he cannot die . . ., offered up himself a sacrifice." Here the reason why Christ assumed humanity is that according to his impassible divine nature he could not do a work which entailed his death![62] But Zwingli hastened to add that the sacrifice is demanded of humanity and that because none of us could offer it on account of original sin, the Son of God graciously stepped in for us. A further point is that we could not in any case make a sufficient payment. In Zwingli's eyes the costliness of the gift assures us of its all-sufficiency.[63]

Calvin's discussion of the humanity of Christ and reconciliation combined various emphases. By his humanity the Mediator teaches us "that he is near us, indeed touches us, since he is our flesh." Along the lines of a patristic insight Calvin also claims that Christ so took "what was ours as to impart what was his to us, and to make what was his by nature ours by grace."[64] Divinity assumed humanity in order to give humanity a share in divinity. Christ's humanity also makes possible his vicarious obedience. The obedience of Christ supplies our lack of righteousness. We are justified by his imputed righteousness. "By the whole course of his obedience" Christ abolished sin and banished the separation between God and us. In this obedience Christ paid "the price of liberation," willingly suffering death and bearing the penalty of sin on our behalf.[65] Taking up a thought of Zwingli, and again echoing the Fathers, Calvin argues that Christ "coupled human nature with divine that to atone for sin he might submit the weakness of the one to death; and that, wrestling

---

[62]Zwingli, *Exposition of the Faith*, 250; cf. Hutchinson, *Works*, 154: "The Deity suffereth no infirmity, which is impossible."

[63]Zwingli, *Exposition of the Faith*, 250.

[64]Calvin, *Institutes*, 2.12.1, 2.

[65]Ibid., 2.16.5.

with death by the power of the other nature, he might win the victory for us."[66]

Among the Anglicans Becon's fifth reason for the Incarnation is that Christ should "suffer for your sake, for your health and salvation." Becon, like Calvin, thinks it important also that Christ fulfilled the law for us.[67] Hooper points out that both deity and humanity were necessary for atonement, for "except the Son of God had been an equal and just redemption, a price correspondent to counterpoise and satisfy the culpe and guilt of man's sin, God would not have taken one soul from the right and justice of the devil."[68] Hutchinson notes that Christ took soul as well as flesh to be a "Redeemer of both." What is not assumed is not healed! The Incarnation enables Christ to take upon himself all the "human infirmities . . . which overflowed the world through sin." Rather fancifully, Hutchinson finds in the mode of Christ's coming into the human world a pointer to the inclusiveness of salvation. Christ became a man, but he did so of a woman! Disguising himself in flesh—the old patristic thesis—Christ reverses the deceitful action of the Serpent and delivers us from bondage: he "did deck and clothe himself with our nature, to deceive and conquer the devil." By his humility he also reverses the pride of our revolt and teaches the humility by which we may return to paradise: "Down therefore, proud stomach; down, peacock's feathers."[69]

The Scots Confession gives a full account of the contribution of Christ's humanity to reconciliation. It links Christ's taking of "body of our body, flesh of our flesh, and bone of our bones," to the power given to believers to be sons of God, "by which most holy fraternity" what we lost in Adam "is restored unto us again." As in Zwingli, stress falls on the fact that "because the only God-head could not suffer death, neither could the only man-head overcome the same, he joined both together in the one person." Christ achieved reconciliation primarily by the voluntary sacrifice in which he even "suffered for a season the wrath of his Father," though remaining "the only well-beloved and blessed Son of his Father, even in the midst of his anguish and torment which he suffered in body and soul to make the full satisfaction for the sins of the people."[70]

The Genevan Catechism makes the familiar points. The honor of being a child of God, which is Christ's by nature, "is communicated to us by gratuitous favour, as being his members." Christ assumed our nature "because it was necessary that the disobedience committed by

---

[66]Ibid., 2.12.3; cf. Heidelberg Catechism, qq. 15-17.

[67]Becon, *The News Out of Heaven*, in *Early Works*, 51-53.

[68]Hooper, *Early Writings*, 49.

[69]Hutchinson, *Works*, 144, 150, 151, 153.

[70]Scots Confession, 8; 9.

man against God should be expiated also in human nature." "It was in respect to the feelings of his human nature" that Christ endured the "dread" and "doom" of the cross. Yet "he did not endure it so as to remain under it"; wrestling with the power of hell, "he subdued and crushed it."[71] The Heidelberg Catechism follows an obviously Anselmian line. "The same human nature which has sinned" must "make satisfaction for sin." Only "by the power of his Godhead," however, can the Mediator "bear, in his manhood, the burden of God's wrath."[72] Christ took upon him "the very nature of man, of the flesh and blood of the virgin Mary," and "bore, in body and soul, the wrath of God against the sin of the whole human race, in order that by his passion, as the only atoning sacrifice, he might redeem our body and soul from everlasting damnation." His "innocence and perfect holiness" cover our sin. Were there no humanity of Christ, there would be for the Reformers no expiation; no justification; no forgiveness; no fellowship with God; no eternal destiny; no faith, hope, or love; no people of God. The humanity could hardly be rated higher. If not abstractly necessary, it is in fact indispensable. Its denial or attenuation makes nonsense of Christian teaching and robs the church of its message and mission.[73]

A point of interest is that Augsburg, followed by the Anglican Articles and the Second Helvetic, speaks of the reconciling of the Father to us. The Belgic says similarly that Christ presented himself to the Father "to appease his wrath by his full satisfaction."[74] Among individual Reformers Hooper states bluntly that "the ire of God" is appeased; and the work of Christ according to Becon was "to pacify God the Father's wrath."[75] Did the Reformers think, then, of an angry Father to placate whom the merciful Son assumes humanity? We must not let the above phrases leave us with this impression. Becon, for example, also traces the coming of Christ to "the immeasurable goodness of this celestial Father"; "God of his own free goodness sent down his only-begotten Son."[76] Luther in the Small Catechism draws attention to the goodness and mercy of the Father and Creator. The First Helvetic Confession says that Christ comes in fulfillment of the eternal council of God, the gracious Father. The Gallican finds in the sending of the Son proof of God's "love and inestimable goodness

---

[71]John Calvin, *Tracts and Treatises*, ed. T. F. Torrance, 3 vols. (Grand Rapids: Eerdmans, 1958), 2:43, 44, 47.

[72]Heidelberg Catechism, qq. 16, 17.

[73]Ibid., qq. 35–37.

[74]Augsburg Confession, 1.3; Thirty-nine Articles, 2; Second Helvetic Confession, 11; Belgic Confession, 21.

[75]Hooper, *A Treatise of Christ and His Office*, in *Early Writings*, 6; Becon, *The Christmas Banquet*, in *Early Works*, 74.

[76]Becon, *The Christmas Banquet*, in *Early Works*, 72, 74.

towards us." The Second Helvetic, like the First, affirms that Christ was "eternally predestinated . . . of the Father to be the Saviour of the world."[77]

To explain the matter, Calvin devotes a whole paragraph to the theme that the Atonement derives from the love of God eternally "grounded in Christ." On the basis of Ro 5:10 he thinks that we may legitimately say that God is made favorable to us by the death of Christ. In the light of Jn 3:16, however, we see that God did not begin to love us when Christ reconciled us. It is because he loved us from eternity that we may be his in Christ. As Augustine aptly put it, Christ's death removes God's hatred of what we were that he had *not* made. What persists is his love of what he *had* made.[78] Against this background the thought of propitiation gives us in fact an enhanced appreciation of the gracious love which in and by the divine humanity of the Son delivered us from the judgment that justly threatened us. "By his love God the Father goes before and anticipates our reconciliation in Christ."[79]

HUMANITY AND RESURRECTION

Conservative theology often attracts the charge of docetism regarding the earthly life of Christ. The situation is reversed, however, when it comes to his resurrection life. At this point those who bring the charge often take refuge in their own form of dualistic docetism, finding difficulty in accepting the full humanity which the biblical and creedal "resurrection of the body" emphatically proclaims. The Reformers had no such inhibitions. Not only did they contend for the real, earthly humanity of Christ which his vicarious work demanded. They contended no less vigorously for his real resurrection humanity, which they viewed as no less essential if salvation were to include eternal life with God.

Coverdale made much of the point that in Christ our own nature, which is mortal, is raised up to an immortal life: "The natural Son of God himself from heaven became a mortal man, to the intent that man's mortal nature, through the uniting thereof with the immortal nature of the Godhead in his own only person, might be exalted to an immortal life."[80] By the resurrection of "the true body of Christ" "we are assured and out of doubt . . . that our own bodies likewise shall rise from death," difficult though it may be to imagine and believe

---

[77]Luther, Small Catechism, in Schaff, *Creeds*, 3:78; First Helvetic Confession, 10; Gallican Confession, 16; Second Helvetic Confession, 11.

[78]Calvin, *Institutes*, 2.16.4.

[79]Ibid., 1.16.3; cf. 16.2.

[80]Miles Coverdale, *Remains*, ed. G. Pearson, Parker Society Publications 14 (Cambridge: Cambridge Univ. Press, 1846), 71.

this. In Christ's resurrection our own "hath a fast and immovable ground."[81] As Calvin puts it, "we are assured of our own resurrection by receiving a sort of guarantee substantiated by his" in view of the fact that he "received immortality in the same flesh that, in the mortal state, he had taken upon himself."[82]

The First Helvetic Confession expresses a similar thought when it states that Christ raised his flesh again so as to give us full hope and trust for the hereafter. So does the Heidelberg Catechism: since Christ's full humanity is raised, his resurrection "is to us a sure pledge of our blessed resurrection." The Belgic Confession resists any suggestion that immortality might destroy the real humanity. Christ has given immortality to "the properties of a real body." "Nevertheless he hath not changed the reality of his human nature; forasmuch as our salvation and resurrection also depend on the reality of his body." The Gallican argues similarly: Christ in bestowing "immortality upon his body, yet he did not take from it the truth of its nature." Christ took humanity in order that our humanity might be saved and raised up in him. The Scots Confession does not doubt "but the selfsame body, which was born of the Virgin, was crucified, dead, and buried, and which did rise again, did ascend into the heavens." The Anglican and Irish stress the fact that in his resurrection, ascension, and session Christ "took again his body, with flesh, bones, and all things appertaining to the perfection of man's nature." The Second Helvetic maintains that Christ's body was not "so deified that it put off its properties, as touching body and soul." Christ "did not rise up another flesh, but retained a true body," ascending "in the same flesh." He thus "restored life and immortality" to us who share his humanity. We, too, will be endowed with "glorified bodies" as he is.[83]

The reference to glorified bodies is a reminder that although the Reformers were at great pains to preserve the reality of resurrection humanity, they were also aware of the distinction that Paul made between the natural body and the spiritual body.[84] The immortality that humanity acquires in Christ is something for which God destined it by creation. There is thus no intrinsic contradiction between humanity and immortal glory. The contradiction came with sin,

---

[81]Ibid., 141-49.

[82]Calvin, *Institutes*, 2.16.13.

[83]First Helvetic Confession, 10; Heidelberg Catechism, q. 45; Belgic Confession, 19; Gallican Confession, 15; Scots Confession, 11; Thirty-nine Articles, 4; Irish Articles, 30; Second Helvetic Confession, 11.8, 10-11, 13, 15.

[84]Heinrich Bullinger, *The Decades*, ed. T. Harding, Parker Society Publications 7-10, 4 vols. (Cambridge: Cambridge Univ. Press, 1849), 1:175-76; Hugh Latimer, *Works*, ed. G. E. Corrie, Parker Society Publications 34, 2 vols. (Cambridge: Univ. Press, 1844), 2:53; Coverdale, *Remains*, 177.

which brought humanity under the conditions of affliction and mortality.[85] Christ in his resurrection brings humanity in all its fullness to perfection and beatitude in eternal fellowship with God. "This my body, raised by the power of Christ, shall again be united with my soul, and made like unto the glorious body of Christ." I shall then "possess complete bliss . . . therein to praise God for ever,"[86] being "made perfectly blessed in the full enjoying of God to all eternity."[87]

For the Reformers the humanity of the risen Christ had a particular bearing on his intercessory ministry. They stressed this ministry from the very outset in opposition to the supposed need for the intercession of Mary and the saints. Zwingli in his Sixty-Seven Articles confesses Christ as our only Mediator. The Bern Theses describe him as our only Mediator and Advocate. Augsburg finds in Scripture "one Christ the Mediator, Propitiatory, High-Priest, and Intercessor." The First Helvetic refers to Christ our Brother as our true High-Priest at the right hand of the Father.[88]

The Anglican Becon says of Christ at God's right hand: "Yet shall he not be there idle . . . . For he shall there continually pray and make intercession to God his Father for you."[89] Hooper describes it as Christ's office "to pray and to make intercession for his people." "This intercession of Christ only sufficeth." It is "the office only of Christ to be the mediator for sin, and likewise to offer the prayers of the church to his Father."[90] Calvin points out in his *Commentary on Hebrews* that "it belongs to a priest to intercede for the people," and he speaks of Christ's "continual intercession." He makes the same point in the *Institutes*. "Clothed with flesh" Christ fulfills the office of a mediator, and having washed away our sins he "obtains for us that grace from which the uncleanness of our transgressions and sins debars us." He is an "everlasting intercessor," and on this basis there may be "trust in prayer" and "peace for godly consciences." Having "opened the way into the heavenly kingdom," he appears before the Father's face as our constant Advocate and Intercessor and "sits on high, transfusing us with his power." He can perform this office only as the Son of God who as the Son of Man has accepted solidarity with us, assuming humanity on our behalf.[91]

The Gallican Confession takes up the theme of Christ's sole advocacy, and the Belgic expressly relates it to his humanity: Christ our

---

[85]Cf. Belgic Confession, 14; Scots Confession, 3.

[86]Heidelberg Catechism, qq. 57-58.

[87]Westminster Shorter Catechism, q. 38.

[88]Sixty-Seven Articles, 19-21; Bern Theses, 11; Augsburg Confession, 1.21; First Helvetic Confession, 10.

[89]Becon, *The News Out of Heaven, Early Works,* 55.

[90]Hooper, *Early Writings,* 31, 34, 35.

[91]Cf. Calvin, *Commentary on Hebrews* 7:25 with idem., *Institutes,* 2.15.6; 16.16.

only Mediator and Advocate "became man . . . that we might have access to the divine Majesty." His love for us dispels the fears that might drive us to Mary and the saints. Verses are adduced from Hebrews (2:17-18; 4:14ff.; 10:19, 22; 7:24-25) to prove his solidarity with us and the sufficiency of his priestly work. In virtue of his humanity he represents us; in virtue of his deity he has power with the Father, and "who will sooner be heard than the own well-beloved Son of God?"[92] The Genevan Catechism points out that as Christ gives us access to the Father, we are made "his colleagues in the priesthood." "He appears in the presence of God as our advocate and intercessor."[93] The Heidelberg Catechism lists it as the first benefit of Christ's ascension that he is "our Advocate in the presence of his Father in heaven." The Westminster Shorter Catechism states that "Christ executeth the office of a Priest, in his once offering up of himself . . . and in making continual intercession for us." The Second Helvetic makes an irenic gesture: "We do neither despise the saints nor think basely of them," but it insists no less firmly: "We, in all dangers and casualties of life, call on him alone, and that by the mediation of the only Mediator, and our Intercessor, Jesus Christ." "God and the Mediator do suffice us."[94]

CONTROVERSIES

1. Communication of Attributes

Confessing the true humanity of Christ, the Reformers stood together in endorsing the creeds and early councils, in rejecting heresies old and new, and in stressing the significance of the humanity in revelation, reconciliation, and resurrection. Yet the humanity of Christ also opened up conflict between the Lutherans on the one hand and the Reformed on the other. This conflict centered on the reciprocal communication of the divine and human attributes, which the Lutherans understood in what the Reformed regarded as a more realist and Eutychian sense, the Reformed in what the Lutherans condemned as more nominalist and Nestorian terms.

Both groups taught the communication of attributes but differed widely in their interpretation of its consequences. On the Lutheran side we find a succinct summary in the Formula of Concord, which recognizes that each nature retains its own essential attributes, but

---

[92]Gallican Confession, 24; Belgic Confession, 26.

[93]Geneva Catechism, in Calvin, *Tracts and Treatises*, 2:43, 48; cf. Calvin, *Institutes*, 2.15.6.

[94]Heidelberg Catechism, q. 49; Westminster Shorter Catechism, q. 25; Second Helvetic Confession, 5.3-5.

maintains that "from the personal union . . . flows everything human that is said and believed of God, and everything divine that is said and believed of the man Christ." On the Reformed side Zwingli allows that "things which are said of one nature are often attributed to the other."[95] Calvin thinks it biblical that things that Christ "carried out in his human nature are transferred improperly, although not without reason, to his divinity." Since the child of the Virgin, though human, is also the divine Son, it is right, for example, that we should call Mary the mother of God. Bullinger states similarly in the Second Helvetic: "We do reverently and religiously receive and use the communication of properties drawn from the Scripture." On the other hand he warns against drawing speculative inferences from the communication. Thus we are not to say "that the divine nature in Christ did suffer, or that Christ, according to his human nature, is yet in the world, and so in every place."[96]

For the Lutherans the problem with this apparent agreement was that the Reformed seemed to accept only a verbal communication. The Lutherans insisted in reply that the union does not make "only common names and titles." To say that "God is man and man is God" is more than "a phrase, and a certain mode of speaking." By rejecting the reality of the communication the Reformed were dividing the unity of the person. They inclined to Nestorianism in fact even though condemning it in words.[97]

The Reformed, on the other hand, thought that the Lutherans were carrying the communication far beyond what Scripture allows. By defining the communication as taking place between the natures, the Lutherans jeopardized the integrity of the natures. In the Reformed view, the Lutherans inclined to Eutychianism in fact even though they repudiated it in words, rejecting the idea "that the divine and human nature are commingled into one essence, and the human nature is changed into Deity, as Eutyches has madly affirmed."[98]

Zwingli, of course, aggravated the debate by the crass way in which he thought he could attribute certain words and works of Christ to his divine nature (e.g., miracles) and others to his human nature (e.g., thirst) even while rightly ascribing all of them to the one person. Calvin's attempt at correction on this point came, perhaps, too late to help. Calvin recognized that certain passages in the Gospels refer clearly to the deity and others no less clearly to the humanity. He also saw, however, that many passages "comprehend both natures at

---

[95]Formula of Concord, Epitome, 8: Affirmative 2 and 5 (translation slightly emended); cf. Zwingli, *On the Lord's Supper*, 213.

[96]Cf. Calvin, *Institutes*, 2.14.2 with Second Helvetic Confession, 11.8-9.

[97]Formula of Concord, Epitome, 8: Negative 5-7; cf. Calvin, *Institutes*, 2.14.4.

[98]Formula of Concord, Epitome, 8: Negative 2.

once" and that these "set forth his true substance most clearly of all."[99]

The important truth for which Calvin was contending was that the communication is not to be viewed or advanced as an abstraction. It does not stand in its own right. It is a fact only in virtue of the unity of the person. Zwingli had this in view when he insisted that "the unity of the person continues in spite of the diversity of the natures," for it was the person of the eternal Son that "assumed humanity in and by its own power." The Lutherans, too, finally based the communication on "the personal union and highest and ineffable communion" whereby the humanity is "personally united with the Son of God."[100] The human attributes are those of the Word who is also divine, the divine attributes those of the Word who is also human.

2. Calvinistic *Extra*

The somewhat esoteric controversy about the so-called Calvinistic *extra* derived from the debate about the communication of attributes. During the era of the Reformation it took only a more general form. It was not until the next century that dogmaticians on both sides gave their positions more precise formulation. The Reformers themselves simply provided the basic statements on which the later debates rested.

The question concerned Christ's continued functioning as Son of God during the years of his incarnation. Zwingli's contribution is simply that according to his divine nature Christ on earth "is in every respect God with the Father and the Holy Spirit." Calvin goes a little further when he exclaims that "without leaving heaven" Christ willed "to be borne in the virgin's womb, to go about on earth, to hang on the cross, yet he continuously filled the world even as he had done from the beginning." Hooper makes a similar statement: "Remaining always as he was, very God immortal," he "received the thing that he was not, mortal nature." Becon has something of the same point in mind when he says: "He lieth simply in a manger, wrapped in vile clouts, when notwithstanding he is Lord over all things." The Heidelberg Catechism is more explicit: The Godhead, being incomprehensible and omnipresent, "is indeed beyond the bounds (*ausserhalb*) of the Manhood which it has assumed, but is yet none the less in the same also, and remains personally united to it."[101]

---

[99]Cf. Zwingli, *Exposition of the Faith*, 251-52 with Calvin, *Institutes*, 2.14.4.

[100]Cf. Zwingli, *Exposition of the Faith*, 251-52 with Formula of Concord, Epitome, 8: Affirmative 5-6.

[101]Zwingli, *Exposition of the Faith*, 251, cf. 212; Calvin, *Institutes*, 2.13.4; Hooper, *Early Writings*, 17; Becon, *Early Works*, 51; Heidelberg Catechism, q. 48.

To the Lutherans such statements seemed to illustrate the mischievous results of a failure to posit the true communication of attributes. They divided the one Christ into a Christ *in* the flesh and a Christ *outside* (*extra*) the flesh. The distinction of the natures destroyed the reality of the unity of person. The Lutherans agree that the attributes of the divine nature "neither are nor ever become the attributes of the human nature."[102] On the other hand the personal unity is merely a matter of words if it is not the *incarnate* Christ who rules the world along with the Father and the Holy Spirit. The Incarnation is only a partial incarnation if always in the background there is a Christ outside the flesh.

The Reformed, however, contend that the distinction of natures is swallowed up if by communication we attribute to the human nature the eternal being of the Word with God. The Lutheran rejection of the *extra* involves the dilemma that either there is no real incarnation or that the Son, in divesting himself of his divine majesty,[103] ceases in truth to be the Son, as would later come to light in kenosis theories. Here again we must not think of the union or the communication abstractly. The unity is the unity of a real person, and the person is not a corporate person resulting from the union, but the person of the eternal Son who assumed humanity, but who in so doing did not renounce his eternal being as the second person of the Trinity. The Word assumed flesh; flesh did not assume the Word.[104]

An important feature of this debate is that both Lutherans and Reformed were arguing in different ways for the reality of the humanity of Christ. To the Lutherans the *extra* raises doubts as to whether Christ is truly and fully human, whereas to the Reformed the denial of the *extra*, if it does not spatially limit the Word to the flesh, necessarily removes all spatial limitation from the flesh and in this way jeopardizes the true humanity. If neither side can be said to have resolved the inherent difficulty, this is because the Incarnation is a divine action. As it is impossible for us to think how we, being human, might also be divine, so it is impossible for us to imagine how God, being divine, could also be human. Although the Reformers clearly could not solve all the related problems, nevertheless, both as Lutherans and as Reformed, they did not dispute the fact. Their explanations might be inadequate, but with equal force they espoused both the deity and the humanity in the unity of the person.

---

[102]Formula of Concord, Epitome, 8: Affirmative 3.

[103]Formula of Concord, Epitome, 18: Affirmative 11.

[104]Cf. Barth, CD 1/2:165ff.

3. Ubiquity

The ascension of Christ raised the same fundamental question from a different angle and with more pressing implications. At issue now was not the relation of the human nature on earth to the eternal and omnipresent Christ in heaven, but the relation of the human nature in heaven to the eternal and omnipresent Christ on earth. The Lutheran view of Christ's eucharistic presence depended on the communication of the divine attribute of omnipresence. Exalted to God's right hand, Christ as man no less than as God "knows all things, can do all things, is present to all creatures," and can "impart his true body and his blood in the Holy Supper" in a presence which, though not physical, is "most true and indeed substantial."[105] Ubiquity is possible for the human nature because "God knows and has in his power various modes in which he can be any where." It is thus an error to say that "Christ's body is so confined in heaven that it can in no mode whatever be likewise at one and the same time in many places."[106] Inability to explain the mode used by God in no way refutes its facticity. To split Christ into a spatially restricted human nature and a spatially unrestricted divine nature is again to deny the real communication and to be guilty of the Nestorian heresy. At the same time it involves the serious error of refusing to believe that God in his omnipotence can "effect that the body of Christ should be substantially present at one and the same time in more places than one."[107]

The Reformed for their part argued from the time of Zwingli that between the Ascension and the Return, according to Scripture and the creeds, Christ in his human nature is in heaven alone. Zwingli puts it plainly: "The body of Christ must truly, naturally, and properly be in one place," and now "according to its proper essence the body of Christ is truly and naturally seated at the right hand of the Father." Christ is undoubtedly present at the Eucharist, but according to his divine nature, which is ubiquitous.[108] Hooper, too, insists on the spatial restriction of the body: "If Christ have a true body, it must occupy place." So does Coverdale: "Christ sitteth at the right hand of God by his humanity, but circumscribed in place, and is not everywhere." If bodies are not in a place, he says, "they be no where" and are therefore "nothing at all." Only "after his Godhead" is Christ everywhere.[109] Calvin does not abandon Zwingli's basic contention that ubiquity is incompatible with corporeality and that there is thus

---

[105]Formula of Concord, Epitome, 8: Affirmative 11-12.

[106]Ibid., 7: Affirmative 5; Negative 11.

[107]Ibid., 7: Negative 13.

[108]Zwingli, *Exposition of the Faith*, 255; cf. 219.

[109]Hooper, *Early Writings*, 158; Coverdale, *Remains*, 157, 160-61.

no literal bodily presence in the Eucharist. The Consensus Tigurinus maintains that "Christ, regarded as man, must be sought nowhere else than in heaven." The Gallican, Belgic, Scots, and Second Helvetic follow suit.[110]

Nevertheless, although the Reformed continue to reject a literal bodily presence, which would have to be visible, they recognize the element of truth in the Lutheran position and make strenuous efforts to find common ground. Calvin in the Genevan Catechism speaks of the eucharistic "communication of Christ's body and blood," of the Lord's body having the virtue "spiritually to nourish our souls," and even of eating "the body and blood of the Lord." The Gallican Confession accepts a feeding with the substance of Christ's body and blood "by the secret and incomprehensible power of the Holy Spirit," thus approximating to the Lutheran "substantial presence" and "omnipotent power." The Second Helvetic confesses that "though in body he be absent from us in the heavens, yet [he] is present among us, not corporally, but spiritually," i.e., by the Spirit. The Heidelberg Catechism, too, teaches a true partaking of the body and blood "through the working of the Holy Ghost," though adding that "his true body is now in heaven."[111] Calvin develops the theme at some length in the *Institutes*, combining a concern for true corporeality (i.e., true humanity) with an equal concern for communion with Christ's body by "the secret working of the Spirit." To argue for a literal presence is to fall into Eutychianism. Yet as "the very same Christ who, according to the flesh, dwelt as Son of man on earth, was God in heaven" (the Calvinistic *extra*), so "the whole Christ is present, but not in his wholeness. For . . . in his flesh he is contained in heaven until he appears in judgment."[112]

Once again, to Lutheran eyes, the Reformed seemed to be overthrowing the unity. Where Christ is in deity, there he surely is in full humanity also. Or is Christ divided? Against the Reformed it might also be brought that they grant to the humanity of Christ infinity in time. Surely, then, there is no solid reason why they should so vociferously dispute its infinity in space. They do in fact display some uneasiness regarding the space-time distinction, but since they regard immortality as God's original plan for the race, it does not contradict full humanity in the same way as would freedom from localization in space. What might be implied by a spiritual body they do not

---

[110]Calvin, *Institutes*, 4.17.16-17; Consensus Tigurinus, in Calvin, *Tracts and Treatises*, 1:21; Gallican Confession, 36; Belgic Confession, 35; Scots Confession, 11; Second Helvetic Confession, 21.10.

[111]Geneva Catechism, in Calvin, *Tracts and Treatises*, 2:89; Gallican Confession, 36; cf. Belgic Confession, 35; Second Helvetic Confession, 21.10; Heidelberg Catechism, qq. 79-80.

[112]Calvin, *Institutes*, 4.17.30-31.

discuss. Their main concern is that the Lutherans press the personal unity to the point of an illegitimate fusion. This has as its unavoidable consequence either an absorption of the humanity into the deity or a deifying of the humanity. Once again the Lutherans seem to blunt the point that the one person is the person of the Son who assumes humanity.

Behind the divisions, however, there is still a basic agreement. All of the Reformers wish to uphold both the unity and the distinction, so that the difference is finally one of emphasis rather than substance, in spite of the heavy charges that are launched on both sides. As regards the humanity, the Lutherans have a stronger sense of the humanity at the Eucharist, but paradoxically the Reformed focus more sharply on the humanity at the right hand of God. Either way, the humanity retains its central significance.

It must also be noted that for all their divergent explanations the Lutherans and Reformed agree that the matters at issue are ultimately beyond human comprehension. As regards the Incarnation itself, the Scots Confession speaks of a "most wondrous conjunction"; and the Formula of Concord says that "next to the mystery of the Trinity, this is the chiefest mystery."[113] As regards the eucharistic presence and operation, Calvin refers to "a secret too lofty for either my mind to comprehend or my words to declare"; and the Belgic Confession, allowing that Christ "works in us all that he represents," states that "the manner surpasses our understanding . . . as the operations of the Holy Ghost are hidden and incomprehensible."[114] With this thesis the Saxon Visitation Articles have no quarrel, for even as they insist on a reception of "the true and natural body of Christ . . . and the true and natural blood," they also admit that we receive them "in an inscrutable and supernatural manner."[115]

CONCLUSION

The data show incontestably that the Reformers had no less vital an interest in the humanity of Christ than any theologians today. Yet they would have regarded many of the related concerns of modern theologians as a sorry confusion of priorities and a negation of truly scientific theology. A generation obsessed with its own interests, e.g., sex and politics, often seems to suggest that unless we can construe Christ in terms of these interests, we do not accept his full humanity or do justice to it. Christ must be subjected to this or that notion or definition of humanity. In contrast the Reformers, drawing more

---

[113]Scots Confession, 7; Formula of Concord, Epitome, 8: Affirmative 12.
[114]Calvin, *Institutes*, 4.17.32, cf. 33; Belgic Confession, 35.
[115]Saxon Visitation Articles, 1.4-5.

strictly from the biblical materials, formed a very different concept of Christ's humanity and very different reasons for focusing on it. As they saw it, Christ's humanity means his solidarity with us, not in our broken relationship to God, to others, to self, and to the world, but in the experiences and consequences of it. It means his vicarious bearing of these consequences with a view to restoration of the broken relationship. The Reformers' concern, then, was not one of purely historical curiosity, though it involved a commitment to history, nor of tailoring Christ to a given notion of humanity or a preconceived program. It was an existentially soteriological concern. Christ assumed humanity in order to heal humanity.

Being soteriological, the Reformers' concern did not blind them to the fact that the humanity, although essential, is not of itself enough. We may begin with Christ below, but we ascend to Christ above. Only a human Mediator, in truly human form and representing humanity, can give revelation, make reconciliation, and ensure resurrection. But he cannot do this as man alone. We know the gracious God, enjoy reconciliation, and have assurance of resurrection, not merely because a true man lived and died and rose again, but because the eternal Son became this true man. For the hearing and answering of prayer and for strengthening in our human weakness, we certainly need an advocate who knows the problems of human life to which we are exposed, but we also need an intercessor who knows the Father's mind and has the Father's ear. The historical Jesus is not just the man Jesus. He is the eternal Word who has come into the world and the race as the man Jesus.

The Reformers had their difficulties with the Incarnation, as the controversies show. Nevertheless, they did not make the mistake of stressing either the humanity at the expense of the deity or the deity at the expense of the humanity. With their biblically soteriological orientation they saw that the Christian message has neither point, validity, nor credibility unless both be true. To tilt the scales either one way or the other is not just to do theological harm but to destroy the Gospel. To study and present the humanity without its soteriological focus can have the same result. The presentations of the Reformers might sometimes be complex but always they had a firm realization that the Gospel is no academic game, no mere matter of antiquarian research, no sphere of speculative imagining. It is a life and death affair, eternal life and eternal death. We can and should give the humanity its essential place, but always in this life and death context and therefore along with the deity in the unity of the person of the eternal Word. For it was this Word, the Word that was with God and was God, who "for our sake and our salvation" was made flesh and dwelt among us. This is Jesus, true man, but also true God. There is no other.

Tradition and Innovation:
The Use of Theodoret's *Eranistes* in Martin Chemnitz' *De Duabus Naturis in Christo*

Robert A. Kelly

Assistant Professor of Systematic Theology
Waterloo Lutheran Seminary

One of the perennial debates in Protestant Christology is that between Lutherans and Reformed over the *communicatio idiomatum*. It began with Luther and Zwingli debating the presence of the incarnate Christ in the Eucharist. In order to defend their teaching of the real presence of the whole Christ, the Lutherans developed their teaching of the *genus maiestaticum* and the ubiquity of Christ's body. As Jaroslav Pelikan points out, the most damaging charge against which the Lutheran scholastics had to defend themselves was that the resulting Lutheran Christology is, at least incipiently, Eutychian.[1] This has been the charge leveled especially by the Reformed theologians of the sixteenth and seventeenth centuries and their descendants. Others have stated that, if Lutheran scholastic Christology is not Eutychian, it most certainly favors an Alexandrian interpretation of Chalcedon. A somewhat different view is offered by Richard Muller, who remarks that the Christology of Lutheran Orthodoxy is an "attempt to move beyond the dichotomy between Antioch and Alexandria. . . ."[2]

If Muller is correct in this assessment, then most of the credit for serving as the architect for the advance should go to Martin Chemnitz, Superintendent of Braunschweig from 1567–86 and one of the principle authors of the Formula of Concord. Chemnitz has long been recognized as the significant figure in the transition from the theology of Luther and Melanchthon to the theology of the Lutheran scholastics, as seen in the old saying, *Si Martinus non fuisset,*

---

[1]*The Christian Tradition*, Vol. 4, *Reformation of Church and Dogma (1300–1700)* (Chicago: Univ. of Chicago Press, 1984), 353-54.

[2]*"Communicatio idiomatum/communicatio proprietatum,"* in *Dictionary of Latin and Greek Theological Terms Drawn Principally from Protestant Scholastic Theology* (Grand Rapids: Baker, 1985), 73.

Martinus vix stetisset (If [the second] Martin had not come, [the first] Martin could not have stood). This is especially true in the Christological controversy of the 1560s and 70s, for Chemnitz' *De Duabus Naturis in Christo* . . .[3] established a Lutheran approach to the real presence, ubiquity, and the communication of attributes that does not share in the more radical and cruder excesses of Johannes Brenz and the Würtembergers.[4]

In spite of this sort of recognition of Chemnitz' role, little research has been done on the sources he used to bring concord to Lutheran theology, and especially his development of a specifically Lutheran scholastic Christology. In addition, while Lutherans have always claimed to be faithful to the orthodox consensus of the great ecumenical councils, and while some work has been done on the use and influence of patristic theology in Luther and Melanchthon,[5] little has been done to examine how the influence of early Christian theology was passed on to Lutheran Orthodoxy through the work of Chemnitz.

Two questions thus present themselves for study: (1) What early theologians have had a major influence on Chemnitz, and how has he appropriated the thought of these writers? (2) Does the *De Duabus Naturis in Christo* of Chemnitz actually move Lutheran Christology beyond the dichotomy of Antioch and Alexandria as hypothesized by Muller, or does Chemnitz simply follow the Alexandrian path, as has usually been claimed? To explore this latter question, it would be especially interesting to examine how a theologian of the Antiochene tradition has been used by Chemnitz. This study will therefore focus on Chemnitz' use of Theodoret of Cyrus, the most significant proponent of the Antiochene Christology between 430 and 451. In order to keep the essay within manageable bounds, we will limit the examination to the writing of Theodoret which Chemnitz knew to be by

---

[3]Leipzig, 1578, hereafter cited as DNC with page references from the 1580 Leipzig ed. Eng. trans. by J. A. O. Preus (St. Louis: Concordia, 1971), hereafter cited as TNC.

[4]For discussion of the development of Lutheran Christology from Luther through Chemnitz, see Theodor Mahlmann, *Das neue Dogma der lutherischen Christologie: Problem und Geschichte seiner Begründung* (Gütersloh: Gerd Mohn, 1969). For a study of Lutheran Orthodox Christology after Chemnitz, see Richard Schröder, *Johann Gerhards lutherische Christologie und die aristotelische Metaphysik, Beiträge zur historischen Theologie* 67 (Tübingen: J. C. B. Mohr [Paul Siebeck], 1983). For Luther's Christology, see Marc Lienhard, *Luther: Witness to Jesus Christ: Stages and Themes in the Reformer's Christology,* trans. Edwin H. Robertson (Minneapolis: Augsburg, 1982).

[5]See, e.g., Peter Fraenkel, *Testimonia Patrum: The Function of the Patristic Argument in the Theology of Philip Melanchthon, Travaux d'Humanisme et Renaissance* (Geneva: Librairie E. Droz, 1961); and E. P. Meijering, *Melanchthon and Patristic Thought: The Doctrines of Christ and Grace, the Trinity, and the Creation,* vol. 32 of *Studies in the History of Christian Thought* (Leiden: E. J. Brill, 1983).

tion to the writing of Theodoret which Chemnitz knew to be by Theodoret and most cites, the *Eranistes*,[6] which Chemnitz cites under its Latin titles, *Dialogi* and *Demonstrationes per syllogismos*. By examining Chemnitz' use of this specific treatise, we hope to gain some clues about Chemnitz' appropriation of Antiochene Christology in general.

I

In examining the use of early theology generally in the *De Duabus Naturis*, the reader is struck at once by the large number of citations of patristic writers throughout the book. The overwhelming authorities for Chemnitz' work are the Scriptures and "the ancients." The total number of patristic references, quotations, and allusions is more than a thousand, compared to less than forty for Luther and Melanchthon combined. This is not to say that Luther and Philip have little influence, for the issues discussed in *The Two Natures in Christ* arise out of Luther's idea of the real presence and his Christology and out of controversy between Lutherans and Reformed. All the same, it is obvious that when citing authorities other than Scripture, Chemnitz' arguments are almost never based on Philip or Luther, sometimes based on "the scholastics," but over and over again on theologians from Ignatius to John of Damascus.

While Chemnitz cites more than sixty early theologians, over half of his references are to five writers: John of Damascus is most cited, followed closely by Cyril, then Athanasius, Augustine, and Theodoret of Cyrus, who is often cited as Justin.[7] In analyzing this list we see several names that should be no surprise: Augustine would be expected to be high on any list of citations in a Latin theologian; given the usual assumption that Lutheran Orthodoxy was Alexandrian in

---

[6]Text in J. P. Migne, ed., *Patrologia cursus completus, series graeca*, 161 vols. (Paris, 1857–66), vol. 83, col. 27-336 (hereafter MPG); Eng. trans. in *A Select Library of the Nicene and Post-Nicene Fathers*, ed. Philip Schaff and Henry Wace, 28 vols. (Grand Rapids: Eerdmans, 1974), 2d ser., 3:160-249 (hereafter NPNF).

[7]According to Johannes Quasten, *Patrology* (Utrecht; Brussels: Spectrum; Westminster, Md.: Newman Press, 1950–), 3:548-49 (citing J. Lebon, M. Richard, and M. Brok), and Frances M. Young, *From Nicaea to Chalcedon: A Guide to the Literature and Its Background* (Philadelphia: Fortress, 1983), 272 (citing Lebon and R. V. Sellers), the *Expositio rectae fide* and *Quaestiones et responsiones ad orthodoxos* attributed to Justin Martyr are from Theodoret and were probably composed prior to the Nestorian controversy. Chemnitz uses these writings more than thirty times, citing them as Justin while recognizing that they are probably not by Justin (cf. TNC, 121; DNC, 116). After the leading five, the next most quoted, and these significantly less than the previous group, are, in order, Irenaeus, Origen, Gregory Nazianzus, Ambrose, and Leo. These are followed by Epiphanius, Hilary, Gregory Nyssa, Tertullian, and Basil.

its Christology, Cyril and Athanasius are far from out of place. One remarkable point is Chemnitz' heavy reliance on the Greek tradition, even outside of the expected Alexandrians. Perhaps Lutheran theology is more influenced by Eastern sources than is often noted.[8] Even more interesting is the significant presence of John of Damascus as Chemnitz' leading authority[9] and the influential presence of Theodoret.

If we look at Chemnitz' use more specifically, we see that in chapters 1-12, which discuss definitions and the hypostatic union in general, Damascenus is most used, followed by Athanasius, then Cyril, Theodoret, and Augustine. In chapters 13-16, where the *communicatio idiomatum, genus idiomaticum* is presented, the five are used almost equally, with Cyril, Athanasius, and Theodoret slightly ahead. In the section that discusses the *genus apotelesmaticum*, chapters 17 and 18, Damascenus is used almost twice as much as the other four combined, mainly because chapter 18 focuses on the Monothelite Controversy. In the crucial section where Chemnitz discusses the controversial *genus maiestaticum*, chapters 19-33, Cyril is used the most, with Athanasius and Augustine not far behind and Damascenus and Theodoret, who are used about equally, the least of the significant five. This is as one would expect, with the Alexandrians most used; yet the influence of Theodoret and John of Damascus is still felt.

II

Theodoret was born about 393, educated in Antioch, and in 423 elected bishop of Cyrus. In the controversy with Cyril over the teaching of Nestorius, Theodoret was one of two bishops requested by John of Antioch to prepare a refutation of Cyril's *Twelve Anathemas,* in which Theodoret takes Cyril to task for his apparent Apollinarianism. Cyril's answer to Theodoret is contained in his *Epistle to Euoptius.* At the Council of Ephesus Theodoret was one of the Antiochene leaders and was not reconciled to Cyril and the reunion settlement until 434. Not long after he became embroiled in the Eutychian controversy and was deposed at the "Robber Synod" in 449. There was opposition to his appearance at Chalcedon, where one session was devoted entirely

---

[8]For discussion of Chemnitz' use of Greek theology in a related doctrine, see G. L. C. Frank, "A Lutheran Turned Eastward: The Use of the Greek Fathers in the Eucharistic Theology of Martin Chemnitz," *St. Vladimir's Theological Quarterly* 26 (1982): 155-71. Cf. also Henry Edwards, "Justification, Sanctification and the Eastern Orthodox Concept of *Theosis," Consensus: A Canadian Lutheran Journal of Theology* 14, no. 1 (1988): 65-80.

[9]Pelikan, *The Christian Tradition,* 4:354-55, notes the importance of Damascenus for Lutheran Christology.

to his case. After pronouncing an anathema on Nestorius and declaring Mary *Theotokos*, he was reinstated. He died about 466. Theodoret's writings against Cyril were condemned as part of the "Three Chapters" at the Fifth Ecumenical Council in 553.[10]

Theodoret's Christology was shaped by his training in the school of Antioch, his controversy with Cyril over the *Twelve Anathemas*, his attacks on Eutychianism, and his own condemnation by the "Robber Synod." Of the writings used most often by Chemnitz, the *Expositio rectae fidei* probably dates from the period prior to the Nestorian controversy and the *Eranistes* from the period between Ephesus and Chalcedon. In these two documents, then, Chemnitz would be exposed to Theodoret's Antiochene Christology both in exposition and in polemic.

The *Eranistes*, which seems to be written to demonstrate the weaknesses of some of the Eutychians' favorite slogans,[11] is presented as three dialogues (thus its Latin title) between Orthodoxus, who represents Theodoret's point of view, and Eranistes, who represents a Eutychian monophysite point of view. This name is given to his opponents, Theodoret says, because, "after getting together from many unhappy sources their baleful doctrines, they produce their patchwork and incongruous conceit."[12]

Each dialogue consists of an encounter between the two where Orthodoxus shows the illogic of Eranistes' position, followed by a florilegium of quotations from earlier theologians that supports the position taken by Orthodoxus. The florilegia include quotations from Ignatius, Irenaeus, Hippolytus, Methodius, Eustathius of Antioch,[13] Athanasius, Damasus of Rome, Ambrose, Basil, Gregory Nazianzus, Gregory Nyssa, Flavianus of Antioch, Amphilochius of Iconium, Theophilus of Alexandria, Gelasius of Caesarea, John Chrysostom, Cyril of Jerusalem, Antiochus of Ptolemais, Hilary, Augustine, Severianus of Gabala, Atticus of Constantinople, and Cyril of Alexandria. One novel feature of these florilegia is that they conclude with citations from Apollinaris (and the third also with Eusebius of Emesa) which show that even that notorious heretic would not stoop to the position of the Eutychians. After the three dialogues the *Eranistes* concludes with a series of syllogisms which restate the points of the dialogues.

---

[10]Biographical information taken from Quasten, *Patrology*, 3:536-37; Young, *Nicaea to Chalcedon*, 266-71; and Aloys Grillmeier, *Christ in Christian Tradition*, vol. 1, *From the Apostolic Age to Chalcedon (451)*, trans. John Bowden, 2d ed. (Atlanta: John Knox, 1975), 488-95.

[11]Young, *Nicaea to Chalcedon*, 272, 283.

[12]NPNF, 2d ser., 3:160; MPG, 83:28.

[13]Often cited as "Eustachius" by Chemnitz in DNC.

The main point of the first dialogue is that the divine nature of the Son is immutable. Orthodoxus' argument begins with agreement that the one substance of the Trinity is immutable. Since the Son shares this substance, the Son is immutable. There follows from this a long discussion of the meaning of John 1, with the conclusion that "the Word was made flesh" cannot imply mutation, but must apply assumption. What was assumed was "not a body only, but also a soul,"[14] that is, a whole human nature.

The second dialogue proceeds to demonstrate that the divine and human natures are joined in union in Christ without confusion. Orthodoxus holds that confusing the two natures or believing that there is only one nature actually destroys both natures. The union must be understood as a true union but without confusion of the natures. Here Orthodoxus attacks Eranistes' inconsistency of approach and brings forth passages from the Gospels which show Christ doing human actions or having human feelings that cannot be ascribed to divinity. If Eranistes were correct, where was the human body that did these things and the human soul whose feelings animated the body's actions? In the summary of this dialogue in the *Demonstrationes*, Theodoret says,

> Now the divine nature is simple and incomposite, but the body is composite and divided into many parts; therefore it was not changed into the nature of Godhead, but even after the resurrection though immortal, incorruptible and full of divine glory, it remains a body with its own circumscription.[15]

The point of the third dialogue is to counter the Eutychian argument raised by Eranistes that Orthodoxus and the Antiochene position cannot help but attribute our salvation to a mere man or involve the impassible divinity in suffering. Orthodoxus begins again with the Trinity. Since the divine substance is impassible and the Son shares in the divine substance, then the divine Logos is impassible and the passion and suffering of Christ must be attributed to the human nature and not to the divine. The Godhead is by nature incapable of suffering. Those who ascribe suffering to the divine nature are blasphemers. To conclude the *Eranistes*, Theodoret states,

> When we say that the body or the flesh or the manhood suffered, we do not separate the divine nature, for as it was united to one hungering, thirsting, aweary, even asleep, and undergoing the passion, itself affected by none of these but permitting the human nature to be affected in its own way, so it was conjoined to it even when crucified,

---

[14]NPNF, 2d ser., 3:246; MPG, 83:321.
[15]NPNF, 2d ser., 3:247; MPG, 83:328.

and permitted the completion of the passion, that by the passion it might destroy death; not indeed receiving pain from the passion, but making the passion its own, as of its own temple, and of the flesh united to it, on account of which flesh also the faithful are called members of Christ, and He Himself is styled the head of them that believed.[16]

III

How has Chemnitz made us of the *Eranistes* in his own argument? To answer that question we now turn to examine the specific *loci*.

As indicated above, in the first section of *The Two Natures*, in which Chemnitz sets down the basics of Christology, Theodoret is the fourth most used Father. The first use of the *Eranistes* occurs in chapter 6, "How we can in a useful and Scriptural way teach and clarify the doctrine of the hypostatic union . . . by using the similes of the union of light and the sun, of iron and fire, and of the soul and the body." Chemnitz has adopted Damascenus' term *perichoresis* as the best to describe the mode of the union and is using that term to make the point that the human nature contains the whole Logos. He says, "It is not as if the Deity is enclosed in a kind of vessel, as Gregory of Nyssa is quoted by Theodoret as saying, but through interpenetration (περιχώρησις)."[17] This citation gives us an example of one of Chemnitz' most common uses of *Eranistes*, that is, as a source of quotations from earlier theologians. It appears that Theodoret's florilegia in *Eranistes* are one of the collections of patristic texts that Chemnitz found quite helpful and made great use of.

Chemnitz' next use of the *Eranistes* is in chapter 9, which is a discussion of the terminology of Scripture and the ancient church. Here Chemnitz makes use of Theodoret in his own right and as a source of earlier theology:

> Therefore, the Word was made flesh, not by conversion or commingling but, in accord with the interpretation of Scripture, by assumption. Nearly all the ancients, as Theodoret tells us, took their explanation of the term ἐγένετο from these proof passages: "Christ is made (ἐγένετο) sin" (2 Cor. 5:21), and a "curse" (Gal. 3:13) in that He carried our sin and took the curse upon Himself. [18]

As stated above, Theodoret argues that the Incarnation does not involve a change in the deity and bases his interpretation of the

---

[16]NPNF, 2d ser., 3:249; MPG, 83:336.

[17]TNC, 96; DNC, 88; citing NPNF, 2d ser., 3:208; MPG 83:193. Note that *perichoresis* does not appear at MPG 83:193.

[18]TNC, 116; DNC, 110.

phrase "the Word was made flesh" on the two passages from Paul and several supporting quotations from earlier theologians. In this case, one of Theodoret's main points has been understood and incorporated by Chemnitz.[19]

Chapter 9 also contains several examples of Chemnitz using Theodoret as a source for quotations, especially from Irenaeus.[20] There is also the first example of a variation of this type of use. In discussing terminology Chemnitz says that it is useful to see how the ancient church used terms less carefully before the Nestorian and Eutychian controversies. In this regard Eustathius, Athanasius, Nyssa, Amphilochius, Basil, Nazianzus, and Augustine[21] are cited from the *Eranistes*. A final interesting use of Theodoret as a source of quotations occurs in chapter 9. Chemnitz says, "Theodoret in *Dialogus III* cites this statement: 'He is above composition and above separation.'"[22] What Chemnitz does not say is that this quotation comes from one of the sections where Theodoret is using the writings of Apollinaris against the Eutychians. These are the words of Apollinaris![23]

In chapter 12, which introduces the concept of the *communicatio idiomatum* and the three *genera*, Chemnitz' use of the *Eranistes* revolves around justifying the use of *koinonia* as an explanation of the meaning of *communicatio*. Theodoret provides a quote from Gregory of Nyssa that says, "The King of kings comes εἰς κοινωνίαν, into communion, with our nature."[24] Chemnitz also cites Theodoret as an authority for speaking "of the 'interchange and communication' of the attributes within the person" and for using *koinonia* for all three *genera*. In *Eranistes* Theodoret does say that "the peculiar properties of the natures are shared by the person,"[25] but to claim Theodoret, at least the Theodoret of the *Eranistes*, as a supporter of all three *genera* of the sharing of properties seems to stretch the data. Theodoret is quite willing to speak of each nature communicating its properties to the one person without confusing or mixing the

---

[19]It is interesting here that Chemnitz' interpretation of Gal 3:13 is more moderate and more influenced by mainline patristic interpretation than Luther's. Cf. LW 26:276-91; WA 40/1:432-52, where Luther interprets the ἐγένετο quite literally.

[20]TNC, 122-24; DNC, 118-20.

[21]TNC, 127-28; DNC, 124-25. Note that Chemnitz attributes the quote from Augustine to "Hilary, Athanasius, Ambrose, and Cassian" (TNC, 128; DNC, 125) and that TNC errs in citing the quotation as from Dialogue 1. The correct citation is Augustine in Dialogue 2, MPG, 83:209; NPNF, 2d ser., 3:213.

[22]TNC, 138; DNC, 138.

[23]NPNF, 2d ser., 3:242; MPG, 83:309.

[24]TNC, 159; DNC, 158. I have altered the word order of TNC to reflect more accurately Chemnitz' manner of inserting Greek into his Latin text.

[25]NPNF, 2d ser., 3:233; MPG, 83:277.

natures, but it would be difficult to show any other sort of *communicatio idiomatum* explicitly stated in the *Eranistes*.

The *communicatio idiomatum, genus idiomaticum* is the subject of the section of *The Two Natures* which includes chapters 13-16. Within this segment are four points where the *Eranistes* is used. The first of these is in chapter 14, where Chemnitz is trying to show how the *genus idiomaticum* has been taught in the past, especially in reference to the unity of the person. Several sentences from the second and third dialogues are cited to show how Theodoret taught that each nature had its own qualities or attributes that are communicated to the person. In each case Chemnitz seems to have conveyed Theodoret's meaning accurately, though we must also recognize that Theodoret uses these statements as part of an argument proving that the divine nature did not suffer in the passion of Christ—an argument quite different from that which Chemnitz is making at this point in *De Duabus Naturis*.[26]

Chapter 15 focuses on distinguishing the natures, and the *Eranistes* is used twice as a source of quotations from earlier theologians. At one point Athanasius is cited from Theodoret, distinguishing the humanity from the deity.[27] Later Theodoret is used as a source for statements from Irenaeus, Hippolytus, Athanasius,[28] and Amphilochius that show how the ancients were more careless in their use of terminology before the Nestorian and Eutychian controversies. In each of these cases the writer cited has made statements that seem to Chemnitz to over-separate the two natures and so gave unintended comfort and support to the Nestorian heresy.[29] Thus, Chemnitz criticizes quotations that Theodoret was using to support his case.

At the conclusion to chapter 16 on the use of the first *genus*, Chemnitz takes conscious issue with the *Eranistes*:

> As a result of what has been said we can judge what to think concerning the disputation of Theodoret, who in his dialogues rejects the proposition that the Logos, or God, suffered and died for us in the flesh, and he only permits us to say that Christ suffered in the flesh, as Nestorius also contended. . . . To be sure, Theodoret believed in the one person of Christ who is both God and man, but he was afraid that if we should say that God suffered, the divine nature which is

---

[26]TNC, 186; DNC, 186.

[27]TNC, 199; DNC, 200. It appears that some of the following citations from Chrysostom, Eustathius, and others may also be taken from or based on the florilegium at the end of Dialogue 3.

[28]Chemnitz attributes one sentence of Athanasius to Eustathius. TNC, 206 n. 84 is incorrect.

[29]TNC, 204; DNC, 206-7.

impassible might be thought to have been changed into a possible nature. But these worries are vain, says Vigilius, since the Scripture itself speaks this way (Rom. 5, 1 Cor. 2, Acts 20). When we add a statement concerning the traps we must avoid, we can easily escape these dangers, as Cyril does in his explanation of the 13th Anathema. We say that God suffered, not that the divine Logos in His own nature endured the piercing of the nails, but that His body sustained that which was made proper for it. For God, who could not suffer, was in the body which did suffer.[30]

This is a most interesting passage. Chemnitz takes issue pointedly with the third dialogue, yet comes to a conclusion which, except for the phrase, "We say that God suffered," could have been drawn from that very text. This is a very odd way of asserting that God suffered if it can be summarized with the words, "For God, who could not suffer, was in the body which did suffer." How, in fact, does Chemnitz differ in content from Theodoret, with whom it seems important to take issue? He goes on in the next two paragraphs to imply that the difference is merely verbal, as was the difference between Cyril and John of Antioch, and that the fears of either side were not realized.

The problem seems to be that Chemnitz has some memory of Luther's *theologia crucis* Christology, in which God *does* suffer in Christ in the Crucifixion,[31] but he hears more strongly the voice of "the ancients" and "the scholastics" who demand that God be immutable and impassible. The result seems to be a God who may be said to suffer but who actually does not. While objecting to Theodoret, Chemnitz has incorporated one of the main points of the *Eranistes* into Lutheran Christology, primarily because this Antiochene theme had become mainline Christology.

Where Chemnitz might be thought to differ from Theodoret regarding the suffering of God in Christ is in his greater emphasis on the *genus apotelesmaticum,* in which the two natures cooperate in communion with one another in the hypostatic union in the work of salvation. This *genus* Chemnitz takes up in chapters 17 and 18. In applying the *genus apotelesmaticum* to the suffering of Christ Chemnitz says:

When Christ in his human nature suffers and dies, even this takes place in communion with the divine nature, but not with the result that the divine nature in itself also suffers and dies. For this is the property only of the human nature. But the divine nature is present

---

[30]TNC, 212; DNC, 215.

[31]Cf., e.g., Luther's analysis of the heresy of Nestorius in *On the Councils and the Church,* LW 41:100-105; WA 50:587-91, where Luther identifies the unwillingness to allow God to suffer in Christ as arising from the same source as the unwillingness to call Mary *Theotokos,* namely, confusion over the *communicatio idiomatum.*

personally in the suffering human nature and wills this suffering for the human nature. The divine nature does not turn away from the suffering but permits the human nature to suffer and die, yet strengthens and sustains it so that it can endure the immeasurable burden of the sins of the world and the total wrath of God, thus making those sufferings precious before God and saving for the world.[32]

In the end, what Chemnitz says seems little different from the conclusion of the *Eranistes*. The distinction is that Chemnitz is perhaps more interested in maintaining the communication of attributes without saying that divine nature suffers, while Theodoret is more interested in maintaining the impassibility of divine nature without dividing the union.

The one appearance of the *Eranistes* in these two chapters is as a source for a quotation from Irenaeus. Chemnitz uses the Greek text of Irenaeus in the florilegium to the third dialogue in order to correct the current Latin version.[33] One could question whether Chemnitz' Latin rendering of the text is any more "accurate" than the text he was criticizing.[34] At any rate, he does provide the full citation in Greek so that the reader can make his or her own judgment. Chemnitz' conclusion from the quotation would probably be acceptable to Theodoret:

> They therefore err and sin who attribute the work of redemption only to Christ's human nature and exclude the divine nature from this work and imagine that the human nature suffers but the divine nature was entirely inactive in the work of our redemption.[35]

In this whole discussion it is likely that Chemnitz' intended target is not Theodoret at all, but Francisco Stancarus and others who similarly followed Lombard.

In the crucial section on the *genus maiestaticum*, which makes up the rest of the work, Chemnitz cites or refers to Theodoret approximately forty times, excluding the material in chapter 25. Of these, about eighteen are references to the *Eranistes*, primarily from the florilegia, mostly from dialogues 2 and 3, with very few from dialogue 1. In chapter 25, which is entirely citations from prominent early theologians, most of the material in the Theodoret section is from dialogues 2 and 3 of the *Eranistes*, supplemented from Scripture commentaries and the *Compendium haereticorum fabularum*. In

---

[32]TNC, 216; DNC, 218.

[33]TNC, 224-25; DNC, 229.

[34]Cf. the Latin at MPG, 83:283, with DNC, 229. Cf. also the English rendering of NPNF, 2d ser., 3:235, with TNC, 224-25.

[35]TNC, 225; DNC, 229.

addition, portions of Athanasius, Eustathius, Hippolytus, Amphilo-chius, and Gregory of Nyssa in chapter 25 are cited from the *Eranistes*.[36]

In chapter 21, in which Chemnitz asserts that the human nature "has a communion corresponding to the union and attributes which are suitable to the divine nature,"[37] the *Eranistes* is used as the source for two key statements from Athanasius. Chemnitz is making two points to support his argument:

> First, those things which Scripture predicates as given to Christ according to his human nature in this highest category are not created gifts, but are attributes which belong to the deity itself. Second, those things are given to Christ not according to the divine but according to the assumed human nature, or with respect to the human nature.[38]

Athanasius is brought forth as support for the second point. After a citation from the orations against the Arians, Chemnitz says that dialogue 1 contains "this rule of Athanasius: 'Whatever the Scripture says that Christ received in time pertains to the humanity and not the deity.'"[39] Further on Athanasius is cited again from Theodoret: "When Christ says, 'The Father has given life to the Son,' it must be understood that life is given to the flesh."[40]

We should note first of all that the first of these citations is not of dialogue 1 but of dialogue 2,[41] and is an interpretation of the text there rather than a quotation. Theodoret's Athanasius says, "When-ever then the Scripture says that the Son received, and was glorified, it speaks because of His manhood, not His Godhead."[42] Theodoret

---

[36]In addition, Chemnitz uses a great deal of material from the *Expositio rectae fidei* throughout this section and in chapter 25 in particular. One interesting observa-tion is that, while Chemnitz will disagree with Theodoret as Theodoret, he never disagrees with Theodoret as "Justin."

[37]TNC, 7; DNC, 264.

[38]TNC, 259; DNC, 267.

[39]TNC, 260; DNC, 268.

[40]Ibid. The text of TNC attributes this correctly to Dialogue 3, though DNC says Dialogue 1. See following note.

[41]If this citation is of Dialogue 1, it is an extremely free paraphrase at best, the closest reference being a statement that interprets Jn 1:1 as indicating the divinity and Jn 1:14 as showing the humanity (NPNF, 2d ser., 3:178; MPG, 83:92). One wonders why, if the policy of TNC was to clean up Chemnitz' erroneous citations (cf. TNC, 11, which tries to shift blame to the printer—must the Missouri Synod also hold Chem-nitz to be inerrant?), this citation was not corrected rather than making TNC, 266 n. 2 purposely ambiguous. Chemnitz himself cites correctly at TNC, 350; DNC, 381.

[42]NPNF, 2d ser., 3:204-5; MPG, 83:181. This citation also raises questions about TNC's use of quotation marks, which do not appear in DNC. Did Chemnitz really mean to imply in his method of citation what the use of quotation marks implies to the modern reader? Again, TNC seems to want to make of Chemnitz something that

intends these words to be an example of Athanasius distinguishing the two natures after the union. Chemnitz uses his interpretation of them to show that the power and rule which Scripture describes as being given to Christ should be understood as being given to his humanity.

In chapter 22 where Chemnitz affirms that there is no commingling or confusion of the natures, the *Eranistes* is infrequently cited. True, other citations from Theodoret appear,[43] but one might expect to see more of a writing one of whose major points is the *inconfusus*, beyond its being used as a source for some of Theophilus of Alexandria's anti-Origen polemic.[44]

Chapter 23 then sets out what Chemnitz considers the true mode of the *genus maiestaticum*. In this chapter the florilegia of the *Eranistes* are used as sources for statements from earlier theologians. One reference to Nazianzus in the first dialogue is incorrect.[45] Another set of citations is used to show that the ancients taught that "the mode of the communion is true and real and yet takes place without commingling, conversion, abolition, or equating." These include material from Hippolytus and Athanasius from the second dialogue and from Flavianus, Nazianzus, and Apollinaris from dialogue 3.[46] While Chemnitz' point is certainly not Theodoret's point, Chemnitz seems to honor the meaning of the original author as well as Theodoret.

Chemnitz also notes that Theodoret "speaks of the body of Christ as full of divine glory and as sending forth rays of light, . . ." and interprets this with a statement from Augustine.[47] Indeed, toward the end of the second dialogue, Orthodoxus says:

> What has already been said indicates the body perfectly plainly; for what is seen is a body; but I will nevertheless point out to you that even after the assumption the body of the Lord is still called a body. . . . It was not changed into another nature, but remained a body, full however of divine glory, and sending forth beams of light. The bodies of the saints shall be fashioned like unto it. . . . But if the bodies of the saints preserve the character of their nature, then also the body of the Lord in like manner keeps its own nature unchanged.[48]

Does Chemnitz' use of Theodoret's words violate Theodoret's intent? I think that there can be little doubt that Theodoret would have been uncomfortable with the concept of the ubiquity of Christ's glorified

---

he did not make of himself.

[43]The *Expositio* at TNC, 272; DNC, 282-83.

[44]TNC, 272; DNC, 283.

[45]TNC, 292; DNC, 309. Neither TNC nor I have been able to find the actual source.

[46]TNC, 297-98; DNC, 316.

[47]TNC, 299; DNC, 317.

[48]NPNF, 2d ser., 3:200; MPG, 83:165.

body, even in Chemnitz' moderate expression of the idea. Yet it does appear that Chemnitz may have in the *genus maiestaticum* hit upon an approach that could be acceptable to Theodoret as a description of how the body can be full of divine glory and send forth beams of light, so long as the body remains a body.[49]

Chapter 24 focuses primarily on scriptural passages that support the *genus maiestaticum*, but it does contain one reference to Theodoret in the section on Col 2:9:

> With this Paul understands also all [the Logos's] attributes when he uses the term "the whole fullness of the Godhead." He says that it dwells in the body or the assumed nature of Christ, just as Athanasius, Augustine, and Theodoret, who explain the adverb "bodily" or *corporaliter* not as a transfusion of the natures or a commingling of the essences but as a hypostatic or personal union.[50]

This is probably a reference to Theodoret's commentary on St. Paul,[51] but may also have the *Eranistes* in view.

Within the section on the *genus maiestaticum* chapter 25 holds a special place. This chapter consists almost entirely of citations from the theologians of the early church, though it also includes material from Bernard and Luther, which Chemnitz uses to support his teaching on the *genus* and his claim that the Lutheran Christology is not an innovation but a continuation of the teaching of the early church. This method in itself reminds one of the florilegia in the *Eranistes*. With these citations Chemnitz wishes to make ten points, of which numbers 6, 9, and 10 are the most controversial:

> 6. In the union not only does the humanity of Christ possess and retain its own essential attributes wherewith He is similar to His brothers in all things, yet without sin, and not only is the humanity adorned with created, finite, habitual, formal, and inherent gifts, but also because of the personal union with the divine nature of the Logos it has the entire fullness of the Godhead dwelling in itself personally, so that it has thus been endowed and enriched also with divine power, authority, activity, wisdom, knowledge, grace, a life-giving life, glory, and divine majesty and universal lordship, by means of which it cooperated in the duties of the Messiah, as we have explained. These are and remain qualities of the deity.
>
> But we have shown by the testimonies of Scripture and of all the ancient church that these attributes can also be said to have been

---

[49] A Reformed theologian of the time might have argued that this is precisely the problem with Lutheran Christology, that the body does not remain a real human body. While this criticism does, I think, apply to some Lutheran theologians of the sixteenth century, it does not cling to Chemnitz when the DNC is read in its entirety.

[50] TNC, 314; DNC, 335.

[51] *Interpretatio in quatuordecim epistolas S. Pauli*, MPG, 82:35-878.

given, handed over, bestowed upon, and communicated, in time, not to the divine, but to the assumed human nature in Christ; not only *in concreto*, that is, with reference to the person only by the use of concrete terms, but also these attributes can rightly be said to be given to the Son of Man, using the terms which denote the human nature of Christ as it is personally united with the Logos. . . .

However, the human nature does not receive or possess them abstractly, that is, if this nature is considered by itself, apart from the union, or in the union, by, through, in, or according to itself; but the human nature receives them only through the plan of the personal union, as we have tried to explain. . . . [T]hese properties are communicated to the assumed nature, not by confusion of the essence or natures, but through the plan of the union, as in the case of heated iron, without any commingling, conversion, equating, or abolition of the natures and their essential attributes. . . .

9. The humanity is worshiped with the same adoration as is given to the divine nature of the Logos.

10. The whole Christ, God and man, each nature, divine and human, is present with the members of the church as their Head.[52]

How does Theodoret's *Eranistes* help Chemnitz advance these ten points? In the section of quotations attributed directly to Theodoret, Chemnitz begins by citing material from dialogue 2 that speaks of the resurrected and ascended body of Christ. The thrust of these quotations is that while the body is glorified, it remains a human body, yet the glory of Christ's risen body is much greater than will be that of the bodies of the risen saints. This section ends with the quotation "We call the body of the Lord divine, life-giving, lordly."[53]

If we look at the context of these citations in the *Eranistes*, we see Orthodoxus engaged in pressing Eranistes to admit that the two natures are unconfounded. Eranistes is trying to defend his position that the human nature was changed into the substance of the Godhead. First he holds out that this occurred at the conception,[54] then he says at the Resurrection.[55] This leads to debate over the incorruptibility of the resurrected body, in which Orthodoxus gets Eranistes to agree that disease, health, corruption, and death are accidents of the body which cease at the Resurrection. Orthodoxus then says (in a passage quoted by Chemnitz), "So the body of the Lord rose incorruptible, impassible, and immortal, and is worshipped by the powers of heaven, and is yet a body, having its former limitation."[56]

---

[52]TNC, 389–90; DNC, 433–34.

[53]TNC, 372; DNC, 411.

[54]NPNF, 2d ser., 3:197; MPG, 83:157.

[55]NPNF, 2d ser., 3:198; MPG, 83:157.

[56]NPNF, 2d ser., 3:199; MPG, 83:164.

At this point Eranistes shifts his "dating" to the assumption of Christ into heaven. Orthodoxus will have none of this and maintains that in order for Christ to be seen by the angels and humans at the judgment or to sit upon the throne of judgment and divide sheep from goats, he must have a limited nature rather than an unlimited nature. Eranistes questions whether one can speak of a body after the Ascension, and Orthodoxus replies that what is spoken of Christ after the Ascension demands a body. He then holds, in another passage quoted by Chemnitz:

> It was not changed into another nature, but remained a body, full how-ever of divine glory, and sending forth beams of light. The bodies of the saints shall be fashioned like unto it. . . . It is therefore according to quality, not according to quantity, that the bodies of the saints shall be fashioned like unto the body of the Lord.[57]

The argument then moves to the Eucharist as an image of the Incarnation as archetype. Orthodoxus and Eranistes agree that the bread and the wine are called Christ's body and blood after the conse-cration. Orthodoxus then maintains that just as the "mystic symbols" do not lose their own nature yet are regarded as what they have become, so Christ's body, though changed by the Resurrection, remains a human body. Eranistes concludes from this that, just as the bread is called the body of Christ, so the glorified Christ should be called God, not body. Orthodoxus replies,

> You seem to be ignorant—for He is called not only body but even bread of life. So the Lord Himself used this name and *that very body we call divine body, and giver of life, and of the Master and of the Lord,* teaching that it is not common to every man but belongs to our Lord Jesus Christ Who is God and Man. "For Jesus Christ" is "the same yesterday, to-day, and forever."[58]

In addition to the section on Theodoret, the *Eranistes* appears in chapter 25 as a source for material in the sections on Athanasius,[59] Eustathius,[60] Hippolytus,[61] Amphilochius,[62] and Gregory of Nyssa.[63]

---

[57]NPNF, 2d ser., 3:200; MPG, 83:165. Note that this is a passage that Chemnitz has used before, TNC, 299; DNC, 317.

[58]NPNF, 2d ser., 3:201; MPG, 83:168. Emphasis indicates the words cited by Chem-nitz, TNC, 372; DNC, 411.

[59]TNC, 350; DNC, 381-82.

[60]TNC, 350; DNC, 382.

[61]TNC, 351; DNC, 383.

[62]Ibid.

[63]TNC, 353; DNC, 385.

In chapter 26, on the terminology of the ancient church, there is a quotation from Theodoret which is unidentified.[64] Part of this quotation uses wording similar to a statement in the second dialogue,[65] but the rest is quite different from anything in the *Eranistes*. Either Chemnitz is quoting another writing where Theodoret uses similar language or he has interpreted the lines from dialogue 2. If the latter is the case, he has made Theodoret say more than the text actually says.

Chapter 28 discusses the session of Christ at the right hand of God, the interpretation of which was at issue in the late sixteenth century. The *Eranistes* is used in this chapter as a source for quotations from Athanasius, Eustathius, and Chrysostom.[66] As always, Chemnitz' citations are more paraphrases than quotations, but of the four passages presented here Chemnitz only misunderstands one. In the last citation from Chrysostom in dialogue 2, Chrysostom is speaking about God's dealings with humanity, while Chemnitz cites the passage as the Father's dealings with the human nature of Christ.[67]

Two statements from the second dialogue of the *Eranistes* appear in chapter 29, where Chemnitz demonstrates that Christ is to be worshiped in both natures. Chemnitz uses both to make the point that the body of Jesus is glorified and worshiped.[68] Both of these citations come from an important section of dialogue 2 where Eranistes is maintaining that the body of the Lord is changed into the divine substance after the Ascension and Orthodoxus is holding that the body is still a body. In the first, Orthodoxus agrees that the body of the Lord is "incorruptible, impassible, and immortal, and is worshipped by the powers of heaven, and is yet a body having its former limitation."[69] Theodoret obviously says, as Chemnitz, that the body of the Lord is worthy of worship, but Chemnitz leaves out the end of the sentence that limits the body.

In the second citation, Eranistes has tried to use the idea of the change of the bread and wine into the body and blood of Christ in the Eucharist in order to defend his position. Orthodoxus counters that the "mystic symbols" do not change their nature but are worshiped as "what they are believed to be." This corresponds to the human nature of Christ:

---

[64]TNC, 400; DNC, 442. TNC has no footnote, so one assumes that the editor was unable to discover the source.

[65]NPNF, 2d ser., 3:200; MPG, 83:165; a quotation Chemnitz has used.

[66]TNC, 408-9; DNC, 448-50.

[67]Cf. TNC, 409; DNC, 450; with NPNF, 2d ser., 3:210; MPG, 83:200-201.

[68]TNC, 420; DNC, 465.

[69]NPNF, 2d ser., 3:199; MPG, 83:164.

> For that body preserves its former form, figure, and limitation and in a
> word the substance of the body; but after the resurrection it has become
> immortal and superior to corruption; it has become worthy of a seat
> on the right hand; it is adored by every creature as being called the
> natural body of the Lord.[70]

Once again, Theodoret does say that the body of Christ is worshiped,
but is making a different point—that this worshiped and glorified
body is still a body. The human nature is still the human nature.
Chemnitz has also made a significant alteration in the text. While
Theodoret says, "the body of the Lord," Chemnitz concludes the citation, "the body of God," a change that one doubts Theodoret would
have approved of at the time he wrote the *Eranistes*.

One of the most important chapters in Chemnitz' argument is
chapter 30, "That the entire person of Christ is present in the church
according to both natures."[71] The *Eranistes* makes three appearances
in this chapter: as a support for one of Chemnitz' points, as the source
of a quotation from Nazianzus,[72] and as one of the weapons of
Chemnitz' opponents. In making the point that Christ's body was
glorified to the highest degree of glory, Chemnitz cites the passage
about the glory of the saints being like Christ's in quality but not in
quantity which we have seen before.[73] Chemnitz then cites several
other early theologians and returns to Theodoret. Here Chemnitz
includes the whole of the point Theodoret was trying to make in
dialogue 2:[74]

> But because our bodies will be conformed to the glorious body of our
> Savior Jesus Christ (Phil. 3:21), the glory of Christ's body by reason of
> the general glorification . . . is of the same kind ($\kappa\alpha\tau\grave{\alpha}\ \tau\grave{o}\ \pi o\hat{\iota}o\nu$) as the
> glory of the other glorified saints, although it excels in glory to an
> indescribable degree ($\kappa\alpha\tau\grave{\alpha}\ \tau\grave{o}\ \pi\acute{o}\sigma o\nu$) as Theodoret says. . . . Since the
> body of Christ, neither in the union or in glory, is changed into an
> infinite or immeasurable essence, therefore, in and of itself, even in
> glory, it is delimited by the attributes of its own nature and it is in one
> place in the manner of glorified bodies, as I have said, except for the
> honorable state of the personal union.[75]

While Chemnitz left out the statements about the limitations of
bodies in previous uses of this passage, here he has included

---

[70]NPNF, 2d ser., 3:201; MPG, 83:168.

[71]TNC, 7; DNC, 467.

[72]TNC, 451; DNC, 506.

[73]TNC, 428; DNC, 474.

[74]NPNF, 2d ser., 3:199-201; MPG, 83:164.

[75]TNC, 430; DNC, 477.

Theodoret's main point in his own argument. That, of course, will make his argument for ubiquity more difficult, but Chemnitz seems to want to maintain the continuing full humanity of the human nature even while he maintains the presence of Christ in both natures.

Wh en Chemnitz takes on his opponents' patristic interpretation in chapter 30, Theodoret is among those listed as used by the opponents to prove that the body of Christ, even in glory, is finite and local. Chemnitz states that the ancients did use such terminology but did not mean what his opponents mean by them. The one specific citation from the *Eranistes* is from Gregory of Nyssa in the florilegium to dialogue 2: "Who would say that the infinity of the Logos is contained in and circumscribed by the dimensions of the flesh as by a vessel . . . ?"[76] Chemnitz makes three statements about the use of such quotations. First, writers such as Theodoret never intended by these quotations to deny the real presence of the body of Christ in the Eucharist, but in fact taught just such a presence. Second, what the ancients were arguing was the inconfusion of the two natures, which Chemnitz also argues. Third, the ancients recognized different modes of the presence of the whole Christ. Here Chemnitz seems not to contradict Theodoret.

In chapter 32 Chemnitz speaks of the exaltation of the human nature. The *Eranistes* is used as the source for a citation from Amphilochius which supports the contention that "the reality of the substance of Christ's human nature is not abolished, even if in those events which are inseparable from the immutable law of nature something happens by divine omnipotence which is not only above and beyond but even contrary to the law of nature."[77]

The final chapter of *De Duabus Naturis in Christo* discusses the state of humiliation of Christ. Here Theodoret is brought forward as one who interpreted the humiliation in the same way as Chemnitz proposed.[78] This is demonstrated both in quotations from the florilegia of the *Eranistes*[79] and from Theodoret's own words.

CONCLUSIONS

In examining the various uses Chemnitz makes of Theodoret's *Eranistes*, we have seen at least three different types: (1) Chemnitz makes extensive use of the florilegia as a source for quotations from earlier theologians, some of which seem to be otherwise unavailable

---

[76]TNC, 457; DNC, 515. Cf. NPNF, 2d ser., 3:208; MPG, 83:193.
[77]TNC, 479-80; DNC, 542.
[78]TNC, 492; DNC, 556.
[79]Ibid., and TNC, 494; DNC, 559.

to Chemnitz; (2) Chemnitz cites Theodoret as support for various of his own arguments; and (3) Chemnitz cites Theodoret so as to take issue with him. In using the *Eranistes* as a source of patristic citations —and we should note that Chemnitz' translations of Theodoret's Greek are always "dynamic equivalent" at best and sometimes paraphrases or interpretations—Chemnitz at times says that some of the statements and phraseology of these ancients can no longer be used because more precision is needed in the post-Chalcedonian period. In these cases Chemnitz gives a negative valuation to material that Theodoret seems to have regarded positively. On most occasions Chemnitz gives the same positive value to statements from the florilegia as Theodoret, even on those occasions when he is using the words of the ancient theologian to make a different point.

When dealing with Theodoret's own words, Chemnitz most often uses Theodoret to support his arguments. Has Chemnitz simply used quotations out of context to suit his own purposes, or was he actually influenced by the content of Theodoret's Christology? In some cases Chemnitz has left out Theodoret's main point in order to use a supporting statement. On the other hand, there are also instances where that main point was used later, such as Theodoret's argument for the continued "bodiness" of the body of the Lord. At points when Chemnitz is arguing against the Reformed, Theodoret seems a bit embarrassing; when Chemnitz is arguing against less moderate Lutherans, Theodoret is helpful. Even in those cases when Chemnitz is using Theodoret's words to support an argument quite different from the arguments of the *Eranistes*, with the possible exception of the ubiquity of Christ's body, he does not seem to be twisting or changing the meaning of Theodoret's expressions.

Chemnitz on occasion disagrees with what Theodoret has said. This is in line with Chemnitz' opinion that the opinions of the ancients are important but ought not to determine contemporary theology—only Scripture is the *norma normans*.[80] Yet, Chemnitz' stated disagreements with Theodoret seem more formal than material. On the key occasion regarding the suffering of God, Chemnitz incorporates Theodoret's point into his own manner of expression. Thus Theodoret was again useful to him in bringing more radical Lutherans back toward the patristic center.

Of course, this also led to giving up one of the crucial insights of Luther's *theologia crucis*: the crucified God.

The result is that Muller's point is supported by Chemnitz' use of the *Eranistes* of Theodoret. Chemnitz not only relies on Alexandrian theologians for important aspects of his Christology, but also includes

---

[80]Cf. TNC, 455; DNC, 511.

one of the most learned and eloquent of the Antiochenes. In the way in which Chemnitz describes and limits the *genus maiestaticum*, Theodoret's concern for the *inconfusus* is upheld and a plausible explanation for the life-givingness of the flesh of our Lord is offered.

The All-Sufficient Jesus in Heinrich Müller's
Geistliche Erquickstunden
(*Moments of Spiritual Refreshment*)

Gary R. Sattler

Interim Pastor
First Presbyterian Church of Covina, California

I will not leave my Jesus. If only I have my Jesus, I surely have what will give me eternal joy. Without Jesus heaven is hell, life is death, but with Jesus the earth is already heaven, scorn is honor, poverty is wealth, death is life. I will not leave my Jesus. . . . [1]

There are only two things which cannot be separated, Jesus and the poor sinner. . . . When I sin I separate myself from Christ, in wrath from his gentleness, in arrogance from his humility. But he rushes after me. Do you want to know why? The sinner is Christ's shadow. Can you separate the shadow from the body? The shadow goes before the body, the body pursues the shadow. I do not know Jesus in his redemption, so I flee on ahead; Jesus knows me well in my need, so he comes after me. I seek hell, heaven follows me.[2]

HEINRICH MÜLLER AND REFORM ORTHODOXY

Heinrich Müller was born in Lübeck, Germany, on 18 October 1631. He was a Lutheran theologian and pastor in the Arndtian tradition. After receiving his doctorate in theology from the University of Helmstedt in 1653, Müller became professor of Greek at the University of Rostock. In 1662 he was named professor of theology there as well. As pastor of St. Mary's Church in Rostock and as superintendent of the city's *ministerium* from 1671, he was well known for his concern for the needy, the sick, widows, and orphans. At his funeral in 1675 it was said that he had worked himself to death in the care of souls.

---

[1] Heinrich Müller, *Geistliche Erquickstunden oder drei-hundert Haus- und Tischandachten*, 3d ed. (Hamburg: Agentur des Rauhen Hauses, 1855), #300. (My translation.) Scripture references in this essay are translated from Müller's German.

[2] Ibid., #62.

Müller is one of a group of Lutheran theologians, occasionally referred to as "Lutheran reform orthodox," who were particularly concerned with the spiritual renewal of the Lutheran church through revitalized laity and clergy dedicated to a rigorous devotional life, watchfulness over the state of one's inner being, and the rejection of things "worldly." He came under no small amount of criticism for styling the baptismal font, the pulpit, the confessional, and the altar (the celebration of the Lord's Supper) as *"die vier stummen Kirchengötzen"* (the four dumb idols of the church) because, in his opinion, people had come to feel that the simple observation of churchly customs was sufficient for salvation. He was solidly in the tradition of Perkins, Arndt, and Lütkemann, and he numbered among his friends Christian Kortholt, Christian Scriver, and the Pietist Philipp Jakob Spener, to whom he once wrote of his relationship to the church, "We shall heal Babylon. Oh, that it only wanted to be healed."[3]

It has been argued that there was never a reform orthodoxy per se.[4] Such arguments notwithstanding, there was, in fact, a group of Lutheran pastors and theologians—in contact with one another—with a particular concern for, and attitude toward, the renewal of the church and a revitalized Christian life for individuals within the church. It is my opinion that the members of this so-called reform orthodox movement and the so-called Pietists were, in fact, of one movement. I believe that only the appearance of Spener's *Pia Desideria* and its subsequent gift of the word "Pietist" (a word first used in mockery) to the churchly vocabulary of the seventeenth century, and Francke's remarkable (and controversial) achievements at Halle shortly thereafter, have obscured the obvious and close connections between the "reform orthodox" and the Pietists.

THE *GEISTLICHE ERQUICKSTUNDEN*

Geistliche Erquickstunden, written over a three-year span from 1664 to 1666, is a collection of three hundred brief devotional thoughts on all aspects of the Christian life. Müller's very straight-forward, nontechnical language appealed to a Germany still reeling from the devastation of the Thirty Years' War (1618-1648)—really a series of religious wars fought by most of the states of Europe, and

---

[3]See Gary R. Sattler, *Nobler than the Angels, Lower than a Worm* (Lanham, Md.: Univ. Press of America, 1989), "Introduction," pp. ix-x n. 1.

[4]See Lowell C. Green, "Duke Ernest the Pious of Saxe-Gotha and his Relationship to Pietism," in *Der Pietismus in Gestalten und Wirkungen*, hrsg. von H. Bornkamm, u.a., (Bielefeld: Luther Verlag, 1975), 179ff. Green also cites Johannes Wallmann, "Pietismus und Orthodoxie: Überlegungen und Fragen der Pietismus Forschung," in *Geist und Geschichte der Reformation. Festgabe Hanna Rückert zum 65. Geburtstag* (Berlin: Walter deGruyter & Co., 1966), 426-31.

primarily on German soil. Germans were emotionally ready for word of a benevolent, powerful, and close-at-hand friend such as the Jesus depicted by Müller in *Geistliche Erquickstunden*, and Müller's hymns, devotional writings, and collections of sermons were found in Lutheran homes throughout Germany. "There can be little doubt," says Stoeffler, "about the fact that Henry Müller was one of the most influential men of his age and that his thought has helped to shape Lutheran piety throughout the seventeenth century."[5]

THE PRESENT, ALL-SUFFICIENT CHRIST—JESUS

The immediate presence of the all-sufficient Christ: this is a central theme in the Pietistic understanding of the second person of the Trinity, particularly in Müller. In fact, there is little direct reference to the Holy Spirit among many Pietistic writers and preachers because Christ, or Jesus, fills the roles frequently ascribed to the Holy Spirit. In *Geistliche Erquickstunden* Müller refers to the Spirit of Christ.[6]

Müller's understanding of Christ can only be extrapolated from his (occasionally exuberant, at times downright florid) depictions of the role of the personal Jesus. That is, Müller nowhere lays out a Christology per se. This, however, in itself reflects his understanding of the role of Christ; that is, Christ is not the object of reasonable speculation or philosophizing, but rather is a personal and present savior, lord, model, and companion. This, the immediate presence of Christ, is simultaneously an inner, mystical presence and a personal presence. Because, like most reform orthodox and Pietistic writers, Müller is concerned with explaining to his audience what this means for them and how they should respond, it is about the personal Christ that Müller writes most. That is, for the Christian, Christ is primarily understood as the personal *Jesus*.

The personal character of the Jesus/believer relationship in no way reduces the divinity of Christ, however, for we find in Müller's writings a certain fluidity between God and Jesus. That is, Müller will begin a paragraph or sentence writing about Jesus and end it referring to God in such a manner that he in no way differentiates between the two.[7] Characteristic of those with a Pietistic bent, Müller presupposes Jesus as Lord and Savior, as Son of God. He concerns himself, then, not with discussing just who Jesus is, but rather primarily with advising the reader how to relate to Jesus, with how Jesus relates—

---

[5]F. Ernest Stoeffler, *The Rise of Evangelical Pietism* (Leiden: E. J. Brill, 1965), 224.

[6]"For faith is active through love. You, my Jesus, ignite the spark through your Spirit, so it will burn." Müller, *Geistliche Erquickstunden*, #40.

[7]We find, for example, that the sinner is redeemed by the blood of God, the blood of Jesus (ibid., #231); we also find a prayer that runs, "Ah, my God, my Jesus, my faithful God, you [*du*] can and will help me. . ." (ibid., #180).

and wants to relate—to him or her, and with Jesus' actual and potential significance for and in the life of the believer. When Müller does write about Jesus, it is always in reference to the believer (or nonbeliever).

Above all, the Jesus of Müller's devotional writings is a *present* companion, albeit a divine one. In this presence, however, Jesus assumes all sorts of roles and functions, and these are the real clues as to the nature of Christ, a divine and thus ultimately loving and life-fulfilling nature. Who Jesus is for Müller becomes evident most frequently in the details of his relationship with men and women, both believers and nonbelievers.

JESUS, THE ALL-SUFFICIENT ALL-IN-ALL

For the action- and inner-oriented Müller, Jesus' nature must be fulfilled in the life of the believer. That is, Christ must become and remain the believer's all-in-all, lest the Christian, missing out on the sufficiency of Jesus, come up short in this life and the next.[8] To have Jesus is absolute wealth in every way, for Jesus is perfect satisfaction in every area of life.[9] Müller assumes that to have Jesus as one's all-in-all means that one knows him not only as *Christus pro nobis*, but as *Christus in nobis*. "If you love Jesus [to the exclusion of all else], Jesus will rest in your heart. . . . How eager he is for this, more eager than hungry people for a piece of bread!"[10] There is a true mystical communion of the Christian and Christ in which Jesus takes up resi-

---

[8]"What are the goods of this life? A handful of sand. . . . Your friend is lost; nothing lost. Your best friend is in heaven. . . . Your wife and child is [*sic*] lost; nothing lost. They were not, after all, yours. . . . Your husband and father is [*sic*] lost; nothing lost. In heaven dwells the one who is the orphans' father and the widows' judge. Your good reputation is lost; nothing lost. A pure life is the best honor. . . . Your life is lost; nothing lost but weariness and suffering; a better life is there, dying is your gain. But, one thing lost, everything lost. I will not lose Jesus! . . . How can you be well, when you are without Jesus? Heaven itself must be a hell, if Jesus were not there. Jesus found, everything found. Jesus found, heaven found. What more do you want?" Ibid., #37.

[9]"Oh, how rich you are in your Jesus; can say: Jesus mine, everything mine. Let the world rise up and show its wealth; what is all its treasure? A piece of poor earth. What you can show is more precious than heaven and earth. So long as big things are your goal, your money goes down the hole! All beneath Jesus, Jesus over all, and all in all. What the world gives is piecework, what Jesus gives is complete. That brings thirst, this stills it; that unsettles, this calms. Jesus mine, in Jesus all is mine. He is my light in the darkness, that I may not err; my righteousness against sin; my blessing against the curse; my life against death; my salvation against damnation; my protection in distress; my joy in sorrow; my fullness in want; my very own, for apart from him I desire nothing; my all, for in him I find all. The Lord is my shepherd, I shall not want." Ibid., #262. Note both the absolute power and goodness of Jesus and the possessive pronouns.

[10]Ibid., #2.

dence in the believer's heart and influences the person's life. At the same time, the person is expected to exercise his or her will in conjunction with the person Jesus who now dwells with and in him or her.

There are three major competitors with Christ for the believer's ultimate concern and/or attention: the self, the world, and the Devil. The self and the world tend to alarm and entice the believer into abandoning Christ. The world and the Devil threaten the believer with attacks on the person.

Christ's own suffering and death may make a person reluctant to receive him into his or her heart. Who, Müller reminds us, would want anything to do with one who by his very nature will bring affliction into one's life? Finally, however, the absolute power of Christ is manifested in his desire and ability to save the soul of the believer. "How precious and powerful is the blood of Jesus, which is shed for your sins! One little drop counts more than all humanity's sin."[11] From his pursuit of the sinner, to his gift of salvific suffering and death, Jesus is (and indeed must be) each person's all-in-all. "He is like the midpoint, and in him is the concentration of all blessing."[12]

Christ and the Self

The person's own perceived needs and how to meet them are constant sources of anxiety and preoccupation. In fact, the life oriented toward caring for one's own well-being through one's own efforts was an object of attack from virtually all Pietistic writers and preachers. This "practical atheism" led believers ever further from the benefits of Christ and into self-defeating self-reliance. Such anxiety about one's temporal conditions and about caring for oneself is hardly necessary, however, for Jesus meets the believer's every need, albeit in a spiritual-emotional way (but then, what else, finally, is there?): "Am I poor—you are my wealth. . . . Am I in distress—you are my protection. Am I cast out—you are my refuge. Am I sad—you are my comfort and my joy."[13]

But Christ is not only relegated to second place by human anxiety, he is also shoved aside by human desire for pleasure and "the easy life." Here, natural human impulses and the ways and treasures of the world work together to draw the believer away from centering his or her life in Jesus.

The flesh says: Follow me, and do what gives you pleasure. Who would not follow? you say; to live according to all [your] desires, is that

[11]Ibid., #117.
[12]Ibid., #223.
[13]Ibid., #138.

not a glorious life? . . . The world says: Follow me, and do as I do. Who would not follow? you say; it leads to wealth, to honor, and to pleasure.[14]

Given that, as we shall see, the way of Christ is a way of affliction, the way of the flesh, or of natural impulses, is by no means unattractive —not only in and of itself, but by comparison with the difficult calling of Christ. But again, Jesus offers far more than the pleasures of the flesh. "The pleasures of this life please you. O fool! one finds the greatest joy in Jesus. . . . When he enters into your heart with his radiant grace, body and soul rejoice in the living God. You do not believe it because you have never experienced it."[15] Müller goes on to mention how sweet Jesus is to the heart who seeks him, ". . . joy, joy beyond joy . . . ecstasy, ecstasy beyond ecstasy. . . . My heart leaps when I taste your sweetness, and each leap enters heaven. So, my Christian, let the best be the most dear to you."[16] Jesus, then, is the final answer to the basic questions of humankind, to both the negative question, "How shall I avoid or overcome sorrow and anxiety?" and the positive question, "Where shall I find what makes me happiest?"

Christ and the World

Müller, like others of his ilk, finds "the world" to be a dangerous place, a constant threat to the believer's relationship with Christ. Müller knows well that a person's environment has a strong influence. Whether the world entices the person with promises of pleasure or attacks him or her with scorn, it is to be regarded as a potential threat. Here, too, Christ provides the proper response. It is not enough simply to resist or rebuke the world; one must do so in the manner of Christ: ". . . give no offense, and do not lose your temper over its [the world's] bad examples; do not let the world make you impudent, but you make it pious."[17]

Having said this, however, rebukes are indeed in order, for "the easy life" is ever a ready replacement for Christ in a person's heart and life. This sort of "worldly life" is precisely what Christ himself did not live and which, by contrast with his own qualities, he repudiated and cast in a very bad light. "Christ did not live in a worldly way in the world, but rather rebuked it, and made its life a disgrace with his whole unworldly life, its pomp with his lowliness, its arrogance with his humility, its greed with his poverty."[18]

---

[14]Ibid., #144.
[15]Ibid., #223.
[16]Ibid.
[17]Ibid., #117.
[18]Ibid.

The world must be thrown out of one's heart. "What do buyers and sellers have to do with the temple of God? John 2:15. Drive them out with a whip."[19] After all, by comparison with Jesus the world looks quite bad: "It takes, he gives; it casts down, he makes glad; it kills, he gives life." The only reasonable thing to say, then, is "Out, world, Jesus shall have my heart!"[20]

One need not rebuke and forsake the world solely because it is wicked, however. Just as Christ is the positive answer to the concerns of the flesh, so is he also the answer to the challenges and enticements of the world. Müller takes St. Paul's admonition in 1Co 12:31, "Earnestly desire the best gifts," and applies it to Jesus. "Of all the treasures of God, Christ is the most precious."[21] There simply is no contest. If it is wealth one seeks, who can be richer than the Lord of all? If it is honor and glory, what could be better than glory that lasts for eternity? If it is power, who other than one united to Christ can say "I am a lord over Devil, hell and world; no emperor can say this of himself unless he is a good Christian." If it is "good living," "one little drop of divine comfort can give more joy than the whole world."[22] We see here, too, that Christ is indeed Lord in power and in comfort. Thus it only makes sense that Jesus should be a person's all-in-all.

Christ and the Devil

If Jesus is everything to a person, he not only meets personal spiritual needs and is able to overcome the world, he is also the person's shield against the Devil. The believer cannot prevent the Devil from tormenting him or her with wicked and scandalous thoughts, but so long as the believer does not entertain (or act upon) them willingly, his or her faith will act as a shield.[23] In this case, faith and Christ are virtually synonymous. Should the Devil shoot such fiery arrows at the believer, they strike not the believer, but Jesus, his or her shield. Should Satan attack the believer, it is like a person running headfirst into an iron wall.[24] Satan has the desire to hurt us, but not the ability. Even the worst that can happen can be redeemed, as from the death of Jesus came the life of the world. "I overcome the lion through the blood of the lamb. Rev. 16. Is it not too much? The lion must fear the lamb."[25] Simply put, Jesus wants to, can, and will do everything

---

[19]Ibid., #2.
[20]Ibid.
[21]Ibid., #223.
[22]Ibid.
[23]Ibid., #117.
[24]Ibid., #138.
[25]Ibid., #30.

necessary and pleasing in the life of whoever will allow him to take up residence in his or her heart.

Jesus as Savior Through the Cross and Affliction

Jesus always has the sinner's best in mind, but this best is reached only through affliction—both the affliction of the cross and the abuse of the world which Jesus had to endure on humankind's behalf, and the affliction which the believer must endure on Christ's behalf. It is not a matter of the believer assisting Jesus in his or her own salvation (Müller is much too orthodox a Lutheran for that, although he did arouse some suspicion). Rather, the living Jesus is so integral a part of the Christian through his indwelling that the two are truly one.

Jesus, as all in all, is ever the point of reference for understanding whatever may befall the Christian. To be in Christ inevitably means affliction of some sort. The suffering and death of Christ illumine and give meaning to the suffering of believers. Indeed, it is precisely through suffering that redemption, and all that redemption entails, comes. Müller asks, "You are indeed no better than your Jesus; why then do you seek to have a better lot on earth than he had?"[26]

The Christian does more, however, than simply identify with Christ through remembering the historical suffering of Jesus when he or she suffers. Here the personal, mystical nature of the Jesus/ believer relationship becomes evident. The Christian participates in Jesus' pain through his or her own pain.[27] Christ present in the church and in the individual believer gives a transhistorical, trans-spatial dimension to Christian suffering. "The Jews crucified him in his person, the world still crucifies him in his members."[28] This is simply the way things are. "Now do you see that whoever would find Jesus must seek him not among the roses, but among the thorns? In affliction and nowhere else. . . . The best blessing is in affliction."[29]

For the unbeliever, of course, suffering of any sort hardly appears to be a blessing. The fact that it is an element integral to the life of, and in, Christ makes Jesus all the less attractive. "Jesus also says: Whoever would be my disciple must follow me. Who would follow? you say. He leads into distress and death."[30] But, Müller goes on to point out, the one who leads you in knows how to lead you through and out as well.

---

[26]Ibid., #127.

[27]"My affliction [*Kreutz*] assures me that I am as near to God as Jesus. How could I be nearer? The nearer in God your heart is to Jesus, the more [you get] the pain of Jesus." Ibid., #102.

[28]Ibid., #127.

[29]Ibid., #66. Jesus is to be found, "Not in riches, but in lack . . . not in great honor, but in insult and disgrace . . . not in joy and ecstasy, but in blood and tears." Ibid., #127.

[30]Ibid., #144.

He leads through temporal poverty into eternal richness, through temporal shame into eternal glory, through temporal suffering into eternal joy, through temporal death into eternal life, out of hell into heaven. He leads you into the wilderness. Why? So he can feed you with manna and speak to your heart.[31]

Indeed, suffering with Jesus and feeling his pain are signs, not of death, but of life. "If you are a member of the body of Christ, you must also participate in the pain of Christ, otherwise you are not a living member, but a dead one."[32] The Christian not only is unperturbed by suffering, but actually embraces it because it is such an integral part of who Jesus is: "I often wish that my affliction may never leave me. Why? Thus Jesus also will not leave me. Christ and his affliction [Kreuz] will not be separated."[33]

On occasion, Christ himself is the source of pain, as when he chastises, or punishes, the Christian—of course for his or her own good. "I know that where my Jesus punishes, he does so in love; he strikes not where he has not love. Stroke of affliction, stroke of love."[34] Remember that corporal punishment was a standard element of discipline in childrearing and was not seen as cruel or counterproductive, as it frequently is perceived today. Discipline was seen as necessary to break the sinful willfulness, or self-will, of the child (in this case the believer) and was perceived as ultimately for the child's own good. Again we see Jesus playing a personal role in the believer's life, acting like a concerned parent, or friend, or ruler (who functioned in that time period *in loco parentis*).

> Tell me, why does Jesus discipline you? So that afterward he can comfort you. No one pours oil on a hard stone, it must be ground, should it be able to absorb the oil. When is Jesus sweetest to you? When you first have had to bite into a sour apple. If you love the comfort, you must also love the discipline. He heals those of a broken heart. Ps. 147:3. . . . I will not only kiss Jesus' mouth when he comforts me, but also his hand when he strikes me. Blows of affliction are blows of love.[35]

Jesus Conquers, Transforms Death

Finally, of course, the greatest affliction is death. But as the person is one with Christ through faith, death becomes another temporal, and thus temporary, event that leads to true and eternal life. "How

---

[31]Ibid.
[32]Ibid., #127.
[33]Ibid., #66.
[34]Ibid., #196.
[35]Ibid., #46.

blessed is the one who has moved to the kingdom of Christ, from death to life!"[36] Christ transforms death: "In Christ is death no death, but a door to life, not terrifying but lovely, not hideous but glorious, not bitter but sweet."[37]

Because the believer is in Christ, and Christ is in him or her, death becomes the greatest victory. "How powerless Christ was on the cross, and yet showed precisely there his greatest power in that he overcame sin, death, devil, hell and everything evil!"[38] The Christian's inner communion with Christ assures him or her of the unalloyed ("un-worlded," as it were) joy that comes only and finally with his or her temporal demise.

> World, good night, we part with joy. Take what is yours. Leave me what is mine. I will not leave my Jesus. Jesus gained, heaven gained. Good night, you my loved ones; why do you weep? Because my suffering is at an end? Ah, rejoice over it with me, do not keep my Jesus from wiping the tears from my eyes. . . . May Jesus help us![39]

Indeed, as with affliction, the true believer not only has no fear of death, but even desires it because the immediate contact with Christ makes it sweet. "I have the desire to depart and be with my Lord Jesus . . . . Is death bitter? Ah, no. My Jesus has sweetened it for me."[40]

Jesus the Person

Müller, like many Pietistic-minded writers and preachers, drew from Augustine and the more orthodox medieval mystics (e.g., Bernard of Clairvaux, Tauler). His strong Jesus-orientation prevents him from lapsing into the sort of mysticism found in, for example, Meister Eckhart. That is, while Müller can give the title "On Union with Christ"[41] to one of his devotional thoughts, this is a union of *persons*, a union of the *Brautmystik* sort,[42] not a loss of oneself into the godhead beyond God and Trinitarian divisions. In fact, Müller writes here, in the midst of other images, ". . . you are my bridegroom, I your bride, you kiss me with the kiss of your mouth. What you are, that you are to me, what is yours, that is all mine."[43] In this, Müller uses a concept and language common not only to the mystics, but to Luther as well.

---

[36]Ibid., #233.
[37]Ibid., #194.
[38]Ibid., #180.
[39]Ibid., #254.
[40]Ibid., #250.
[41]Ibid., #138.
[42]Ibid.
[43]Ibid.

For Müller, remember, Christ is a *person*. This means that there is simultaneously a union with Christ which is indeed inward and mystical, as well as a union which is more of a person-to-person nature and calls for the active participation of the believer in the divine/human relationship, properly so-called. That is, one not only is "in" Christ (and vice versa) and is moved by the feelings one has for him, one also has Christ as an actual model one can follow. As a wise painter follows a pattern based on what he or she wishes to paint, the Christian says,

> Jesus shall be my model. I Pet. 2:21. His teaching and life shall never leave my memory. . . . If I cannot make it [my image] like his, I will endeavor with all my might to make it somewhat like his. He remains the master, I wish only to be his pupil. He remains the way and maintains the lead, I will see to it that I follow in his footsteps. You most beloved Jesus, enter my heart, that I may form myself according to you, be and remain yours forever![44]

The personhood of Jesus makes it possible to use the human, relational language that Müller loved to intertwine with the language of the inner life. Jesus' personhood gives Müller some*one*, someone specific, to encourage Christians to love. And it provides Müller with, again, some*one*, someone visible, as it were, to whom he could point as evidence of the personal nature and the concrete love of God for humankind. Thus the believer can surrender to Christ in mystical union *with someone*. This surrender, then, can occur not only in passivity, but can, and must, take place in the activity of prayer and action in the regular arenas of life. It looks less like withdrawn contemplation and more like out-and-out love—even to the point of dying for or with one's beloved.

In this sense, Müller is humanity-affirming. The flesh is indeed fallen, but the person nonetheless is both sufficiently valuable to God that Jesus would die for him or her, and Jesus did in fact come to the world as a person. Müller laments that so many a person passes him- or herself off as a Christian, yet actually is not even human, but rather is "a butting ox, a vicious dog, a sly fox, a fierce lion, a lustful ninny [calf], a filthy sow, a poisonous snake, indeed in murder and death a devil."[45] He goes on:

> You put off humanity and want to boast that you have put on Christ. Did not Christ become a person? Can the humanity of Christ be separated from his divinity? Can you put on Christ without the humanity? Idle boasting. No humanity, no Christian. Humanity was created in

---

[44]Ibid., #33.
[45]Ibid., #272.

the image of God, and Christ is the image of the divine nature, in Christ the person is renewed according to God's image and only then begins to be truly human.[46]

Thus we see that it is important that Christ is not only a person figuratively, or as a helpful image to facilitate human relationship with him, but actually, in order to make true humanity possible. The sinner, then, must accept his or her humanity—in all its fallenness—in order to receive Christ—in his perfect humanity—if he or she would be truly human.

If you would be a Christian, see to it that you first become a human being; and if you would be a human being, first become a Christian: Without Christ no person is a human being, and without humanity no person is a Christian. I will work to become a new person in Christ, so that I am both, a person and a Christian. God help me.[47]

Finally, that at last Christ might truly be all-in-all, and even though it means the end of history and of the life of the one praying, the believer says with Scripture, and Müller, "Amen, Come soon, Lord Jesus! Yea, come, Lord Jesus! Amen."[48]

CONCLUSION

In my opinion, Müller's Christology appealed to the masses, not because it was orthodox by Lutheran standards (which it was), or accurate theologically, or even because it was a message of hope and security in the midst of devastation and instability, but because it was on target anthropologically. That is, it reflects the apparently innate human need for fellowship, for meaningful personal relationships. Although there was a clearly mystical strain to Müller's understanding of the divine/human relationship in Christ, it was worked out both in meditation on the Word of God—Scripture—and interaction, regular human-style interaction (spending time together, heartfelt conversation, modeling one's own life after another's, loving, sacrificing oneself for another, etc.), with the Word of God—Jesus Christ. Thus we find a lively but eminently understandable message in Müller's depiction of Christ and his role in the life of the believer.

This understanding of Christ and his role in the Christian's life is current today, particularly in evangelicalism, a movement which—like the Pietism spawned by Kortholt, Fritsch, Scriver, Spener, and Müller following Perkins, Sonthom, Dyke, and Arndt, among others

---

[46]Ibid.
[47]Ibid.
[48]Ibid., #260.

—stresses the inner life, individual and corporate renewal in the church, and a *personal* relationship with God in Christ. What evangelicalism too often lacks in its understanding of Christ, however, and what it can learn from the Christology of Heinrich Müller, is the relentless grace, the constant ingathering, the underlying love that characterizes the essential nature of the present and active Christ. "He loves my soul, he is my Jesus. . . . It must finally be so: Jesus, you have won."[49]

---

[49]Ibid., #300.

The Christological Problem as Addressed by Friedrich Schleiermacher: A Dogmatic Query

Richard A. Muller

Professor of Historical Theology
Fuller Theological Seminary

It is typical of many modern historians of doctrine and theologians that, when they approach the Christology of Friedrich Schleiermacher, they announce either that he denied the divinity of Christ or that he set aside the Chalcedonian formula of two natures in one person and, by implication, denied the divinity of Christ[1] or, somewhat less pointedly, that he did not do justice to the Christological problem and failed to produce the Christ-centered theology that was his goal.[2] C. W. Christian has offered a salutary counter to this claim in his description of Schleiermacher's teaching as a "Christology from below" that, at least in its discussion of the older heresies, evidenced Schleiermacher's "faithfulness to the insights of Chalcedon," even though Schleiermacher believed that "the two-natures doctrine [was] no longer viable in its Chalcedonian form."[3] Martin Redeker goes still further by noting Schleiermacher's assumption of the "agreement between the dogma of the ancient church" and his own teaching and concluding that "Schleiermacher did not fundamentally call the ancient church's doctrine of the two natures into question; he did, however, try to transform it."[4] And, finally, from David Friedrich

---

[1]See J. L. Neve and O. W. Heick, *A History of Christian Thought*, 2 vols. (Philadelphia: Muhlenberg, 1946), 2:113; Bengt Hägglund, *History of Theology*, trans. Gene J. Lund (St. Louis: Concordia, 1968), 357-58; and Karl Barth, *The Theology of Schleiermacher*, ed. Dietrich Ritschl, trans. Geoffrey W. Bromiley (Grand Rapids: Eerdmans, 1982), 67, 103-7; cf. Emil Brunner, *The Mediator*, trans. Olive Wyon (Philadelphia: Westminster, 1958), 85-87, 91-93, 219, 276n, 299-300; idem., *The Christian Doctrine of Creation and Redemption*, trans. Olive Wyon (Philadelphia: Westminster, 1952), 330-32.

[2]Cf. Alasdair Heron, *A Century of Protestant Theology* (Philadelphia: Westminster, 1980), 30-32, with the somewhat mellowed comments of Barth in his *Protestant Thought in the Nineteenth Century: Its Background and History* (Valley Forge: Judson, 1973), 431-32.

[3]C. W. Christian, *Friedrich Schleiermacher* (Waco: Word, 1979), 119.

[4]Martin Redeker, *Schleiermacher: Life and Thought*, trans. John Wallhauser (Philadelphia: Fortress, 1973), 136.

Strauss we have the comment that "Schleiermacher's Christology is a last attempt to make the churchly Christ acceptable to the modern world."[5]

Schleiermacher's actual statements present us with a highly complex picture and, in fact, with a significant inquiry into the problems inherent in the Chalcedonian formula and in the use of the traditional language of Christology, particularly the use of the term *person*. What is more, Schleiermacher himself explicitly states that his doctrine affirms the divinity of Christ and, indeed, that "to ascribe to Christ an absolutely powerful God-consciousness, and to attribute to Him an existence of God in Him, are exactly the same thing."[6] It is one thing to disagree with Schleiermacher and to mount an argument to the effect that "an absolutely powerful God-consciousness" and "the existence of God in" Christ are not the same at all—and quite another to claim that Schleiermacher denied the divinity of Christ or sought to set aside the fundamental dogmatic intention of the classic Christological formulae. The latter was certainly not Schleiermacher's intention. Indeed, it was most certainly Schleiermacher's intention to replace what he felt to be an unusable dogmatic language that did violence to the biblical picture of Jesus of Nazareth with a formulation that was able both to deal with the biblical materials and to state unequivocally that God was indeed somehow "in Christ."[7]

It is far more fruitful, rather than commenting with negative implication on the difference between Schleiermacher's Christology and that of Chalcedonian orthodoxy, to ask historically and theologically, why Schleiermacher argued in the way that he did—particularly in view of the problems that he perceived in the traditional language of person and natures—and why he was convinced that the most suitable way to affirm Christ's divinity in his own time was to argue in Jesus of Nazareth "an absolutely powerful God-consciousness." It also may be fruitful to ask how the doctrinal intention behind Schleiermacher's way of affirming the divinity of Christ evidences common ground with the dogmatic intention of the older orthodox

---

[5]David Friedrich Strauss, *The Christ of Faith and the Jesus of History: A Critique of Schleiermacher's "Life of Jesus,"* trans., ed., and intro. Leander E. Keck (Philadelphia: Fortress, 1977), 4.

[6]Friedrich Schleiermacher, *The Christian Faith*, ed. H. R. Mackintosh and J. S. Stewart (Edinburgh: T. & T. Clark, 1928), 387. On Schleiermacher's Christology see Redeker, *Schleiermacher*, 131-37, and cf. Paul Tillich, *Perspectives on 19th and 20th Century Protestant Theology*, ed. with an intro. Carl E. Braaten (New York: Harper & Row, 1967), 109-13.

[7]See Friedrich Schleiermacher, *The Life of Jesus*, ed. and intro. Jack C. Verheyden, trans. S. MacLean Gilmour (Philadelphia: Fortress, 1975), 79-102.

formulations, particularly the wrestlings of the Fathers of the first five centuries.[8]

The Christological problem certainly lay at the very center of Schleiermacher's theological enterprise, and the work of Christological construction occupied a foremost position in his theological efforts. Schleiermacher's first major work, the *Speeches on Religion to its Cultured Despisers* (1799), offered a series of Christological reflections in the final speech that rejected both eighteenth-century pictures of Jesus—both the portrait of Jesus as a teacher of morality and the portrait of Jesus as human example.[9] As early as 1806, moreover, in the work entitled in its final edition, *Christmas Eve Celebration: A Dialogue*, Schleiermacher engaged in a discussion of the effects of the radical criticism of his time on the New Testament picture of Jesus and, in the persons of Eduard and Ernst, offered a rejoinder based on the nature of the experience of Christ in the Christian community.[10] Nor is the Christological inquiry far from the surface of Schleiermacher's study of the Gospel of Luke (1817).[11] It remains a central issue, fully coordinate with and, indeed, intimately bound to the critical questions in the lectures, eventually published as *The Life of Jesus*, that Schleiermacher offered on five occasions during his academic career (1819, 1821, 1823, 1829, 1832)—and there can be no doubt that the ongoing inquiry undertaken in the lectures on Jesus' life had a major impact on the work of Christological construction found in *The Christian Faith*. Jesus Christ, indeed, the redeeming power of the resurrected Christ, is a central theme in Schleiermacher's preaching. And, finally, the Christological problem is present as an important theme in the lectures on hermeneutics—Schleiermacher held that the underlying unity in faith of the New Testament writers that stands behind their individuality is the "Being and Spirit of Christ."[12] He also insisted that, beyond the usual sphere of hermeneutics, which of its nature deals with the common features of

---

[8]Cf. the arguments in George A. Lindbeck, *The Nature of Doctrine: Religion and Theology in a Postliberal Age* (Philadelphia: Westminster, 1984), 81: "Faithfulness to such doctrines does not necessarily mean repeating them; rather it requires, in the making of any new formulations, adherence to the same directives that were involved in their first formulation."

[9]Friedrich Schleiermacher, *On Religion: Speeches to its Cultured Despisers*, trans. John Oman, intro. Rudolf Otto (New York: Harper and Brothers, 1958); cf. the discussion in Christian, *Friedrich Schleiermacher*, 72-75.

[10]Friedrich Schleiermacher, *Christmas Eve: Dialogue on the Incarnation*, trans. Terrence N. Tice (Richmond: John Knox, 1967); and see the illuminating discussion of the dialogue in Colin Brown, *Jesus in European Protestant Thought, 1778-1860* (Durham, N.C.: Labyrinth, 1985), 110-14.

[11]Friedrich Schleiermacher, *A Critical Essay on the Gospel of Luke*, trans. Connop Thirlwall (London: Taylor, 1825).

[12]Cited in Redeker, *Schleiermacher*, 178.

language, there was a distinctiveness of idea in the New Testament that had to be argued through careful comparative philological study of the New Testament and the Apocrypha. This distinctiveness, and therefore the hermeneutics of the New Testament as well, must ultimately be referred to the impact of Christ's self-consciousness on the self-consciousness of the early Christian community.[13]

Much of Schleiermacher's interest in the critical problems confronting both New Testament scholarship in general and, more specifically, the early nineteenth-century phase of the "old quest" for the historical Jesus, arose, moreover, out of his profound distaste for the eighteenth-century portrait of Jesus as a merely human ethical teacher who brought the world a message about human virtue and the reward of immortality. As Redeker points out, Schleiermacher doubted whether a Jesus whose chief work was bearing and communicating ethical concepts could be capable of redeeming the world from sin.[14] Schleiermacher was also deeply convinced of the error of the critical method when it attempted to drive a wedge between the historical identity of Jesus and the consciousness of Jesus' unique, filial relationship to God found in the New Testament witness.[15]

SCHLEIERMACHER ON THE PROBLEMATIC OF CHRISTOLOGICAL FORMULATION

Schleiermacher begins the Christological portion of *The Christian Faith* with the premise that "Whether we prefer to call Christ the Redeemer, or to regard Him as the one in Whom the creation of human nature, which up to this point had existed only in a provisional state, was perfected, each of these points of view means only that we ascribe to Him a peculiar activity, and that in connexion with a peculiar spiritual content of His person."[16] Christ's activity or redeeming work is unique: there has never been any other individual in whom the "salvation of mankind" and the completion of the creation of human nature has taken place. It follows, therefore, that the description of Christ's person ought to reflect the character of Christ's activity, neither exalting the "dignity" of the person beyond the import of the "activity" nor claiming an activity beyond the capacity of the person. In more traditional language, Schleiermacher calls for a correlation and mutual interrelation between the language of person and work in Christology. He assumes that the doctrinal con-

---

[13]Friedrich Schleiermacher, *Hermeneutics: The Handwritten Manuscripts*, ed. Heinz Kimmerle, trans. James Duke and Jack Forstman (Missoula, Mont.: Scholars, 1977), 125-26, 139.

[14]Redeker, *Schleiermacher*, 134.

[15]*Life of Jesus*, 80.

[16]*The Christian Faith*, 374.

tent of these two topics is identical, although their dogmatic language is different. This identity does not mean, however, that his approach to Christology can either conflate the two topics or develop one rather than the other: such procedures "would involve at once both giving up the (traditional) language of the Church, and making a comparison between our statements and other treatments of the doctrine more difficult."[17] Traditional Christological language, therefore, plays a crucial albeit dual role in Schleiermacher's exposition of the doctrine of Christ.

Moreover, Schleiermacher was also intent on recognizing that the traditional forms of Christological doctrine stood on the same religious ground that he sought for his own formulations. All doctrines must be regarded as outward expressions of the "religious consciousness" of the believing community. This definition had to be, for Schleiermacher, true in the highest degree for Christological doctrines, inasmuch as "the whole work of the Redeemer Himself was conditioned by the communicability of His self-consciousness by means of speech."[18] The various forms of ecclesiastical Christology, produced out of theological controversy and varied according to the historical conditions of their authors, nonetheless are all rooted in this same "original consciousness" of the activity and dignity of the Redeemer.[19]

Schleiermacher's exposition of Christology, therefore, consists in part of an investigation into the relationship of the traditional language of dogmatics to the Christian religious consciousness as it finds its center in Jesus Christ. As Redeker points out, Schleiermacher recognized with great clarity that

doctrine and reflection . . . are not themselves the foundation but that which has been founded. The certainty of salvation and of faith rests on the existential experience of revelation and not on correct theological understanding and formulation. Christian faith is therefore never faith in correct doctrine and the dead letter but in the living relation between God and man.[20]

Schleiermacher was, of course, concerned with the task of theological formulation, but he recognized that the formulation must consistently and constantly refer to its source in the relationship, held and meditated in the community of belief, between God and human beings—with the result that Christology, the center of Christian

---

[17]Ibid., 375-76.

[18]Ibid., 77.

[19]Ibid., 389.

[20]Redeker, *Schleiermacher*, 40.

doctrine, must be founded clearly on its source in the redemptive experience of the community as it is focused on Christ.[21]

It is also clear, Schleiermacher argues, that the traditional language of one person and two natures, as found in the various creeds and confessions accepted as standards by the Protestant churches, all focus on "the unique personality of the Redeemer" with the specific purpose of describing "Christ in such a way (*frater, consubstantialis nobis*) that in the new corporate life a vital fellowship between us and Him shall be possible, and, at the same time, that the existence of God in Him shall be expressed in the clearest possible way."[22] The basic intention of these formulae, therefore, is the same as his own. Particular formulae may be modified or retained intact depending on their relationship to this fundamental consciousness concerning the identity and significance of Jesus.

Schleiermacher points first to several of the more problematic aspects of the traditional formulae. There is a great lack of clarity in the use of the words *Jesus Christ*. Typically, "Jesus Christ" refers to "the subject of the union of the two natures" and, in addition, to "the divine nature of the Redeemer from all eternity before its union with the human nature." The latter usage carries with it the difficulty of placing the primary identity of the "person" prior to the union and making the union an "act" of the person rather than "an element that goes to constitute the person."[23] This approach is quite foreign to the New Testament, continues Schleiermacher, which almost universally refers to the "subject of the union" rather than to "the divine element before the union." Even so, *Christ* is not a name but a title added to the name of Jesus—so that *Jesus* always refers to the human subject in whom God was revealed.

Far more troublesome to Schleiermacher even than this equivocal usage of the words, *Jesus Christ*, is the equally equivocal and far more confusing application of the term *nature*, without further qualification, both to the divinity and to the humanity of Jesus.[24] "Any other expression," he comments, "that was used indifferently of both [the divinity and the humanity] would lead one to suspect that such a formula was bound to become the source of many confusions."[25] The divine and the human are not, after all, in any way alike. What is more, the word *nature* is particularly ill-suited to such usage—inasmuch as *nature* and *God* are most typically contrasted or set over against one another. *Nature* usually indicates the finite, the corpo-

---

[21]Cf. Schleiermacher, *Speeches*, 148-52, 246-50, with *The Christian Faith*, 371-76.

[22]*The Christian Faith*, 391.

[23]Ibid., 392.

[24]Ibid., 392-93.

[25]Ibid., 392.

real, the various, and the conditioned realm of human existence. "Over against this divided and conditioned we set God as the unconditioned,"[26] and, in so doing, make the term *nature* inapplicable to God. Only in heathen polytheism, where the concept of the divine is divided up into a series of finite beings, can the term *nature* be applied equally well to the divine and the human—and the "heathen sages" knew well enough to place the One of their theological reasonings "beyond all existence and being."[27]

The linguistic problem extends to the juxtaposition of *nature* with *person*: typically, comments Schleiermacher, a nature is the larger category and may be shared by numerous individuals; but in the church's Christological language, one person is said to have two natures. The latter is a "formula" created for dogmatic use, but it has little capability of addressing the individuality of Christ and cannot "achieve a living presentation of the unity of the divine and the human in Christ."[28] The churchly usage, "nature," in no way indicates a generic class in which other individuals subsist and can only cause difficulty in the identification of Jesus' humanity. Schleiermacher was also painfully aware that metaphysical discussion of the divine nature was viewed as impossible in his own time on philosophical grounds, granting the Kantian critique of rational metaphysics. The demands of language pressed him toward another usage.[29]

ISSUES AND PROBLEMS OF PATRISTIC ORTHODOXY IN THE LIGHT OF SCHLEIERMACHER'S CRITIQUE

One of the lessons taught by the history of doctrine is that even the best and most influential of the dogmatic decisions of the church generate new problems at the same time that they settle old ones. There is probably no more striking example of this lesson than the dogma of the two natures in the person of Christ. The various Trinitarian and Christological heresies of the early church all proposed, in one way or another, a Christ who was incapable of providing the promised redemption from sin, world, and death, at least as far as the majority of theologians and the councils of the patristic era were concerned. The fundamental intention of the Fathers, then, was to produce and support soteriologically adequate doctrinal formulae. It was not the case that their chief concern was to settle the problem of the divinity and humanity of Christ and, then, to ask how the resultant description of the Redeemer could be used as a guide to

---

[26]Ibid.

[27]Ibid., 393.

[28]Ibid., 394.

[29]Cf. Christian, *Friedrich Schleiermacher*, 119.

understanding the work of salvation. Rather, they invariably moved from the assumption of a reconciling work in Christ to the question of formulae that could deal adequately with the person who was believed to have performed the work.[30] It is hardly an accident, therefore, that we find throughout the writings of the Fathers hints of the "Anselmic" thesis that the Mediator is constituted as a single divine-human person because such a person is required for the reconciliation of the human with the divine.[31]

It is worth remembering here that all of the patristic Christological heretics were, at least initially, well-intentioned bishops and theologians who attempted, albeit unsuccessfully, to provide formulae that would solve or at least deal linguistically with the problem of the identity of Jesus Christ as Word incarnate. The Chalcedonian Formula offered a solution to the specific problems of the patristic era that has stood the test of time. But it also created a set of Christological problems that remain with us today.

First, a brief review of the problems removed by Chalcedon: the Christ of Paul of Samosata and the Adoptionists was not enough different from the prophets of the Old Testament and, in the terms provided by the Logos theology of the second century, not a full enough embodiment of the divine Word. The Christ of Arius, as we learn from Athanasius' polemic, was the embodiment of a Logos incapable of the ultimate task of joining human beings to God. The task was such that it could not be accomplished by an intermediate being. The Christ of Apollinaris, satisfactory in its identification of the Logos or Son as fully divine, was incapable of offering a human Jesus who was "like us in every way." The Christ of Eutyches was so utterly divine that the humanity of Christ, the place where the divine nature touches our human life, could hardly be identified as having any attributes of its own. The Christ of Nestorius—at least as understood by Nestorius' adversaries—had so little connection between his divinity and humanity that he could hardly be understood as a unified individual.

The doctrine of the two natures, divine and human, conjoined in one person without change, confusion, division, or separation, the divine being consubstantial (*homoousios*) with the Father, the

---

[30]Cf. Robert C. Gregg and Dennis E. Groh, *Early Arianism: A View of Salvation* (Philadelphia: Fortress, 1981); Jaroslav Pelikan, *Jesus Through the Centuries: His Place in the History of Culture* (San Francisco: Harper & Row, 1985).

[31]E.g., Irenaeus, *Against Heresies*, 5.21.1-2, in *The Ante-Nicene Fathers*, ed. Roberts and Donaldson, 10 vols. (Grand Rapids: Eerdmans, 1973), 1:548-549 (hereafter ANF); Athanasius, *On the Incarnation of the Word*, §8-11, in *A Select Library of the Nicene and Post-Nicene Fathers*, ed. Philip Schaff and Henry Wace, 28 vols. (Grand Rapids: Eerdmans, 1974), 2d ser., 4:40-42 (hereafter NPNF); Augustine, *Enchiridion*, 33-36, in NPNF, 1st ser., 3:248-50.

human being consubstantial with us, that was produced by the Council of Chalcedon, definitively set aside all of these Christological problems. Together with the so-called *Tome* of Leo I and the *Dogmatic Letters* of Cyril of Alexandria, it offered, if not a single, cohesive statement of how the divine-human person of Christ must be understood, certainly the boundaries between which all genuinely churchly Christological discussion must take place. After Chalcedon, there can be no legitimate Christological formula that so separates Christ's humanity from his divinity that it is impossible to understand him as a single subsistent or individual—nor can there be any legitimate Christological formula that so collapses or merges one nature into the other as to leave the person of Christ either purely human or exclusively divine or to identify the person of Christ as a *tertium quid*, a "third thing," neither divine nor human. Doubtless, the formula has served the church inestimably over the centuries by barring the way to each and all of the various unworkable patristic solutions to the Christological problem.

From another point of view, however, the Chalcedonian Formula has created a whole new set of Christological problems. It led a good many late patristic authors to ask how the person of the divine-human Christ can be truly a unified person if he has two wills. As Schleiermacher points out, the problem is insoluble: does "Christ as one person formed out of two natures [have] two wills according to the number of natures, or only one according to the number of the person"?[32] If there is only one will, then one of the natures is incomplete, as the proponents of Chalcedonian orthodoxy noted in debate with the monothelites. But the side of orthodoxy could make no better case for its view of Christ's person: as Schleiermacher points out, a person in whom there are two wills possesses no genuine unity, even if the wills are said to agree in all that they will. Mere "agreement" can never be unity; and in fact, "one or the other will is always simply a superfluous accompaniment of the other, whether it be the divine that accompanies the human or vice versa."[33]

Similarly, Schleiermacher continues, since reason and will are usually understood as operating together, the problem of personal unity also arises in relation to the rational faculties of Christ. How can a unified individual be possessed at the same time of an operative divine reason that knows all things simultaneously and of an operative human reason that knows individual things in succession; and what kind of unity can arise if either the divine or human reason is equated to the other, whether by the divine knowing in a human fashion or the human in a divine? Once again, if there is only one

---

[32]*The Christian Faith*, 394.
[33]Ibid.

reason, one of the natures is incomplete, and if there are two, they can hardly be brought into such a relationship as would indicate a genuine union of the divine and the human in one individual.[34] In other words, the orthodox doctrine fails in its own intentions, being unable to offer a convincing explanation of the unity of the divine-human person of Christ.

Nor is the problem merely a result of the change of meaning in the term *person* between the fifth and the nineteenth century. Schleiermacher very carefully reads "person" as a unified individual, and the problem to which he directs his readers' attention is one that the patristic formulae embodied and that caused most of the Christological controversies of the patristic era. He can even summarize his critique in such a way as to demonstrate that the patristic language of person and natures must result in its own heresies:

> Now if "person" indicates a constant unity of life, but "nature" a sum of ways of action or laws, according to which conditions of life vary and are included within a fixed range, how can the unity of life coexist with the duality of natures, unless the one gives way to the other, if the one exhibits a larger and the other a narrower range, or unless they melt into each other, both systems of ways of action really becoming one in the one life?[35]

In other words, once the Christological problem is stated in terms of the union of two natures in one person, it will lead (and, historically, did lead) either to a doctrine of the dominance of one nature over the other (Apollinarianism, monothelitism) or to a doctrine of the mingling of natures (Eutychianism) or to an unconvincing claim of union on grounds of the proximity of the natures (Nestorianism).

At a somewhat more rarified level than either the problem of monophysitism or the problem of monothelitism, debate over the union of natures led Leontius of Byzantium to question how Christ could be a unified person if there were two subsistents or *hypostases* in his person. His query led to the declaration, in explanation of the Chalcedonian formula, that the human nature was anhypostatic or not individually self-subsistent but subsisted in the person or *hypostasis* of the Word. Monothelitism, the doctrine that Christ had one will, and that divine, had broken against the Chalcedonian rule that Christ was perfect in his humanity, in all things like us. After all, a genuine human being has a will. Leontius, therefore, refused to contemplate the union of the natures at the expense of Christ's human will. He argued, instead, that Christ's humanity has all of the

---

[34]Ibid.
[35]Ibid., 293.

attributes and aspects of genuine human life except full, individual self-subsistence.

This concept of an anhypostatic human nature, however, for all its technical orthodoxy, has always seemed to some theologians—most notably, Duns Scotus and I. A. Dorner—to stand in the way of a full humanity as well. After all, a genuine human being has its own subsistence. Anhypostasis can easily seem to be a reprise, on a far more rarified level, of the Apollinarian or monothelite views, which preserve the union by taking something away from the humanity. Individual self-subsistence is so rarified a notion that it may be passed over by most students of the Christological problem. Nonetheless, taking it away from Christ's humanity does leave Christ without a crucial characteristic of human nature that every other human being has. As Schleiermacher noted, this identification of the *person* as prior to and creative of the union interferes with our appropriation of the biblical approach to Jesus as an individual human subject.[36]

The problem of an anhypostatic human nature in Christ provides clear entry into the difficulty inherent in the person/nature language of Christology in general: as Schleiermacher well argued, "nature" cannot be univocally applied to the divine and the human. And when it is so applied, in the interest of drawing the two together into a unity, the tendency is to view the divine as somehow cancelling the limitations of the human, inasmuch as humanity "manifests itself everywhere as a definite, limited consciousness, but the divine nature excludes limitation."[37] The moment that such a cancellation occurs in a doctrinal formulation—and this does appear to have occurred typically in the Alexandrian version of the two natures Christology, even in the form given it by Leontius—the problem of Docetism arises.

Much after the fashion of the orthodox church Fathers of the fourth and fifth centuries, modern students of the two natures formula tend to read the Gospel narratives with the question, "Which nature is operating now?" at the back of their minds. Are Christ's miracles divine acts? When he eats and drinks is he performing human acts? When Jesus states that he is ignorant of the date of the end time, is this a human statement and is he really ignorant—or, as Hilary of Poitiers insisted, is he speaking in such a way as to limit the revelation of what he actually must know? What died on the cross—was it the human nature only; or was the divine nature, deathless by definition, somehow inexplicably involved in the death of Jesus of

[36]Ibid., 392.

[37]*Life of Jesus*, 82. It is worth noting that Schleiermacher's analysis of the problem of the natures identifies the reason for the nineteenth-century interest in an ontically-conceived kenosis of the divine nature: the divine limits itself in order to bridge the gap between itself and the limitations of humanity.

Nazareth; or can we speak of a "crucified God"? And, finally, if we read the text of the Gospels in such a way as constantly to identify "divine acts" and "human acts"—acts performed by one nature or the other—have we done in the name of Chalcedon precisely what both Chalcedon and the Gospel narratives tell us not to do, divide up the person of Christ and refuse to understand Jesus of Nazareth as a unified individual?

Under the terms of Chalcedon, both the Alexandrian and the Antiochene approaches to the individuality and unity of the God-man were considered to be orthodox—this despite the fact that their approaches to the issue of the unity of Christ's person differed greatly. The so-called "Word-flesh" Christology that arose out of the Alexandrian school held for an ontological union of the divinity and humanity of Christ. It argued, in all of its forms or modifications, that the becoming of the Logos in the flesh was more than an indwelling and that, although the Logos remained essentially unchanged in the transaction, the human nature of Christ experienced a transformation that was to be the foundation of the *theopoiesis* or redemptive "divinization" of human nature. In other words, a change, ontologically conceived, occurred in the human nature of Jesus because of its assumption into the person of the Logos or Son.

The various heresies of an Alexandrian tendency—Arianism, Apollinarianism, Eutychianism, monophysitism and monothelitism —all shared, whatever differences there were between them, a conception of the union between the divine and human that so changed the nature of Jesus' humanity that the larger church found their arguments insupportable. The Antiochene school, and perhaps Western, Latin theologians like Augustine and Leo, tended away from the ontological view of the union of natures and tended toward a conception of the union as moral. The great heresy of the Antiochene model, Nestorianism, so barred the ontological association of the two natures with one another that it appeared to deny the union of the natures. Within the bounds of the orthodox language of Chalcedon—and of the orthodoxy that preceded it—both Antiochene and Alexandrian perspectives were permitted. The concept of a moral union of the natures, dating back at least to Origen's theory that the human soul of Jesus had a moral affinity for the Logos and clung to it eternally, certainly belonged to the range of possibility within patristic orthodoxy, as witnessed by the Christology of Theodore of Mopsuestia. Ontologically conceived union of natures is not the only option— and, if numbers or statistics have any relevance in doctrinal formulation, it may be useful to note that the Alexandrian perception of the union as ontological bred more problems than did the Antiochene notion of a moral union.

One other point must be noted concerning the problems and solutions found in patristic Christology: the doctrinal point made by Athanasius, Hilary, Ambrose, Augustine and others that has come down to us under the curious name of *extra calvinisticum*.[38] Athanasius, who held strongly to the apologetic tradition of the early church and whose most noteworthy Christological treatise, *On the Incarnation of the Word*, is in fact the second half of an essay in apologetics, emphasized the work of the *logos asarkos*, the Logos apart from and beyond the flesh.[39] Not only could Athanasius argue that the Logos performed its revelatory work prior to its assumption of the flesh, he could also argue that the Logos, as infinite and omnipresent God, was not contained by the flesh when united with it, but continued to be omnipresent and continued in its providential functions during the time of the Incarnation.[40] The point carried over as a central emphasis of Reformed or Calvinist theology in the sixteenth century, whence its rather curious name.[41]

The *extra calvinisticum* directs our attention to the rather difficult element of the Christological problem—at least from the point of view of the union of the natures—that the Logos, granting its omnipresence, infinity, and incorporeality, was no more present ontologically in Palestine during the lifetime of Jesus of Nazareth than it was, at the same time, present in China. As the Fathers of the first five centuries well understood, union between Christ's divinity and humanity cannot be considered in the way we would consider the union of two finite, temporal, and physical things—such as two boards glued together. When an infinite, spiritual, and eternal nature is joined to a finite, physical, and temporal nature, the union must be such that it is suitable to the character of both: in other words, it cannot be a merely physical union. Nor, of course, can it be a union by way of physical containment, as if the human nature of Jesus were like a bottle into which the Logos had been poured.

These latter considerations raise the issue of the intention of the Fathers that lay beyond the difficulties inherent in their language. For if the language of person and natures (or of *hypostasis* and *physeis*) did lead to the various problems noted above, it is equally clear that, with the exception of the final problem of patristic Christology, the doctrine of *anhypostasis*, the Fathers rejected all of the problematic

---

[38]See E. David Willis, *Calvin's Catholic Christology: The Function of the So-Called Extra Calvinisticum in Calvin's Theology* (Leiden: Brill, 1966), for a serviceable discussion of the term.

[39]Athanasius, *Against the Heathen*, §35, 40-43, 47, in NPNF, 2d ser., 4:22-23, 25-27, 29-30.

[40]Athanasius, *On the Incarnation of the Word*, §17-18, in NPNF, 2d ser., 4:45-46.

[41]Cf. Calvin, *Institutes*, 2.13.4.

conclusions to which their vocabulary and its philosophical implications had led. Although the term *person* as used by the writers of the
early church has only an indirect relationship to the contemporary
usage of "person," it is clear from the tendencies of patristic debate
that the Fathers did intend to speak of Jesus of Nazareth as what
Schleiermacher called "an Ego which is the same in all consecutive
moments of its existence."[42] The Fathers, after all, affirmed Jesus to be
a single subject, and they rejected Nestorius' language of two *prosopa*.

We can infer this intention as lying behind some of the efforts of
Fathers like Hilary of Poitiers and Gregory of Nazianzus to deal with
such issues as the weakness, hunger, thirst, and particularly the ignorance of Jesus: these issues caused them great difficulty precisely
because they wrestled with the question of the identity of the divine-
human individual, Jesus of Nazareth.[43] The problem in both cases is
that the tendency of these authors to allow the dominance of the
divine nature leads to the assumption of an abridgment or partial
abolition of the limitation of a function or faculty typical of human
life in general. In a very real sense, the problem encountered by the
Christology of Hilary and Gregory on this point concerns the inability
of their formulae to bear the full weight of meaning. Both writers
sought to argue the fullness of Jesus' divinity and humanity and, in
addition, the spiritual and physical unity of his individual life, but
the insistence on language of two natures or two *physeis* stood
directly in the way of the achievement of that end: unity is achieved
—unity of ego, in the rationalization of Christ's ignorance as feigned
—but at the expense of a totally convincing view of the humanity of
Jesus of Nazareth.[44]

The Fathers of the church and the great patristic dogmatic formulae
—whether the basic person/substance formula of Tertullian in its
application to Christology or the formula of Chalcedon—when set
into the context of the insistence of the Fathers on the concepts of the
logos asarkos and the so-called *extra calvinisticum*, also tend away
from a rigid identification of the nature or character of the union
between the divine and the human in Jesus. We find, after all, a
balance in the language of the Fathers between use of the language of
becoming, the "assumption" of the flesh, and language of indwelling,
a "tabernacling" in the flesh. And when the language of becoming is
used, we encounter, typically, an insistence that there can be no

---

[42]*The Christian Faith*, 393.

[43]Cf. Hilary of Poitiers, *On the Trinity*, 9.71-75; 10.47, 55-56, in NPNF, 2d ser.,
9:179-81, 194-95, 197-98; with Gregory of Nazianzus, *Oration IV*, 15-16, in NPNF, 2d
ser., 7:315.

[44]Cf. J. N. D. Kelly, *Early Christian Doctrines*, 2d ed. (New York: Harper & Row,
1960), 298, with Aloys Grillmeier, *Christ in Christian Tradition: From the Apostolic
Age to Chalcedon (451)*, (New York: Sheed and Ward, 1965), 289-91.

change in the Logos: in "becoming flesh" the Logos did not cease in any way to be Logos; and whatever change took place was a redemptive change in the flesh, certainly not an ontological change in the Logos or a reduction of Jesus' humanity.

The final question that confronts us, then, is the question of Schleiermacher's doctrinal intention as compared and contrasted with the doctrinal intention of the early church and, in particular, of the person/nature language which Schleiermacher debated. As Schleiermacher's preaching indicates, he in no way intended to undercut the redemptive power of God as present and manifest in Jesus of Nazareth. What is more, his entire dogmatic exercise in *The Christian Faith* is predicated on the assumption that the redemptive power of God in Christ can be mediated to the Christian community as the basis of its new life. In addition, and more importantly, Schleiermacher's approach to the Christological problem had as its basic intention a statement of the mode of divine presence in Christ that would both satisfy an understanding of the character of the redemptive work to be accomplished in Christ's person and affirm the necessity of Jesus' humanity remaining a humanity no different from ours, except for sin. In all fairness, this last description of doctrinal intention must be recognized as standing well within the bounds of the patristic doctrinal intention. It is also the case that Schleiermacher's Christological construction, resting as it does on an alternative to the person/nature language of the early church, cannot be judged heterodox or otherwise unsuccessful on the basis of that language: he cannot, in other words, be classed as teaching Adoptionism or a Nestorianism or some other doctrine defined as problematic on patristic grounds because the language of natures is as inherent to the patristic heresies as it is to patristic orthodoxy. All that we have left with which to evaluate Schleiermacher's Christology is his doctrinal intention.

SCHLEIERMACHER'S POSITIVE CHRISTOLOGICAL FORMULATION

If we move beyond the question of person and natures to the positive Christological construction found primarily in Schleiermacher's *The Christian Faith*, what we encounter is a model of Jesus as the archetypal man, the human *Urbild*, whose relationship to God assures the superiority of Christianity to all other religions.[45] As Richard R. Niebuhr has pointed out, the difficulty that many modern theologians have with Schleiermacher's formulation arises not from the genuine untenability of a view that argues both the nature of

---

[45]*The Christian Faith*, 377-78, 400; and see Tillich, *Perspectives*, 110.

religion as a fundamental aspect of human consciousness and the superiority, indeed, the uniqueness of Christianity as grounded in the religious consciousness of Jesus—but rather from the positivistic assertion of the dialectical and neo-orthodox theologians of the twentieth century that no human phenomenon can be "the vehicle of God's self-disclosure."[46] Indeed, it appears to have been the great burden of Schleiermacher's Christology—undertaken in the interest of rescuing the New Testament witness to Jesus of Nazareth from the toils of obscure and somewhat problematic dogmatic language and, in addition, in the interest of reaffirming the spirit of the patristic inquiry—to argue that incarnation meant *precisely* that something in the phenomenal order *could* become the vehicle of divine revelation! In other words, Schleiermacher's Christological efforts have been misunderstood and unappreciated not only because of the continuing dominance of person/nature language in conservative Christian circles but also because of the antagonism to religion and religiosity, to emphasis on the phenomenological order and to a focus on the human, an antagonism hardly characteristic of earlier ages of the church, but typical of neo-orthodoxy in the twentieth century.[47]

The problem is easily seen in the somewhat cryptic declamation made by Barth in his *Protestant Theology in the Nineteenth Century*:

> It can be asked whether what [Schleiermacher] wanted to say about the relation of God and man could possibly also be said in the form of Christology. And it can, moreover, be asked whether Christology can possibly serve as the form for what Schleiermacher wanted to say. The Christology is the great disturbing element in Schleiermacher's [theology], not a very effective disturbance, perhaps, but a disturbance all the same. What he wanted to say might perhaps have been said better, more lucidly and concisely, if he had been able to say it in the form of a circle with one center, instead of an ellipse with two foci. But Schleiermacher could not avoid this element of disturbance. . . . Jesus of Nazareth fits desperately badly into this theology of the historical "composite life" of humanity, a "composite life" which is really after all fundamentally self-sufficient.[48]

---

[46] Richard R. Niebuhr, *Schleiermacher on Christ and Religion: A New Introduction* (New York: Scribner, 1964), 176-77.

[47] Cf. the discussion of the use of the term *religio* in the theology of the Reformers and of the Protestant orthodox in Richard A. Muller, *Post-Reformation Reformed Dogmatics*, vol. 1. *Prolegomena* (Grand Rapids: Baker, 1987), 112-21; and note the approach to religion, broader and more adequate than that evinced by neo-orthodoxy, in Gerardus van der Leeuw, *Religion in Essence and Manifestation*, trans. J. E. Turner, new foreword by Ninian Smart, 2 vols. (Princeton, N.J.: Princeton Univ. Press, 1986), 1:23, and John Macquarrie, *Principles of Theology*, 2d ed. (New York: Scribner, 1977), 149-73.

[48] Barth, *Protestant Thought*, 431-32.

It can be asked in return—on behalf of Schleiermacher—whether the elliptical form of theology and, preeminently, of Christology, with a divine focus and a human focus, is not in fact necessary in Christian theology. And it can, moreover, be asked whether a theology with one center, a center that has been abstracted from the toils of human *Historie* into a divine *Geschichte*, is free of Christological disturbance only because it avoids the great problems confronting a critical, historical reading of the text of the New Testament. Finally, it must also be asked whether a theology with one center is indeed capable of dealing with the divine address and human response that *is* religion or with the reconciliation of divinity with humanity and humanity with divinity that *is* the fundamental Christological and soteriological message of Christianity.

Schleiermacher's conception of Jesus as the *Urbild* of the new humanity, guided in all things by his unique sense of dependence on God is, after all, not unlike the pre-Nicene Christologies of the Apologists and Irenaeus. Justin Martyr, for example, appears, frequently, to understand the Logos as indwelling in the fully human Jesus in a manner "similar in kind to [his] universal presence, though much greater in degree," and in such a way that Jesus' whole humanity was "animated and enlightened by the Word."[49] Irenaeus, like Justin, speculated very little about the nature or character of the union of the Logos with humanity in Jesus. His concern was to identify Jesus as truly divine and truly human, the complete humanity of the Redeemer having been fashioned by the creative Logos in the womb of Mary, in order that Jesus might be the archetype of the new humanity, the Second Adam who recapitulates and thereby renews humanity under himself as its new federal head.[50] What is more, in the absence of the rather abstract person/ nature vocabulary of the later patristic period, Irenaeus often spoke of the conjunction of divinity and humanity in Christ in terms of "the God" and "His man"—emphasizing the character of Jesus as archetype of the new humanity and as, over against the Gnostic proclamation, eminently human.[51] (There is a certain irony, thus, in Barth's charge that Schleiermacher's Christological efforts "transformed *pistis* into *gnosis*," granting that Schleiermacher's concept of Jesus as *Urbild*, like Irenaeus' antignostic teaching concerning the archetypal Man, cast its emphasis on the fullness of Jesus' humanity.[52])

In the all-too-brief Christological section in his *Speeches*, Schleiermacher rested his Christology firmly on a principle of mediation and

---

[49]Kelly, *Early Christian Doctrines*, 146-47.

[50]Cf. Irenaeus, *Against Heresies*, 5.14.2

[51]Ibid., 5.14.1, 4; 21.3; and cf. Kelly, *Early Christian Doctrines*, 148.

[52]Cf. Barth, *Protestant Theology*, 432.

on the assumption that the relation of Jesus to God was such that, in Jesus, the problem of human finitude was overcome: Jesus, in other words, had a "consciousness of the singularity of His knowledge of God and His existence in God" that "was at once the consciousness of His office as mediator and of His divinity."[53] The archetypal character of Jesus thus resides in his mediatorial function as it, in turn, rests on the presence of divinity in and to his consciousness in such a way as to deliver him from the limitations of human sinfulness and finitude.

The Christological model that Schleiermacher presents, therefore, granting both the radical interpenetration of the dogmatic categories of "person" and "work" noted above and the reconstruction of Christological language around the problem of mediation—on what Christ does rather than on who Christ is—is clearly that of a "Christology from below."[54] Here again we recognize the philosophical and epistemological constraints placed on Schleiermacher by Kant as well as the intellectual difficulties caused for theology in the early nineteenth century by the continuing popularity of both supernaturalism and rationalism: not only did the person/nature language of classical Christology become problematic in the new philosophical setting of the early nineteenth century, the very "starting-point" of traditional Christologies in the divine appeared inappropriate. There was, certainly, some precedent for a Christology resting on the problem of mediation, particularly in the Reformed tradition,[55] but never before was there such strong pressure to replace entirely a "Christology from above" with one generated "from below."

As Keck has noted, Schleiermacher provided his contemporaries with a view of theology that freed them "from supernaturalism's extraneous God and externally grounded truth (miracles and inspired scripture), and from rationalism's inability to deal constructively with the reality of the Christian church and its actual history."[56] Schleiermacher was able to offer a view of Christianity and of Christ in which "the truth of Christianity" was not understood as something "'inserted' into human history," but was seen as an integral part—indeed, the highest part and the goal—of human existence.[57]

The identity of Jesus, as known through the grounding of the religious consciousness of the believing community in his God-consciousness, consists in the sinless condition of his ideal humanity,

---

[53]Schleiermacher, *Speeches*, 247.

[54]Cf. Christian, *Friedrich Schleiermacher*, 118-21.

[55]See Richard A. Muller, *Christ and the Decree: Christology and Predestination in Reformed Theology from Calvin to Perkins* (Durham, N.C.: Labyrinth, 1986; repr., with corrections, Grand Rapids: Baker, 1988), 27-33, 37, 74, 133-36, 146-47.

[56]In Strauss, *The Christ of Faith*, lii.

[57]Ibid.

in the necessarily related "constant potency of his God-consciousness," and in his mediatorial ability to draw "believers into the power of his God-consciousness."[58] The latter, moreover, is possible because of the character of Jesus as *Urbild* or archetype: Christ is "the one in Whom the creation of human nature, which up to this point had existed only in a provisional state, was perfected"—or, as the pre-Nicene Fathers, particularly Irenaeus, would have argued, Christ is the image of God, the prototype, according to whom humanity was created and in whom it will be ultimately perfected.[59] Christ is known as divine, therefore, in and through the church's apprehension of his perfect relationship with the Father as the effective ground of all human reconciliation with God.

(It is noteworthy that Schleiermacher's assumptions regarding Christ's absolute or utter sense of dependence are grounded not in a reconstruction of the self-consciousness of the historical Jesus but rather in the consciousness of Christ's identity that is mediated in and through the community of faith. Schleiermacher recognized that the Gospels do not offer, either singly or as a group, "a connected presentation of the life of Jesus,"[60] and that the self-consciousness of Jesus is known in and through the Gospels not directly by a critical, biographical reconstruction, but in and through its impact on the community in which the Gospels were composed.[61] In other words, the original impress of Jesus' God-consciousness, as witnessed in the New Testament, parallels and ratifies the impress of Jesus' God-consciousness on the ongoing community of belief. As Schleiermacher comments in his *Brief Outline*, the New Testament consists in "the normative documents which concern the action and effect of Christ both on and with his disciples, and also those which concern the common action and effect of his disciples toward the establishment of Christianity."[62])

The usual critique of Schleiermacher's Christology—that he did not do justice to the divinity of Christ—ought, perhaps to be reread and reassessed "from below": the issue is not merely that Schleiermacher's critics remain dissatisfied with his replacement of an ontic with an experiential divine presence in Christ, but that they also have difficulty with the very humanness of Christ's divinity and its potential analogy with "divinity" of the reconciled human race. Schleiermacher's point is, after all, that Christ is the archetype and prototype of the new humanity in whom what is provisional in all other

[58]Schleiermacher, *The Christian Faith*, 385, 425.

[59]Ibid., 374; cf. Irenaeus, *Against Heresies*, 4.20.1; 33.4; 5.16.1, 2; and see Dominic Unger, "Christ's Role in the Universe According to St. Irenaeus," in *Franciscan Studies* 26, no. 1 (1945): 3-20, 114-37.

[60]Schleiermacher, *Life of Jesus*, 43.

[61]Schleiermacher, *Hermeneutics*, 125-26, 139.

[62]Schleiermacher, *Brief Outline*, §105.

human beings is fully realized. Christ brings into the world something absolutely unique but which is nevertheless intimately linked with "the corporate life" of humanity.[63]

His divinity, therefore, is not something that must lie absolutely beyond the bounds of human possibility but must, instead, be identified as the divine possibility for humanity. This assumption, in turn, leads Schleiermacher to the comment—in adumbration of the critiques to which his Christology would be subjected—that objections to the "ideality" of Christ as Redeemer might easily lead to "hope" that the development of the religious consciousness of the human race will someday "pass beyond Christ and leave Him behind." It is the case, however, that the Christian faith "knows no other way to a pure conception of the ideal than an ever-deepening understanding of Christ" and that such a development would mean the end of Christianity.[64] It is clearly not Schleiermacher's intention to diminish the "peculiar activity" and "exclusive dignity" of the Redeemer or in any way to deny that "the spontaneity of the new corporate life is original in the Redeemer and proceeds from him alone." Indeed, he assumes that all other religions "are destined to pass over into" Christianity, inasmuch as Christianity, in its Christ, has and experiences the "highest development" of which the race is capable.[65]

There are, certainly, difficulties and problems with Schleiermacher's Christology—and most of them were pointed out almost immediately by Ferdinand Christian Baur and, following in his steps, David Friedrich Strauss.[66] Both thinkers questioned the ease of Schleiermacher's transition from the pious consciousness of Christ belonging to the Christian community to the datum of the Incarnate Christ as a unique event in history. Baur noted that, if the external history of Jesus was a reflection of the development of the religious self-consciousness of the believing community, then Christ is in some sense "every man" and not the unique event that he must be in order to achieve the ends of a proper Christology.[67] They questioned also the means by which the historical Jesus was identified, first, as the ideal or archetypal humanity, and second, as ideal humanity, as the object of anyone's consciousness. Baur in particular argued that Schleiermacher had failed to prove any philosophical necessity for a historical Jesus at the foundation of his formulations about Jesus'

---

[63]Schleiermacher, *The Christian Faith*, 386.

[64]Ibid., 378.

[65]Ibid., 374, 377-78.

[66]Cf. the discussion in Peter C. Hodgson, *The Formation of Historical Theology: A Study of Ferdinand Christian Baur* (New York: Harper & Row, 1966), 43-54, with Strauss, *The Christ of Faith*, lx-lxxxii, and especially 28-37, 59-68, 159-69.

[67]Baur, as cited in Hodgson, *Formation*, 14.

ideality and Christian God-consciousness. Strauss could conclude his criticism with the very pointed remark, "true reality is lacking from [Schleiermacher's] Christ; he is only a memory from a long-forgotten time, like the light of a distant star which still strikes the eye today although the body from which it shone has been out for years."[68]

Such criticisms are hardly negligible. What can be said on Schleiermacher's behalf, however, is that they are modern problems that function on an utterly different level than the Christological problems of person/nature language that he strove to avoid. Nor are they problems that have been set aside by modern alternatives to Schleiermacher's teaching, whether those of Baur and Strauss in the nineteenth century or those of various twentieth-century theologians. If the link between Schleiermacher's concept of individual and communal consciousness of Jesus Christ as the ideal, and the historical identity of Jesus of Nazareth, seems tenuous, it nevertheless adumbrates and parallels the problem of the historical Jesus that remains with us after the demise of the "old quest." The theologically interpreted and understood Christ present already in the earliest church's testimony, recorded in the Gospels, is not always easily linked with the historical Jesus—certainly not in any universally satisfactory reconstruction.

Schleiermacher responded to the criticism in his *Letters to Lücke* by noting that his starting point in consciousness was not a problematic transition from the ideal to the particular but rather an examination of the empirical data of the faith. It belongs to the Christian consciousness of God to know that it is derivable only from Christ and that Christ was constituted as the particular historical person he was "through the divine power dwelling in him."[69] Faith cannot, Schleiermacher insisted, be "derived from knowledge or philosophy" —and since he had not replaced the historical Christ with a philosophical construction, but had, instead, approached the historical Christ via the church's consciousness of his relationship to God, he was no "gnostic," as Baur had claimed.[70]

Schleiermacher's Christology, then, stands as an attempt, perhaps as the most important modern attempt, to overcome the historical, biblical, and metaphysical difficulties inherent in the language of traditional orthodoxy—without losing the grounds achieved by ancient orthodoxy. Even if the criticisms leveled by Baur and Strauss are taken as irrefutable in every point, they must be taken as criticisms affecting not only Schleiermacher's but also any Christology

---

[68]Strauss, *The Christ of Faith*, 167.

[69]Schleiermacher, *On the Glaubenslehre: Two Letters to Dr. Lücke*, trans. James Duke and Francis Fiorenza (Chico, Calif.: Scholars, 1981), 45-47.

[70]Ibid., 27, 36-37, 63, 71-72, 77. The parallel between Baur's criticism and Barth's should be noted.

that assumes the universal soteriological significance in and for the believing community of the historical human being, Jesus of Nazareth. Schleiermacher, arguably, did offer (despite the criticism) a way of historical, phenomenological, and theological approach to the church's underlying motivation in formulating its Christology that presents both the reason for the church's perception of the ongoing redemptive significance of Jesus Christ and a way of understanding— of course without the kind of philosophical proof required by Baur and Strauss—how God could be in Christ reconciling the world to himself and how Christ could also be a genuine human being holding out the promise to all human beings of a renewed fellowship with God.

The terminological shift from traditional orthodoxy to Schleiermacher's statements concerning the humanity and divinity of Christ is so great that the question of orthodoxy naturally arises. Schleiermacher's understanding of the problems confronting the traditional language in the modern world can hardly be faulted. And the positive, constructive nature of his intentions is undeniable. Those who have labeled his thought as heterodox or unsuccessful and incapable of sustaining a genuine Christology or genuinely Christocentric approach to theology have greatly overstated their case, if only to defer inquiry into the problematic elements in their own Christologies. Those who have asked objectively the question of the success or failure of his approach in the context of traditional Christological language encounter the difficulty of Schleiermacher's acknowledgment, on the one hand, of the intention behind the traditional language, and his rejection, on the other, of the language itself—on precisely stated and very cogent theological grounds, indeed, for the sake of the profoundly biblical and traditional intention that Jesus Christ be understood as an individual subject. The final verdict has not been pronounced on Schleiermacher's Christology. We are left both with a renewed sense of the difficulty of formulating a Christology in contemporary language and with the distinct impression that the century and a half separating us from Schleiermacher has in no way diminished the importance of his contribution to the discussion.

The Person of Christ:

Contemporary and Literary Views

Psychological Evaluations of Jesus

Vernon Grounds

President, Evangelicals for Social Action

A meticulous scholar with an impressively wide range of interests, Paul Jewett in his life and service has been steadfastly Christocentric. It is therefore fitting that in expressing our gratitude for his significant ministry we explore various dimensions of Christology. An aspect of Christological speculation that might be regarded as slightly esoteric has to do with psychological evaluations of Jesus. Earlier in our century certain scholars were concerned, both positively and negatively, with Jesus' psyche. Since most of their discussions are entombed in books now rarely read, I have seized upon the privilege of contributing to this *Festschrift* as an opportunity to perform a very minor resurrection. Because of the dubious value of those discussions, one might question the advisability of, if not exactly resurrecting dead issues, at least disinterring some skeletal remains. Yet scholarship is rightly dedicated to the task of preventing the past from being forgotten, and the past can often speak sagely to the present. In any event, my purpose in this essay has been to exhibit a few specimens of Christological speculation which, to risk one more figure of speech, will thus be exhibited like bees in amber for curious readers to contemplate.

A SPECTRUM OF CHRISTOLOGIES

It was at Caesarea Philippi that Jesus asked his disciples, "Who do men say that I am?" That question has echoed on through history. Who is he anyway, this Questioner whose question has elicited an astonishing range of diverse answers? Examine the chapter headings of John Wick Bowman's 1970 *Which Jesus?* They indicate how widely interpretations of our Lord differ: "(1) The Apocalyptic 'Son of Man'; (2) The Existentialist Rabbi; (3) The Essene-like 'Teacher of Righteousness'; (4) The Nazorean Scheming Messiah; (5) the Para-Zealot Revolutionary; (6) The Church's Resurrected Lord; and (7) The Prophetic Suffering Servant-Messiah."[1] Or consider the answers to that question Jesus asked as they are given in John Hayes' 1976 *Son*

---

[1]John Wick Bowman, *Which Jesus?* (Philadelphia: Westminster, 1970).

of God to Superstar: Twentieth-Century Interpretations of Jesus: "(1) Jesus: The Historical Figure; (2) Jesus: The Christ of Orthodoxy; (3) Jesus: The Apocalyptic Visionary; (4) Jesus: The Constant Contemporary; (5) Jesus: The Jew from Galilee; (6) Jesus: The Proclaimer Calling to Decision; (7) Jesus: The Messianic Suffering Servant; (8) Jesus: The Political Revolutionary; (9) Jesus: The Black Messiah; (10) Jesus: The Messianic Schemer; (11) Jesus: The Founder of a Secret Society; (12) Jesus: The Qumran Essene; (13) Jesus: The Sexual Being; (14) Jesus: The Creation of the Early Church."[2]

Compare those interpretations with the views discussed by Jaroslav Pelikan in his 1985 *Jesus Through the Centuries: His Place in the History of Culture*: "(1) The Rabbi; (2) The Turning Point of History; (3) The Light of the Gentiles; (4) The King of Kings; (5) The Cosmic Christ; (6) The Son of Man; (7) The True Image; (8) Christ Crucified; (9) The Monk Who Rules the World; (10) The Bridegroom of the Soul; (11) The Divine and Human Model; (12) The Universal Man; (13) The Mirror of the Eternal; (14) The Prince of Peace; (15) The Teacher of Common Sense; (16) The Poet of the Spirit; (17) The Liberator; (18) The Man Who Belongs to the World."[3]

How can we explain this astonishing divergence of beliefs and opinions concerning Jesus? Obviously a monocausal explanation is impossible; a multicausal analysis is called for. Yet out of all the factors that might be adduced, one seems of primary importance. Christological speculation, more often than not, is a mirror of a given era; it reflects the dominant philosophy, the ideologies and concerns of the *zeitgeist* that happens to prevail in a certain epoch. As Hanna Wolff remarks perceptively in her *Jesus the Therapist*, "Each and every Christian age has seized the figure of Jesus and overlaid it with its own unconscious wishes and uncritical conceptions."[4]

Assuming, then, that Christological speculations tend to mirror the changing *zeitgeist*, it is by no means surprising that in our own century, permeated as it has been by the epochal work of Sigmund Freud, Jesus has been seen, both negatively and positively, in the light of psychology. Positively, he has been seen as the model of a healthy-minded, remarkably insightful counselor. Negatively, he has been seen as an engrossing case study of mental illness, an emotionally disturbed person needing therapy. What I propose doing is to make available for contemporary students, first, a statement of the positive evaluation; second, some of the more drastic negative evaluations;

---

[2]John H. Hayes, *Son of God to Superstar: Twentieth Century Interpretations of Jesus* (Nashville: Abingdon, 1976).

[3]Jaroslav Pelikan, *Jesus Through the Centuries: His Place in the History of Culture* (New Haven: Yale Univ. Press, 1986).

[4]Hanna Wolff, *Jesus the Therapist*, trans. Robert R. Barr (Oak Park, Ill.: Meyer-Stone, 1987), 159.

third, critiques of the negative case; and, finally, views of contemporary psychotherapists who have a high estimate of Jesus from the standpoint of their profession.

THE POSITIVE CASE

Repeated analyses of the Gospel records have been made in an attempt to fathom our Lord's psyche, his mental health, his emotional dynamics, his controlling convictions, his goals and ambitions, his attitudes and values. Many of these analyses are examples of the grossest eisegesis, with inferences drawn that completely lack textual support. More often than not these interpreters have been like artists painting portraits over a Rembrandt canvas and thus concealing the original figure. Their eisegesis is, as a rule, a learned exercise in imaginative extrapolation. Albert Schweitzer flatly declares, "We possess no psychology of the Messiah"; indeed, Schweitzer challenges the possibility of legitimately extracting any "natural psychology"[5] from the Gospels. But his objections have been ignored by biographical reconstructionists who have deduced psychologies of Jesus in keeping with their own presuppositions and prejudices.

The most ambitious effort of the genre is perhaps that of G. Stanley Hall, who served Clark University as both president and professor of psychology. Published in 1917, his two imposing volumes entitled *Jesus, the Christ, in the Light of Psychology* constitute a remarkable tour de force that endeavors to liberate the true Jesus from his imprisonment in orthodox theology. "This indeed is the task of the psychology of Christianity now, to gird itself to a work not unlike that of late so often and so brilliantly done in other fields, but here inspired by the new hope that we may really resurrect the Jesus so long buried in the Gospels."[6] Psychology, Hall confidently avers, provides "the new key . . . now able to unlock the very secret soul of Jesus himself, which has never been understood before."[7] Looking back on the Christological research and reinterpretation of "the great historical critical movement best marked by the Tübingen school," Hall declares that "the inevitable next step" in understanding Jesus "must be psychological." Casting himself in the role of "a pioneer in a new domain," he voices his belief that "the psychological Jesus Christ is the true and living Christ of the present and the future."[8]

---

[5]Albert Schweitzer, *The Quest of the Historical Jesus*, trans. W. Montgomery (London: A. & C. Black, 1931), 9, 331-32, 334; cf. 361.

[6]G. Stanley Hall, *Jesus, the Christ, in the Light of Psychology*, 2 vols. (Garden City, N.Y.: Doubleday, Page & Co., 1917), 1:312.

[7]Ibid., 2:413.

[8]Ibid., 1:xxv.

Approaching the Gospels from this ποῦ στω, Hall "is not chiefly concerned with questions of historicity." The actual occurrence of the alleged events in the life of Jesus is for him "a matter of relative indifference." They have "a higher symbolic value" far transcending their facticity.[9] Providentially, the development of "analytic psychology" has negated the argument of Strauss and others that myth and legend render the Jesus story worthless. Invite criticism to do its task relentlessly. There remains "a supremely precious psychological residue in Christianity," and the higher psychology will illuminate "the mystery of the death and Resurrection of Jesus," unearthing the motives that inspired this "ideal embodiment of humanity in his prime to voluntarily subject himself to every psychic and physical torture and finally to the most disgraceful death."[10] In carrying out its laudable labor of rescue and reinterpretation, the higher psychology will trace the development of Jesus' conviction that he stood "nearer than any other to God," a conviction that "constituted his divine sonship." Hence while Adolf Harnack insists "that no psychology can ever tell us how Jesus attained this insight,"[11] the higher psychology can ascertain how Jesus came to incarnate "all the good tendencies in man," demonstrating those ideals that "constitute the true psychological essence of Christianity . . . the very truth of truth," truth that will abide, "even if his historical existence were disproven."[12]

So the Virgin Birth, since a "belief in its literalness would not meet the criteria a modern psychology would test it by,"[13] can nevertheless be affirmed on a symbolic level far above that of crass biology. So too the parables of Jesus will at last be understood for what in fact they are. The higher psychology will help readers to realize that during our Lord's prepublic years, in his solitary musings he had come to symbolize much of his physical and social environment by investing their items with higher meanings, so that the parables

give us glimpses of how in his own marvelous, if primitive, method of growth all things had come to speak to him of something above themselves. They give us perhaps the best of all examples of how the human soul works its way to truth in a prelogical stage, when imagination and intuition are everything and logical concatenation has not yet begun its work of coordinating and harmonizing insights in different directions.[14]

---

[9]Ibid., 250.

[10]Ibid., 153-54.

[11]Ibid., 2:339.

[12]Ibid., 1:244.

[13]Ibid., 258-59; cf. 268, 278, 286.

[14]Ibid., 2:519.

It follows of course that the parables, which permit us to "see farthest into Jesus' own heart," will be regarded as "in a sense Binet tests of spiritual insight," since "for genetic religious psychology they serve as moron-finders. A parable is a patent, postulating a latent meaning, always requiring some psychoanalysis, as does a dream."[15]

What holds good for the parables holds good as well, Hall maintains, for the miracles of Jesus. The higher psychology will perceive how at the outset of his public career, if the Temptation narrative is considered from a psychological perspective, Jesus resolved to spurn miracle-working and thaumaturgy, doing wonders "in the domain of soul." For he had become aware that "There are abundant powers waiting to be set free, and this master psychologist of the kingdom within would work his magic in this domain only. Even all his healing would be psychotherapy alone, and should be done chiefly as a symbol of a more inner psychic regeneration from the obsession of sin."[16]

Thus the higher psychology will not deny that Jesus did in fact perform healings. On the contrary, it will selectively endorse the historicity of some Gospel "miracles." It will account for these, however, on a naturalistic premise. "His fame and the charm and magnetism of his personality proved very effective therapeutically in Galilee, which abounded with neurotics, and in an age when cure was exorcism. Thus, besides being a physician of the soul, Jesus found himself more and more revered as a physician of the body."[17]

Because genuine miracles are impossible, i.e., divine interventions that modify the operation of nature's laws, the higher psychology will be compelled to deny a physical resurrection, and deny it dogmatically: "The Jesus that arose and ascended was not a reanimated cadaver. . . . His body mouldered like ours. The postmortem Jesus had no vestige of historicity." This means, consequently, that "psychology does not pronounce on the historicity of the Resurrection as an objective fact, but it magnifies the unquestioned belief in it which became ineluctable and the chief source of power in the early Church."[18] Is the Resurrection, then, to be buried in the graveyard of dead beliefs? By no means! "It must ever be to us a predominantly psychological fact, truer to the nature and needs of the soul than to the canons of historical research."[19] And what if mystery together with a measure of uncertainty remains despite the basic certainty that "this is all at bottom psychology"?

---

[15]Ibid., 522-23.
[16]Ibid., 1:307.
[17]Ibid., 2:371.
[18]Ibid., 697.
[19]Ibid., 699-700.

Psychology with its special sections on illusions of perception, on the life of feeling and will, on the individual and the movement of groups and races of all men, has yet much to learn and is still in its infancy, but it is already big with the promise and potency of larger and more cogent explanations here, which far from weakening faith will give it a higher sanction and a larger scope with strict conformity to science.[20]

Meanwhile, however, a verdict can be rendered that will reassure Christians if they are disturbed by Hall's reinterpretation of their faith. What emerges from a fearless investigation of the Gospels in the light of psychology is, he affirms, a towering Figure, "the Supreme Master of all who have ever known or utilized consummately the higher powers of man."[21] And this Supreme Master stands on the horizon of history as the Supreme Model. "Here we have phenomena of an altitude which, though many have approached, none has ever yet attained, so that the psychology of Jesus remains the unique psychology of humanity at the acme of its insights and in the supreme *actus purus* of moral efficiency."[22]

THE NEGATIVE CASE

We turn from this quintessential piece of liberal theology which argues the positive case for our Lord's psychological health to a related work which provides detailed information regarding the negative case. Here we appreciatively utilize the research done by William E. Bundy, who in 1922 published *The Psychic Health of Jesus*, a critical study of scholars he labels "pathographers." Forerunners of today's psychobiographers, they differ in their diagnoses of our Lord's mental and emotional condition but in common focus their attention on his belief-system concerning his own person and his messianic role. According to Bundy, they are primarily concerned with the question of Jesus' self-consciousness. This is indeed

of paramount importance in the pathographic issue. In certain serious forms of mental alienation, particularly in paranoia, it is the subject's estimate of his own ego that constitutes the surest symptom of his psychic derangement. It is here that that deplorable divergence from reality, actuality, concrete condition and circumstance begins which is convincing in determining the subject's state as morbid. The inmate of the institution for the insane imagines himself a president, a king, a general, a millionaire, a Messiah, or even a god, with all the pertaining pretentions, prerogatives, and plans.[23]

---

[20]Ibid., 714.

[21]Ibid., 425.

[22]Ibid., 436.

[23]William E. Bundy, *The Psychic Health of Jesus* (New York: Macmillan, 1922), 199.

Whatever the specific reasons they adduce for their diagnoses, these pathographers agree that Jesus suffered some form of serious mental imbalance. Thus O. Binswanger, though taking sharp issue with this approach, remarks that "in recent times the effort is in vogue to stamp the heroes of religious history, in particular Mohammed, the Apostle Paul, Martin Luther, and even Jesus . . . as psychopaths, hysterics, and epileptics. . . ."[24]

One investigator of our Lord's inner life is Emil Rasmussen, a Danish philologist and onetime student of theology. He published *Jesus: Eine vergleichende psychopathologische Studie* in 1905. This was a German translation of the Danish edition that had been issued a year previously. He begins his examination by stating "that the old alternative, Jesus was either the one whom he gave himself out to be or he was the greatest imposter who ever lived . . . is false. There is a third possibility: a man may not be the one he represents himself to be, and yet not be an imposter; he may be beside himself, insane."[25] And that third possibility is the one Rasmussen adopts. He advances a kind of syllogism in which "the minor premise precedes the major":

1. Jesus was a prophet.
2. All prophets are epileptic to a greater or lesser degree.
3. Therefore Jesus was an epileptic.[26]

And Rasmussen argues that epileptics are hopelessly egocentric; warped in their ethical judgment; paranoid, since they view the whole world as hostile; afflicted with hallucinations, and often end their lives as suicides.[27] Hence Rasmussen expresses with reference to Jesus, "a genuine sympathy for an exceedingly unfortunate nature with a tragic yet splendid fate."[28] But he insists that our Lord, psychologically considered, was an emotionally warped epileptic.

A second pathographer whom Bundy studies is Dr. de Loosten. That name is a pseudonym for George Lomer, who was the head physician at the Holstein Provincial Institute for the Insane in Neustadt. His 1905 book-length analysis is entitled *Jesus Christus vom Standpunkte des Psychiaters, Eine kritische Studie für Fachleute und gebildete Laien*. There is no need to rehearse in detail the tendentious arguments he advances. His conclusion summarizes his entire case.

---

[24]Ibid., 211-12.
[25]Ibid., 57.
[26]Ibid., 63.
[27]Ibid., 62.
[28]Ibid., 67.

Suffering from birth on under a hereditary burden Jesus was probably a half-caste, who as a born degenerate attracted attention even in early youth by his exceedingly pronounced self-consciousness which was combined with a highly gifted intelligence and a meagerly developed sense for family and sex. . . . His self-consciousness was aggravated in a slow process of development that ended in a fixed system of delusions, the particulars of which were determined by the intense religious bent of the time and his own one-sided preoccupation with the Scriptures of the Old Testament.[29]

While he makes no professional classification of Jesus' pathology, de Loosten stroke upon stroke paints the picture of an individual afflicted with paranoia.

Bundy next examines the views of William Hirsch, a doctor of medicine, indeed a specialist in mental diseases. In 1912 he published *Religion and Civilization: The Conclusions of a Psychiatrist*. A radical freethinker, he vehemently denounces all supernaturalism and biblical faith in particular. "Christianity," he fulminates, "was the greatest hindrance, the most persistent obstacle which civilization has had to overcome." He stigmatizes it as "a curse and blight to the human race."[30] Yet he does not regard Jesus as an imposter. On the contrary, "Christ was thoroughly honest and was convinced himself of the truth of every word he uttered."[31] Not a liar, certainly not Lord of Lords, Jesus was psychotic. "All that we know of him corresponds so exactly to the clinical aspect of paranoia, that it is hardly conceivable how anybody at all acquainted with mental disorders, can entertain the slightest doubt as to the correctness of the diagnosis."[32] The evidence lies on the surface of the Gospels. Consider the "I am" assertions Jesus made, his claims to be the unique Son of God, and, beyond that, even his delusive belief in his own deity. Thus, in Hirsch's opinion, "no text book on mental diseases can give a more typical description of delusions of grandeur, gradually developing and infinitely increasing, than is offered by the life of Jesus Christ."[33] Incontestably, therefore, Jesus was paranoid.

The fourth and last of the pathographers whom Bundy discusses is the most formidable advocate of the thesis that Jesus was demented. Dr. C. Binet-Sanglé, professor in the school of psychiatry at the University of Paris, actually devoted four volumes to his microscopic examination of *La Folie de Jésus*, which appeared between 1908 and 1915. A megalomaniac—that is the judgment he pronounces on our

[29]Ibid., 77-78.
[30]Ibid., 79.
[31]Ibid., 81.
[32]Ibid., 82.
[33]Ibid., 83.

Lord. Jesus, he surmises, undoubtedly had visions before his baptism, but that event precipitated a psychotic reaction. "The hallucination at the Jordan marks the entry of Jesus, son of Joseph, into the ranks of the incurables. Henceforth nothing is able to restrain him in the expression of his delirium, neither the injuries of the priests and the soldiers nor the majesty of the Sanhedrin and the Praetorium, not even the suffering of the cross."[34] After that hallucinatory experience, Jesus was obviously out of touch with reality. "Blinded by his vanity, convinced that the world would be effaced before him, the theomega-lomaniac was constantly wounded, offended, and humiliated by those with whom he came in contact."[35]

Bypassing Binet-Sanglé's interpretation of other events in our Lord's life that reinforce the paranoia diagnosis, we notice only his comment regarding Jesus' practice of solitary devotion. "In the intimacy of his consciousness he played the part of king and God and abandoned himself to the contemplation of his work and the adoration his own ego."[36] The appropriate term for Jesus is, consequently, not *megalomaniac* but, preferably, *theomegalomaniac*, since his was "a psychic affection where this excessive pride is combined with an extreme piety."[37] No wonder, then, that as he concludes his fourth volume Binet-Sanglé engages in self-congratulation: "I have reached the end of the task which I set for myself and I believe that I can say that for alienists, medical men, for all learned and sincere persons, the insanity of the founder of the Christian religion is a demonstrated truth."[38]

Bundy puts in a few terse words the implications of this psycho-pathological interpretation of the Gospels: "The whole Christian world worships an insane Jew who was crucified 2000 years ago."[39]

CRITIQUES OF THE NEGATIVE CASE

Epileptic, paranoiac, theomegalomaniac—how is this pathographic denigration of Jesus to be evaluated? Much as it may offend those of us who adhere to traditional Christology, or even if it offends a liberal interpreter of Jesus like G. Stanley Hall, do the facts compel us to accept its central thesis? Was the man portrayed in the Gospels not just a human being? Was he a tragically defective human being who today would probably be hospitalized? Or can these early twentieth-century excursions into psychobiography be dismissed as biased,

---

[34]Ibid., 97.
[35]Ibid., 102.
[36]Ibid., 189.
[37]Ibid., 94.
[38]Ibid., 107.
[39]Ibid., 86.

tendentious, utterly wrong, a misreading of the available data which is devoid of credibility and validity?

In undertaking a refutation of pathography, Bundy points out that, for one thing, exegetically and hermeneutically its conclusions are indefensible and that, for a second thing, its diagnosis of Jesus is psychologically unwarranted. To select one crucial instance of exegesis, these diagnosticians insist that the statement in Mk 3:21, "He has lost His senses" (NASB), occurs in a context which describes Jesus' frenzied ministry and the unsuccessful efforts of family and friends to force him to stop. That passage in itself, they contend, proves their thesis. Renowned New Testament scholar Bernhard Weiss protests, however: "The whole account does not exhibit the least trace of any mental alienation, but plainly proves the easily understood care and anxiety which, if somewhat limited, was exceedingly well-intentioned, bestowed on the member of the family who had been too long removed from the others."[40] Though other instances of highly debatable exegesis and indefensible eisegesis could be cited, for our purposes this one typical instance will suffice.

It must be noted, though, that Bundy's refutation of Jesus' alleged mental illness requires in his opinion the abandonment of the Fourth Gospel as a dependable source of information. If Jesus actually engaged in the grandiose self-assertions John records, then, Bundy concedes, the psychobiographers have incontestably established their case. Yet this concession to textual criticism does not carry with it, he argues, the jettisoning of that account. Instead, in his view, these egocentric words ascribed to Jesus in the Fourth Gospel are only early Christian convictions and confessions, originally in the third person, set in the first person in the mouth of Jesus. Hence this Gospel remains "one of the most significant and remarkable documents of primitive Christianity."[41]

As for the psychiatric diagnosis of a historical character 1900 years after his death, most theorists and therapists dismiss it as an impossible undertaking. Bundy cites, for example, Dr. H. Schaefer, who was quite contemptuous of this whole approach: "Pathography is at a very low rate of value, even in the estimate of its psychiatric colleagues; many still reckon it among the unprofitable occupations."[42] Another therapeutic professional, Dr. Theodore Ribot, sees Jesus as the antithesis of a mentally deranged individual. He places him instead among the greatest of great human beings, integrated and one-directional, marked by "unity, stability, and power." What fundamentally distinguishes these great personalities among whom Jesus towers "is

---

[40]Ibid., 160.
[41]Ibid., 135.
[42]Ibid., 267.

a mighty, inextinguishable passion which enlists their ideas in its service. . . . They present a type of life always in harmony with itself, because in them everything conspires together, converges, and consents."[43]

While Bundy's refutation of the pathographers we have glanced at is itself convincing, it seems advisable to highlight one document which he alludes to and summarizes briefly, Albert Schweitzer's 1913 dissertation for his medical doctorate, *The Psychiatric Study of Jesus*. In short compass (the text of the English translation runs only forty pages) Schweitzer with surgical incisiveness exposes the baselessness of the allegation that Jesus was emotionally ill. To be sure Schweitzer, like Bundy, rules out the Fourth Gospel as a historical source and feels free to dismiss as unhistorical passages such as Luke's account of our Lord's interaction with the temple priests when he was a boy of twelve. Overlooking Schweitzer's critical views, however, let us set down his four devastating conclusions:

1. The material which is in agreement with these books is for the most part unhistorical.

2. Out of the material which is certainly historic, a number of acts and utterances of Jesus impress the authors as pathological because the latter are too little acquainted with the contemporary thought of the time to be able to do justice to it. A series of wrong deductions springs also from the fact that they have not the least understanding of the peculiar problems inherent in the course of the public ministry of Jesus.

3. From these false preconceptions and with the help of entirely hypothetical symptoms, they construct pictures of sickness which are themselves artifacts and which, moreover, cannot be made to conform exactly with the clinical forms of sickness diagnosed by the authors.

4. The only symptoms to be accepted as historical and possibly to be discussed from the psychiatric point of view—the high estimate which Jesus has of himself and perhaps also the hallucination at the baptism —fall far short of proving the existence of mental illness.[44]

In the light of these conclusions one can objectively declare that Schweitzer has given the *coup de grâce* to the claim that Jesus was a pathological case. And that claim, as advanced early in our century by pathographers like Rasmussen, Binet-Sanglé, and de Loosten (these are the three Schweitzer deals with) has become as the century draws

---

[43]Ibid., 253.

[44]Albert Schweitzer, *Psychiatric Study of Jesus*, trans. Charles R. Joy (Boston: Beacon, 1948), 75.

to a close a largely forgotten aberration in the history of psychology and theology.

EVALUATIONS OF JESUS BY CONTEMPORARY PSYCHOLOGISTS

What is the judgment of more recent practitioners in the field of mental health regarding our Lord's psyche? Is he viewed as unbalanced and deranged, obviously in need of intensive therapy? No doubt such appraisals continue to be made, though, if they are, they have not attracted much attention. On the contrary, Jesus has frequently been eulogized as a model of healthy-mindedness and, far from needing therapy, a therapist from whose remarkable insights even sophisticated post-Freudians can profit. Thus, for example, the eminent American authority W. S. Sadler, in his 1936 *Theory and Practice of Psychiatry*, remarks, "The sincere acceptance of the principles and teachings of Christ with respect to the life of mental peace and joy, the life of unselfish thought and clean living, would at once wipe out more than one-half the difficulties, diseases, and sorrows of the human race."[45] Sadler's opinion is endorsed by Fritz Kunkel, who in his 1943 *In Search of Maturity* says simply, "Jesus of Nazareth was the greatest psychologist of all times."[46] A tribute like that may understandingly be dismissed as greatly overblown, yet it is possible to duplicate such an appraisal from a surprisingly large and diverse number of sources. Suppose we mention only three; and to show the international scope of this more than positive reaction to our Lord's life and ministry as set forth in the Gospels, we will give the judgments of Hanna Wolff, a German; Frank Lake, an Englishman; and one more American, James T. Fisher.

To start with Fisher, consider a long passage from his 1951 autobiographical *A Few Buttons Missing*. It is very obviously a studied piece of rhetoric open to the charge of exaggeration and extravagance. But we must bear in mind that it has been published under his own name by a distinguished professional.

> Not until I took up the study of psychiatry did I pause to consider deeply the significance of religious ritual and to ponder its value to the world. . . . I examined many patients who could recite long passages from the Bible—but none who could honestly understand the basic philosophy of what he was reciting, and none who had lived in accordance with the rules being quoted. . . . I could never be entirely satisfied with my role as a psychiatrist—struggling to find a safe pathway so

---

[45]William S. Sadler, *Theory and Practice of Psychiatry* (St. Louis: C. V. Mosby, 1936), 1073.

[46]Fritz Kunkel, *In Search of Maturity* (New York: Scribner, 1943), 12.

that I might lead a few lost souls out of the wilderness of mental abnormality. . . . What was needed, I felt sure, was some new and enlightened recipe for living a sane and satisfying life. . . .

I dreamed of writing a handbook that would be simple, practical, easy to understand, and easy to follow. It would tell people how to live—what thoughts and attitudes and philosophies to cultivate, and what pitfalls to avoid, in seeking mental health. I attended every symposium it was possible for me to attend, and I took notes on the wise words of my teachers and of my colleagues who were leaders in their field. And then, quite by accident, I discovered that such a work had already been completed. . . .

If you were to take the sum total of all authoritative articles ever written by the most qualified of psychologists and psychiatrists on the subject of mental hygiene—if you were to combine them, and refine them, and cleave out the excess verbage [sic]—if you were to take the whole of the meat and none of the parsley, and if you were to have these unadulterated bits of pure scientific knowledge concisely expressed by the most capable of living poets, you would have an awkward and incomplete summation of the Sermon on the Mount. And it would suffer immeasurably through comparison.[47]

Consider, next, the appraisal of Frank Lake in his 1966 simply monumental *Clinical Theology*, a landmark in the integration of Christianity and psychotherapy. "Model-makers in the field of human personality," he writes, seek a pattern of human normality. Freud, Adler, and Jung, from their analysis of patients as well as their self-analyses, "inferred, *as an act of faith*, a model of normal man. . . . Three quite different norms resulted." Lake himself is convinced that Jesus is the long-and-vainly-sought-for model of normality: ". . . only one member of the species retained His true humanity," and he appeared on

the human scene uniquely in order to perform His task of demonstrating normality. As Martin Niemöller said once in Travancore, "Jesus Christ is human, we are not. . . ." He is the "Logos," God's interpretive word to man about his own essential nature. If this is true, and it is the basic affirmation of the Christian faith, then we cannot know either what we are, or what we are meant to be, or how this is to be achieved through interpersonal relationships, unless we look first at Him.

It is Jesus, then, who "provides us with a pattern of the norm for our humanity."[48]

---

[47]James T. Fisher and Lowell S. Hawley, *A Few Buttons Missing* (New York: Lippincott, 1951), 271-74.

[48]Frank Lake, *Clinical Theology* (London: Darton Longman & Todd, 1966), 138-39.

Consider, finally, the appraisal of Hanna Wolff, who moves in a therapeutic tradition akin to that of Carl Jung. Jesus, she declares,

> has discovered valid, basic laws of psychic existence. Indeed, he has emphatically installed them at the very center of his speech and activity. That is why we have been able, without contrivance, to adopt elements of that speech and action as governing paradigms for an understanding and treatment of the problems of human beings today. In Jesus and in psychotherapy, then, we see the same, entirely specific, humane image of the human being. Apart from Jesus himself, of course, we as yet possess no concretization of that image.[49]

Subject these positive appraisals to critical discount as one may, they nevertheless compel us to acknowledge that, considered from the perspective of psychology, the Jesus of the Gospels is an extraordinary person, at the very least an intuitive genius. Perhaps, in fact, he belongs in a *sui generis* category that lends credence to the answer traditionally given to the question, "Who do men say that I am?"

---

[49]Hanna Wolff, *Jesus the Therapist*, 152-53.

Jesus' Humanity and Ours in the Theology of Karl Barth

Elouise Renich Fraser

Associate Professor of Systematic Theology
Eastern Baptist Theological Seminary

From my teacher Paul K. Jewett, I have inherited a love for words. Not just any words, but the right words. Not out of the need to define or describe all things comprehensively, but out of desire for the object of every theologian's longing—to know God, which is to love God. This essay is both an expression of gratitude and a contribution to our common struggle as theologians to find the right words.

Our words give us away. Some would argue that in his doctrine of humanity, Karl Barth has given away his male bias against females. But perhaps it is more accurate to say that he has given away the painful reality that the one human being he longed to know and describe above all others was the one human being for whom he had the most trouble finding the right words. In this essay I want to demonstrate that Barth's inability to find the right words for our common humanity is directly linked to his inability to find the right words for Jesus' humanity.

The discussion centers on the irreversible priority of male over female,[1] which I take as basic to Barth's understanding of cohumanity. I will argue that irreversible male priority is incompatible with Barth's own theological definition of humanity, that it compromises the freedom of the *imago Dei*, and that it results from a questionable shift in Barth's Christological focus. After showing the inadequacy of Barth's descriptions of both male and female humanity, and of Jesus' humanity, I will suggest that the priority of the other is a better way of thinking about what it means to be human. My approach differs from

---

[1]Excellent analytical summaries of Barth's position can be found in Paul K. Jewett, *Man as Male and Female: A Study in Sexual Relationships from a Theological Point of View* (Grand Rapids: Eerdmans, 1975), 69-82; and Christina A. Baxter, "The Nature and Place of Scripture in the Church Dogmatics," in *Theology Beyond Christendom: Essays on the Centenary of the Birth of Karl Barth, May 10, 1886*, ed. John Thompson (Allison Park, Pa.: Pickwick, 1986), 33-62. For Barth's discussion of irreversible male priority see *Church Dogmatics*, 4 vols., trans. and ed. Geoffrey W. Bromiley and Thomas F. Torrance (Edinburgh: T. & T. Clark, 1956-75), 3/2:285-324.

most other treatments of this part of Barth's thought in two ways. First, it is an internal critique, based on criteria suggested by Barth himself. Second, my analysis attends in particular to Barth's retelling of biblical narrative. This is because I take Barth as a narrative theologian whose primary resource for reflection on theological convictions is biblical narrative.[2]

ORDER AND RECIPROCITY

Barth's argument for irreversible male priority falls within the larger context of his anthropological definition of humanity.[3] Here Barth develops the idea of cohumanity. To be human is to exist not in isolation, but with other human beings. It is to live not just with God as covenant partner, but with each other in a way that corresponds to covenant partnership with God. As Barth puts it,

> That real humanity [Mensch][4] is determined by God for life with God has its inviolable correspondence in the fact that its creaturely being is a being in encounter—between I and Thou, man [Mann] and woman. It is human [menschlich] in this encounter, and in this humanity [Menschlichkeit] it is a likeness of the being of its Creator and a being in hope in Him.[5]

Although cohumanity is a central idea in Barth's discussion, it is not clear how cohumanity is to be understood. On the one hand, Barth describes the basic form of humanity as I-Thou encounter which is characterized at every point by reciprocity:[6] reciprocal seeing

---

[2]Barth's narrative method is complex. For full discussion, including the various elements of Barth's particular narrative approach, see Elouise Renich Fraser, "Karl Barth's Doctrine of Humanity: A Reconstructive Exercise in Feminist Narrative Theology" (Ph.D. diss., Vanderbilt Univ., 1986).

[3]Barth defines humanity several ways in the doctrine of creation, with the first setting the context for the others. He defines what it means to be human in terms of relationship to the Creator (a theological definition), relationship to each other as creatures of this God (an anthropological definition), relationship of soul to body, and relationship to time.

[4]Barth's characteristically deliberate choice of words has been rendered invisible in the English translation of both Mensch and Mann as "man." Barth normally uses Mensch to refer to human beings or humanity in general, and Mann to refer to males. Exceptions highlight Barth's understanding that the male is human only in relation to woman. Throughout this essay I have used the terms "humanity" and "human being," not simply in order to be inclusive, but to make clear Barth's own careful distinction between Mensch and Mann.

[5]Barth, Church Dogmatics, 3/2:203.

[6]The English translation of Barth's term gegenseitig alternates throughout between "mutual" and "reciprocal." Given Barth's intention, the better choice is "reciprocal." The idea is not that something is done together or simultaneously, or

and being seen, reciprocal speaking and hearing, reciprocal aid, and reciprocal gladness in this encounter. On the other hand, Barth describes the concrete form of this cohumanity as male and female, characterized not simply by differentiation and relatedness, but by the irreversible order of male preceding female. Barth's critics have generally seen a contradiction between reciprocity and male priority and have proposed various ways of resolving the tension. Some attempt to make reciprocity the heart of Barth's discussion of male and female and to see male priority as an intrusion into or compromise of Barth's basically liberating insights into human relationships, including those between male and female.[7]

While there are reasons to think reciprocity might lie at the heart of cohumanity, evidence favors the conclusion that irreversible order is more basic than reciprocity. Neither Barth's appeals to the immanent Trinity as the original source of every I-Thou relationship, his use of covenant as an organizing metaphor in the doctrine of creation, his emphasis on the necessity for reciprocity within human relationships, nor his rejection of an orders of creation approach to human relationships is incompatible with this conclusion.[8] In each case, reciprocity is an essential characteristic of relationship. However, in the final analysis, reciprocity is subordinate to irreversible order. Order sets the context for reciprocity, and reciprocity serves not equality or egalitarianism, but order.

In addition, Barth's structuring of male-female relationships according to irreversible male priority is but part of a larger pattern that runs throughout Barth's doctrine of creation. Irreversible order prevails both in the "cosmological border" of the world as heaven and earth and within what might be called center stage, that is, humanity itself as it exists within this border. In both settings, irreversible orders of various kinds witness to the divine-human relationship. In

---

that both partners share equally in every aspect of the relationship. Rather, Barth speaks in terms of a give and take that is better conveyed by words like "reciprocity" and "reciprocate."

[7]For examples of critics who argue that reciprocity or a fellowship of equals is the new insight Barth should have retained, see Jewett, *Man as Male and Female*; Clifford Green, "Liberation Theology? Karl Barth on Women and Men," *Union Seminary Quarterly Review* 29 (Spring and Summer 1974): 221-31; Emma J. Justes, "Theological Reflections on the Role of Women in Church and Society," *Journal of Pastoral Care* 32 (March 1978): 42-54; Cynthia McCall Campbell, "*Imago Trinitatis:* An Appraisal of Karl Barth's Doctrine of the *Imago Dei*, in Light of His Doctrine of the Trinity" (Ph.D. diss., Southern Methodist Univ., 1981). Others who note the tension between reciprocity and order include John C. Bennett, review of *Church Dogmatics* III.4, by Karl Barth, in *Union Seminary Quarterly Review* 18 (November 1962): 74-79; Kathleen Bliss, "Male and Female," *Theology* 55 (June 1952): 208-13; Robert E. Willis, *The Ethics of Karl Barth* (Leiden: E. J. Brill, 1971), 384-85.

[8]For full discussion see Fraser, "Barth's Doctrine of Humanity," 162-99.

the case of male and female, irreversible male priority is essential to the reflected image of God in humanity. While the male is not God in relation to the female, the pattern by which male relates to female reminds us of the way in which God is with us, always taking initiative for the relationship. Further, insofar as male and female embody this relationship of irreversible order, they are in fellowship with each other, thus reminding us also of the fellowship God enjoys within God's own Trinitarian being.

If irreversible male priority is the structure within which cohumanity is to be defined and experienced, then one cannot simply ignore or pass over male priority and make reciprocity basic to male-female relationships.[9] To overlook order in the paradigmatic case of male and female is to run the risk of missing and thus perpetuating other less visible problems in Barth's understanding of cohumanity. Ironically, one also runs the risk of missing some of Barth's creative and challenging insights into the human situation. It seems one cannot pick and choose in this matter. For Barth, the primary meaning of cohumanity is an irreversibly ordered duality in which one partner (male) always has priority over the other partner (female).

AN INTERNAL CRITIQUE OF MALE PRIORITY

Barth's concept of irreversible male priority can be assessed theologically from at least three directions, each of them suggested by Barth himself. Two have to do with implications flowing from the content of this idea. The third has to do with the way Barth carries out his reflection, and it provides a way of seeing where Barth misses the mark, as well as a possible alternative.

The *first major criticism* draws on Barth's theological definition of humanity, which provides the larger context for his anthropological definition. According to Barth, only in light of our ongoing relationship with God can we understand our ongoing relationships with each other. In relation to God, to be human is to exist within the history of God's gracious, initiating movement toward us, and of our grateful, responsive movement back toward God. No matter what is said about relationship to each other, it must already be entailed in this description of our relationship to God.

Our first criticism, then, is that irreversible male priority is incompatible with Barth's own theological definition of humanity. This can be seen in two ways. First, Barth's theological definition implies that all human beings stand in solidarity before God—equally needy but

---

[9]Stuart D. McLean almost completely dismisses the significance of Barth's views on male and female in his otherwise careful analysis of Barth's doctrine of humanity. See "Creation and Anthropology," in Thompson, ed., *Theology Beyond Christendom*, 139 n. 1.

also equally hopeful and capable of relationship with God. Barth's Christological reflection supports and clarifies the significance of this point. In the Gospel narratives, all human beings are leveled insofar as none of them is specially favored in his or her encounter with Jesus. All are needy, even those who minister to Jesus. Apart from divine deliverance, all are threatened by nonbeing. This leveling of human beings in their encounter with Jesus points to the leveling of human beings in relation to God. Natural and historical dualities of life have no significance when one stands before God. This is true not just of humanity in general, but of male and female in particular. All stand before God in need of a Savior.[10]

But there is more to this solidarity than relationship with God. The encounter with Jesus indicates also one's status in relation to other human beings. Just as outer distinctions ultimately count for nothing before God, so they ultimately count for nothing with each other. This does not mean that there are no distinctions between male and female. Rather, it means that if distinctions between male and female carry no weight in relating to God, they carry no weight in relating to each other as creatures of God. What is needed is not to see male priority as a special reflection of the priority of God, but to see all human beings standing together before God and before each other, equally needy and equally hopeful. Whatever the *imago Dei* is, it cannot, according to Barth's own theological definition, single out any group of human beings for special treatment on the grounds that they, by virtue of some outer distinction, occupy a more godlike position than any other. Only one human being ever qualified for special status in relation to God, but even he renounced this possibility in favor of solidarity with other human beings.

Second, Barth's theological definition demonstrates that irreversible priority has but one theologically justifiable context—divine grace. The content of Barth's theological definition supports this point. Gratitude toward God is not automatically demanded of human beings. Only in the context of grace already shown is the expectation of gratitude natural, justifiable, or even intelligible. The irreversible priority of God over humanity is not an arbitrary principle imposed upon human beings. Nor is it immediately observable and thus self-explanatory within the realm of human life. Rather, it appears and has meaning only in the retelling of the story of God's eternal and constant demonstration of grace toward humanity.

Barth's insistence on male priority has no such context. Barth appeals to the givenness of male priority within Scripture and within human experience, presumably in a way similar to the way God's grace is already given in the very fact of human existence. However,

[10]Barth, *Church Dogmatics*, 3/2:295, 320–21.

the question as to why, on theological grounds, there is male priority is not answered by a story about male initiative toward females, a story whose rationality obligates females eternally or even temporally to return gratitude to males. Barth's claim to find within the story of Jesus some basis for male priority will be discussed later in this essay. The point here is that Barth's retelling of the story of God and humanity conveys the dynamic of grace and gratitude and thus supports the concept of the irreversible priority of God over humanity. His discussion of male priority, on the other hand, conveys neither a corresponding dynamic nor a corresponding story by which to make the idea of male priority natural, justifiable, or even intelligible.

The *second major criticism* has to do with Barth's understanding of the *imago Dei*. Barth finds in the priority of male over female a sign pointing to the way God relates to humanity. If Barth were saying that something in the dynamic of human relationships images the Creator, there would perhaps be no problem. Barth might even point to male-female relationships as the primary (because virtually inescapable) instance of this. Instead, he argues that the *imago* is located in human relationships according to a specific pattern. While Barth does not write the actual script, he does draw up clear role configurations—one set for males and the other for females. Males are primarily the initiating, responsible I and are only secondarily Thou in relation to females; females are primarily the subordinate, responsive Thou and are only secondarily I in relation to males. Only within these limitations can one speak of the *imago Dei*.

The theological issue can be clarified by recalling the way Barth speaks of the kingdom of God.[11] Here is a concept which, like the *imago Dei*, finds its fullest embodiment in the person and work of Jesus. The narratives about Jesus convey the event character of this kingdom. The kingdom is not a concept to be defined abstractly, or controlled by means of exhaustive analysis. Rather, it is a happening to be described as well as anticipated by retelling the story of the one who most fully embodies it. It does not restrict itself to the structures of this age, but subverts them. It is dynamic and unpredictable, though it never loses its character as the kingdom of this particular God.

In a similar way, the *imago Dei* is properly an event, fully embodied in Jesus, and fragmentarily (though really) embodied in human relationships. If human beings "have" or "are" the *imago*, it is only as a capacity, though as an essential capacity, which graces human existence. The *imago* is not seen in the formal structure of human

---

[11]See, for example, Barth's discussion of the kingdom of God in *The Christian Life: Church Dogmatics*, 4/4, *Lecture Fragments*, trans. Geoffrey W. Bromiley (Grand Rapids: Eerdmans, 1981), 233-60.

relationships, but becomes visible in the dynamics of interpersonal encounter as it occurs in everyday life. While this encounter happens between male and female, it also happens within other kinds of relationship.

The suggestion being made is that Barth has compromised the freedom of the *imago Dei*. Instead of defining the *imago* as a free and spontaneous (though recognizable) event, he has fixed a set of specific boundaries within which this event takes place. While Barth has not reduced the *imago* to a lifeless concept, he does seem to have inoculated it against any surprise moves from within or without. The movement of Barth's thought in his lengthy excursus on the *imago* is particularly telling in this regard.[12] Barth clearly recognizes the relational aspect of the *imago*. However, by the end of the excursus, it is also clear that he views the *imago* as a possession, something to be owned, and perhaps even measured in terms of an ideal.[13] It begins to resemble timeless truth, rather than a dynamic concept Barth wants to rejuvenate through imaginative reflection on and redescription of the biblical text.

Finally, the *third major criticism* has to do with the grounding of Barth's concept of irreversible male priority. An implication of the first major criticism, discussed above, is that the priority of God over humanity and the priority of male over female are not necessarily linked. Indeed, Barth never claims that his argument for male priority proceeds from the priority of God as such. While he links the two priorities, he does so only indirectly and with many qualifications. On what grounds, then, does Barth argue for male priority? In the course of his discussion, Barth appeals to a number of supporting arguments. He appeals to the importance of order in the creaturely realm. He finds that Scripture assumes such an order between male and female, not just explicitly, but implicitly as well. He finds confirmation in ordered patterns of word usage in Scripture. The constitution of human beings as soul and body offers further illumination and support. Finally, observation and a little knowledge of life will surely keep one on the right track in this regard.

As important as these supporting arguments are, none of them forms the foundation for Barth's position. Here, as always, Barth's chief appeal is to Christological reflection. However, there is a significant difference between his appeals at this particular point and his earlier appeals within the doctrine of creation. In his theological definition of humanity and in the first part of his anthropological definition (the basic form of humanity as cohumanity), Barth's primary

---

[12]Barth, *Church Dogmatics*, 3/1:191-206.
[13]Ibid., 202-5.

focus is on Jesus as an individual.[14] Jesus is the one human being among many, the one whose individual humanity defines the meaning of all human being. Barth bases his earlier reflection on Jesus' humanity as witnessed to in the New Testament, but especially in the Gospels. However, when he comes to the last part of his anthropological definition (the concrete form of humanity as male and female), Barth shifts his focus from Jesus as an individual to Jesus and his community. This Christo-ecclesiological foundation now becomes Barth's point of reference for reflection on the concrete form of cohumanity. Instead of referring all human beings to Jesus as an individual, Barth now refers males to Jesus as Lord of the church, and females to the church.[15] Hence the male is primarily I and the female is primarily Thou in their encounter with each other.

Barth had, in his exegesis of Genesis 1 and 2, already prepared for this shift by saying that just as the man is never without his woman, so Jesus is never without his community.[16] But the full implications of this point do not emerge until his formal discussion of human beings as creatures of God. Given Barth's hermeneutical standpoint, this connection of male and female with Jesus and his community has apparent legitimacy. Barth's standpoint is not that of the primal pair in the Garden, but what he identifies as the truly "primal" history, the event of the Word of God revealed.[17] Hence the basic patterns of the New Testament witness to Jesus and his community cast light all the way back to creation itself, affirming the natural coherence and intelligibility of the Creator's work. Thus, in every part of his doctrine of creation, Barth expects to find, and does indeed find, signs that point to that which gives creation its unity.

However, Barth's method involves working chiefly from one Christological viewpoint at a time. In the doctrine of creation that viewpoint is the humanity of Jesus. The story of Jesus as this particular human being forms the basis for Barth's retelling of the story of creation, particularly the story of human beings as God's creatures. The viewpoint of Jesus' lordship over his community belongs properly to the doctrine of reconciliation, and that story forms a part of the basis for Barth's retelling of the story of reconciliation. Barth seems, in his discussion of the concrete form of humanity, to be looking ahead to the doctrine of reconciliation.[18] The objection is not that

---

[14]Ibid., 55-71, 132-62, 203-22.

[15]An exception to this, which nonetheless reinforces the different status of man and woman, is Barth's exegesis of 1Co 11:1-16. Here he refers both man and woman to Christ—the man to Christ as superordinate and the woman to Christ as subordinate (ibid., 311-12).

[16]Ibid., 205.

[17]Ibid., 3/2:157.

[18]Christina Baxter notes this also in "Scripture in the Church Dogmatics," 35, 58.

themes of reconciliation are alluded to in creation, or even that one viewpoint illuminates the other. Rather, it is that Barth's premature shift of focus to the viewpoint of reconciliation does not allow for the full playing out of the significance of Jesus' humanity within the creaturely realm. Insofar as this shift violates Barth's intention to focus on the humanity of Jesus as an individual, it is questionable, if not unwarranted.

FEMALE AND MALE HUMANITY

Of several ways in which this shift affects Barth's discussion of male and female, one is particularly relevant to this essay.[19] It has to do with Barth's characterization of female and male humanity. It is instructive to read Barth's description of the man and the woman of Genesis 2 in conjunction with his later discussion of cohumanity.[20] The comparison yields the conclusion that Barth has inadequately characterized both the humanity of the woman and the humanity of the man, not primarily because he insists on male priority, but because, even within that frame of reference, he has not found language to describe either the man or the woman as both I and Thou in their encounter with each other. Even though Barth places cohumanity within the context of male priority, he still seems to argue that being human means one is both I *and* Thou in any given relationship. One may not be I and Thou to the same degree within that relationship, but one must be in some way both I and Thou if one is to exist as human rather than inhuman. Barth's identification of the male as primarily I and secondarily Thou, and the female as primarily Thou and secondarily I, would seem to bear this out as his intention.

However, in his discussion of Genesis 2 Barth describes the woman not simply as primarily Thou, but as *only* Thou. She is included in the story only as responsive partner to the man. Apart from this, she has no status as human. Barth's several special definitions of woman confirm this. For example,

The simplest and most comprehensive definition of woman is that she is the being to which man [*Mensch*], himself becoming male [*Mann*], can and must say in the exercise of his freedom that "this" is now the helpmeet which otherwise he had sought in vain but which

---

[19]Others include Barth's absolutizing of the relative, the centrality of marriage, and his use of Scripture. For discussion see Fraser, "Barth's Doctrine of Humanity," 200-222.

[20]This comparison is indirectly suggested by Barth himself, insofar as the language he uses in describing the man and woman of Genesis 2 anticipates his later description of I-Thou encounter.

had now been fashioned and brought by God. . . . This, then, is woman —the one who is so near to the man [*Mensch*] who through her existence has become man [*Mann*], and is therefore so indispensable to him for his own sake. If she were not this to him; if she were neutral, distant and dispensable in relation to him; if she were to him another being, human [*menschliches*] but only feminine, she would not be woman.[21]

Even as the completion of the man, however, this woman is characterized more by what she does *not* do than by what she does. To be human is to engage in reciprocal seeing and being seen. Yet here the seeing is all one-sided; the man as I looks for the woman as Thou and recognizes her. The woman does not actively choose to be seen by the man but is brought to him and presented for him to see, quite apart from any choice on her part. To be human is to engage in reciprocal speaking and hearing. Yet the only voice heard is that of the man, who talks about the woman and speaks his Yes in her presence, but to God, not to her. Thus she does not actually receive his communication, but overhears it. Since she is silent, the man can hardly be said to have heard her own speaking. The woman's most eloquent message is conveyed by her "still, quiet, soft and silent" presence.[22] To be human is to engage in giving and receiving reciprocal aid. However, the chief help in this story comes from the woman, who by her presence somehow helps the man to his full humanity. Finally, and most importantly, to be human is to choose each other in freedom and gladness. Yet clearly the choice and the rejoicing are all the man's. The woman not only does not choose the man, but completes her humanity by refraining from choice.

One might argue that Barth presupposes that the woman is I, since he claims that her humanity as such is presupposed by the Ge 2 account.[23] However, it is not clear on what grounds the woman's humanity might be presupposed. The man's humanity is implied by his I-Thou encounter with God; the woman in Barth's retelling of Ge 2 is not encountered as a living subject by God, but is a passive object —created, and then presented for the man's approval. Barth argues that humanity is not simply a gift, but a task; yet as he describes the woman of Ge 2, she does not take even the first step (reciprocal seeing) in the task of being human. Her alleged humanity is not problematic, even though she, like the man, is also without a partner

---

[21]Barth, *Church Dogmatics*, 3/1:300-301 (English translation unchanged). Similar definitions are on pp. 303 and 309.

[22]Ibid., 329. Elsewhere, Barth sees silence as significant only within the context of speech. See his comments on Jesus' silence before Pilate in vol. 3/2:340.

[23]Ibid., 3/1:303.

in the beginning. The only part of being human for which this woman seems to be prepared is the giving of aid to the man.

Turning to Barth's description of the man, one might expect that if anyone is human in this encounter, it is the man. According to Barth, the male's humanity is completed by God's creation of the female and by the male's own free and glad choice of her. Anticipating his discussion of cohumanity, Barth says that the man has sought, found, recognized, and accepted the woman—not under pressure from without, but as an act of his own freedom.[24] The man is now prepared to enable the woman to complete her humanity (which is also somehow presupposed), just as he has, by choosing her, completed his own.

However, Barth's failure to describe the woman as I in her encounter with the man is matched by failure to describe the man as Thou in his encounter with the woman. As retold by Barth, there is in Ge 2 no point at which the man, as Thou, opens himself to being seen by the woman, is spoken to or even actively listened to by the woman, or is freely chosen by the woman. Although the man receives aid from her, this is not in response to his self-revelation of need; and although the man is subordinate and passive in God's creation of woman, this hardly counts for an encounter with her. Even in his relation to God the man is not fully Thou, since he needs the help of the woman's example in this.

It might appear, then, that Barth has clearly assigned man the role of I, in relation to the woman as Thou. However, even this is debatable. It is true that the man chooses the woman freely and gladly. But the significance of this choice is dimmed by ways the man has not been I in relation to the woman. The man looks at the woman God brings to him; but this is similar to the way he looked at the animals. She is shown to him. It is difficult to make this into an encounter involving reciprocal seeing; the man is not looking the woman in the eye. The man does not address the woman directly but talks about her to God. Since she is silent, he cannot listen actively to her spoken self-disclosure. Since he most needs aid and receives it from the woman, it is difficult to name how he, as opposed to she, is actively taking initiative for the relationship, beyond his choosing of her.

In sum, Barth's descriptions of the man and woman of Ge 2 do not fit Barth's own analysis of cohumanity. Barth does not offer a description of what it means for woman to be I in relation to man, not even secondarily I. Nor does he offer a description of what it means for man to be Thou in relation to woman, not even secondarily Thou. In addition, his description of the man as I is weak. Only with reference to the Song of Songs does Barth describe both man and woman as

---

[24]Ibid., 291.

fully reciprocal partners, but he takes this to be an expression of eschatological hope, the exception which proves the rule.[25] The rest of the time, Barth seems to work with two different definitions of humanity —male humanity and female humanity. According to Barth's own analysis of cohumanity, these can only be forms of inhumanity insofar as each partner does not in some way participate in being both I and Thou within any given encounter. Barth's special definitions of woman bear this out. They are flat and idealistic, lacking in that free give and take over a period of time which is, according to Barth, essential to human existence. The same is true of his description of the man as I. It lacks the risk, conflict, and uncertainty of true initiative and leadership. The man seems to be I simply by virtue of being male, and the woman Thou by virtue of being female.

JESUS' HUMANITY

I began by suggesting that Barth's inability to find the right words for our common humanity is directly linked to his inability to find the right words for Jesus' humanity. We turn now to Barth's description of Jesus' humanity, particularly as embodied in his relation to other human beings, since it is from within this context that Barth proposes to develop his understanding of humanity. Barth is not concerned with the humanity of Jesus as such, since this is not the standpoint of the Gospel accounts. Rather, he is concerned with Jesus' humanity insofar as it is seen in the story of divine deliverance.

Almost immediately the problem with reference to Jesus' humanity becomes visible and can be stated in terms similar to those used of the problem with reference to male and female. Just as Barth does not describe both male and female as both I and Thou with each other in the task of being human, so he does not seem to describe Jesus as both I and Thou in the task of divine deliverance. Barth refers to Jesus in relation to others as I, not as Thou. In his work of salvation, Jesus as the Second Adam is I to the fallen Adam, who is Thou.[26] Jesus is "the archetypal human being whom all threatened and enslaved humans and creatures must follow."[27] He is the head of the body, the one in whom all others have their identity as recipients of divine grace. Only as companions of Jesus do other human beings have their true existence. There is an irreversible order between Jesus and the rest of humanity.

For the existence of the human being [des Menschen] Jesus is not in any sense fortuitous, secondary, or subsequent. It is the true and origi-

---

[25]Ibid., 312-13.
[26]Ibid., 3/2:215.
[27]Ibid., 144.

nal object of the divine election of grace. Apart from God Himself there is nothing that was before it. In the decree of God it is the first thing to which everything else is related and which everything else can only follow.[28]

Barth is emphatic in denying to Jesus the position of Thou. He says that in the New Testament witness Jesus emerges as "a supreme I wholly determined by and to the Thou."[29]

Barth's shift in focus from Jesus as an individual to Jesus and his community reinforces his emphasis on Jesus as I, and is congruent with his emphasis on the male as I. Barth seems to be laying a foundation for the humanity of Jesus (as he is engaged in the work of salvation) to support the male as primarily I and the female as primarily Thou. However, there is a significant difference between Barth's descriptions of the male-female relationship and his description of Jesus in relation to others. When describing male and female, Barth attempts to carry through explicitly his view of male as primarily I and female as primarily Thou. In his account of the relation between Jesus and others, however, Barth combines *assertions* about Jesus as the strong I with seemingly contradictory *descriptions* of Jesus as a strong Thou. The clue that this is the case lies in several pointed similarities between Barth's description of woman as Thou and his description of Jesus' activity in the work of salvation.

First, both Jesus and the woman come from the other. Not only are they physically from the other, but more significantly, the meanings of their lives are determined by the need of the other. In the case of Jesus, this need is salvation; in the case of the woman, it is completion of the man's humanity. Second, both move toward the other. They serve the other, in that everything they do is directed toward meeting the need of the other. Neither Jesus nor the woman considers taking any other role than service for this other. There is no thought of independent action or the fulfillment of one's own potential. Third, neither suffers loss of identity in this service. On the contrary, both Jesus and the woman find true self-identity only in the context of existence on behalf of the other. Finally, both accept this as a task given by God. Jesus' existence is defined by the fact that he is the elect of God, the one chosen to bear the sin of others. The woman's existence is defined by her being doubly chosen. She is the elect of the man and ultimately the elect of God for the man, chosen to complete the man's humanity.

Other similarities between Jesus and the woman are not directly associated with what it means to be Thou, but they support the suggestion that Barth sees Jesus as a strong Thou, in correspondence

---

[28]Ibid., 144-45.
[29]Ibid., 216.

with the woman. For instance, both Jesus and the woman are related to others who are at once alien and familiar. Jesus is related to human beings who are alien because sinful and guilty, yet familiar because even sin cannot obliterate those essential marks of humanity that Jesus shares with his companions. Woman is related to man, in contrast with whom she has an alien origin and nature; her origin is alien because it is outside the man's control, and her nature is alien in its relative autonomy from his. Yet this distance does not prevent the man from recognizing in her something familiar, a part of himself. The second similar pattern is found in Jesus' and the woman's lack of need when compared with the others whom they aid. Jesus' lack of need is his sinlessness. At this point he has no need for reciprocal aid from his companions; they alone are in need of deliverance from sin.[30] The woman's lack of need is seen in Barth's assertion that "in some sense" the woman is human from the beginning. The man's humanity needs completion in that his isolation or solitude has yet to be broken.

Given these similarities between Barth's descriptions of both Jesus and the woman as Thou, the dissimilarity between the same descriptions only underscores the painful truth about Barth's woman. Unlike Jesus, her status as Thou is not based on or connected to her identity as I. Jesus' service to others is portrayed in the language of active solidarity with others. He does not merely offer aid from without or intervene when things are out of control; rather, he interposes himself, gives himself, puts himself in the place of others. In contrast, the woman's help to the man is described as passive existence for the man. Although Barth tries valiantly to make the woman's nonchoice and nonactivity carry the weight of choice and activity, she still serves the man more by her passive presence than by active engagement in life with him. Jesus puts himself in the place of others, in solidarity with them; the woman keeps her place in relation to the man. Jesus allows himself to be determined by the need of others, exercising the free and glad choice of a powerful I. The woman has no such choice but is chosen by God for the man and then chosen a second time by the man.

---

[30]Barth is not saying that Jesus had no reciprocal relationship at all to others. His point here is that the Gospel narratives never portray Jesus as needy in the sense of being sinful. They do portray him as an individual who is both with and from others, but in such a way that he participates in their sin only through voluntary solidarity. On this point see Thomas W. Ogletree's discussion in *Christian Faith and History: A Critical Comparison of Ernst Troeltsch and Karl Barth* (Nashville: Abingdon, 1965), 175-80. Ogletree argues that Barth has left the notion of reciprocity out of Jesus' humanity. While it is true that Barth is inconsistent at this point, it is not true that he omits reciprocity entirely. Rather, the reciprocity of I-Thou encounter is at work in Barth's description of Jesus' humanity as Jesus engages in the work of divine deliverance.

The point is that Barth has not listened to the way Jesus in his humanity is both a strong I and a strong Thou in the work of salvation. He thus misses what his retelling of the story of Jesus makes clear in spite of everything: one cannot be a strong and powerful I unless one is also a strong and powerful Thou. The one entails the other. Given Barth's insistence that Jesus is supremely and only I, one might have expected to find Jesus portrayed as a leader who takes forceful initiative and responsibility for his fallen, helpless companions. Indeed, Jesus does take initiative for fallen humanity. But according to Barth, this means nothing more or less than his free and glad decision to relate to them as Thou, to be identified with them in their guilt and misery. It is precisely Jesus' public role as Thou that gives both offense and credibility to his salvific activity. All of this seeming compromise of Jesus' identity as Savior is exactly what makes him a powerful I, the image of God who is for others. What is true of Jesus' humanity is true of ours. It is impossible to draw a sharp line between what it means to be I and what it means to be Thou in relation to other human beings. Barth's description of humanity is inadequate insofar as it does not recognize that every human being, including Jesus, is both I and Thou in relation to every other human being.

THE PRIORITY OF THE OTHER

But there is more beneath the surface of Barth's retelling of the story of Jesus. What is true of Jesus' humanity is also *not* true of ours. Jesus' humanity is not identical to ours. Only Jesus, in his particular work of salvation, fully embodies what it means to be human in relation to others. As Barth puts it, only Jesus is "totally for others." All other human beings are at best "with others." Barth makes much of the repetition in the New Testament of the simple prepositional phrase "for us," which describes the direction and focus of Jesus' salvific activity. In his relationships with others, Jesus is totally for them. This is ultimately demonstrated in his crucifixion "for our sakes." However, it is also demonstrated in his encounters with others along the way to the Crucifixion. From the very beginning, the Gospel accounts are profoundly other-oriented in their witness to Jesus' work of salvation.

Once again, Barth misses the point. In shifting his focus away from Jesus as an individual to Jesus and his community, Barth shifted his attention away from the Gospel accounts and onto the Pauline Epistles and Ge 2 in order to make a case for irreversible male priority.[31] My suggestion is that he thereby missed the logic of the Gospel

---

[31]For further discussion see Fraser, "Barth's Doctrine of Humanity," 220-32.

accounts, even though that logic can be heard beneath the surface of his retelling of the story of Jesus. According to this logic, truly human encounter happens when one acknowledges the priority of the other, not the priority of the male. Though Barth's fascination with the idea of irreversible male priority is egregious, it is not without at least one feature that confirms this suggestion. That is, the positive impulse that drives male priority is to be the good of the male-female relationship, not the selfish advantage of the male. Stronger confirmation comes, however, from looking once again at Barth's theological definition of humanity. The line of thinking suggested here is already anticipated in Barth's description of the way both Jesus and other human beings relate to God. That is, just as Jesus and other human beings acknowledge the priority of the *divine* Other, so in human relationships they acknowledge the priority of the *human* other. If the priority of God is the inner logic of one's acknowledgment that to be human is to be with God, the priority of the other is the inner logic of the acknowledgment that to be human is also to be with others.

The meaning of the priority of the other is not found by simple transfer of terms used of irreversible male priority. This is not priority based on structural differentiation. It is not the priority of one particular person or group over any other, whether on the basis of gender or some other distinction such as race, religion, economic status, age, or even experience in life. While distinctions like these are constant, tangible reminders of the inescapability of the other, they are not the basis for irreversible ordering of some over others as special reminders of the priority of God. This is not priority based on the assumption that some are needier than others. It is neither the priority of those who seem to have the most to give nor of those who seem to need the most. The priority of the other is not hierarchically determined according to measurable signs of any kind. To establish such a hierarchy would be to invite the static preconceptions and stereotypes that plague Barth's idea of irreversible male priority.

Barth himself offers a way of describing in a positive way what it means to acknowledge the priority of the other. The image of the neighbor, the good Samaritan of Lk 10 who has compassion on his needy companion, appears at various points throughout the doctrine of creation as a way of understanding the dynamics of cohumanity.[32] To affirm the priority of the other is to accept, freely and gladly, the particular help which I need from another person, and to give to him or her, freely and gladly, the help needed from me. This concrete

---

[32]Barth develops the meaning of the neighbor extensively in his discussion of the command to love the neighbor. See *Church Dogmatics*, 1/2:401-54. For further discussion of the neighbor as a model for cohumanity, see Fraser, "Barth's Doctrine of Humanity," 249-56. See also Fraser, "Is Karl Barth My Neighbor?" *TSF Bulletin* (May-June 1986), 11-14.

service, both received and given, is essential to human existence, not just for us as we are "with others," but also for Jesus who is "totally for others." It has nothing to do with irreversible patterns of initiative and response or with attained or fixed priorities of any kind. Instead, it reflects a pattern running throughout the history of God and humanity, the pattern of God taking up, at great cost and great risk, the cause of all human beings including Jesus. This does not mean that one person or group assumes the role of God. Rather, it is simply one human being, even the hated and feared foreigner, reminding another in some concrete, human way, that we are not alone in this world. To be with each other in these sometimes small, but often costly and risky ways reflects the way in which God is with us. These encounters bind us to each other in solidarity which freely and gladly accepts our dependence on each other and offers each other aid in the task of being human. This is genuine I-Thou encounter.

Given the theological assessment undertaken in this essay, this alternative to Barth's irreversible priority of males has several strengths. First, the priority of the other is compatible with the idea that all human beings stand in solidarity not just before God, but before each other—equally needy, equally hopeful, and equally capable of reflecting together the *imago Dei*. Second, the priority of the other has a theologically justifiable context, the story of the compassionate neighbor. This story, which runs through both the biblical text and the stories of our lives, becomes visible and has meaning in the retelling of the story of Jesus as the full embodiment of the compassionate neighbor. This story conveys the everyday dynamic of one person taking up the cause of another in such a way that we discover we are not alone in this world. Third, in its rejection of all predetermined roles, the priority of the other allows for the free, spontaneous, and often surprising appearance of the *imago Dei* within the ordinary and the extraordinary affairs of daily life. Finally, the priority of the other reflects explicitly the relational dynamics of Jesus' humanity as he went about the work of our salvation. Instead of reading the patterns of Jesus and his community back into the meaning of cohumanity, this pattern for Jesus' humanity and ours casts light not just on the relational dynamics of Jesus and his community, but also on the meaning of the church as a human institution.

By drawing on Barth's own thinking in proposing this alternative, I am not suggesting that Barth had it right all along and just did not recognize it. Rather, I hope to underscore an underlying tension in Barth's discussion, one that is more far-reaching than any tension between order and reciprocity. The problem becomes visible once one recognizes that Barth's concept of reciprocity already carries within itself the patterns of irreversible order. In Barth's description of

cohumanity, the perspective of the initiating, primary I predominates. Barth is not describing cohumanity as the encounter of two
people, each of whom is both I and Thou in this encounter.[33] Barth's
understanding of cohumanity thus leaves the door open for the
inhumanity of patronizing, benevolent superiority on the one hand,
and equally controlling, manipulative subordination on the other,
regardless of the gender of the partners involved. Even though Barth
sees the danger with reference to male-female relationships, his
description encourages the kind of thinking that lies behind these
forms of inhumanity. This is at least partly because Barth does not
refer male and female, in precisely the same way, to the full humanity of Jesus. In the end, the most frustrating tension in Barth's
doctrine of humanity is not the apparent tension between irreversible
male priority and reciprocity, but the less visible tension between two
kinds of priority—irreversible priority based on distinctions of any
kind, and the priority of the other which binds us irreversibly to each
other, equally needy and equally hopeful.

---

[33]For further discussion see Fraser, "Barth's Doctrine of Humanity," 174-83.

The Temptation, Sinlessness, and Sympathy of Jesus: Another Look at the Dilemma of Hebrews 4:15

Marguerite Shuster

Pastor, Knox Presbyterian Church
Pasadena, California

Heb 4:15, in its familiar insistence that Jesus is able to sympathize with our weaknesses because he has in every respect been tempted as we are, yet without sin, is a prime example of the consequences of the orthodox doctrine that Jesus is indeed wholly man and wholly God. God cannot be tempted (Jas 1:13). Human beings are not without sin (Ro 3:23). Yet both temptation and sinlessness are attributed to Jesus, in the same sentence, without defense or explanation—a state of affairs that has hardly been characteristic of the later deliberations of the church!

Many of the issues that have occupied theologians examining this verse and its implications are not the direct concern of the present article. It will not deal, for example, with the theoretical question of whether Jesus *could* have sinned (even most authors who answer that question affirmatively at the same time deny that he *actually* sinned)[1]; or with whether the humanity the Son assumed was the

---

[1]For arguments from diverse points of view that Jesus could have sinned, see Karl Heim, *Jesus the World's Perfecter*, trans. D. H. van Daalen (Philadelphia: Muhlenberg, 1961), chap. 7; John A. T. Robinson, *The Human Face of God* (Philadelphia: Westminster, 1973), 94; Helmut Thielicke, *The Evangelical Faith*, trans. and ed. Geoffrey W. Bromiley, 3 vols. (Grand Rapids: Eerdmans, 1977), 2:376-80; Carl Ullmann, *The Sinlessness of Jesus*, trans. Sophia Taylor (Edinburgh: T. & T. Clark, 1901), 158; and Ronald Williamson, "Hebrews 4:15 and the Sinlessness of Jesus," *Expository Times* 86 (1974): 4-8, who considers it conceivable that Jesus actually did sin. On the other side we find Karl Barth, *Church Dogmatics*, trans. and ed. Geoffrey W. Bromiley and Thomas F. Torrance, vol. 1/2 trans. G. T. Thomson and Harold Knight, 4 vols. (Edinburgh: T. & T. Clark, 1956-75), 1/2:158; Friedrich Schleiermacher, *The Christian Faith*, ed. H. R. Mackintosh and J. S. Stewart (Edinburgh: T. & T. Clark, 1928), 413, who claims, "where the inward possibility of sinning is posited, there too is posited in addition at least an infinitely small amount of the reality of sin, in the form of a tendency"; and Peter T. Forsyth, *The Person and Place of Jesus Christ* (Philadelphia: Westminster, 1910), 302-3: "Among all his potentialities that

unfallen humanity none of us has experienced or the fallen humanity we know all too well (a question sometimes argued with reference
to the claim of Gregory of Nazianzus that what Christ did not assume
he could not thereby heal).[2] Nor will it take up the philosophical
issue of whether any possible metaphysical or historical argument
can make a valid judgment regarding the person of Christ or even
regarding what particular acts must be deemed sinful (the problem
being that what has a suprahistorical point of reference cannot be
fully evaluated from within history but may perhaps be grasped only
by faith).[3] This article, rather, is concerned simply to ask if the temptation of Jesus can be conceived in such a way that Heb 4:15 truly serves
the purpose for which it was apparently written: that of both strengthening and comforting believers. Jesus' sympathy provides little
comfort if his temptation was so remote from ours that we cannot
conceive his understanding our trials from within. His sympathy
provides little strength if he capitulated under pressure just as we
capitulate, or if, because of his victory, he scorns us for our failures.

INADEQUATE APPROACHES

Several approaches that have had varying degrees of popularity do
not meet the criteria I have set in the preceding paragraph. Perhaps
the most common, and also the most orthodox, has been to give
$\pi\epsilon\iota\rho\alpha\sigma\mu\acute{o}\varsigma$, as related to Jesus, simply the meaning "testing" (which is,
indeed, a legitimate force of the word), and to understand it as
including "temptation" only in the sense of solicitation by another to
do evil (as when the Devil tempted Jesus in the wilderness). This

---

of sin was not there; because potentiality is only actuality powerfully condensed. . . ."
Forsyth, however, takes the interesting position that the force of Jesus' temptation
may have been related to his not knowing that he could not sin (p. 301). Donald
Baillie, *God Was in Christ* (New York: Scribner, 1948), makes the impossibility an
extreme case of what we say about any good person, that such a one is "incapable" of
an underhanded act; while Hugh R. Mackintosh, *The Doctrine of the Person of Jesus
Christ* (New York: Scribner, 1912), 37, emphasizes "the fruit of continuous moral
volition pervaded and sustained by the Spirit."

[2]The poles here (apart from the ones established by those who do not scruple to
suggest Jesus' actually sinning) are set by the careful wording of Ro 8:3, on the one
hand, which speaks of Jesus assuming the *likeness* of sinful flesh; and the view of
nineteenth-century theologian Edward Irving, who insisted that the Son took on
fallen human nature (see Mackintosh, *Person of Jesus Christ*, 277). Barth, *Church
Dogmatics*, 1/2:153-56, and Dietrich Bonhoeffer, *Christology*, trans. J. Bowden
(London: Collins, 1971), 111-13, both make exceedingly convoluted attempts to have it
both ways.

[3]In Barth's words, "The incarnation is inconceivable, but it is not absurd . . ."
(*Church Dogmatics*, 1/2:160). See the very full and helpful discussion in Reinhold
Niebuhr, *The Nature and Destiny of Man*, 2 vols. (New York: Scribner, 1946), vol. 2,
chap. 3.

approach safeguards absolutely Jesus' purity because it keeps the locus of the πειρασμός entirely external, making it an objective occurrence without any fundamental subjective component. But this is not what we human beings normally label as temptation. I recall once being handed a joint—a marijuana cigarette—at a party. The one who handed it to me may have been tempting me in one sense of the word, but since I had no interest in smoking it, I experienced nothing of the internal struggle in passing it by that we usually consider to be temptation. If that is the only way in which Jesus experienced temptation, then the claim that he can sympathize with us because of what he has gone through carries no force. As Thielicke put it, "If he had not been horrified and shaken by the power of temptation, there would have been no temptation."[4]

Another tack, especially favored in the popular literature that seeks to free Christians from self-destructive guilt-riddenness about every ungodly thought that passes through their minds, is to define sin narrowly and suggest that not having wrong inclinations, but only willfully entertaining or acting upon those inclinations, is sinful.[5] By that definition, Jesus could have been tormented by every sort of fleshly desire, proud ambition, and rebellious impulse against the Father without ever actually sinning. But such a view goes flatly against what Jesus himself taught when he said, for instance, "anyone who looks at a woman lustfully has already committed adultery with her in his heart" (Mt 5:28). Sinlessness is not constituted by a sharp disjunction between thought and act—not even if Jesus were capable of the sort of disjunction of which we have ourselves proved incapable. The desire to sin is sin, and no dictum of mental hygiene can change that fact.

The most radical approach is simply to deny Jesus' sinlessness, insisting that Jesus must have been involved in sin in order to be able to defeat it in a way meaningful and of help to us.[6] Only if he knew sin experientially could his sympathy for our struggles ring true, it is

---

[4]Thielicke, *Evangelical Faith*, 2:378.

[5]Note also the narrow interpretation of Hugh Montefiore, *A Commentary on the Epistle to the Hebrews* (London: Black, 1964), 92: "Probably by sin our author means conscious and deliberate disobedience. . . ."

[6]See Williamson, "Hebrews 4:15 and the Sinlessness of Jesus." Williamson develops his argument by citing texts in Hebrews (e.g., 2:10; 5:8, 9) related to Jesus' growth and learning, asking how one can be "made perfect" if one has been wholly free from sin at the start. See also John Knox, *The Humanity and Divinity of Christ* (Cambridge: Cambridge Univ. Press, 1967). Knox also emphasizes the "developing character" of Jesus' goodness in Hebrews and says, "there is no way of distinguishing Jesus' humanity from ours which does not deny the reality of his manhood in every sense which makes the affirmation of it significant" (p. 106). However, contra Williamson and Knox, immaturity or lack of knowledge or experience is not the same thing as sin: growth and development can be pure.

said. Consider, however, the well-meaning friend or therapist who reassures one that one's impulses are perfectly "normal," at least in the sense of being an unavoidable part of the human condition. While a part of us may be comforted by such reassurances, many times we will find another part of us resisting the comfort. Something in us does not want to be told that what we know is wrong is really okay. We are more and not less suspicious if we know that the person sympathizing with us presumes to understand very well where we are because she has not only experienced the same temptation but has actually succumbed to it. As Reinhold Niebuhr argues, the perfect ideal is *not* irrelevant to our limited human condition. We are not in fact absolutely conditioned or limited but do sometimes transcend our circumstances; and there is no predetermined point at which sin can justify itself.[7] A sympathy based on common failures does not strengthen us in dealing with temptation. Further, the consistent scriptural witness denies any sin in Jesus (Jn 8:46; 2Co 5:21; Heb 7:26-27; 1Pe 2:22; 1Jn 3:5).

If it is true that we cannot identify with a Jesus for whom temptation was a strictly external matter, but that we are forbidden by Scripture and self-knowledge from defining sin narrowly enough to allow him supposedly innocent evil impulses; and if we acknowledge that we are not really strengthened in our own struggles by the sympathy of those who have succumbed to the sin we are fighting; where shall we turn next? Before taking up the matter of Jesus' real sympathy for us, let us look again at the nature of πειρασμός and the nature of suffering.

Πειρασμός

We have already noted that πειρασμός has the force both of "testing" or "trial" and of "temptation"; but we commonly experience and label as temptation only those circumstances, solicitations to do evil, or impulses that arouse in us some internal desire to do wrong. Thus Knox has stated the problem of temptation as follows:

> Is not sin the presupposition or precondition of temptation even when our resistance or God's grace keeps it from being, in overt act, its consequence? Am I really tempted if I do not, however briefly or tentatively or slightly, consent? Have I been really tempted if I have rejected only that which entirely repels me or that from which I stand entirely aloof?[8]

Similarly Thielicke: "susceptibility to temptation is always itself sin, the tempter having already gained a foothold in the ego which is

---

[7]*Nature and Destiny of Man*, 2:75.

[8]*Humanity and Divinity of Christ*, 47.

tempted."[9] Both see temptation without sin as being, logically, a contradiction in terms.[10] But is that conclusion firm?

As background for tackling that question, we must first affirm that Jesus' temptation rests upon his experiencing the needs, limitations, and frailties of a human's body, mind, and circumstances.[11] Those circumstances include the fact that humankind in general is fallen and the world riddled with evil, which impinges upon everyone living in the world, including Jesus.[12] Jesus was neither a phantom nor insulated from the world by a plastic bubble. Thus, when he says in Mk 10:18 that only God should be called good, his words should not be heard as "a veiled confession of moral delinquency." "What Jesus disclaims, rather, is *God's* perfect goodness. None but God is good with a goodness unchanging and eternal; He only cannot be tempted of evil, but rests for ever in unconditioned and immutable perfection."[13] To be subject to limits and weakness and to be affected by evil surroundings is not in itself, however, to have sinned.

Second, we must acknowledge that some temptations would be excluded by Jesus' sinlessness, sins of a sort that relate to questions the author of the letter to the Hebrews was not asking, and hence of a sort that appear not to have been in his mind. Among these would be sins

---

[9]Helmut Thielicke, *Theological Ethics*, ed. William H. Lazareth, 3 vols. (Philadelphia: Fortress, 1966), 1:287.

[10]Thielicke, however, affirms Christ's sinlessness, as a part of the mystery of his deity.

[11]One seventeenth-century commentator (David Dickson, *The Epistle to the Hebrews* [1635; reprint, Edinburgh: Banner of Truth Trust, 1978]) listed the trials to which Jesus was subject as poverty, contempt of the world, being forsaken by friends, exile, imprisonment, hunger, nakedness, watching, weariness, pain, dashing of mind, heaviness of heart, dolor, anguish, perplexity of spirit, and the wrath and curse of God.

[12]See Brooke Foss Westcott, *The Epistle to the Hebrews*, 3d ed. (London: Macmillan, 1903), 108: "Christ assumed humanity under the conditions of life belonging to man fallen, though not with sinful promptings from within." Also Barth, *Church Dogmatics*, 1/2:152: "He was not a sinful man. But inwardly and outwardly His situation was that of a sinful man. He did nothing that Adam did. But He lived life in the form it must take on the basis and assumption of Adam's act." Karl G. Kuhn, "New Light on Temptation, Sin, and Flesh in the New Testament," in K. Stendahl, ed., *The Scrolls and the New Testament* (New York: Harper & Bros., 1957), 94-113, argues further that the concept of πειρασμός has its roots in a state of war between two powers in the world—God and Satan—which allows no neutral position and which means that it is, therefore, specifically believers who are subject to temptation, nonbelievers already being on the other side of the battle.

[13]Mackintosh, *Person of Jesus Christ*, 37. Heim, *Jesus the World's Perfecter*, chap. 7, similarly argues that the Father's goodness is beyond the battle, but Christ's purity is within it. Schleiermacher, *Christian Faith*, 415, takes a more extreme view, arguing that even the smallest amount of struggle involves sin. (The sort of struggle I see as sinless will be elaborated below.)

springing from impulses corrupted by original sinfulness.[14] Also excluded would be sins arising out of sins already committed.[15] Such a limitation does not rob the statement that he was tempted in all ways καθ'ὁμοιότητα of all meaning (whether the words are taken to mean "according to the likeness of our temptations" or "according to his likeness to us"). In no case can we conceive of him undergoing every possible temptation or being precisely like each of us in every detail. Surely the author intended no such rigid literalism.[16] Rather, the point is simply that Jesus entered fully into our human existence, without special privilege or protection.

Third, while denying that Jesus' being "made perfect" implies prior sinfulness (see note 6), we do not need to exclude the positive function of testing in confirming him in righteousness. Jesus, the Second Adam, by successfully withstanding temptation, achieved in this way what the First Adam did not. The possibility of this achievement depended upon his being subject to human frailty and death. Only so could he experience the full meaning of obedience to the Father as a perfect Son in human flesh.[17] Further, we tend to have a healthy suspicion of the reliability of the virtue of those who have lived fully protected lives. We have no confidence in what they might do under pressure. As Mark Twain once put it, the weakest of all weak things is a virtue which has not been tested in the fire. The whole possibility of confirmation in righteousness, though, depends on there being a genuine internal response to temptation that does not deepen but rather repels sin.

Fourth, while it can be argued, and with reason, that succumbing to temptation ultimately increases the hold of temptation and sin on one's life, it is also true that succumbing provides at least temporary respite from one's struggle. The promise of relief is the reason for yielding. Even false hopes for relief are still hopes, and to that extent energizing. Suffering without hope is worse and creates increased pressure to grasp any imagined solution. Thus, it can equally legitimately be argued that only the sinless can experience the full inten-

---

[14]Jean Héring, *The Epistle to the Hebrews*, trans. A. W. Heathcote and P. J. Allcock (London: Epworth, 1970).

[15]James Moffatt, *A Critical and Exegetical Commentary on the Epistle to the Hebrews* (Edinburgh: T. & T. Clark, 1924), 59. Also Westcott, *Hebrews*, 108. Westcott, however, considers it possible that the author's phrase χωρὶς ἁμαρτίας might refer not to the outcome of Christ's temptation but rather to a limitation of this sort upon it.

[16]John H. Davies, *A Letter to Hebrews* (Cambridge: Cambridge Univ. Press, 1967), 49.

[17]Arthur H. Curtis, *The Vision and Mission of Jesus* (Edinburgh: T. & T. Clark, 1954), 131-33.

sity of temptation. "He who falls yields before the last strain."[18] Further, our complicity often obscures even the fact that we are being tempted and thus makes us bewildered by our sin, a bewilderment Jesus does not show. To find the nature of sin obscured by sin, or to experience sin as inevitable, is to fail to know it aright and to miss its full horror, a horror that comes with recognizing that sin is finally gratuitous.

We return to our question, then: How can we conceive temptation without sin? I would suggest that, not just in Jesus' case, but in most cases in a world marred by sin, the outer and the inner aspects of πειρασμός are united around the fact of suffering and that it is suffering (which is not in itself sinful) that initially gives external circumstances or internal longings their tempting power.[19] Take just two examples from the realm of admittedly sinful humanity. When testing is external and visible, as when someone is being tortured, it is perfectly obvious to everyone why a person might be tempted to make whatever "confession" is required to obtain relief. But, to turn to a superficially trivial case, suffering is not absent from the life of the overweight person drawn almost irresistibly to the chocolate mud pie. He obviously is not dying from physical hunger. However, those who cannot control their eating usually are suffering from some much deeper hunger, some gnawing emptiness for which food provides a supposed remedy. The intensity of the struggle comes from the nontrivial nature of the underlying suffering.[20] To fail to recognize that suffering is to be unable to grasp the true nature of the problem. Now it happens that in the letter to the Hebrews, temptation in fact generally refers to the temptation to *avoid suffering*, most specifically the temptation to avoid it by engaging in disobedience or apostasy.[21]

---

[18]Westcott, *Hebrews*, 60.

[19]Emil Brunner, *The Christian Doctrine of Creation and Redemption*, trans. Olive Wyon (London: Lutterworth, 1952), 108, remarks that human sin would be demonic if self-originating, apart from an outside force of temptation and an element of frailty or sensuality, but that through sin temptation comes to reside within. My point will be that that element of frailty—susceptibility to suffering—provides an internal foothold for temptation prior to any sin being committed.

[20]Thus I do not sharply differentiate, as does, for example, Ullmann, *Sinlessness of Jesus*, 125, allurements and sufferings, as if they were fundamentally different sorts of temptation. Allurements, in my judgment, generally promise either to alleviate present suffering or to prevent future suffering (though I grant that the need from which they gain their power may be hidden).

[21]Donald A. Hagner, *Hebrews* (San Francisco: Harper & Row, 1983); Heinrich Seesemann, "πεῖρα, κτλ," in Gerhard Kittel and Gerhard Friedrich, eds., *Theological Dictionary of the New Testament*, trans. G. Bromiley, 9 vols. (Grand Rapids: Eerdmans, 1964-74), 4:23-36. See also Moffatt, *Hebrews*, 59.

TEMPTATION AND SUFFERING

It is almost axiomatic that in a world marked by the Fall, sin and suffering are not precisely correlated. Even if we affirm that suffering can ultimately be traced back to the effects of sin and the consequent curse of creation, a particular instance of suffering cannot necessarily be attributed to one's individual sin. To the contrary, as 1Pe 4:15-16 says, "If you suffer, it should not be as a murder or thief or any other kind of criminal, or even as a meddler. However, if you suffer as a Christian, do not be ashamed. . . ." It is possible to suffer on account of one's faith; and it is also possible to suffer as pure victim, buffeted in one's frailty by the sins of others or by "natural" forces. Further, it not only is not sinful or unworthy, but is positively necessary that, *other things being equal*, one desire to avoid or stop suffering. We call people who seem to get some sort of gratification out of suffering masochists, not saints. Courting suffering for its own sake simply increases its power in the world.

Now take the case of Jesus. We have affirmed that as a man, he was subject to the needs, limitations, and frailties of a human being in this world. He knew physical hardship, frank torture, and the spiritual sense of being abandoned by God. He had a body with nerve endings like ours, emotions that tore him as do ours. That is what it means for him to have been fully human. As Kierkegaard put it, although he freely assumed the "disguise" of human flesh, he came to a certain extent under the power of the disguise, which led to a literal reality of human suffering as intense as if he had been arrested and imprisoned by others.[22]

Not only was Jesus fully subject to every form of human suffering; but one can further argue that he was *more* subject to suffering, on the grounds that the pure—victims and those not hardened by sin—are the only ones who experience evil for what it is, since they have not been taken captive by it.[23] Says Ronald Goetz:

> Christ knows sin as only God can know it: as sin's pure victim. He knows what sin is, precisely because he has not been enticed by its lies. Only the pure victim can truly grasp the truth about sin, for only the victim knows that all of sin's supposed delights are opiates which

---

[22]Noted in Emil Brunner, *The Mediator*, trans. Olive Wyon (Philadelphia: Westminster, 1947), 331-32.

[23]See, for instance, J. K. S. Reid, "Tempted, Yet Without Sin," *Evangelical Quarterly* 21 (1949): 161-67. In a somewhat curious argument, Ceslaus Spicq, *L'Epître aux Hébreux*, 2 vols. (Paris: Librairie Le Coffre, 1952), 2:296 n. 2, carries this thought to an extreme, suggesting that Jesus' very perfection made him more susceptible to all sorts of suffering, of body and of emotion, than others: he identifies perfection with heightened sensitivity even to heat and cold, for example.

deaden the conscience of the sinner, both to his own malignancy and to the agony he inflicts upon others. . . . It is fashionable to suppose that sinners understand sin because "experience is the best teacher." The street-smart ones have a thing or two to teach the children of light about life. What a lie this is. It is not the sinner who knows what sin is. If he did, he would go mad.[24]

The pain that comes from seeing evil truly cannot be relieved by any of the supposed rationalizations or justifications for evil which we use to hide its scope and depth and dominance.

We must repeat the contention that a proper labeling of suffering as evil not only may but must lead, *other things being equal*, to a desire to avoid or stop it.[25] Pain is a warning signal, pointing to something wrong somewhere. To feel no repulsion is not to know, in any humanly meaningful sense, what it signifies.[26] Indeed, the greater Jesus' experience of suffering, the more strongly he must have been repulsed by it and the greater must have been his normal, healthy, sinless desire for escape from it.

Temptation comes when the possibility presents itself of escaping or avoiding suffering (albeit temporarily) *in the wrong way* and with the knowledge that refusing evil will often lead to the increase of earthly suffering. (Which is to say that "other things" are, more often than not, *not* equal.) Jesus had spread before him—by the Devil in the wilderness; by Peter, who chastised him for speaking of suffering and death; by his own soul in the Garden of Gethsemane—the possibility that his mission could be carried out without suffering, that all this pain was not only terrible but unnecessary.

If his body and heart and mind cried out for relief, as he was faced with these supposed options, with all the intensity that ours do, and more besides, since he did not have the temporary relief of capitulation, should we not call that real temptation? (Note Heb 5:7 for the strength of Jesus' feeling: "He offered up prayers and petitions with loud cries and tears to the one who could save him from death. . . .") And yet there is no sin as long as he does not ever, even for a moment, will the accomplishing of that relief by disobedient, sinful means.[27] Indeed, as we have intimated, temptation is perhaps

---

[24]"A New Innocence," *The Christian Century* 99, no. 34 (November 3, 1982): 1095.

[25]Contra Schleiermacher, *Christian Faith*, 415, who denies the legitimacy of any desire or repulsion in response to an awareness of pleasure and pain, because desire or repulsion involves struggle: "the beginning of sin must lie between the moment at which pleasure and pain exist in this sinless way and that at which struggle begins."

[26]See Adolf Schlatter, *Das christliche Dogma* (Stuttgart: Calwer Vereinsbuchhandlung, 1923), 314-15.

[27]C. F. D. Moule suggests the following analogy: "In a desperately long battle, a soldier may yearn with every muscle in his weary body to gain the relief of desertion; but it is possible for him at the same time, never to deviate a hair's breadth from the

greatest exactly at this infinitely narrow boundary between the intense desire to be free of suffering and the sort of capitulation to evil manifested by an inner resonance with a forbidden means. As soon as one experiences the inner resonance, which comes before conscious awareness of having made a choice, at least that much sin is felt as inevitable and at least that much of the struggle is over. But as long as Jesus did not disbelieve God and embrace another, seemingly better or easier way, the struggle continued and there was no sin.[28]

Note the subtlety of the problem here: as Ullmann rightly says, any evil that tempts a non-Satanic nature will *appear* good.[29] But temptations deceive. It it not correct to say with Forsyth that "the only temptation with real power for [Jesus] was a temptation to good—to inferior forms of good"[30] (for instance, to bring in the kingdom by raising an army rather than by dealing with human sin and guilt). At least as far back as Plato, it has been recognized that choosing inferior goods produces not just a smaller quantity of good, but evil. Even if, as Thielicke suggests,[31] Jesus' temptation had been to yield, not in antithesis to his calling, but to further it, his disobedience to God would of course have nullified fulfillment of the calling. We cannot say that because Jesus was faced with alternative *goods*, he could have chosen either alternative and yet have remained sinless. Everything rested upon his unswerving obedience to the Father, counter to the pressing, natural, uncorrupt, but tempting impulses of his flesh. His temptation was not something safely outside and distant, but felt as one feels the stab of a knife or the terror of fear or the desolation of abandonment. But suffering temptation and temptation produced by suffering is not in itself sin, nor does it require that sin have a prior foothold.

SYMPATHY

Let us see, then, how this understanding of Jesus' temptation might meet the goal of bringing us both comfort and strength in our struggles. To emphasize the reality of Jesus' suffering and desire to escape from suffering as a common feature of his human experience and ours provides the beginning of a way to conceive his genuine sympa-

---

steady 'set' of the current of his loyalty to his country or his cause. Physically—even mentally—he may consent to the relief he longs for, but the 'set' of his will remains constant in its direction" (quoted by Robinson, *Human Face of God*, 91).

[28]One might see in the perfect, πεπειρασμένον, an indication of the *duration* of Jesus' tempting/testing: Heb 4:15 does not suggest that he faced only a single hurdle.

[29]*Sinlessness of Jesus*, 124.

[30]*Person and Place of Jesus Christ*, 303.

[31]*Evangelical Faith*, 2:378.

thy for us. Unless he felt something of the pressure we feel, we tend to count his experience as irrelevant to our own and to see any sympathy as looking more like the condescension of a winner toward a loser.

However, the argument has often been mounted that since it was by his sovereign choice that the Son shared in our existence, he was not trapped in it as we are; and thus his experience was fundamentally different from ours. Take the famous example of Tolstoy, who sought to show his love for his serfs by putting himself on the same social footing and sharing in their life-style. Despite his efforts and whatever hardships he suffered in consequence, his serfs did not acknowledge his actual solidarity with them. The essential thing was missing. Tolstoy, being of the aristocracy, was free at any time to go home.[32] Must we say the same with respect to Jesus?

Granting that the Son freely and out of love chose to become incarnate, it does not necessarily follow that, like Tolstoy, he could at any moment, and without deadly consequence, retreat to the security of heaven. Once a choice has been made, one cannot always simply retract it. Father Damian freely went to Molokai; but having contracted leprosy, he could not thenceforward act as if nothing had changed. Recall Kierkegaard's contention that Jesus in some sense came under the power of the incognito he assumed. Consider the possibility that having come to us, he could not thereafter escape suffering without disobedience to the Father, without sinning. His solidarity with us was real. At that point the battle was no sham.

We acknowledge, though, that Jesus won the battle. Does it then follow that he will scorn us when we lose it? In this regard, it is precisely Jesus' difference from us, his sinlessness, rather than his similarity to us, that makes full sympathy possible.

To see why, take the opposite case, that of sinners who overcome particular temptations. Gordon Liddy wrote in his autobiography of how he managed to overcome his excessive boyhood fears by confronting them. To overcome his fear of rats, he ate one; to conquer his fear of electrical storms, he lashed himself sixty feet up on a seventy-five foot pin oak in the midst of violent wind and lightening; and so on. As a result of the fact that he was able to triumph over his own weakness, he became contemptuous of those who did not.[33]

Similarly, consider the case of a much-decorated hero of the Vietnam War, who in this place shall remain nameless on the grounds that he has surely already suffered enough. He was held as a prisoner

---

[32]This example is noted by Heim, *Jesus the World's Perfecter*, 80, and Thielicke, *Evangelical Faith*, 2:379.

[33]Noted in Robert C. Roberts, "Compassion," *The Christian Century* 100, no. 1 (January 5-12, 1983): 15.

of war for more than seven years, during which time his captors used all their brutal skill to get him to talk. A man of iron will, he resisted every assault, though he will never fully recover from the injuries inflicted upon him. Others held captive in the same place lacked his strength. They capitulated, sooner or later, and said whatever needed to be said to alleviate their pain.

The day finally came when many of them—the hero and others— at last came home. All were warmly welcomed; and those who had capitulated under pressure were not punished. Now, what is significant at this point for our argument is that the hero was very critical of the government for letting his weaker brothers off. He hadn't given in; they shouldn't have either. He wanted them to pay for their failure. We can, perhaps, understand his feeling? On the outside, it looks like a reasoned concern that if there are no consequences for breaking down under torture, people will break down sooner and sooner threaten the national security. But deep on the inside we might suppose that he wondered, at least for a moment, if holding out had been worth the cost, when those other guys got off scot free.

Under such circumstances, only one who is not the captive of the deceptions of sin and is not in competition with us is really free to be sympathetic.[34] Only such a one is not afraid that someone, somehow, may have gotten a better deal. Only such a one sees clearly that succumbing to temptation does not in fact deal with the underlying evil which is the source of the temptation. Eating a gooey dessert may actively prevent one from dealing with the real source of one's emptiness. "Confessing" to the enemy gives aid precisely to those who have caused one's pain. The promises held out by tempters are lies. The relief they promise is finally illusory. Like all the Devil's bargains, they trade short-term gains for long-term losses. But we sinners keep missing that truth. Participating in sin does not increase sympathy but dulls it by obscuring the idea of evil.[35] And personal guilt prevents us from escaping ourselves, from emptying ourselves sufficiently to offer sympathy freely to others.[36]

Thus, exactly because Jesus truly suffered and was truly tempted but was not finally deceived, he is able to sympathize with us in our weaknesses and temptations. Knowing both our pain and the ultimate deadly futility of the expedients we choose, he neither condemns nor excuses us. His sympathy, which gives both comfort and strength, depends precisely upon his both being, and not being, a human being like us.

---

[34]Regarding competition as obviating sympathy, see Donald P. McNeill, Douglas A. Morrison, and Henri J. M. Nouwen, *Compassion* (Philadelphia: Westminster, 1983), 20.

[35]Westcott, *Hebrews*, 60.

[36]Forsyth, *Person and Place of Jesus Christ*, 302.

Therefore, since we have a great high priest who has gone through the heavens, Jesus the Son of God, let us hold firmly to the faith we profess. For we do not have a high priest who is unable to sympathize with our weaknesses, but we have one who has been tempted in every way, just as we are—yet was without sin. Let us then approach the throne of grace with confidence, so that we may receive mercy and find grace to help us in our time of need. (Heb 4:14-16)

The Order of Temptations in *Paradise Regained:* Implications for Christology

Anthony C. Yu

Carl Darling Buck Professor in the Humanities
The University of Chicago

The story of the temptations of Jesus has been variously treated in the New Testament. Mark, in its characteristic terseness, devotes only two verses to the subject (1:12-13) that amount to no more than a summary. Providing a much lengthier account, the other two of the Synoptic Gospels agree on all essential features but diverge partially in the order of presentation. Both Matthew (4:1-11) and Luke (4:1-13) begin with the temptation of changing stones to bread; thereafter Matthew follows with the temptations of Jerusalem's temple and of empire, whereas Luke reverses the order and ends the account with the episode of the temple's pinnacle.

That the biblical account forms the basic plot of *Paradise Regained* is familiar to all students of Milton. Why the poet chose to follow Luke's version instead of Matthew's is, however, a question that continues to intrigue, particularly in view of the latter book's preeminent position in the canon and in the history of biblical interpretation before the challenge to its priority was mounted by critical scholarship. In seeking to understand the poet's choice, modern criticism of Milton has often sought to establish the preference for Luke's order on the basis of its correspondence with other aspects of Christian doctrine or exegesis. Thus for those who would see in Jesus' experience a victorious recapitulation of that undergone by the first human couple in Paradise, Milton's is a poem that perfectly mimes the "triple equation" obtaining between Luke's account and the temptations of Eve, the elaboration of which itself is derived directly from 1Jn 2:16 (the lust of the flesh [bread/hunger vs. fruit/desire], the lust of the eye [sight of fruit vs. sight of empire], and the pride of life).[1] For other critics who would argue that the wilderness experience of Jesus provides the inaugural ordeals that launch him on his public ministry, the three temptations of both source and poem essentially test the

---

[1] Elizabeth Pope, *Paradise Regained: The Tradition and the Poem* (New York: Russell & Russell, 1947).

readiness of the incarnate Christ in relation to the offices he must assume: prophet, king, and priest.[2] In such a view, the poem's structural pattern is finally determined by the venerable practice of typological exegesis of Scripture.

In any attempt to address this problem of the poet's inventive use of his source, there can be little doubt that Milton is both steeped in the lore of Christian theology and profoundly responsive to antecedent tradition. Even for seventeenth-century England, a period marked by the greatest proliferation of writers embodying the most successful union of religious and literary sensibilities, Milton still remains a near unique example of poetic prowess and theological acumen. His mature compositions, as modern scholarship has thoroughly documented, consistently enlist talent and erudition to probe and illumine many of the cardinal but vexing themes of his faith.

Even with such commonplace allowance for the decisive role of theology in shaping Milton's poetic art, however, it is hard to acknowledge that the plotting of *Paradise Regained* owes its organizing principle primarily to the poet's desire to honor a particular strand of tradition. Once the Lukan account is chosen as the more appropriate source, of course, the biblical text would impose its own formal constraint on the poetic construct. Indeed, the poem everywhere suggests that its author is very much aware of the impingement made by traditional exegesis (triple equation, typology) on his source. Nonetheless, it is difficult to believe that a poet daring enough to rearrange Scripture (as when he makes Adam's request for a mate in *Paradise Lost* 8.363-66 and 383-91 the initiative to woman's creation, a request subsequently endorsed by the Deity's own assessment of the essential privation in man's solitary condition [PL 8.445, citing Gen 2:18]) would write in mere conformity to a prior schema of interpretation, however crucial and estimable that schema might be. Milton, in other words, must have seen something in the Lukan account itself, in contrast to the Matthean, that is more genial to the conception of his poem, to the way he wants to tell the story of Christ's temptations. In that regard, moreover, the typological correspondence to prophet,

---

[2]The definitive study here is Barbara Kiefer Lewalski, *Milton's Brief Epic: The Genre, Meaning, and Art of "Paradise Regained"* (Providence, R.I.: Brown Univ. Press, 1966). Cf. also Howard Schultz, *Milton and Forbidden Knowledge* (New York: Modern Language Assoc. of America, 1955), and "A Fairer Paradise? Some Recent Studies of *Paradise Regained*," ELH 32 (1965): 275-302; Michael Fixler, *Milton and the Kingdom of God* (London: Faber and Faber, 1964). In the most recent book-length study of the epic, John T. Shawcross of *Paradise Regain'd: Worthy T'Have not Remained So Long Unsung* (Pittsburgh: Duquesne Univ. Press, 1988) reaffirms the structural schematics of both Pope and Lewalski. His own interpretation of the poem's structure, however, is based on this understanding: "the first temptation investigates man's relationship with the self; the second, with community; the third, with his God." See pp. 45-58.

king, and priest by itself hardly provides a binding order of presentation, since this sequence of office varies interchangeably among biblical commentators and even within the discourse of a single author.

This brief study of the order of temptations in *Paradise Regained*, therefore, seeks to address the problem by focusing once more on the poem's internal constraints, on how the poet seems to have crafted his story in response to the particular biblical text. At the same time, the study will compare certain aspects of the poem to one possible but neglected source, *The Combate Between Christ and the Devill Expounded*, by the Puritan divine William Perkins (1558-1602).

The choice of Perkins is dictated by both the man and the work. Though he died six years before Milton was born, Perkins and his writings were held in such high esteem in England and on the Continent that they continued to exercise a strong influence on the circle of Puritan thinkers gathered at Cambridge.[3] His collected works were found in the library of Nathan Paget (1615-79), a physician who befriended Milton and who might have leased his house to the poet in 1651.[4] Written as a homily on Mt 4:1-11, *The Combate* is arguably the longest treatment of Christ's temptations by a Protestant thinker prior to Milton's own poem. Indeed, as we shall see, there are important similarities surfacing in both Perkins' and Milton's thought on the subject that might indicate a certain common context of understanding.

One notable thread of that context concerns the exact meaning of the title "Son of God," which Jesus was declared to be by the voice from heaven during the baptism episode. In Matthew, that episode is followed at once by the account of the temptations. Like many precritical commentators who envisage a literal and direct continuity of the Gospel narrative at this point, Perkins' discussion of the events in the first part of chapter 4 rests on the assumption that the narrative continuity betokens a deeper inner logic linking the two episodes. The temptations of Jesus arise from a necessity that can be differently discerned in either the divine or the demonic perspective.

As far as the Devil is concerned, the baptism of Jesus provides the immediate cause of his action. That incident precipitates a crisis of knowledge because he needs to know what is the true identity of this person whose lineage has received such a miraculous, public declaration. Thus Perkins writes:

> . . . hee [the Devil] knew well, that if Christ were the true and proper sonne of God, then hee must needs be the true Messias; and if he were the annointed of God, then also hee it was that must accomplish that

[3]Christopher Hill, *Milton and the English Revolution* (New York: Viking, 1977), 32-37.
[4]Ibid., 492-95.

old and ancient promise made to our first Parents for the bruising of the serpents head. This was the thing that of all other the Devill was most afraid of, and could not indure to heare. . . .[5]

That similar reasoning underlies Milton's portrayal of Satan's character and motivation is apparent from the first moments of his brief epic. Although Luke inserts some sixteen verses of genealogy of Jesus (3:23-38) between the episodes of his baptism and temptation, it is clear as well that Milton's conception of his story at this particular point seems to presume the Matthean logic, since he does not envisage a break between the two incidents.

In contrast, however, to Matthew's genealogy which stresses Jesus' Jewish descent by linking him only with Abraham and David, the Lukan catalog traces Jesus' forebears back to the original creation, to Adam now named by the evangelist (3:38) as the descendent or son "of God" (τοῦ θεοῦ). Such broadening of the line of descent places an emphasis on the common humanity of Jesus that in turn might have given further impetus to the debate on the meaning of sonship structured in the poem. If Adam already enjoyed such a nomenclature, what is so special about this late descendent of his when he is declared to be "son of God"? Thus upon introducing Jesus as "the Son of Joseph" who came to the river Jordan "as then obscure, / Unmarkt, unknown" (PR 1.24-5),[6] the narrative immediately switches to Satan, who happens to be circling the air above the earth and thus has overheard the divine proclamation of Jesus' status. Haunted by the threat of the protoevangelium and the more recent realization that "the Womans seed / . . . is late of woman born" (PR 1.64-65), Satan tells his crew that "Who this is we must learn, for man he seems / In all his lineaments, though in his face / The glimpses of his Fathers glory shine" (PR 1.91-93). Throughout the poem, then, the burning issue for Satan is whether he can discover the exact identity—and hence the nature—of this man Jesus. The frustration of his repeated attempts understandably drives him to ever more desperate and dangerous means.

---

[5]William Perkins, "The Combate between Christ and the Devill Expounded," in *The Vvorkes*, 3 vols. (London: I. Legatt, 1626-31), 3:382. Hereafter page number will be indicated in the text immediately after citation.

[6]All citations of Milton are taken from *The Student's Milton*, ed. Frank Allen Patterson (New York: Appleton-Century-Crofts, 1930). Cf. Perkins' comment at this point: ". . . so long as Christ was a private man he lived with Joseph and Marie a private life; but being baptized, and thereby installed into the office of Mediator, he returns not to Bethlehem or Nazarett where he was borne and brought up, but gets him presently into the wildernesse, there to encounter Satan" (3:374). Citations of *Paradise Lost, Paradise Regained,* and *Samson Agonistes* in this essay are abbreviated as PL, PR, and SA respectively.

If *Paradise Regained*, in comparison with the "cosmic grandeur" of its epic antecedent, appears "bleakly simple" to a modern critic,[7] the biblical source of Milton's poem is even more stark and laconic. According to Matthew's matter-of-fact narration, "then was Jesus led up of the spirit [identified more specifically by Luke as the Holy Spirit] into the wilderness to be tempted of the devil."[8] There is no explanation offered either before or after the episode as to why Jesus must undergo such an experience. The ostensibly motiveless character of the narrative, in fact, is what renders it especially hospitable to interpretation, for exegetical theology has always felt obliged to plumb the fateful significance of this simple and yet highly dramatic encounter between the incarnate Christ and his tempter.

The history of biblical exegesis has long advanced the opinion that the temptation experience provides an indispensable initiation readying Christ for his entire redemptive ministry. Thus John Calvin offers two reasons for "Christ's withdrawal into the wilderness: the first, that after a fast of forty days He should as a new, indeed a heavenly, man advance to the pursuance of His task, and the second, that only after He had been tested by temptations, after His preliminary training, would He be equipped for such an arduous and distinguished mission."[9] On the other hand, a writer like Perkins directly links the temptations to the nature of the redemptive task itself, for Christ must somehow undo satanic success wrought in the first humans.

> And therefore was Christ led by the spirit to encounter with the Devill, that hee might performe this one work of a Mediator, namely in temptation overcome him, who by temptation overcame all mankinde.
>
> (Perkins, 3:373)

Keenly sensitive to the symmetrical analogy joining the two Adams and all the nuanced ramifications of this Pauline theme, Milton's poem gives explicit and emphatic definition to his self-appointed task at the very beginning.

> I who e're while the happy Garden sung,
> By one mans disobedience lost, now sing
> Recover'd Paradise to all mankind,
> By one mans firm obedience fully tri'd
> Through all temptation, and the Tempter foil'd

---

[7]Hill, *Milton and the English Revolution*, 414.

[8]All biblical citations in this essay quote the AV.

[9]*A Harmonie of the Gospels Matthew, Mark and Luke*, trans. A. W. Morrison, 2 vols. (Grand Rapids: Eerdmans, 1972), 1:133.

> In all his wiles, defeated and repuls't,
> And *Eden* rais'd in the wast Wilderness.
>
> (1.1-7)

The key words in this sentence are *man, obedience, temptation,* and *paradise,* all of which forging thematic links with the former and longer epic of *Paradise Lost.*

Concerning the person of Christ, the brief epic gives unambiguous focus to his humanity. As far as the poetic narrator is concerned, the long promised "Greater Man" of *Paradise Lost* has finally appeared and is now the subject of this poem. Even when he is mentioned by God, Jesus is described as "This perfect Man, by merit call'd my Son" (1.166). Concerning his work, what is stated in the poem sheds light also on what is not. While critics fret about the lack of any reference to the Crucifixion in *Paradise Regained,* the Father specifies what task is assigned to Christ. In the poem's precise context, Jesus is not charged with saving humankind from the penalty of disobedience, for that would involve the Atonement, but only with the recovery of Paradise, the edenic condition lost to the first couple when they fell but subsequently promised to Adam as a displaced, internal state: "A Paradise within thee, happier farr" (PL 12.587). To accomplish this, Jesus is sent forth to "resist / All . . . sollicitations" of the Devil, "Winning by Conquest what the first man lost" (PR 1.154).

The limitation of the poetic action is thus grounded first upon the crucial fact that Christ is seen to be a man and that he is expected to accomplish this part of his earthly mission as a man. Though military metaphors show up in the Father's speech, they are not meant to associate the subject of his discourse with the preincarnate Son's heavenly warfare that crushed the revolt of Satan (PL 5 and 6). The battle plan prescribed here is "By one mans firm obedience fully tri'd / Through all temptation," the completion of which would signal the defeat and repulsion of the Tempter. If in *Paradise Lost* Milton sought to construct a poetic theodicy based on the fundamental premise that evil can never limit, stymie, or exhaust the resourcefulness of the good, hence the Divine is continuously depicted as capable of action that transforms, saves, and salvages, his intentions in his brief epic seem no less fervent in striving to uphold the honor and wisdom of his God.

To "justifie the wayes of God to men" within his second epic's highly specific confines, however, requires another attempt at the justification of human nature. He has to show, bluntly put, that God did not make a mistake or fall short of his own ideal in the creation of Adam and Eve. It is not enough, as the received tradition of Christian theology has generally held, that a uniquely costly means of redemption was devised for man's salvation even prior to the Fall[10]; and thus the entire line of theological argument epitomized by the so-called *felix culpa* motif, in my judgment, has but limited appeal to Milton's thinking. His reticence to devote any major poetic effort to the treatment of Christ's passion may signal a similar reservation on his part. Because primal human failure is for Milton an ineradicable fact of history as he knows it, he feels much more obliged, when the opportunity arises in a poem like *Paradise Regained*, to demonstrate that a human qua human[11] can withstand the most seductive and severe test of temptation. Only this can redeem the worth and wisdom of the original creation. This concern explains the prominent allusions to Job in the poem that all critics have noticed, but Job's qualified success seems only to intensify the zeal of Milton's God. The man Jesus now occasions a new and decisive wager with the Devil.

> To show him worthy of his birth divine
> And high prediction, henceforth I expose
> To Satan; let him tempt and now assay
> His utmost subtilty. . . .
> He now shall know I can produce a man
> Of female Seed, far abler to resist
> All his sollicitations. . . .
>
> (1.142-52)

The ability to resist is premised on a paradox of Christian existence favored by Milton: strength derived from the weakness of utter dependence on the Divine.[12] Though the wilderness experience is planned by the Father as a staging moment when Christ "shall first

---

[10]Book 3 of *Paradise Lost* makes high drama of the Deity's self-deliberations in the persons of the Father and the Son. The poetic utterances that foreordain humanity's redemption may have the ring of Calvinism, but the theological cast of Milton's prose and poetry is not easy to pin down, as it runs the gamut of Reformed theology—mainstream and radical, Calvinist and Arminian. See Hill, *Milton and the English Revolution*, 233-340; Dennis Richard Danielson, *Milton's Good God: A Study in Literary Theodicy* (Cambridge: Cambridge Univ. Press, 1982).

[11]It is necessary to skirt the consideration here of the two natures of Christ and all the attendant speculative formulas enshrined in the history of Christian thought. Milton's view on the matter is unusual to say the least, if not downright heretical. His position taken in the prose treatise, *On Christian Doctrine*, has been shown to harbor shades of unorthodox opinions such as Nestorianism and Adoptionism. See Lewalski's informative survey in chap. 6 of *Milton's Brief Epic*. On the other hand, *Paradise Regained* is not a poem about the possible varieties of Christology.

[12]Cf. John M. Steadman's account of Milton's use of Paul in *Milton and the Renaissance Hero* (Oxford: Clarendon, 1967), 36: "In his blindness, he takes the Pauline text ('My strength is made perfect in weakness') as a personal motto and inscribes the Greek words ἐν ἀσθενείᾳ τελεῖται in two different autograph albums in 1651 and 1656."

lay down the rudiments / Of his great warfare" before he is actually sent "To conquer Sin and Death" (1.157-59), the mode of operation remains the same throughout the Son's earthly career: "By Humiliation and strong Sufferance: / His weakness shall o'recome Satanic strength / And all the world" (1.160-62).

This second limitation of action that necessitates the poetic emphasis on Christ's passivity[13] finds correlative extension in the constraint of the form in which he is to encounter Satan. Milton's biblical source already stipulates a dialogic confrontation, but the apposite nature of such a meeting is enlarged by the poet's own interpolations. The first lines of Christ's soliloquy as he appears in the poem (1.196-98)—

> O what a multitude of thoughts at once
> Awakn'd in me swarm, while I consider
> What from within I feel my self,—

convey the kind of premonitory intimation that also suggests divine prompting in a literary hero poised on some great enterprise. His utterance looks toward the words of the Miltonic Samson just before the latter proceeds to Dagon's temple:

> . . . I begin to feel
> Some rouzing motions in me which dispose
> To something extraordinary my thoughts. . . .
> If there be aught of presage in the mind,
> This day will be remarkable in my life
> By some great act, or of my days the last.
>   (SA 1381-89)

Samson's utterance in turn recalls the old, blind Oedipus of Sophocles' tragedy. Begging the gods for "some great consummation" (καταστροφήν τινα) for his life, he recognizes, when the end does arrive, his inward stirring as the god driving him on (ἐπείγε γάρ με τοὐκ θεοῦ παρόν—1540) and leads, unassisted, his daughters and his benefactor Theseus to his final resting place at Colonus. The intertextual resonance of Samson and Oedipus strikes an especially suggestive chord, since both their dramas are built on the urgent, desperate need to wrest some meaning from their devastating experience of humiliation and suffering. Only the recovery of a sense of divine purpose will enable each of them to seal his shipwrecked existence with one, climactic heroic act that will at the same time bequeath lasting benefits to his community.

---

[13]Cf. Stanley Fish, "Things and Actions Indifferent: The Temptation of Plot in *Paradise Regained*," in *Milton Studies* 17, ed. Richard S. Ide & Joseph Wittreich (Pittsburgh: Univ. of Pittsburgh Press, 1983): 163-86.

The life of Milton's Christ, of course, has no need of salvage, but like his biblical and classical counterparts, the hero of this brief epic stands at the threshold of a perilous, momentous conflict, of which its imminent occurrence and purpose, however, he is at the moment unaware (PR 1.291-93).[14] In the retrospective and prospective reaches of the long soliloquy (PR 1.196-293) that surveys what Jesus knows of himself, his upbringing, and what he anticipates to accomplish in the world, the hero reveals both political zeal ("To rescue *Israel* from the *Roman* yoke") and a dawning Messianic consciousness ("what was writ / Concerning the Messiah, to our Scribes / Known partly, and soon found of whom they spake / I am"). His knowledge sheds further ironic light on satanic tactics about to be deployed: whereas Satan, perpetually racked by doubt and uncertainty, seeks to acquire a knowledge that would, if granted, confirm his doom, Christ knows the telos of his life, his serenity buoyed by the conviction that divinely prescribed goals are to be achieved only by lawful and timely means. Most important of all, his meditation gives voice to the cherished Miltonic preference, particularly after the failure of the Puritan revolution, for pacific means to do God's work. Instead of seeking to overthrow "proud Tyrannick pow'r" by violence, his Christ holds "it more humane, more heavenly first / By winning words to conquer willing hearts, / And make perswasion do the work of fear" (221-23).

This last and third limitation of the action clarifies the nature of the "deeds / Above Heroic" which the poet seeks to tell. That the temptations of Jesus must in some way reenact the experience of the first human couple but reverse its result is arguably a motif firmly embedded in even the most primitive Christian documents, the two Synoptic Gospels themselves. If in Milton's interpretation of the Fall his Eve and Adam suffer calamitous defeat in a verbal contest over the interpretation of God's specific commandment and prohibition, his poetic Christ can recover Paradise only if he could prove himself to be Satan's superior in this "rematch." If it can be said of his Eve that Satan's "words replete with guile / Into her heart too easie entrance won" (PL 9.733-34; cf. 550),[15] the man Jesus must show himself "greater" in being able to resist and block such entry. Christ's affirmation of "winning words" and "perswasion" thus not only reveals

---

[14]Don Cameron Allen, in *The Harmonious Vision: Studies in Milton's Poetry* (Baltimore: Johns Hopkins Press, 1954), 119, speaks of Christ here standing "on the threshold of an extreme expectancy."

[15]Commenting on the first temptation in the Gospel account, Perkins draws specific parallel with Eve's experience in Genesis: "first hee labours to weaken her faith in the truth of Gods threatning; which done, he easily brought her to actual disobedience" (3:381). A small point of interest here is the word "easily" used by both Perkins and Milton.

his understanding of verbal potency,[16] but it also defines in anticipation the form of action he will take in the coming agon of wit and rhetoric.

Perceiving the limitations that the poet has structured on the action also enables us to see more clearly the shape of its progressive development. The history of biblical interpretation has variously classified the temptations of Jesus. "A former generation" to John Calvin, according to that theologian, understood Matthew's account of the temptations as those of gluttony, ambition, and greed.[17] William Perkins, on the other hand, speaks of "three great conflicts . . . tending to bring Christ to unbeliefe, . . . to presumption, . . . [and] to idolatrie" (3:370). For Milton, however, the overarching issue of all three episodes can still be summed up in the matter of obedience. Since obedience or faith must have its own object, the prominence of Scripture in his biblical source is, for him, no accident, for the Second Adam is there confronted repeatedly with the necessity of deciding what constitutes the proper response to, and use of, the word of God.[18]

In the initial speeches to Christ (1.320ff.; 337ff.) by Satan disguised as an "aged man in Rural weeds,"[19] the attack at once focuses on Jesus' new and publicly declared identity as the Son of God and on the problem of trust in God's providence made more acute by that identity. Satan's challenge to turn stones to bread is occasioned not merely by the attested hunger of Jesus after forty days fasting (Lk 4:2), but it is also built upon the danger of wilderness, a poetic interpolation. So treacherous and desolate is the immediate region in which the two strangers find themselves that Satan, in response to Christ's declared faith in God's guidance (PR 1.335-36), can assert that only a miracle (1.337) can assure his interlocutor safe passage. The logic appears both swift and keen: if you happen to be the Son of God, why not act to relieve your legitimate need, an act that will at the same time deliver you from the environing peril?

---

[16]Some recent articles on this theme are Elaine B. Safer, "The Socratic Dialogue and 'Knowledge in the Making' in *Paradise Regained*," in *Milton Studies* 6, ed. James D. Simmonds (1975): 215-26; Leonard Mustazza, "Language as Weapon in Milton's *Paradise Regained*," in *Milton Studies* 18 (1983): 195-216.

[17]*A Harmonie*, 1:136.

[18]For a comprehensive treatment of this topic, see Mary Ann Radzinowicz, "How Milton read the Bible: The Case of *Paradise Regained*," in *The Cambridge Companion to Milton*, ed. Dennis Danielson (Cambridge: Cambridge Univ. Press, 1989), 207-23.

[19]Cf. Perkins' gloss on the phrase, "the Tempter came unto him": "by which phrase is probable, though not certaine, that the Devill tooke upon him the forme of some creature, and appeared unto Christ" (3:381).

The glosses which Milton has his Christ elaborate on the cited Deuteronomic text (8:3) to counter Satan's ploy bear the symmetry of biblical typology. The wilderness of Israel's experience is archetypical precisely because it has always been the testing ground for the community's faith in God's providential sustenance; hence the fitting allusion to Moses and Elijah, to manna and other heaven-sent provisions. Christ's rebuttal not only rejects any ground for "distrust" but also hoists Satan with his own petard. Instead of gaining the knowledge he seeks on the Son's true identity, he is compelled to reveal something of himself: "I am that Spirit unfortunate" (1.358). The lengthened debate that closes the epic's First Book continues to show satanic semblance unmasked by the Son's discernment, ending with the deft poetic insertion of a theme of patristic theology into Christ's words. With Christ's advent, pagan oracles deemed the mouthpiece of Satan are all silenced.[20] Had Satan been a more alert student of historical theology in the poem's ironic anachronism, this decisive pronouncement of Christ (1.455ff.) might well have been a dead giveaway as one clear indication of the Son's self-revelation. As it was, the poetic "Fiend" was "inly stung with anger and disdain" and ready to try his hand once more.

The redoubled efforts of Satan begin with another demonic council. Belial's suggestion to "Set women in [Christ's] eye and in his walk" (2.153), actually a foil to Satan's greater cunning, is quickly rejected. Biblical history may attest to a string of such prominent figures as Adam, Samson, and Solomon falling prey to their "Wives allurement," but Satan has already perceived that the target of their plotting is "wiser far / Then *Solomon*" (2.205-6). Demonic sexism demands more subtle tactics:

> Therefore with manlier objects we must try
> His constancy, with such as have more shew
> Of worth, of honour, glory, and popular praise;
> Rocks whereon greatest men have oftest wreck'd;

---

[20]Lactantius (*Divine Institutes* 2.16) considers pagan oracles to be devils posing as gods. Origen (*Contra Celsus* 7.3) and other Christian writers sought naturalistic explanations for the prophetic ecstasy of the priestess at Delphi. Milton's fondness for this theme already surfaced in his early poem, "On the Morning of Christ's Nativity" of 1629. The fifth-century Spanish poet Prudentius describes (in his *Apotheosis*) the flight of the pagan gods from their shrines at Christ's birth. But the crucial source for Milton's poetic assertion here seems to be Eusebius, *Preparation for the Gospel* (5.18-36; 6.7), which details pagan denunciations of the oracles and their silence upon Christ's first advent. Plutarch in two dialogues (*De E apud Delphis* and *De defectu oraculorum*) also speaks of the decline of Delphi. Cf. treatment in Bernard le Bovier de Fontenelle, *Histoire des Oracles* (1687), Caps. 2-3; Robert M. Grant, *Gods and the One God* (Philadelphia: Westminster, 1986), 62ff.

> Or that which only seems to satisfie
> Lawful desires of Nature, not beyond.
>
> (2.225-30)

The appeal must now be directed not merely to what is publicly acknowledged as praiseworthy but most importantly to what his adversary himself deems attractive. Milton's interpolation makes clear how the poet wants the episode of one temptation to prepare for and lead into the next.

The victory of Christ during the first temptation episode apparently has not solved the problem which occasioned the temptation itself: still ravaged by hunger, he is appropriately pondering again on the relationship between the needs of nature and God's support. Inasmuch as Satan starts again with the scene of a banquet, the symbol of food may lead the reader to think that it is a repetition of the first temptation. Considering the issues raised, however, one can readily see that it truly belongs to the second temptation (or groups of temptation). The temptation to empire that sums up this episode concentrates on what are the lawful possessions of the Son of God.

The appeal is skillfully double-edged. As the Son of God (and if it was indeed true), Jesus would assume natural lordship over the entire cosmos. But even as man, he is also the head of all creation in the great chain of being. Our recognition of the manifold magnitude of Christ's possessions gives clue to both the length of this episode and its order in the poem.

William Perkins reveals a bit of the theologian's concern for rational explanation and his own amusing literalism when he comments thus on the Devil's reported attempt to show Christ the kingdoms of the world.

> This he could not doe actually: for there is no mountain so high in all the world, whereon if a man were placed, he could see one halfe or one quarter of the kingdomes of the world, as they are seated and placed upon the face of the earth; nay, if a man were set in the Sunne, and from thence could looke unto the earth, yet he could not see past the half thereof. And therefore we must know, that the Devill did this in a counterfeit vision; for herein he can frame an imitation of God.
>
> (3:397)

What leads Perkins to devise a solution of "a counterfeit vision" supplied by Satan is precisely the inclusiveness of the biblical assertion: showing Jesus *all* the kingdoms of the world and the glory of them, the Tempter says, "*All* these things will I give thee." Since Milton's poem necessitates his miming the action of Satan, the poet's means of conveying a developed sense of this "all" is to break up the episode into several segments. Only thus can his poem give scope and substance to the meaning of what such kingdoms and their respective glory entail.

If the first temptation essentially seeks to seduce Christ into a misuse of his miraculous powers should he be the divine Son, the second temptation is in every sense a critical test of how Jesus understands his own humanity. For the entire group of temptations that occupies Books 2 and 3 can be summarized as the temptation to autonomy on the part of the human creature, to bestow priority on one's own need and law. It is not the transgression of limits but the aggregation of what is within bounds to oneself that defines this temptation. Thus Satan asks:

> Hast thou not right to *all* Created things,
> Owe not *all* Creatures by just right to thee
> Duty and Service, nor to stay till bid,
> But tender *all* their power?
> (2.324-27; emphasis mine)

To this rhetorical affirmation of the Son's licit dominion, it is no accident that the key word describing the manner of Jesus' response is "temperately" (2.378), for as in other poems, the doctrine of temperance serves as the cornerstone of Milton's effort in delineating one crucial aspect of human perfection. Temperance will serve as his Christ's choicest weapon in crushing all forms of wealth, honor, glory, and popular praise that Satan can offer precisely because it is a virtue which, in its concrete exercise, defines his unfailing submission to God's providential will. It is thus a virtue that gives unity to the life of the preexistent Son and the incarnate Christ. More than the typical Puritan advocacy of frugality or the doctrine of Aristotelian magnanimity oft cited from *The Christian Doctrine* (2.9), temperance substantiates the Pauline doctrine of kenosis (Php 2:5-11), which declares that Christ "being in the form of God" did not cling to or grasp after (ἁρπαγμὸν) that "equality." If the church's teachings often stress this notion of voluntary self-emptying of divine prerogatives and attributes as the distinctive character of the Incarnation, Milton's epic here places the emphasis squarely on the meaning of how Jesus as man "humbled himself, and became obedient unto death."[21]

The form that obedience takes entails extending that original surrender further into the human sphere: the resolute and persistent refusal to insist on one's rights ("That which to God alone of right belongs"—3.141), an astonishing, hard truth when seen in the total drift of Western civilization. The entire course of the Son's

---

[21]For a recent study of this important topic, particularly in relation to PL, see Michael Lieb, *The Sinews of Ulysses: Form and Convention in Milton's Works* (Pittsburgh: Duquesne Univ. Press, 1989), 38-52.

incarnational sojourn, the motion toward human existence, may be construed as one long, arduous, and (in the poet's view) triumphant effort to reverse—and thus remove—all internal and external inducements to godlike aspirations on the part of the human creature. As befits the teachings of the Gospels, the sustained focus is trained therefore on the internal conquest of self ("he who reigns within himself, and rules / Passions, Desires, and Fears, is more a King"—2.466-67). Consistent with the received paradox of Christian existence ("That who advance his glory, not thir own, / Them he himself to glory will advance"—3.143-44), the normal orders and expectations of ethics and politics are reversed ("who best / Can suffer, best can do; best reign, who first / Well hath obey'd"—3.195-96).

Given this perspective, Christ's rejection of all satanic overtures becomes understandable and consistent. The lavish banquet spread by Satan well exceeds "lawful desires of Nature"; the riches that he claims to be his are "impotent" because they lack "Virtue, Valour, and Wisdom." As for military conquests and popular praise which should be the definitive goal of one's "thirst for glory," especially if one like Christ is endowed with "God-like Vertues" (3.21), such imperial theme is at once countered by the poet's favored examples of "patient *Job*" and "Poor *Socrates*" who "For truths sake suffering death unjust, [live] now / Equal in fame to proudest Conquerours" (3.98-99). Even the more specific urging for Christ to claim his legitimate heritage ("to a Kingdom thou art born, ordain'd / To sit upon thy Father *David's* Throne"—3.152-53) by delivering Israel from the hated Roman yoke, and to which enterprise Satan promises the Parthian for assistance, is met by Christ's insistence that his time "hast not yet come."[22] He will no more usurp the sole prerogative of the Father, "in whose hand all times and seasons roul" (3.187), than indulge in wanton excesses.

Satan's final effort in completing the temptation is the proffering of wisdom, the extension of mind and knowledge as a broadening of rule (4.221-30). Jesus' rejection of classical learning and its stern denunciation trouble modern ears, but we need to remember the premise of that rejection. It is not merely the appeal to the Bible as the compendium of knowledge, a theological commonplace since patristic times,[23] or the inferiority of pagan learning. It is rather the strict subordination of knowledge's end in relation to the particular user. "Other doctrine" is "granted true" (4.290) by the Son, but he in his situation has no need of such. The acknowledgment of receiving

---

[22]See Mother M. Christopher Pecheux, "Milton and *Kairos*," *Milton Studies* 12 (1979): 197-212, for a recent study of this theme in Milton.

[23]See Lewalski's thorough discussion, *Milton's Brief Epic*, 281-302.

"Light from above, from the fountain of light" abrogates any necessity for him to seek such knowledge and its purported benefit as Satan describes it—"These rules will render thee a King compleat / Within thy self, much more with Empire joyn'd" (4.283-84)—because Jesus has already demonstrated a vastly superior understanding of what the kingship over self truly means. As we have seen over the long course of this temptation, Satan's conception of empire contrasts completely with Christ's. If the characteristic thrust of the Tempter's suasion is for self-aggrandizement ("nor to stay till bid"), the disposition of Jesus throughout is exactly the reverse ("Shall I seek glory then, as vain men seek / Oft not deserv'd? I seek not mine, but his / Who sent me, and thereby witness whence I am"—3.105-7). Any attempt to put self ahead of God's providential order, even if it is in the name of service to God, idolizes in fact creaturely status and interest, the equivalent of worshiping Satan. This was, after all, the ultimate thrust of Satan's bidding in both source and poem (4.166-69). Milton, by amplifying the brief account of the Gospels into several episodes, has made the far-reaching implications of such bidding abundantly clear.

Against the "temperance invincible" of the Son, Satan's range of reactions—surprise, bewilderment, fear, and rage—may in part resemble that of the unsympathetic reader. How could any putative Son of God be so exasperatingly passive ("What dost thou in this World?"—4.372), so seemingly wanting in human energy and motivation? Satan's behavior, as the Miltonic simile of "surging waves against a solid rock" reveals, now becomes increasingly destructive and, ironically, self-destructive. His predicament stems from his failure to discover, on his terms, the Son's identity, and from his unwillingness to heed his adversary's warning that such discovery might spell disaster for him (3.200-201). His final assault on the pinnacle, unleashing the latent violence of his character, uses a physical dilemma (the poet's invention) to force a spiritual one.

The Gospel account tells nothing of the pinnacle's danger or difficulty, but the rapid epanalepsis of Satan's challenge ("there stand, if thou wilt stand; to stand upright / Will ask thee skill"—4.551-52) confronts Christ with two treacherous alternatives: he could be physically killed[24] or he could act in presumption of God's preservation. In either case, Satan thinks he would win by learning "In what degree or meaning" his adversary is called the Son of God.

Despite Christ's success in standing, which results in Satan's simultaneous "fall," the problem of Sonship and its precise meaning persists and continues to divide the opinion of the critics. For some,

---

[24]Cf. George Williamson, *Milton and Others* (Chicago: Univ. of Chicago Press, 1965), 81-83; Allen, *Harmonious Vision*, 111.

the moment is a decisive revelation of divinity, when the hero's self-knowledge converges with the knowledge sought by his antagonist in one dramatic utterance.[25] For others, the scene is an anticipatory, symbolic enactment of his crucifixion, when he fulfills his priestly role and function of offering himself as a sacrifice.[26] There are even those who would argue that the inherent ambiguity of the cited biblical text in Christ's answer ("Tempt not the Lord thy God") and of the context (what is the referent of "the Lord thy God"?) makes it impossible to affirm a definitive solution.[27]

In view of the drift of this essay's argument, I would side with the emphasis on Christ's human success in undergoing the third temptation.[28] The statement, "Tempt not the Lord thy God," must once more be understood in the context of the biblical injunction to obedience (Dt 6:16). When the wandering Israelites demanded water from Moses, they were accused of "putting the Lord to test" by asking the question, "*is* God still with us?" (Ex 17:7). If the entire experience of temptation, as Michael Lieb so aptly describes it, can be considered a "descent" of Jesus into himself by confronting "the human dimension of his personality,"[29] the succinct quotation of Scripture to rebut the satanic misuse of Scripture represents the most signal triumph in that dimension. Though perched on an "uneasie station," Christ would rather risk death than risk forcing the hand of his God. His physical success in standing, whether because of skill (the satanic conjecture) or "Godlike force" with which he is "indu'd" (the angels' closing hymn of praise), justly serves as the transparent metaphor of his spiritual victory, his crowning act of obedience as the "Greater Man."

Because of the constraint of space, I have avoided discussing thus far the difficult issue of Miltonic understanding of the two natures of Christ. The poet's unorthodox views are by now familiar. He has argued in chapter 16 of *The Christian Doctrine*, when commenting on the Gethsemane episode, that "the presence of an angel would have been superfluous, unless the divine nature of Christ, as well as

---

[25]Cf. Arnold Stein, *Heroic Knowledge* (Minneapolis: Univ. of Minnesota Press, 1957), 225.

[26]So Lewalski, *Milton's Brief Epic*, 303-21.

[27]Thus the clearly deconstructionist reading of Lawrence W. Hyman, "Christ on The Pinnacle: A New Reading of the Conclusion to *Paradise Regained*," in *Milton Quarterly* 18 (1984): 19-22.

[28]Cf. Dick Taylor, "Grace as a Means of Poetry: Milton's Pattern for Salvation," *Tulane Studies in English* 4 (1954): 87-88; Thomas Langford, "The Nature of the Christ of *Paradise Regained*," *Milton Quarterly* 16 (1982): 63-67.

[29]Michael Lieb, *Poetics of the Holy: A Reading of "Paradise Lost"* (Chapel Hill: Univ. of North Carolina Press, 1981), 72.

his human, had needed support."[30] Could not the same understanding inform the magnificent climax of the poem?

An affirmative answer to the above question is exceedingly
tempting, though not without a formidable barrier. Even allowing for
the poet's penchant for advancing his own peculiar views on sundry
theological issues, no student of his can presume that Milton has
forgotten the plain scriptural assertion that "God cannot be tempted"
(Jas 1:13). If Jesus triumphed at last over Satan in theophanic form,
how could he be said to have "aveng'd / Supplanted Adam" by exercising that "one mans firm obedience fully tri'd"?

On the other hand, the research of Barbara Lewalski has helped us
see that Milton's understanding of the *communicatio idiomatum* in
the hypostatic union exceeds the norms of orthodox theory, in such a
way that "whatever Christ says of himself, he says not as the posses-
sor of either nature separately, but with reference to the whole of his
character, and in his entire person, except where he himself makes a
distinction. Those who divide this hypostatical union at their own
discretion, strip the discourses and answers of Christ of all their
sincerity."[31]

If this understanding is applied to *Paradise Regained*, the Christological implications may seem radical but not out of character. As
Milton has made it clear in his previous epic, his poetic theodicy is
built on "the paradox central to the Christian affirmation that man
who bears the image of God must also live by the realization that he
is not like God."[32] His shorter epic devoted to dramatizing one crucial
episode in the earthly life of the Son of God must now show how he
redeems Adamic failure to live in accordance with that paradox. The
Son in his earthly existence, even by satanic testimony, appears to be
most godlike (1.91-93). Thus the saving irony emerging from the
temptations of Jesus is that the most characteristic action of this
"godman" (Milton's preferred designation of the incarnate Christ in
The Christian Doctrine is θεάνθρωπος) is his adamant rejection of all
godlike affectations. Amidst the manifest plurality of meanings
inherent in the phrase, "the Son of God," Satan's quest is to pin down
a definitive significance for his adversary. The Miltonic Christ, however, is one who resists to the end any hint of wishing to bear that
title "in higher sort" (4.198). The Son, who possesses the fullest semblance to the Father, who embodies in the greatest plenitude the
divine image, is he who eschews all such profession and pretension,
who aspires, in short, not to be God. Only this sort of self-emptying

[30]Patterson, *Student's Milton*, 1010.

[31]*The Christian Doctrine*, chap. 14, cited by Lewalski, *Milton's Brief Epic*, in her
discussion on p. 153.

[32]See my discussion in "Life in the Garden: Freedom and the Image of God in
Paradise Lost," *Journal of Religion* 60 (July 1980): 255ff.

and self-giving, in the poet's thinking, can merit the promise of corresponding divine elevation:

> Therefore thy Humiliation shall exalt
> With thee thy Manhood also to this Throne;
> Here shalt thou sit incarnate, here shalt Reigne
> Both God and Man, Son both of God and Man.
>
> (PL 3.313-16)

It is a Christology of which its many ramifications have yet to be appreciated by the Christian community.

The clarification of the nature of temptations enacted in the poem also helps us understand the order of their presentation. In the poet's conception the first and third temptations essentially revolve around a single issue, but the temptation to empire has to be stretched out to achieve its full impact. Moreover, the temptations of stones and empire involve no satanic appeal to Scripture, whereas the pinnacle episode has the Tempter quoting directly from the Hebrew Bible. The head-on confrontation of the contestants' use of Scripture over an invented hazard provides the opportunity for swift, potent climax. The Lukan order thus cannot be reversed without undercutting the literary effectiveness of mounting theological tension. In *A Harmonie of the Gospels* John Calvin writes:

> There is nothing very remarkable in Luke putting in second place the temptation which Matthew places last, for the Evangelists had no intention of so putting their narrative together as always to keep an exact order of events, but to bring the whole pattern together to produce a kind of mirror or screen image of those features most useful for the understanding of Christ.[33]

By choosing Luke over Matthew, Milton may yet have proven himself a more imaginative theologian and, in consequence, a better poet, when he can offer his readers so meticulously wrought a "screen image" of the Christ whom he and they both seek to understand.

---

[33]Calvin, *A Harmonie*, 1:139.

Ethics and Christology

The Sort of Friend We Have in Jesus

Lewis B. Smedes

Professor of Theology and Ethics
Fuller Theological Seminary

"Friendship is the allay of our sorrows, the ease of our passion, the discharge of our oppressions, the sanctuary to our calamities, the counsellor of our doubts, the clarity of our mind, the emission of our thoughts, the exercise and improvement of what we meditate."[1]

On reading Jeremy Taylor's lyrical tribute to friendship, we may be roused to special gratitude that Jesus should count us as his friends. "No longer do I call you servants, for the servant does not know what his master is doing; but I have called you friends, for all that I have heard from my Father I have made known to you" (Jn 15:15).[2]

When our Lord says that he *calls* his disciples his friends, I assume he means that they *are* indeed his friends. More, I assume that he extended his gracious gesture to all who are his servants. And, a critical point, I assume that he not only counts us as *his* friends, but that he wants to be *our* friend as well. I assume, too, that Jesus does not merely mean to *be*friend us; he does not give us a helping hand the way he might *if* he were our friend. Nor, I assume, does he mean merely that he is *not* our enemy, as in, "Who goes there, friend or foe?"

And surely he means more than to be amicable, or friendly, toward us. Amicability is an important sort of friendliness that we ought to show to one other; to be surly, sulky, crabby, brusk, discourteous, rude, testy, and generally uncivil is a moral fault, even if not an outrageous one. Thomas, for one, includes affability in this sense among the moral virtues,[3] though, of course, he does not mean that friendship is no more than affability.

---

[1] Jeremy Taylor, "The Offices of Friendship," *Works*, 15 vols. (London: Ogle, Duncan, 1822), 11:302.

[2] Scripture citations in this essay are from the RSV.

[3] "Now one man behaves towards another, in serious matters, in two ways. First, as being pleasant in this regard, by becoming speech and deeds; and this belongs to a virtue which Aristotle calls friendship, and may be rendered affability." *Summa Theologica*, 2a-2ae, quest. 60, art. 5, from *Basic Writings of Saint Thomas Aquinas*, ed. Anton C. Pegis, 2 vols. (New York: Random House, 1944), 2:465. Cf. also *Summa Theologica*, 2a-2ae, quest. 114, art. 2.

It is the likelihood that Jesus meant to be a genuine friend that, while it fulfills a pious need, does bring one up short intellectually. Jesus' vast superiority to us in both status and authority makes friendship with him problematic. Most of our friends are people who live and work more or less on the same level we do. So we may ask: what sort of friend do we have in Jesus? Or what sort of friendship is appropriate between Jesus, the Lord and Savior, and all those who obey him as Lord and praise him as Savior?

Can Jesus be our friend in the ordinary ways in which ordinary people are friends? Or does he have a unique friendship in mind such that his friendship with us transcends and perhaps redefines our notion of what friendship can be, redefines it so thoroughly that we really should give it another name?

It is possible that Jesus did not have ordinary notions of friendship in mind, but instead a uniquely biblical notion, a notion of friendship that transcends any natural friendship. Maybe he was transforming *philos* in the same way that *agape* transcends *eros*. Maybe the sort of friendship he offers is as different from the sort of friendship we have with each other as the sort of love that led God to sacrifice his Son for unworthy sinners is different from the convivial love that Plato celebrated in the *Symposium*. The possibility at least recommends that we poke around for a bit to see if we can come up with a biblical theology of friendship that disqualifies our ordinary notions of friendship from being paradigmatic for friendship with Jesus.

If we began with the apostle Paul, we would finish quickly, for he never speaks of friendship. He knows people as brothers and sisters in the Lord, as servants and masters in the flesh, and as his spiritual children. But none as friend. Does his silence tell us anything?

St. Paul's very silence may make us wonder whether there is not something about friendship that makes it, at the most, a relationship so inferior to what we know in Christ that Christians are advised to seek other sorts of relationships with people, more sacrificial, disinterested, inclusive, indiscriminate, and selfless relationships than friendships are. In fact, the very question has been explicitly raised anew in a scholarly way by Gilbert Meilander.[4] There is something unchristianly clubby about friendship, Meilander observes; we choose our friends because we like them, we prefer them above other people, and we relate to them because they have attractive features that we admire. Friendship is a preferential, a reciprocal, a rather exclusive relationship. We do not love our friends with the indiscriminate, selfless, sacrificial love of Christ. So perhaps friendship has been overcome rather than endorsed by Christ.

---

[4]Gilbert Meilander, *Friendship: A Study in Theological Ethics* (Notre Dame, Ind.: Univ. of Notre Dame Press, 1981).

Jeremy Taylor resolved the tension ambiguously by first explaining that "Christianity hath new christened [friendship] and calls this charity." Thus, it might seem, friendship has been taken up into and transformed by love. But the learned divine then explains that "Christian charity is friendship to all the world; . . . charity is friendship expanded like the face of the sun when it mounts above the Eastern hills."[5] In our natural condition, we are too limited to be friends with the unscrubbed, unlovely, and unsaved world. But possessed by *agape,* we receive the Spirit's push to be friends of everyone. So the baptism of friendship into charity comes down to this: *agape* enlarges our field of friends. On the one hand, charity sanctifies natural friendship, but, on the other, friendship naturalizes charity.

I mentioned Meilander's concern and Taylor's solution in view of St. Paul's silence about friendship. But friendship does get a mention by other biblical writers. It is certainly pertinent that God himself, as well as Jesus, called a human being his friend: "But you, Israel, my servant, Jacob, whom I have chosen, the offspring of Abraham, my friend." God seems to prefer Abraham as a friend above other people who were only his servants, like Jacob, and thus, no doubt, above any of the ordinary creatures who were his children or his servants but not his friends. Who does not remember Abraham walking beside the Angel of the Lord, negotiating with him as with an equal for the souls of Sodom? God's friendship with Abraham was based on something specially admirable that he saw in him. (In somewhat the same way, perhaps, that the Greek gods selected only the heroic among men as their friends?)

Aristotle observed that the noblest kind of friendship was based on admiration of one another's natural virtues. But what God admired in Abraham was not his virtue but his faith. True, if we thought in a Thomistic style, we could call faith a supernatural virtue and thus suppose that the biblical concept of friendship—even with God— shares the conventional assumption that friends are friends because they prefer one another over others. At least, it does not indicate a radical new basis for friendship even with God, let alone with one another, or with Jesus. Still, anyone who believes the Pauline doctrine of justification by grace alone will be hard put to pursue the line of thought that God is our friend because he sees something in us that spurs him to prefer us above others.

While the Bible does not offer us much to go on if we seek a specifically biblical theology of friendship, it does give us David and Jonathan, a classic portrait of true friendship. I will mention their friendship later, in another connection. Enough here simply to observe that if their friendship is a paradigm of Jesus' friendship with

---

[5]Taylor, *Works*, 11:302.

us, we would have to raise the same questions that are being raised here. For, deep and true as it was, their friendship was an exclusive, preferential, and reciprocal relationship between two relatively equal persons.

All of this leads me to give up—for now—trying to locate Jesus' friendship with us within a biblically informed theology of friendship. We certainly have not come up with anything that illumines what sort of friendship we would have with Jesus were it *sui generis*, a friendship that has no similarity to ordinary friendship.

This is the moment, then, for us to take a longer look at the conventional notions of friendship and ask again how, in the light of what we already know friendship to be, we should expect Jesus to be our friend. Since Aristotle's observations on friendship in the *Nichomachean Ethics* have long been the starting point for serious discussions of friendship, he offers a reasonable place for us to begin.

The philosopher observed that there were three basic types or levels of friendship. One of them is based on the pleasure that friends get from each other. Another is based on the use that friends have for each other. And the third and noblest friendship is based on the admiration friends have for each other's virtues.

For Aristotle, then, *philos*, the love of a friend, friendship, was a species of *eros*, the love that seeks union with another in order to fill a need within one's self. "Without friends," he wrote, "no one would choose to live, though he had all other goods."[6] And the friends we love are persons who are "either good, or pleasant, or useful to us." What distinguishes *philos* is its reciprocity; friends are either good or pleasant or useful to *each other*. Christian piety finds all three of Aristotle's levels of friendship most fitting for a friendship with Jesus.

Take Aristotle's first level of friendship, pleasure, and the way friends seek each other out because they enjoy one another. Does it not match the joy that the pious Christian seeks in intimacy with Christ? Does not Franck's hymn express a genuinely Christian piety of pleasure:

> Jesus, Priceless Treasure,
> Source of purest pleasure,
> Truest friend to me.

Or take the second level, usefulness. Aristotle says that friends, at one level, "use each other for their own interests."[7] And then sing Criven's most favored hymn:

---

[6] Aristotle, *Nichomachean Ethics*, 8.1155a5, in *The Basic Works of Aristotle*, ed. Richard McKeon (New York: Random House, 1941).

[7] Ibid., 11621b.17-18.

> What a friend we have in Jesus,
> All our sins and griefs to bear;
> . . . .
> Can we find a friend so faithful
> Who will all our sorrows share?
> Jesus knows our every weakness,
> Take it to the Lord in prayer.

Jesus is indeed a useful friend!

Aristotle's third level of friendship, that based on virtue, is no less congenial to piety. It deserves some special attention if only to notice that the erotic, self-seeking, self-loving notion of friendship commonly attributed to Aristotle needs some qualification. The distinction between self-love and other-love gets fudged here. For a friendship based on admiration of virtue sounds like the purest sort of other-love. It is a love for persons for their own sake, not for what they can do for us nor for the pleasures we enjoy in their presence. We love them only as we admire their virtue.

And yet, the love of a friend for his or her virtue is not simply an aesthetic admiration of the beautiful form of goodness. We want some of our friend's virtue to rub off on us. "For when a good man becomes a friend to another he becomes that other's good; so each loves his own good, and repays what he receives by wishing the good of the other. . . . There is a saying 'caring is sharing,' and these qualities belong especially to the friendship of good men."[8]

What could be more akin to why we need Jesus for a friend? We love him in the sense that we admire his virtue. "I love thee, Lord, yet not because I hope for heaven, nor yet since they who love thee not, must thereby burn eternally. . . . Not with the hope of gaining aught; not seeking a reward, but as thyself has loved me, O ever-loving Lord" (Francis Xavier). But, as in Aristotle's friendship of virtue, we do not simply admire him in deep appreciation of his glory. We want to "grow up in him," as St. Paul says, have his "mind" in us (Php 2:5), that we "may know him and the power of his resurrection, and may share his sufferings, becoming like him in his death" (Php 3:10), and thus let his virtue become our virtue.

The resemblance between Aristotle's friendship of virtue and our friendship with Jesus stops here, however. For in Aristotle the friendship of virtue assumes a friendship between two good persons who admire each other and desire to share the virtue each has. But it would take an arrogant person indeed to assume that Jesus would wish to be her friend in order to grow in virtue through close association with her.

---

[8]Ibid., 1158a7.

Our problem, once again, focuses on the reciprocity that marks ordinary friendships. How, in the light of it, can a real friendship be carried on between two such unequals as a saved sinner and his Lord and Savior?

Reciprocity runs as a common assumption through Aristotle's three levels of friendship: friends enjoy each other, are useful to each other, and admire each other's virtue. When there is no reciprocity, friendship dies. And reciprocity implies a certain equality, enough to persuade James Olthuis to say simply, "Friends are equals."[9] How can we imagine a reciprocating friendship with Jesus when we are so acutely aware of our inequality that, on seeing him, we would hardly offer our hand to him; we would fall flat on our faces before him?

Can we have a reciprocating friendship with the Lord of heaven and earth? Consider the Jesus whom John the apostle saw "clothed with a long robe and with a golden girdle" and "eyes . . . like a flame of fire" and a voice "like the sound of many waters" and a face "like the sun shining in full strength." Can we have a reciprocating friendship with that one? John, at least, was not moved by what he saw to put his arms around his good friend Jesus and walk off to have a good talk in the glen. Quite otherwise. "When I saw him I fell at his feet as though dead" (Rev 1:12-17).

It is not as if friends are always completely equal. Aristotle says, and it is obvious, that most friendships are to some extent unequal. But the bigger the difference gets, the less chance the friendship has of surviving. This is notably true with the gods "because they are furthest above us in respect of all good things"; so "where there is a great gulf, as between God and man, friendship becomes impossible."[10] What does this say about friendship with Jesus?

Are we faced with the inescapable tension that we always have in relating in any familiar way to the Christ who is both divine and human? And can we resolve the tension by relating to the human Jesus as friend and the divine Jesus as the awesome God before whom we tremble? I do not think so.

For one thing, few of us are up to making such refined distinctions within our pious feelings. For another, the Jesus who calls us his friends is simply Jesus, the whole self, one person, the incarnate Lord, walking on earth and risen in glory and power. In any case, it is not only his deity that creates the enormous inequality between us. He is, one person, the Lord of us all, the glorified Savior, one Lord, one friend.

True, if we could get a new understanding of God as our friend, maybe the question of friendship with Jesus would be moot. Sallie

---

[9]James Olthuis, *I Pledge You My Troth* (San Francisco: Harper & Row, 1975), 110.
[10]Aristotle, *Ethics*, 8:1158a9.

McFague offers us a suggestion. McFague specifically recommends "friend" as metaphor for God as well as for Jesus. She observes that familial metaphors for God do not work well for many people anymore. Many women are uneasy with God as Father. Some men are uneasy with God as Mother. And people whose earthly parents have been abusively cruel find it terribly hard to think of a loving God as either Father or Mother. But everyone thinks well of a friend. So, if only for its more universal appeal, "friend" may be the metaphor of choice for God.[11]

But if the metaphor "friend" tells us what God is like, what does it tell us? Does the metaphor affect our theology? The answer is yes, considerably. Our divine friend is not the God "up there" of traditional theism, even less the God "down there," the Ground of Being, the Abyss of Paul Tillich's theology. He is instead the God walking alongside of us, not so much leader as fellow traveler, not so much parent as fellow worker, not so much commander as comrade.

Christian piety has seldom been prevented by the doctrine of God's transcendence from intimate experience of the God who is a close friend. Pious songs of close familiarity with God still tug at the hearts of Christians:

> And he walks with me and he talks with me,
> and he tells me I am his own,
> and the joy we share as we tarry there,
> none other has ever known.

And then there is the lovely Latvian spiritual:

> My God and I, go in the fields together,
> we walk and talk, as good friends should and do.

Who does not want God at his side, walking and talking as a good friend should?

But what if the metaphor of friendship becomes the dominant metaphor? How could the God who is the friend alongside of us be congruent with the God of Isaiah's vision, he whom Isaiah saw "sitting on a throne, high and lifted up," with seraphim flying about the throne singing, "Holy, Holy, Holy is the Lord of Hosts" (Isa 6)? Can the "friend" metaphor cope with such a God? Or will it edit him to fit?

And can we who are saved sinners have as friend one who is Divine Savior? Not if we let conventional notions of friendship define our metaphor. McFague agrees: "Friends do not and cannot save one another; rather, they work together for common goals in

---

[11]Sallie McFague, *Metaphorical Theology* (Philadelphia: Fortress, 1982), 177ff.

such a way that each is encouraged, empowered, and enlivened to do what each is able to do for the good of the whole."[12] Well now, we at least get a hint of where the "friend" metaphor could lead if it becomes more master than servant of our theology.

So we are back at square one: if we assume that friendships are by nature reciprocal and that reciprocity implies that friends are relatively on the same level, how should we think of Jesus as friend? Can a Lord be a friend?

Human lords do not readily make human friends. They cannot afford reciprocity; they need people who are willing to be of use to them in pursuit of their ends without asking for friendship in return. Doris Goodwin observed of Franklin Roosevelt, for instance, that "for all his warmth and capacity to make friends instantly, FDR was a man without a deep commitment to anyone . . . rarely gave himself" to those who found him charmingly friendly.[13] Desmond Morton was one of many who risked their foreign office careers to keep Winston Churchill secretly informed during the days of his exile from power, but William Manchester quotes him as saying, "The full truth, I believe, is that Winston's 'friends' must be persons who were of use to him. The idea of having a friend . . . because he liked him, had no place."[14]

But if human lords do not indulge in friendships, the Divine Incarnate Lord might. But *could* he? That is, would we still have a friendship in the ordinary sense with the *Lord* Jesus?

There have been good friends who were vastly unequal. John F. Kennedy and Lem Billings were good friends from the time they were scalawags together in school until President Kennedy was shot in Dallas. But something had to give. Jack Kennedy's father felt that friendship had to give. One night at dinner, when being president was still only Jack's ambition, his father said to Lem, "From now on you must think of Jack less as a friend and more as a potential candidate for president of the United States." But Jack's sister Eunice felt that, even after Jack was president, the inequality between the president and Lem Billings was not so great as to make friendship impossible: "Sometimes friendships have to have an equal level of respect to continue on. If you're always pulling someone along, it's a different kind of relationship. But you never pulled Lemmie anywhere because he has so much talent of his own. Lem was always an equal to Jack. In friendship you must have an equal amount of affection

---

[12]Ibid., 186.

[13]Doris Kearnes Goodwin, *The Fitzgeralds and The Kennedys* (New York: Simon & Schuster, 1987), 459.

[14]William Manchester, *The Last Lion: Winston Spencer Churchill* (New York: Little, Brown, 1988), 374.

and respect for another, and they had that."[15] So if Eunice Shriver saw things accurately, Lem Billings and Jack Kennedy were equals of a sort. And it is commonly known that when he was with his old friends, Jack Kennedy took off his presidential hat. Friendship was a sort of intermezzo between roles.

David and Jonathan were unequals, one the royal heir apparent and the other a fugitive from the king, yet true friends of classic format. But *in* their intimacy, their commitment to one another as friends, they put aside their inequality; in the fields, neither was son or enemy of the king, but they were equals, giving and receiving, reciprocally and preferentially.

In short, where human friendship happens between rulers and ruled, there is usually a suspension of the inequality. Or, they enjoy an equality of the mind and spirit that could not be overcome by the gap in status. But can Jesus suspend his lordship for a while in order to act as a friend on weekends? Or could we ever claim any sort of equality with him on other terms that overcome the true and great disparity between us? Perish the thought.

We have tested the waters of ordinary friendship enough, I think, to see that if Jesus is a good friend, he is not a friend in the ordinary sense of the word. Perhaps what he offers as friendship is not less, but infinitely more than any human friend can offer. Yet it is good to note that the conditions that he sets for friendship with him are daunting.

Go back, for instance, to the context in which Jesus called us his friends. Notice that Jesus plainly said that to be his friends we must accept an inequality ordinary friendship could not tolerate.

The reason he gave for calling us his friends was that he shared his Father's secrets with us. Sharing secrets implies a kind of camaraderie. Masters keep their servants in the dark, as if to underscore and maintain their inequality. Jesus shared his secrets with his disciples, so it seemed appropriate to call them friends: "I have called you friends, for all that I have heard from my Father I have made known to you" (Jn 15:15).

But the camaraderie is acutely conditional. And the condition is that we honor our enormous inequality: he is Master, after all. And we will be his friends only if we are at the same time his obedient servants: "You are my friends *if you do what I command you.*" At once, friendship with Jesus not only tolerates, but requires, an inequality that ordinary friendship cannot normally tolerate.

Clearly, Jesus will not have the "friendship" metaphor define the relationship he offers us. There is a stitch in the fabric that is enough

---

[15]Quoted by David Michaelis in *The Best of Friends* (New York: Morrow, 1983), 168.

like friendship—sharing secrets, for example—for Jesus to call us his
friends. The hitch comes when we call him *our* friend; for to call *him*
friend we must also call him Master. And so what goes for friendship
in ordinary life is a very limited metaphor for friendship with Jesus.

We are not fellow travelers; he is leader and we are followers. We
do not walk side by side; he is always before us. We are not equals; he
is vastly superior. He is the sort of friend we could not long endure in
ordinary life with ordinary people; few people can remain friends for
long with someone who accepts them by grace, "in spite of what they
are." Surely, Jesus is a friend without compare, and the sort of friend
he is to us will be different from Aristotle's notion of what every
friend will be to another friend.

The main difference, it seems to me, will be experienced on the
moral level. This is interesting because Aristotle's main discussion of
friendship occurs in his *Ethics*. Aristotle's *Ethics* are mainly descriptions of excellence, and an excellent person is a person with friends, if
only because others will admire and want to share his virtues. So for
the most part he only describes the sort of relationship that excellent
people have when they are friends. But he does not focus much on
the moral obligations that friendship entails for friends. Certainly he
does not strongly stress the sacrificial side of friendship. I do not
mean that Aristotle does not appreciate the sacrifices friends make for
each other. I only mean that friendship, as he sees it, is not built on a
willingness of a superior person to sacrifice for an inferior person. It
is grounded rather in a desire to enjoy the pleasure and admire the
virtue of another who is rather much one's equal.

When we think of Jesus as a friend, we think precisely of such
moral dimensions as his commitment, his grace, and his sacrifice.
Most basically, he is the committed friend. No human friendship
lasts long without an unspoken commitment to stick with each other
in preference to others. But human friendships do not necessarily
endure: we stop getting pleasure from each other, stop getting benefit
from each other, stop admiring each other's virtue; a friendship based
on reciprocity, alas, has tentativity built in. But friendship with Jesus
abides because he keeps a promise that few friends dare even make,
though most good friends might wish such a promise could be the
abiding bond of their friendship. It is a promise that no loss of pleasure, no discovery of character flaw, not even disloyalty or betrayal
will undo. "I shall be with you to the end of the world," he said. And
this is a commitment human friends simply do not have it in them
to make to one another.

He is also the forgiving friend. Human friendships tend to die
when one friend betrays another. We do not always have the spiritual energy to forgive, and it is not always prudent to restore the
friendship. But he forgives. And he reconciles his friends to himself.

Always. There is no friend whose betrayal cuts so deep an arroyo that he does not bridge it with forgiveness. And he forgives with style; he forgives with a grace that does not demean the forgiven friend. In human relationships, it would be hard to be a friend of Francis Thompson's "Hound of Heaven": "Thou, of all earth's clotted clay, the dingiest clot; whom wilt thou find to love ignoble thee, save Me, save only Me." Not possible, unless the hound be also the Good Shepherd.

He is also the listening friend. He called us friends because he had shared his Father's secrets with us. But we call him friend because he listens to our secrets. And he invites us to speak without fear that we might bore him and wear out our welcome with our petty petitions and our silly sins. If we are his friends because he tells us what we need to know, he is our friend because he listens to what we need to tell him.

Jesus suggests that he, as a truly good friend would, lays down his life for his friends. "Greater love has no man than this, that a man lay down his life for his friends," he said (Jn 15:13). And then he went on to say that he called us his friends. Odd thing, actually, for according to St. Paul, Jesus laid down his life for us when we were still enemies and not yet friends (Ro 5:10). No matter, however, for what Jesus clearly meant was that the love that might lead one to die for one's friends was the kind of love he had for his friends. And if he would die for us before we became his friends, he would certainly be the sort of friend who would go to sacrificial extremes to support and sustain us as friends.

The end of all this is that Jesus is not an ordinary friend, and friendship with him does not meet the usual conditions of ordinary friendship. If reciprocity and relative equality characterize, as they ordinarily do, all good human friendship, then Jesus will not be to us what even a good human friend is. For whatever it is like to experience him as a friend, it is also, and at the same moment, the experience of a saved sinner worshiping a divine Savior, a mere servant obeying a sovereign Lord, and a worshiping devotee on her face before his great glory. To call him friend is not a license to cut him down to our measure of a friend. And yet, in those invisible bonds of moral consistency, kept commitment, gracious forgiveness, untiring listening, and ultimate sacrifice, he is the best friend one can ever have.

It is a paradoxical relationship. And perhaps no hymn captures the paradox of friendship with a Creator and Redeemer better than Robert Grant's:

> Frail children of dust, and feeble as frail,
> In Thee do we trust, nor find Thee to fail,

Thy mercies how tender, how firm to the end,
Our Maker, Defender, Redeemer, and Friend.

It is a sort of friendship Aristotle could not imagine, the kind one is granted only with an incarnate God.[16]

---

[16]I regret that I did not discover Paul J. Wadell, *Friendship and the Moral Life* (Notre Dame, Ind.: Notre Dame Univ. Press, 1989), in time to include a discussion of its valuable contribution in the above article.

Anselm and the Modern Mind

M. Eugene Osterhaven

Professor of Systematic Theology, Emeritus
Western Theological Seminary

One of the striking developments that has taken place in the area of social morality during the professional career of Paul King Jewett has been the shift in thinking on the subjects of crime and punishment and their relation to each other. When Dr. Jewett began teaching, the prevailing mood in penology was one of broad-mindedness and toleration, even leniency. Some centuries earlier, brutality and unspeakable torture, perpetrated by the authorities in the name of justice, had been the usual manner of handling criminals. In reaction to that, the nineteenth century witnessed the fruition of a romantic idealism which, in the name of humaneness and enlightened morality, in one way or other explained away wrongdoing and regarded punishment as the last despicable display of a crude barbarism. Although on the world scene that trend had reached its zenith and was declining by the end of the Second World War—totalitarianism, left and right, had given it the *coup de grâce*—nationally that period is best remembered by a number of judgments rendered by the "Warren Court" of a generation ago. In those decisions of the Supreme Court of the United States of America the rights of offenders were interpreted by many to be of greater consequence than those of victims.

A reaction was predictable. In the last two and a half decades there has been a notable shift to the right that some decry as a denial of hard-earned human rights and a retreat to medievalism and others hail as a return to sane principles of social justice. The clamor against crime and for punishment, the election of "law and order" candidates to public office on all levels of government, and numerous court appointments, not to mention public opinion polls, are evidences of the change in national sentiment. In most parts of the country today it would be political suicide for a politician to espouse positions taken by a majority some years ago. Concrete evidence of the new mood was the appointment in 1965 of The President's Commission on Law Enforcement and Administration of Justice,[1] the revision over a

---

[1] The report *The Challenge of Crime in a Free Society*, was published at the United States Government Printing Office, Washington, D.C., in February 1967. Karl

decade ago of the United States Criminal Code, and the creation by Congress in 1984 of the United States Sentencing Commission. In these two latter actions stricter guidelines were established for judges in meting out sentences and paroling offenders. The former leeway given judges in sentencing some 40,000 federal defendants a year was taken away in the attempt to improve the criminal justice system. Although 158 federal judges and defense attorneys throughout the country protested that the new regulations were unconstitutional, at its first sitting in 1989 the United States Supreme Court upheld the Commission by a vote of eight to one.

That one-sided message of the frequently divided court was a sharp reminder of the drift of opinion concerning crime and punishment and their relation to each other. The conservative drift was not first of all the result of hard thinking about principles of morality and justice, but rather of displeasure with the crime rate, which had risen 300 percent between 1955 and 1973, a time that marked a turning point in public attitude. Ironically, these "were precisely the years when society was at its greatest pains to humanize the justice system, make rehabilitation programs work and allow indeterminate sentences to relax the law's supposedly heartless rigidity."[2] It was the deterioration of society that determined the decision. Theory developed out of practice as moral principles were brought out into the light and reexamined.

A modern thinker who gave attention to moral problems in general and the relation of crime to punishment in particular was C. S. Lewis. In an essay on punishment he refers to the wide objection to punishment and, by implication, to the theory that Christ bore our punishment and thus satisfied the justice of God.[3] The objection to the latter theory stems from a conviction about punishment in general. There was a time when it was thought that sin deserves punishment, that the two are riveted together because God is holy and just. Where there is sin, or crime, there is intrinsic guilt, and guilt requires punishment. God must punish sin because of his nature; he cannot and will not clear the guilty.

Today, said Lewis, instead of that theory of retributive punishment, other reasons are given for dealing with offenders: restoration, or reformation, and deterrence. When he wrote, in England before the days of Margaret Thatcher, Lewis claimed that almost none of his compatriots any longer believed in retributive justice; rather, they held what he called the "humanitarian" view, seen by Lewis as a

---

Menninger's popular *The Crime of Punishment* (New York: Viking Compass Edition, 1969) was first published in 1966, when the Commission's report was being prepared.

[2]Lance Morrow, "On Crime and Much Harder Punishment," *Time* 112, no. 12 (September 18, 1978): 54.

[3]C. S. Lewis, *God in the Dock* (Grand Rapids: Eerdmans, 1970), 287-94.

dangerous illusion. He urged a return to the retributive theory of justice, not only for the sake of society, but for the sake of individuals. The humanitarian view claims that to punish someone because that person deserves it is barbarous and cruel, and thus immoral. According to this view, the only legitimate motives for punishment are deterrence and restoration. Where this is coupled with the notion that crime is pathological, Lewis held, then punishment is intended to be therapeutic. Thus we no more punish the wicked but heal the sick.

Lewis claimed that this thinking deprives one of the rights of a human being. The reason is that it removes the concept of desert from punishment, and it is that concept of desert that is the only connecting link between punishment and justice. It is only as deserved or undeserved that a sentence can be just or unjust.

> There is no sense in talking about a just deterrent or a just cure. We demand of a deterrent not whether it is just but whether it will deter. We demand of a cure not whether it is just but whether it succeeds. Thus when we cease to consider what the criminal deserves and consider only what will cure him or deter others, we have tacitly removed him from the sphere of justice altogether; instead of a person, a subject of rights, we now have a mere object, a patient, a "case."[4]

This distinction becomes clearer, Lewis claimed, when we ask who is "qualified to determine sentences when sentences are no longer held to derive their propriety from the criminal's deservings. On the old view the problem of fixing the right sentence was a moral problem,"[5] and the judge who made the decision was trained in law, a science which has to do with rights and duties and which originally was thought to be dealing with eternal principles. Society's conscience was controlled by these, and if "justice" got too rough, juries would refuse to convict until there was reform, as happened in eighteenth-century England. This was possible as long as people thought in terms of desert, the rightness of the law, and moral questions about which all people have an opinion because they are human beings, rational-moral creatures.

When the concept of desert is abandoned, Lewis argued, this is all changed. Then the interest becomes whether the sentence deters or cures. But these are not questions on which all people have a right to an opinion because they are human beings. They are questions only experts can answer—psychiatrists, perhaps. If crime is in fact a form of disease, then any mental state that rulers decide to label "disease" can

---

[4]Ibid., 288. Another fine treatment of the concept of desert is in Robert William Dale, *The Atonement* (London: Hodder & Stoughton, 1878), 377-79.

[5]Lewis, *God in the Dock*, 288.

be treated as crime, as we have seen in totalitarian countries. Commenting on this reasoning of Lewis, Morrow noted, "The KGB understands the logic."[6]

Lewis claimed that when the idea of desert is surrendered as archaic and vindictive, the jury system becomes obsolete because sentences are taken from the hands of "jurists whom the public conscience is entitled to criticize" and placed in the hands of "technical experts whose special sciences do not even employ such categories as rights or justice."[7] This is the thinking that is responsible for suspended sentences, the abolition of capital punishment and churches petitioning governments to that end, the reduction of penalties for crimes, the fact that few criminals serve their entire sentences, and the demise of the belief that the punishment must fit the crime. However, when forgiveness looms larger in jurisprudence than punishment, the whole foundation of justice is undermined. The resulting chaos in society is similar to what happens in a home when forbearance and forgiveness supplant discipline.

Whether or not Lewis is correct in his thinking, one thing is certain: public opinion has swung in his direction, back to older conceptions of the relation of crime to deserved punishment. That shift to the right in penal theory has had important bearing on Christian theology, which, while having its foundation in the self-disclosure of God in his Word, is influenced by its environment. The proverb, *"Tempora mutant et nos mutamur in illis*: times change and we are changed in them" is apropos here. The theology of the church has often been so sensitive to earthly change that it has drifted from the rock to which it had been anchored.

That was seen vividly in certain theological theorizing on the Atonement when Paul Jewett began his teaching career. A case in point is the trilogy of Vincent Taylor, a prominent British theologian, on the death of Christ. In a work entitled *Jesus and His Sacrifice* the author rejects the notion of propitiatory sacrifice as "too crude"[8] and holds that the rationale of biblical sacrifice is "the bestowal of life [as] the fundamental idea in sacrificial worship."[9] Popular aversion to the biblical teaching of sacrificial offering is understandable but wrong: "Only if we think of sacrifice as a means of appeasing God is the conception out of place."[10]

In *The Doctrine of Atonement in New Testament Teaching* he continues this line of argument. We should not think "in legal terms . . .

[6]Morrow, "On Crime and Much Harder Punishment," 54.

[7]Lewis, *God in the Dock*, 289.

[8]Vincent Taylor, *Jesus and His Sacrifice* (London: Macmillan, 1937), 74.

[9]Ibid., 57

[10]Ibid., 304.

[but] intelligently believe that first, last, and always [God] is Love, and that Fatherhood is the highest category under which we can conceive or think of him." Then "we restore freedom to the Godhead."[11] He repudiates substitutionary atonement but affirms "representative action."

> Perhaps the most striking feature of New Testament teaching concerning the representative work of Christ is the fact that it comes so near, without actually crossing, the bounds of substitutionary doctrine. Paulinism, in particular, is within a hair's breadth of substitution. If, moreover, we read Mark 10:45 by itself ("a ransom for many"), apart from Mark 14:24 ("my blood of the covenant"), a similar claim, although with less justice, can be made for certain aspects of the teaching of Jesus, and, indeed, for not a little of New Testament doctrine concerning redemption, purchase, and mediatorial action. In fact, a theologian who retires to a doctrinal fortress guarded by such ordnance as Mark 10:45, Romans 6:10f., 2 Corinthians 5:14, 21, Galatians 3:13, and 1 Timothy 2:5f., is more difficult to dislodge than many New Testament students imagine. Now this argument is not intended as a defense of substitution. On the contrary, in the earlier discussions we have given reasons, which we believe to be conclusive, for rejecting such teaching. The fortress can be outflanked, captured, and dismantled. The point of our argument is the *significance* of the fact that New Testament teaching about the representative work of Christ is almost, but not quite, substitutionary. . . . We need a category of representative action.[12]

Taylor continues:

> In claiming that the work of Christ is sacrificial we are far removed from propitiatory ideas which are sub-Christian in their character and implications. We are, however, certainly in the realm of expiatory ideas, if we use this adjective, as the New Testament encourages us to use it, of the covering, canceling, or annulling of sins which stand between ourselves and the blessedness of fellowship with God.[13]

He concludes his argument by quoting another author who claims that "we are now hundreds of miles from the thought of vicarious punishment."[14] It is not surprising, then, to hear Taylor, in a subsequent work, repudiate the doctrine of imputation which the Bible (e.g., Ro 4) and historic Protestantism place at the heart of the doctrine of salvation.

---

[11]Vincent Taylor, *The Doctrine of Atonement in New Testament Teaching* (London: Epworth, 1940), 283.

[12]Ibid., 289.

[13]Ibid., 290.

[14]Ibid., 293.

[I]mputation . . . can never be anything else than an ethical fiction. . . .
[R]ighteousness cannot be transferred from the account of one person
to another. Righteousness can no more be imputed to a sinner than
bravery to a coward or wisdom to a fool. If through faith a man is
accounted righteous, it must be because, in a reputable sense of the
term, he is righteous, and not because another is righteous in his
stead. . . . Reformation teaching . . . cannot be said to have been successful in surmounting the ethical difficulties of justification.[15]

It is little wonder that Emil Brunner, having emerged from that
kind of theological milieu when he wrote *The Mediator*, penned the
following:

Superficiality makes its own God—a God who is of the kind it likes. So
long as we continue to reject the scriptural ideas of divine holiness, of
divine wrath, and of divine righteousness in punishment, the process
of decay within the church will continue.[16]

Brunner was a part of the biblical-theological revival that began in
Europe at the time of the First World War and in this country two
decades later.[17] It was a time of the rediscovery of the Bible as the
Word of God rather than the ripest fruit on the tree of human
achievement; of the justice and holiness of God and of his necessary
judgment on sin; of the exceeding sinfulness of sin, with a biblical
apprehension of its guilt and pervasive corruption; of the church as
the body of Christ created by the Holy Spirit; of the person of Christ, as
the church of the fourth and fifth centuries had defined it; and of his
work, as described mainly by Anselm and the Reformers of the
sixteenth century.

It is Anselm, archbishop of Canterbury, more than anyone else, to
whom we are indebted for our understanding of the theological
meanings of sin, satisfaction, and the death of the Savior. This is not
because only he saw the biblical motifs which he wrote into a comprehensive statement, for Athanasius and Ambrose before him, and
others later, spoke of substitution and satisfaction. Nor was it because
of the indefectible character of his essay, for there are passages in it
which nobody takes seriously today. It is rather because of his selection, grasp, arrangement, and articulation of these fundamental
truths that *Cur Deus Homo* made an enormous impact on the thinking of the church and determined its future course in interpreting the

---

[15]Vincent Taylor, *Forgiveness and Reconciliation* (London: Macmillan, 1941), 57.

[16]Emil Brunner, *The Mediator*, trans. Olive Wyon (New York: Macmillan, 1934),
468.

[17]Dr. Jewett's dissertation is entitled *Emil Brunner's Concept of Revelation*
(London: J. Clarke, 1954).

Atonement. After Anselm, thought about the work of Christ was not the same as it was before his time.

The problem Anselm addressed is: "By what reason or necessity God was made man, and by his death, as we believe and confess, restored life to the world."[18] After disposing of earlier theories which he saw as unsatisfactory, he said that there must be some rational necessity for the incarnation and death of Christ. To say that it is God's will that salvation be effected in a certain manner is insufficient; there must be a reason for it, some absolute necessity.

As he laid out his argument, he began with the premise that humanity was made for eternal fellowship and happiness with God and that our wills ought to be subject to his. They are not subject to him, however; thus we fail to give God his due, robbing him of the honor he deserves. This cannot go unnoticed and unpunished lest the moral order of the universe be disturbed. Those who fail to appreciate this have not yet considered the gravity of sin, Anselm says in what may be the essay's most famous line.[19] Future obedience does not pay past debt, for we should always give God his due. Nor can we repay God by penances or any other kind of satisfaction for the dishonor we have done him.[20] Yet the divine honor must be vindicated. Justice demands that sin be punished, for God is God, and he cannot call sin anything other than that which it is.

In certain of the writings of the fathers of the early church, this Godward aspect of the Atonement appeared in the suggestion that something in the very nature of God requires atonement. Yet none carried this thought to its conclusion. Some tended to see God administering a law like that of Rome; others wished to defend God against the charge of injustice toward the Devil; still others showed that God does not and cannot take sin lightly. While appreciating the work that had been done before him, Anselm tried to dig deeper. He probed the question of what the Atonement meant to God himself.[21]

An important point in the discussion is the relation of God's attributes to his being. If they are arbitrary in God, he might be able to

---

[18]St. Anselm: Proslogium; Monologium; Cur Deus Homo, trans. S. N. Deane (LaSalle, Ill.: Open Court, 1951), 1.1.15.

[19]Ibid., 1.20.21.

[20]John McIntyre notes that "by a single stroke St. Anselm here destroys what had obviously become a misconception of the early medieval penitential exercises, namely, that of themselves, apart from the work of Christ, they achieved forgiveness for the sinner. He thus strikes a blow for evangelical theology, for justification by God's free grace in Christ as against justification by works, the importance of which has not been fully realized" (St. Anselm and his Critics: A Re-interpretation of the Cur Deus Homo [Edinburgh: Oliver and Boyd, 1954], 78).

[21]McIntyre claims correctly that Anselm is "more concerned with the effects of sin upon God than upon man" (ibid., 69).

forgive sin by an act of will alone, for there would be no absolute necessity for the satisfaction that Anselm had in mind. On the other hand, if they are more ultimate than God, he would have to pay deference to them in his actions. That would mean that he is not sovereignly free. In Anselm's thought, God's attributes are identical with God himself. The old question whether God wills what is right because it is right, or whether something is right because God wills that it be right, is put to rest. Both voluntarism and Platonism are wrong. "The moral notions are neither more ultimate than God's nature, nor are they willed to be what they are, as it were, arbitrarily by Him. On the contrary, they are co-eternal with Him, existing integrally to His very Being."[22]

Having created humanity in his image, God does not desire to lose his work. He will not suffer defeat. Yet sin remains a horrendous fact that demands settlement. Because sin belongs to humanity, it is by humanity that satisfaction must be made if God's handiwork is to be saved. But humanity is weak through sin and is completely unable to make satisfaction. Only God can do that, and he did it in the person of his Son, who is both God and man. As a sinless man, though he owed to God the obedience of his life, he was under no obligation to die as God-man. If he were to die, it is because of his own free will. Here, then, was the possibility of satisfaction. Because Christ's life and death have infinite value and outweigh all sins, his death could be a satisfaction for the sins of the world. Whereas the whole created universe could not provide the satisfaction necessary for sin, the Godman could make that compensation. When he had made it, forgiveness was possible, for forgiveness is indissolubly connected with satisfaction.

Among the many interpretations of Anselm on the Atonement, John McIntyre's is sympathetic and, in my judgment, accurate.[23] A central concept in Anselm's theory is the meaning that he gives the term *satisfaction* and the propriety of its use in theological discourse. It is true, as McIntyre states, that Anselm borrowed the term from the church and society of his day, which had given it long usage. However, he gave it a specialized meaning that is more religious than legal,[24] and the thought that he desired to convey through the use of the term is thoroughly biblical.

While it is not at all difficult to raise questions about Anselm's treatise, the fact remains that he identified and scrutinized the great issues that have to be dealt with when God, sin, and salvation are

---

[22]Ibid., 100.

[23]McIntyre's response to the adverse criticism of Albrecht Ritschl, Adolf von Harnack, and Robert S. Franks is found in *Anselm and His Critics*, 90-95.

[24]Ibid., 76-95.

considered. As a result, he left a legacy from which the church and society continue to draw.

In the contemporary debate over crime and punishment and their relation to each other, those issues are again on center stage. The rising crime rate and the exposure given it by the media are bound to continue to hold the spotlight on them. This will show, with increasing clarity, the relevance and the importance of the close relationship between criminology, on the one hand, and ethical and theological concerns, on the other. It is impossible to think profoundly and consistently about the one apart from the others.

If Anselm and Lewis are correct in their conviction that in the moral order sustained by God wrongdoing necessitates divine reaction against it, that conviction has important consequences for both theological and criminological theory. When a sufficient number of members of church and society become convinced that the positions taken by Anselm and Lewis square with reality, those positions will be reflected in church doctrine and civil law. That has happened in the past, and change in that direction is evident in our time. We have observed this change in the movement in penology from more lax to more stringent attitudes toward crime and punishment, in the switch from leniency and indulgence in sentencing to the creation of a federal sentencing commission, and in the adoption of a stricter penal code. These developments do not mean, one may hope, that a scourge of vindictiveness has swept over society, although they could mean that; but they may indicate a new awareness that our system of social justice must affirm the conviction that there is a fundamental difference between right and wrong, that human beings make decisions between the two daily, and that they are responsible for their decisions. The new mood suggests the belief that the distinction between right and wrong is, at bottom, not merely the consequence of arbitrary human judgment but rather the certainty that we are part of a higher order, one ordained by God.

That order, revealed in the divine self-disclosure recorded in the Bible, is the special concern of the science of theology. Theology, however, is not interested only in a higher order; it is also as deeply interested in the human condition, and it has a special concern for the moral and spiritual healing of persons. It is not surprising, therefore, that, with the drift to the right in criminology, there has been a similar movement in theology in general and in the doctrine of the death of Christ in particular. Emil Brunner's restatement of the penal satisfaction theory of the Atonement was the first of many studies that took Anselm's position essentially. Atonement must be understood primarily in its relation to God the Father and his necessary aversion to sin. A new appreciation for the biblical teachings of the holiness of God and the exceeding sinfulness of sin has brought a wholesome emphasis on the necessity of dealing with sin, so that reconciliation between God and humankind might become a reality.[25] We find evidence of this emphasis in the literature of the evangelical movement, whose remarkable rise in America in the second half of the twentieth century is due in large part to its willingness to take a long, hard look at fundamental Christian doctrine.[26]

Paul King Jewett has been a leader in contemporary evangelical theology. His career demonstrates a profound familiarity with and dedication to the moral ideals and principles on which our civilization and its culture have been built. In an unostentatious but effective way he has contended for them, thus demonstrating his linear descent from the Archbishop of Canterbury and the writers of Holy Writ. The basic concerns that claimed their attention have been his, and they are the great issues that confront society today.

---

[25]A Buddhist who had heard that Christianity teaches the forgiveness of sins knew nothing about the doctrine of the death of Christ which has made forgiveness possible. His perceptive comment was, "The forgiveness of sins seems too simple, almost trifling and immoral." On the basis of what he knew, he was right.

[26]The several monographs of Leon Morris on the work of Christ are a prime example.

Jesus and Political Authority

Richard J. Mouw

Provost and Professor of Christian Philosophy and Ethics
Fuller Theological Seminary

What does Jesus have to do with political leadership? In what sense, if at all, does the biblical portrayal of Jesus of Nazareth—or of the risen and ascended Christ—provide us with a helpful model for understanding the proper use of political authority?

These are the questions that I will address in this essay. But my purpose here is not so much to answer these questions as it is to examine some of the reasons why Christian thinkers have had such a difficult time finding satisfying answers to them. Specifically, I will look at three factors that have given rise to these difficulties. The first has to do with the challenge of finding ways of relating the political dimensions of Jesus' ministry to the content of political theory. The second deals with some important features of contemporary political life. And the third factor is rooted in longstanding Christological disagreements.

My use of the word "difficulties" here is quite intentional. It is not impossible to make significant and legitimate applications of the ministry of Jesus to contemporary patterns of political leadership, but it is difficult. The project is important enough, however, to make it worthwhile to take on the challenges. The need for new manifestations of political righteousness continues to be an urgent one. And the political authority of Jesus is not diminished by the very real puzzles that we face as we attempt to explore the ways in which that authority operates in contemporary political life.

THEOLOGY AND POLITICAL THEORY

The first difficulty is obviously a case in point for a more general problem. Questions about the proper links between our understanding of the ministry of Jesus and issues in political theory have to be viewed against the background of more general questions about the relationship of the Bible's treatment of political topics to the scholarly investigation of contemporary political phenomena.

An understandable but regrettable gap presently exists between the concerns of those who deal with political questions from a perspective that is primarily biblical-theological and those who study political phenomena from within the context of the social sciences. This gap is understandable because the social sciences have experienced rapid theoretical and methodological growth in the past few decades; new disciplines and subdisciplines have emerged so quickly that it has been difficult for individuals, and even communities of scholars, to maintain a sense of perspective. But the gap is also regrettable, since many Christians who direct their scholarly attention to such matters as political behavior, international law, the study of political parties, and the like, have had to pursue their interests with little by way of clear guidance from Christian theologians and philosophers.

The difficulties here are inherent in the task of establishing the kinds of correlations (to borrow Tillich's term) that are necessary if we are to bridge the gap between the biblical message and the contemporary study of politics. The Bible, as we are regularly reminded, is not a textbook of natural science. And neither, we must add, is it a textbook of sociological or political theory. Indeed, it is not a "textbook" of anything. It is the locus and vehicle of God's urgent message to a human race that is desperately in need of good news about the basic questions of the human condition.

But political questions are included within the compass of the Bible's address to the urgent issues of life. The pages of the Bible are full of tales of political intrigue, psalms written by and about rulers, prophetic critiques of political practices and policies, and visions of the future in which political images play a prominent role. The challenge is, of course, to translate these existential dealings into the kinds of themes and concepts and insights that are relevant to topics of political theory.

"Political theory," as I use the term here, refers to a broad area of intellectual discussion of social-political phenomena. It includes that branch of philosophy called "social-political philosophy," as well as the concerns of those scholars in academic departments of politics, political science, or government who deal with matters falling under the rubrics of "normative political theory" and the "conceptual foundations" of the study of politics. Here are some key questions that are important for these areas of academic-intellectual discussion: What is the nature of, and justification for, political relationships? Why ought we to have political structures at all? What are the sources, limits, and ends of political power? How, if at all, are patterns of political authority different from other kinds of authority patterns? What do all political systems have in common? What is "political obligation"? What sort of political system is "best" for human beings? What are the appropriate criteria for evaluating and comparing political systems?

Once we formulate these questions in their most general form, we can begin to see how the Scriptures can be rightly thought of as having relevance—at least of a sort—to such ideas. These questions have to do with basic issues about the nature of reality, human nature, human social relationships, authority patterns, and the like. And the biblical writers are dealing with similar issues, although—to repeat—their mode of address is regularly characterized by a sense of urgency and poignancy.

The fact that the Bible focuses on very concrete political phenomena should not be viewed as constituting an insurmountable problem in our attempts to find links between the biblical message and political theory. After all, political theorists themselves regularly insist that concrete political phenomena are the touchstone of their theorizings. Scientific studies of contemporary political behavior take their starting point from very ordinary people and groups, many of them caught up in urgent and poignant issues of political existence. Those scholars who go beyond empirical studies to formulate more refined theories are themselves under an obligation to show that their models and constructs comport with the concrete political data.

The fact that both the Bible and political theory have a strong interest in concrete political data provides an important consideration, then, in our search for correlations. Political theorists who take the Bible seriously will of necessity operate with an expanded "data base." In conceiving of the proper scope of "political behavior," they will attend not only to the political information they glean from studying the ethnic enclaves and city councils and smoke-filled rooms of contemporary life; they will also be mindful of the political patterns of Moses and Deborah and Jezebel and Daniel and Stephen and John, and of the political patterns of Jesus as well—which brings us back to our central concern here.

John Howard Yoder's 1972 book, *The Politics of Jesus,* is a good place to start in looking at the relevance of Jesus' ministry for a theoretical understanding of political behavior. The very title of Yoder's book announces the relevance. For one thing, it directly addresses the naïveté of those who have been content with a Jesus-without-politics. Indeed, Yoder's book has had an important influence in this regard; many evangelical Christians can testify to the fact that *The Politics of Jesus* has helped to arouse them from their pietistic slumbers.

But Yoder's title also interrupts the musings of those who want a politics-without-Jesus, which is the problem that we are dealing with here. Yoder insists that we cannot properly understand the domain of politics without viewing the political role of Jesus as "normative." And this claim of his is much more than a homiletical ploy designed to stir Christian consciences. It is a challenge to even the most "empirically" oriented political theorists.

One way of reading Yoder is to interpret him as defending what we might call an "authoritative-exemplar" account of politics. On this reading we can, in an important sense, learn what politics is "about" by committing ourselves to becoming followers of Jesus. By assuming the posture of discipleship, we encounter politics in its "purity"; from this perspective we come to view all other modes of political activity as distortions of an ideal mode.

This is, to be sure, to go beyond Yoder's own formulation of his case. But there is much in the argument that he presents in his book that can be expanded in this manner, with the result that his discussion becomes relevant to political theory as such, quite apart from the religious commitments of the theorists involved. Thus, Yoder is right to complain that Christians regularly ignore the way in which "the exemplary quality of Jesus' social humanity" can serve as "a model for our social ethics."[1] But we can also add that the inattention of political theorists in general to the "political behavior" of Jesus leaves them open to the charge that their generalizations are formed on the basis of insufficient data with regard to actual and possible modes of political behavior.

The question of a proper definition of "politics" is near the surface at almost every point in Yoder's discussion: it is present in his claims that Jesus provides us with "a model of radical political action"[2]; that Jesus is "presenting to men not the avoidance of political options, but one particular social-political-ethical option"[3]; and that Jesus is "the bearer of a new possibility of human, social, and therefore political relationships."[4] At a few points Yoder himself explicitly raises this definitional question. In a lengthy footnote, for example, he tells us that Jesus is issuing a fundamental challenge to commonly accepted accounts of the term *polis*,[5] and at another point he puts the case in these rather dramatic terms:

> Jesus chose not only to stumble over diversities of definition but to be crucified on them. He refused to concede that the men in power represent an ideal, a logically proper, or even an empirically acceptable definition of what it means to be political. He did not say . . . , "you can have your politics and I shall do something else more important"; he said, "your definition of *polis*, of the social, of the wholeness of man in his socialness is perverted."[6]

---

[1]John Howard Yoder, *The Politics of Jesus* (Grand Rapids: Eerdmans, 1972), 131.

[2]Ibid., 12.

[3]Ibid., 23.

[4]Ibid., 63.

[5]Ibid., 50n.

[6]Ibid., 112-13.

The applicability of these emphases to basic methodological and conceptual issues in political theory should be obvious. Even from an allegedly "value-free," empiricist point of view, generalizations about what is actual or possible in the realm of politics must be tested against actual or possible political behavior. Many of the claims Yoder makes, then, about the political attitudes and behavior of Jesus seem to count as counterevidence against many widely held theories of politics.

Note also that the political behavior of Jesus—or more specifically, Yoder's claims about the political behavior of Jesus—can serve as counterexamples to existing generalizations even when the theorist in question does not accept the activity and teachings of Jesus as in some sense "normative" or even commendable. Very few contemporary theorists view Hitler as a commendable politician; yet few would dare to propose a theory about how politics or politicians function which did not in some sense "account" for the politics of Hitler. If Jesus did express political beliefs and engage in political activity, then his case, too, provides us with data that are relevant to generalizations about actual political beliefs and activities.

In fact, the relevance of the biblical story for political theory does not even depend on its being taken as "empirical data" in a straightforward sense. Christians thinkers do not have to engage, then, in a full-scale historical apologetic in order to introduce biblical information into the discussion of political themes. Insofar as political theory is concerned with the clarification of political concepts, even purely hypothetical examples may be relevant to the discussion: Plato did not think that the story of Gyges' Ring was a true story, and social contract theorists typically warn us against taking such phenomena as the "state of nature" and the "veil of ignorance" to be historically locatable conditions. Yet in each case these "stories" function as important conceptual tools. The question "What if such-and-such were to occur?" is often an important element in political theoretical discussion.

Yoder's insistence on the conceptual relevance of Jesus' political ministry for a basic understanding of the political sphere, then, has clear implications for the nontheological disciplines. Needless to say, however, not all theologians would agree with Yoder in his understanding of the relation of Jesus' ministry to political life. It is interesting, for example, that Vernard Eller—who, like Yoder, operates with an Anabaptist perspective on such issues—takes a very different line on this topic. Eller insists that when the Christian

steps into the political arena, he must realize that he is on the same footing with every other citizen: his Christian faith gives him no special leading, grants him no special wisdom, confers upon him no special status, results in no special privileges, carries no special advantages. His Bible gives him no more political guidance than it gives guidance in modern physics to the fellow Christian in the laboratory.[7]

On the other hand, it is also interesting that in formally challenging the accepted definitions of "politics," Yoder is aligned with the secular social critic, the late Paul Goodman, who dissented from "the assumption, now appallingly unanimous among the ordinary electorate, professional politicians, most radicals, and even political scientists who should know better, that politics is essentially a matter of 'getting into power,' and then 'deciding,' directing, controlling, coercing, the activities of society."[8] And Goodman continues: "When I question such a universal consensus, I wonder if I am on the right planet. Nevertheless, these persons are deluded. They are taking a base and impractical, and indeed neurotic, state of affairs as if it were right and inevitable."[9]

The narrow, "neurotic" understanding of the scope of political relationships is clearly exhibited in Max Weber's definition of a "political" group as one in which "the enforcement of its order is carried out continually within a given *territorial* area by the application and threat of physical force on the part of the administrative staff."[10] This, from the Yoder-Goodman perspective, only delineates the nature of one kind of political order, namely a sinful or neurotic one.

Yoder is right to reject the commonly held accounts of the nature of the political as too restricted. And he is right to insist that Jesus' mission and authority apply to the political sphere in a way that prods us to broaden and revise our understandings of what constitutes the "normal" and the "neurotic" in the exercise of political power. Christian political thinkers in a variety of related disciplines can perform an important service by exhibiting conceptual clarity on this matter and by offering a full-scale defense of a broader understanding of the scope of, and possible patterns within, the domain of political thought and action.

---

[7]Vernard Eller, *King Jesus' Manual of Arms for the 'Armless: War and Peace from Genesis to Revelation* (Nashville: Abingdon, 1973), 197.

[8]Paul Goodman, *People or Personnel: Decentralizing and the Mixed Systems* (New York: Random House, 1965), 178. See also Paul Goodman, *Like a Conquered Province: The Moral Ambiguity of America* (New York: Random House, 1967).

[9]Goodman, *People or Personnel*, 179-80.

[10]Max Weber, *The Theory of Social and Economic Organization*, trans. A. M. Henderson and Talcott Parsons (New York: Free Press, 1964), 154.

CONTEMPORARY POLITICAL PATTERNS

Even if it can be established that Jesus provides us with an alternative account of what politics is all about, questions still remain as to how we can practice the politics of Jesus in the give-and-take of a political environment like that of North America. Christian ethicists have written surprisingly little on this topic. For all of the talk about "contextualization" on the part of Christian social thinkers in recent years, there has been very little attention given to the context of the power-wielder in North American political life. Christian ethicists have been writing much recently about the need for a contemporary "ethics of virtue"; but we have yet to see any serious Christian attempt to deal with the exercise of the virtues in political office. To be sure, Christian scholars have produced much helpful material about substantive policy issues that are of concern—or ought to be of concern—to political officeholders. But they have not said much about the station and the duties of the officeholder as such.

This subject has not always been neglected. It was given sustained treatment during the Italian Renaissance, especially in the city of Florence. In his detailed discussion of Florentine political thought, Quentin Skinner recounts the themes and nuances of a whole series of fifteenth- and sixteenth-century political advice books, such as Patrizi's *The Kingdom and the Education of the King,* Sacchi's *The Prince,* Carafa's *The Office of a Good Prince,* Pontano's *The Prince,* and, of course, Machiavelli's *The Prince.*[11]

In these "mirror for princes" works, the writers advise rulers on how to achieve the proper patterns of virtue in the exercise of political power. Several of them seem genuinely concerned to provide *Christian* advice regarding the cultivation of political virtue. Indeed, however we may understand Machiavelli's actual intentions in writing his much interpreted—to say nothing of much maligned—political advice book, there can be no doubt that he at least formally acknowledges these same purposes. And even on the worst interpretation of his actual intentions, Machiavelli at least did politicians the favor of focusing exclusively on the exercise of political power, a form of guidance that has been seriously lacking in recent ethical literature.

The kind of attention the conduct of political office deserves is already highly developed with regard to other areas of professional activity. One could even argue that it is somewhat *over*developed in relation to, say, the medical professions. Production of literature in medical ethics has become a virtual industry in the past two decades. A vast proportion of this literature has focused on the practice of

---

[11]Quentin Skinner, *The Foundations of Modern Political Thought,* 2 vols. (New York: Cambridge Univ. Press, 1978), vol. 1, chap. 5.

medicine on the part of physicians: How does the physician relate to his or her patients? What principles ought to guide the physician's decision-making? What is the proper order of priorities having to do with those values that bear on questions of medical intervention by physicians? Medical ethicists have begun, more recently, to broaden the scope of their concerns. But it is still fair to say that much of the existing literature in the field of medical ethics focuses primarily on the character, values, and decisions of individual practitioners.

In political thought, however, ethicists have focused almost exclusively on systems and policies. The patterns of individual political virtue have been pretty much ignored by recent Christian social ethicists. It is not surprising, then, that the ministry of Jesus is not seen as providing a relevant model for individual politicians. Even liberation theologians, who certainly believe that the politics of Jesus has relevance to contemporary political life, do not really have much to say to the specific callings of individual politicians in, say, capitalist democracies. They assume that Jesus' political vision is primarily a prescription for reshaping political-economic structures. They are not very interested in the virtuous pursuit of individual political careers.

The assumptions that have led to this neglect of political virtue are paralleled in widespread attitudes in the larger Christian community. Many ordinary Christian people seem to be firmly convinced that there really is no such thing as a uniquely political pattern of virtue. This skepticism is intimately related to the conviction that politics is essentially a "dirty business": we cannot expect much good to come from the political realm, but it is an important check on human sin. Since the political system is viewed as a kind of holding action, political careers are looked at in much the same terms. Politicians are not expected to produce much positive good; the most we can hope for is that they will not become more corrupt than necessary. Excessive corruption can be avoided if political officeholders have the appropriate personal characteristics—if, for example, they pray and have faith and maintain good family relationships and the like.

On one very widespread Christian assessment of political life, then, there is an important emphasis placed on personal character. But the kinds of virtues singled out are not peculiarly political. They are the traits the folks in the pew want everyone to possess. They would list the same virtues in describing the godly insurance agent, or the godly concertmistress, or the godly football coach. Thus, while these ordinary Christian folks do think that it is possible for politicians to cultivate virtues that bear on the exercise of political power, they do not have much of a notion of what it would be like to display uniquely *political* virtues. This point brings us back to the Christian social ethicists. As we have already observed, they have been much more comfortable advising people on how to be godly physicians than they have been talking about godly mayors.

On the face of things, though, there would seem to be equally good reasons to address both areas. It is not unusual, for example, for Christian ethicists to employ the *imitatio Christi* theme in dealing with the responsibilities of the physician. This is quite appropriate. Jesus was the divine healer. We can plausibly refer to him as the Great Physician. Isn't it obvious that Christian healers today can learn important things from the healing ministry of Jesus?

Of course. But why can't we also use the imitation-of-Christ theme in dealing with the conduct of political office? Doesn't the Bible consistently portray God as Ruler? Isn't Jesus properly thought of as the divine liberator who comes to announce and initiate the reign of God? Of course. And present-day Christian ethicists and political theorists do not deny these things; in fact, they regularly emphasize them.

Why is it, then, that they seem to be so reluctant to move from God-as-Ruler to godly mayor? Why is that comparison more awkward for them than the move from God-as-Healer to godly medical doctor? One obvious reason—and here we come close to the heart of the issue—has to do with the nature of political office in the North American political system.

If we are going to look for symmetry between the medical and the political discussions, then we have to move, strictly speaking, from divine Ruler to human *ruler*, just as we move from divine Physician to human physician. And that is where the rub comes. The writers of political advice books in fifteenth-century Florence could still make such a move. They could slip back and forth, with little sense of awkwardness, between divine Ruler and human ruler, divine King and human king, divine Prince and human prince.

But the conceptual link here, which seemed such a natural one in the past, is not so easy to establish in contemporary North America. It does not seem very natural to refer to our present-day politicians— mayors and members of city councils and legislators—as "rulers." On the national level of government in the United States, for example, political power is shared by three branches of government. Indeed, there is an important sense in which we must locate "the powers that be" of Ro 13, not with this or that individual or group, but with that constitutional system that defines the offices and patterns of accountability of federal government.

The president of the United States is not a "ruler" whom to disobey is to violate the inspired guidelines given by the Apostle. Rather, if the president refuses to accede to legitimate requests on the part of the legislative and judicial officers—as was the case, for example, during the Watergate proceedings—then it is the president who is not fully obeying the properly constituted authorities of Ro 13. Furthermore, since constitutionally defined political power is delegated to public officials by the citizenry, who possess the rights of criticism and review with regard to public policy and conduct, one might even argue that a Christian citizen who refuses to criticize the government officials when that is called for is *failing* to obey the biblically designated "powers that be."

This is a complex system of "rule." It is difficult to think of any officeholder in the system simply as a monarchial leader whose activities can be directly modeled on the actions and attitudes of the divine Monarch. To be sure, the North American diffusion and segmentation of political authority does not completely undercut the Christian appeal to the *imitatio* theme, but it certainly complicates the ethical situation.

The problems posed by the structural complexity of the political system are at least matched by the difficulties caused by the moral complexity of the larger society which that system is designed to govern. A high value is placed on the framing of policies that will effect accommodations and adjudicate disputes among diverse interest groups.

There can be no doubt that in practice a system whose agreed-upon aim is the taming of moral conflict takes its toll on the convictions of those who accept official roles within that system. Indeed, some have argued that the kind of toll exacted here is not peculiar to political life today, but is encouraged by the general theories of organization which have currency in the contemporary intellectual marketplace. It is very common, for example, for "scientific" accounts of organizational leadership to begin by noting that while "trait" theories of leadership were common in the past, it is no longer deemed adequate to account for leadership primarily in terms of subjective traits of personality and character.[12] The proposed alternatives—which, to be sure, seldom avoid all interest in the subjective characteristics of leaders—emphasize such factors as effective "behaviors," or perceived costs and benefits, or the kinds of "environmental constraints" a "systems analysis" can uncover.

There is undoubtedly much to be learned from these approaches. But this is an area that is also fraught with danger. James MacGregor Burns worries about the prevalence of a widespread leadership pattern which he labels "transactional." Here the goal of the interaction between leader and follower is "an exchange of valued things."

---

[12]See, for example, the discussions of theories of leadership in Barbara Kellerman, ed., *Leadership: Multidisciplinary Perspectives* (Englewood Cliffs, N.J.: Prentice-Hall, 1984); and *Stogdill's Handbook of Leadership: A Survey of Theory and Research*, rev. and expanded ed. by Bernard M. Bass (New York: Free Press, 1981).

While this kind of interaction does deserve to be called leadership, Burns insists, it is a kind of relationship in which the goods that are exchanged—whether they are votes, commercial products, money, or labor—are the only valued items; no higher or enduring purpose binds together the parties to the exchange.[13] This can easily degenerate into a "Machiavellian" relationship in which the goal is to "manage and manipulate other persons rather than to *lead* them."[14]

Burns advocates an increase in what he calls "transforming leadership":

> Such leadership occurs when one or more persons engage with others in such a way that leaders and followers raise one another to higher levels of motivation and morality. . . . Their purposes, which might have started out as separate but related, as in the case of transactional leadership, become fused. Power bases are linked not as counterweights but as mutual support for common purpose. Various names are used for such leadership, some of them derisory: elevating, mobilizing, inspiring, exalting, uplifting, preaching, exhorting, evangelizing. The relationship can be moralistic, of course. But transforming leadership ultimately becomes moral in that it raises the level of human conduct and ethical aspiration of both leader and led, and thus it has a transforming effect on both.[15]

This is an account of leadership—at least of an important and necessary kind of leadership—in which the personal traits of the leader are a central ingredient. The transforming leader operates with a vision of the normative possibilities of human conduct, and with conscious aspirations regarding the goals of the leader-follower relationship. Persons who engage in such leadership activities must possess some firm convictions, and they must be willng to join others in a quest for "higher levels of motivation and morality."

Is it possible to exercise transforming leadership in North American politics today? Burns thinks so, although he views some political offices as more receptive to transforming efforts than others: legislatures are, he argues, predominantly "transactional" in their patterns of decision-making, while party and executive leaders have more opportunities for transformational efforts.

Burns's conception of transforming leadership seems to be a fruitful one to explore in our attempts to find the ways in which we can "imitate Christ" in the contemporary political setting. Christian political programs that presuppose an imperial-monarchial framework do not comport well with the contemporary political mood. And that is

---

[13]James MacGregor Burns, *Leadership* (New York: Harper & Row, 1978), 20-21.
[14]Ibid., 446.
[15]Ibid., 20.

perhaps all to the good. Jesus alone is the true and righteous monarch
—the one who reigns over all of the rulers of the earth (Rev 1:5). As
his followers, we can hope only to approximate his thoughts and
policies—and that only in partial and fragmentary ways. This approx-
imation is best expedited, in turn, not by setting ourselves up as
would-be monarchs, but by entering into the kind of dialogue and
cautious experimentation that can nurture broader political sensitivi-
ties than any one human being can generate in isolation.

CHRISTOLOGY AND POLITICAL AUTHORITY

One reason why the notion of "transforming" leadership is an
attractive one for an understanding of Christian political involvement is that it seems to correlate well with the *servanthood* theme in
Jesus' teaching. Indeed, this way of fleshing out the idea of servanthood has clear advantages over the loose and imprecise ways in
which "servant leadership" is sometimes celebrated by Christians.
But it must be admitted that any attempt to spell out the patterns of
the politics of Jesus in terms of transforming leadership will beg some
serious theological questions unless further argument is offered in
support of the very idea of such an attempt. Many theologians would
question, for example, whether the notion of servanthood is itself
deserving of a central emphasis in our understanding of the patterns
of Jesus' political authority.

Let us consider how such a question might arise. In his 1898 Stone
Lectures, Abraham Kuyper spelled out what he took to be a proper
Calvinist understanding of the Christian's political calling by offering
a rather harsh critique of the Anabaptist perspective. Kuyper specifically rejected the Anabaptist notion that the earthly ministry of Jesus
provides us with an ethical model according to which we are to
distance ourselves from accepted patterns of citizenship. Such
distancing wrongly presumes, insists Kuyper, that Jesus came to
replace the Old Testament standards for righteous politics with a new
set of ethical requirements. Kuyper vigorously rejected the argument
that the earthly ministry of Jesus introduced new moral-political
content:

> Can we imagine that at one time God willed to rule things in a certain
> moral order, but that now, in Christ, He wills to rule it otherwise? As
> though He were not the Eternal, the Unchangeable, Who, from the
> very hour of creation, even unto all eternity, had willed, wills, and
> shall will and maintain, one and the same firm moral world-order!
> Verily Christ has swept away the dust with which man's sinful limita-
> tions had covered up this world-order, and has made it glitter again in
> its original brilliancy. Verily Christ, and He alone, has disclosed to us
> the eternal love of Christ which was, from the beginning, the moving

principle of this world-order. Above all, Christ has strengthened in us the ability to walk in this world-order with a firm, unfaltering step. But the world-order itself remains just what it was from the beginning. It lays full claim, not only to the believer (as though less were required from the unbeliever) but to every human being and to all human relationships. Hence Calvinism does not lead us to philosophize on a so-called moral life, as though *we* had to create, to discover, or to regulate this life. Calvinism simply places us under the impress of the majesty of God, and subjects us to His eternal ordinances and unchangeable commandments. Hence it is that, for the Calvinist, all ethical study is based on the Law of Sinai, not as though at that time the moral world-order began to be fixed, but to honor the Law of Sinai, as the divinely authentic summary of that original moral law which God wrote in the heart of man, at his creation, and which God is rewriting on the tables of every heart at its conversion.[16]

The application of Kuyper's comments to our present topic should be obvious. Kuyper does not see the earthly ministry of Jesus as having any special significance for Christian decision-making. The Incarnation adds nothing of substance, in his view, to our understanding of God's will for the patterns of human interaction. The moral-political content of the Gospel accounts is in effect a "republishing" of that which was already available in the Old Testament's display of God's lawful ordering of the creation.

The debate between Kuyper and the Anabaptists has much to do with differing assessments of the politically relevant features of the "career" of Jesus. Kuyper makes much of Jesus' kingly majesty. To show forth the rule of Christ—the key requirement of Christian political involvement in his scheme—is to act in obedience to that divine power that is most clearly displayed in Christ's roles as Creator and as ascended and victorious King. For the Anabaptists, on the other hand, showing forth the divine rule means exhibiting those patterns of servanthood that we see most clearly exhibited in the earthly suffering of Christ. Indeed, we do not properly understand Jesus' victorious kingship unless we define it with reference to his acceptance of powerlessness. "Thus the historicity of Jesus retains," argues Yoder, "in the working of the church as she encounters the other power and value structures of her history, the same kind of relevance that the man Jesus had for those whom he served until they killed him."[17]

Nor do we need to restrict ourselves to Reformed-Anabaptist disputes to find examples of the ways in which different readings of the "career" of Jesus shape various understandings of his political

---

[16]Abraham Kuyper, *Lectures on Calvinism* (Grand Rapids: Eerdmans, 1931), 71-72.
[17]Yoder, *Politics of Jesus*, 162.

relevance. Franciscans see Jesus at his political best in his "incarnational presence" among the poor. Some charismatics call Christians to imitate an earthly Jesus whose ministry was most clearly characterized by the miraculous displays of power in the "signs and wonders" he performed. Still others insist that the example of Jesus driving the money changers from the temple is a model for the crucial project of liberating structures from entrenched systems of economic injustice. It is not my intention to adjudicate these differences here. But I will offer some brief observations about their significance, as a conclusion to this present discussion.

First, it is a good thing to recognize that these theological disagreements do play an important role in arguments about the political relevance of the ministry of Jesus. We conservative evangelicals have long insisted that theological questions about the person and work of Jesus Christ are of the utmost importance in dealing with the basic issues of discipleship. This present discussion supports that longstanding contention with reference to the political arena as well. Traditional questions about Christology and soteriology are not mere diversions from the important challenges of "praxis." They are essential for a clear understanding of the proper shape of our political and economic obedience.

Second, the discussion of the political relevance of Jesus does provide us with an opportunity to evaluate traditional Christological themes with reference to their political embodiments. Kuyper may be right—as I think he is—to insist that the earthly ministry of Jesus has to be viewed against the backdrop of creational patterns. But it must still be admitted that Kuyper's own bold affirmations have a decidedly "imperialist" tone to them. To give the impression, as he seems to do, that our understanding of Christ's heavenly rule need not be informed in any way by the Gospel witness to his incarnational ministry is a serious mistake. When Christians are encouraged to engage in an *imitatio* of a Christ whose rule is depicted in thoroughly transcendent terms, it should not surprise us if those Christians promote the kind of politics that is characterized by attempts at a triumphalist "lording over" their fellow citizens.

Third, the complexities of contemporary political life, along with the difficult challenges involved in formulating perspectives that will be helpful to Christian social scientists, present new opportunities for ecumenical dialogue about important theological issues. Kuyper's imperialist tones do not serve us well in our twentieth-century democracies. But neither do the old Anabaptist formulations, which presupposed fairly clear boundaries between the political and the nonpolitical. The older definitions of "noninvolvement" do not offer very clear guidance to Mennonites and Amish today. Is it "political involvement" for an Amish farmer to serve on the county drain commission? Or as an adviser to the bureau of highways? Can a Mennonite campaign for election to the local public school board? Or accept an appointment to a government task force that will investigate low-cost housing for the poor? Changing political contexts can stimulate Anabaptists and Calvinists—along with Lutherans and Franciscans and liberationists and theonomists—to take a fresh look together at what it means to be political disciples of Jesus Christ.

It is no easy thing to accept the challenge posed in the old gospel song—that we "be like Jesus" both "in the home and in the throng." But the difficult challenges of our present-day political environment do present us with the opportunity to engage in a wide-ranging dialogue about what faithfulness to the person and work of Jesus Christ means to us in the midst of the complexities of contemporary life.

The Beatitudes of the Apocalypse: Eschatology and Ethics

Virgil P. Cruz

Professor of New Testament
Louisville Presbyterian Theological Seminary

INTRODUCTION

Without exception, commentaries on the Apocalypse recognize the existence of seven beatitudes: (1) 1:3; (2) 14:13; (3) 16:15; (4) 19:9; (5) 20:6; (6) 22:7; (7) 22:14. However, one searches those same commentaries in vain for any extensive treatment of them.[1] The result is that, for all intents and purposes, an exegetical famine exists. This is regrettable because these macarisms constitute helpful and succinct statements concerning eschatology and ethics and the interrelationships of these vital Christian motifs, which, by the way, have deeply engaged the heart and mind of Paul King Jewett. As the title of this chapter indicates, my goal is to focus upon this material that has been neglected too long.

An item of prolegomena is the question of an interpretative method for Revelation—clearly a crucial one for, obviously, a priori hermeneutical conclusions profoundly influence exposition. Among the most extensively utilized are:

1. The *preterist method*, which holds that Revelation is concerned fully and exclusively with the author's own day, not with subsequent periods or even with the end time. This is potentially too restrictive, for it may lead to "(1) the ignoring of a truly prophetic character in the book, which gives to it a spiritual outlook not realized within the limits of the history of the Roman Empire; (2) the effort to extend too widely the interpretation of *symbolical* language by circumstances of the writer's era."[2]

2. The *futurist method*, which contends that Revelation is a prophetic writing and therefore deals with the end time and the arrival of the era of the new world. While validly reflecting the writing's future dimension, a thoroughgoing eschatological interpretation

---

[1]This is the testimony of my research assistants, Randy Wilcher and Robert Griffin. Scripture citations in this essay are from the RSV.

[2]Isbon T. Beckwith, *The Apocalypse of John* (New York: Macmillan, 1919), 336.

which does not see in certain symbols allusions to conditions of John's day and/or succeeding generations flies in the face of well-supported evidence to the contrary.

3, The *historicist method*, which views Revelation as an inspired foretelling of the whole of human history (*Weltgeschichte*) or of the history of the church (*Kirchengeschichte*) from the Advent to the Consummation. Although this position insures Revelation's relevance for every generation, its practitioners fail to be sufficiently instructed by historical background and setting; further, freed from these disciplining factors, the method produces numerous creative expositions with, not surprisingly, a paucity of agreement among them.

My conclusions are best summarized under the rubric of Historical-Prophetic. Included in the evidence that supports a historical dimension to the text is John's clear identification with his contemporaries, with whom he shares in a future hope and in the present benefits of Christ, as well as in suffering and persecution (1:5-9). With respect to the symbols of the beasts, significant in Revelation's references to persecution, we may assume an allusion resulting from demands associated with emperor worship, even though this one historical reality does not exhaust their meaning. The author's proclivity for the present tense in describing the land beast's activity (13:11ff.) expresses a linear force which likely harbors allusions to existential confrontation with evil. This is in keeping with the sense of imminent danger that pervades the book. Its repeated admonitions against apostasy as well as calls to perseverance continue the same force. Further, the effect of the seven letters (chap. 2-3), the contents of which can be shown to be initially directed to the specific situations of historical congregations, is to bring the entire book into clear association with John's day.

Likewise, a case for a future dimension can be made.[3] One need only point to such elements as New Jerusalem, the annihilation of evil, and the motif of renewal-recreation, each significant in Revelation and each best understood as an eschatological reality.

Revelation reflects a unique joining of the two dimensions, historical and prophetic, with the result that all of history—past, present, and future alike—is characterized by (1) the fact of God's sovereignty, the dominant, continuing reality; (2) the activity of the anti-God force

---

[3]Henry Barclay Swete, *The Apocalypse of St. John*, 3d ed. (Grand Rapids: Eerdmans, 1909), p. ccxvi. I prefer to refer to the future dimension with the use of the term *prophetic*. In this I am tutored by H. B. Swete: ". . . the author of the Apocalypse was, what he claimed to be, an inspired prophet. . . . [He] is not less able than the prophets of the Old Testament to read the secrets of God's general purpose in the evolution of events, to detect the greater forces which are at work in human life under all its vicissitudes, and to indicate the issues towards which history tends" (ibid).

(symbolized by the three apocalyptic monsters) which, working especially through human followers, directs hostility against God and his people; (3) the struggle of God's people who, though they may even lose their lives, will never be separated from God; (4) the implications of the Christ event through which theodicy is effected.

To be sure, these theological conclusions are perceived by John in a concrete, historical context and, as is true of other apocalyptic writings, the conclusions reflect the author's own situation. Therefore, "their meaning and true use can be apprehended only by approaching them from the standpoint of their origin."[4] However, the historical-eschatological tension in the material, together with a pronounced concern for the time "in between," clearly indicates that his theological conclusions have an ongoing validity. It is not simply that continuing applicability of abstract principles which is inevitably dehistoricizing. Rather, what is apprehended by John finds expression in recurring fulfillments throughout all of history.

Also meriting a preliminary look is the imagery of the apocalyptic monsters. The three beasts of Revelation are among its most significant symbols. They are also pertinent for the present investigation; one or more beasts figure importantly in the immediate context of four of the beatitudes.

John immeasurably facilitates interpretation of the entire complex of beast imagery by clearly identifying one phenomenon in 12:9: "And the great dragon . . . that ancient serpent, who is called the Devil and Satan, the deceiver of the whole world—he was thrown down to the earth. . . ." That grouping of titles, which is a merging of the traditions concerning evil each represents, is unmistakable indication that "the focus of attention here is God's great adversary, the penultimate evil, the anti-God power,"[5] active throughout history from the Garden of Eden (Serpent) through the time of the birth of Christ (12:4-5) and beyond (12:17). Besides destruction and hostility, the nature of Evil is summed up by πλανάω, a term indicating both *modus operandi* and goal.

The beast from the sea and the beast from the land are extensions of the dragon; therefore they symbolize the existence and the activity of the anti-God power in the world and are not to be identified with specific historical rulers or governments. The sea beast, characterized by horns, crowns, a throne, and great authority, symbolizes the activity of the anti-God power as it bombastically seeks to establish its claim to sovereignty. The earth beast in turn points to the destructive activity of the anti-God power in the world carried out through deception.

---

[4]Beckwith, *Apocalypse of John*, 336.

[5]Virgil Cruz, *The Mark of the Beast* (Amsterdam: Academische Pers, 1973), 23.

The earthly allies of the evil triad are indicated by these special terms: *Babylon*—that earthly power that succumbs to the deception of evil and becomes allied with it; *earth dwellers*—contrasted with the followers of the Lamb, they accept the beast's mark which signifies allegiance and are the church of the anti-God power; *kings of the earth*—those individual rulers who accept this evil authority.

Far from representing a visionary flight from reality and an exclusive preoccupation with eschatological solutions, Revelation's repeated calls for obedience and perseverance and warnings against apostasy focus upon ongoing confrontation with evil and upon provisional victories, as well as upon the eschatological triumph. It is in this context that the beatitudes function and are to be understood.

With respect to our examination of eschatology as pertinent for a focus on the beatitudes, it is instructive to note that the author of Revelation expected a future in-breaking, an eschatological completion of the cosmic redemption inaugurated by Christ. Further, he maintained that this expectation guides, disciplines, and inspires the followers of Christ as they face the challenges to their faith in this time in between, during which they are still "in danger of losing their right to participate in the eschatological kingdom by becoming followers of the beast."[6]

Finally, we will understand ethics to be, in general, the inquiry into humankind's moral nature so as to discover what are one's responsibilities and the means by which one may fulfill them. The author of Revelation and his community, heirs to Old Testament moral faith and instruction, would have viewed the will of God as the theocratic foundation of ethics. There is every reason to believe they would hold to the early church's well-attested, profound involvement with ethical concerns. This is the force of John the Baptist's preaching on righteousness, purity, and social concerns. Paramount, of course, is the witness of Jesus Christ, who lifted up Judaism's emphasis upon ethical monotheism, social concerns, and the relation of religion to morality. He pressed for righteousness which exceeded the law. All is summarized in his reflection on the great commandment of love and is at the heart of his proclamation of the kingdom of God, where religion and ethics intersect. As a part of this tradition, Revelation contains explicit as well as implicit moral teaching: calls to abstinence from sin and to rejection of the claims of the beasts, announcements of warnings regarding punishment for disobedience, proclamation of promises of reward for those who with God's help do overcome. The beatitudes of the Apocalypse function precisely in this context of ethical consideration.

---

[6]Elizabeth Schüssler Fiorenza, "Revelation, Book of," *Interpreter's Dictionary of the Bible, Supplemental Volume* (Nashville: Abingdon, 1976), 745.

THE FIRST BEATITUDE

1:3 Blessed is he who reads aloud the words of the prophecy, and blessed are those who hear, and who keep what is written therein; for the time is near.

This initial macarism (beatitude) and its immediate context introduce elements that are foundational for the entire study and recur in subsequent targeted passages. While John here is the speaker-writer, he functions as the last in a sequence of agents of revelation. His source is the angel commissioned by Jesus Christ to convey the message previously received by Christ directly from God. This indication of its divine origin lends affirmation and establishes authority. Especially significant for Christ's role is 1:1a: "The revelation of Jesus Christ, which God gave him to show to his servants." The translation options of the genitive case—of, by, about Jesus Christ—are energetically debated; however, I prefer to hold all together in combination, with each providing complementary nuance of the profound relationship between Jesus Christ and his revelation.

Noteworthy is John's choice of the verb σημαίνω ("and he made it known . . . to his servant John," 1:1b) to indicate the nature of the revelation received. The term tells more for a symbolic rather than a literal message. It also suggests reserve and modesty on John's part without implying that his own imagination gave rise to the message. "All that [John] *saw*" (1:2b, italics mine) is a strikingly appropriate word, for the largely visionary material to follow and to which John witnesses, which remains the word of God, is embodied as well as corroborated in the testimony of Jesus Christ.

1. "Blessed is he who reads . . . and . . . those who hear, and keep what is written. . . ." The reference is surely not to private reading; rather, we may assume that reading and hearing point to a liturgical setting in the community of the faithful. However, very important for our task is keeping in mind the full meaning of *hearing:* the Greek ἀκούω (like the Hebrew שָׁמַע) implies that true hearing necessitates obedience to the message. In this connection, "keeping" may complete a synthetic parallelism as it calls to mind that obedience associated with submission to the commandments, unmistakably implying that here are ethical injunctions to be faithfully observed, moral instruction and not mere prediction. It is also likely that the term *written*, closely associated as it is with the phenomenon of Scripture, was intended to confer here (and in 14:13) high status upon the message.

2. ". . . the words of the prophecy. . . ." Here (and in 22:7) John designates his writing as prophecy. Upon several occasions he also terms himself a prophet.

In his substantial and helpful volume, *New Testament Prophecy*, David Hill presents convincingly this thesis.

> The Book of the Revelation is therefore written out of its time and for its time: the author is not concerned to predict specific historical events in the near or distant future, as is the case with writers of Jewish apocalyptic: rather, he interprets the meaning of the history in which he is involved (with the Church) in terms of a traditional imagery, taken over partly from the Old Testament and partly from Jewish concepts. But if the style and imagery, or some of it, is determined by the apocalyptic tradition, in his interpretation of history and the sensitivity to the actualities of his situation the writer stands in the tradition of prophetic faith and proclamation.[7]

As Christian prophecy, Revelation, in Hill's view, is the means by which "divine judgments and directives are brought to bear upon the life of the church(es). . . . Unfaithfulness and immorality are rebuked, and a call to repentance offered. . . . Exhortations and encouragements are given to believers to remain faithful."[8]

3. ". . . the time is near. . . ." *Time* [καιρός] and *near* [ἐγγύς] are familiar eschatological technical terms. If the reference is to an impending crisis, then they provide motivation for learning and keeping the words of this prophecy. Regarding John's reference to an immediate crisis that has not subsequently taken place in spite of the passage of some one thousand years, Mounce offers this hypothesis: "The most satisfying solution is to take the word in a straightforward sense, remembering that in the prophetic outlook the end is always imminent."[9]

THE SECOND BEATITUDE

14:13 And I heard a voice from heaven saying, "Write this: Blessed are the dead who die in the Lord henceforth." "Blessed indeed," says the Spirit, "that they may rest from their labors, for their deeds follow them!"

1. ". . . voice from heaven saying, 'Write. . . .'" In the absence of information detailing which agent of revelation is in focus here, it may be assumed that the reference is to God, not unlike Johannine usage in the Fourth Gospel (12:28). The command to *write* is found also in 1:11, 19; 2:1, 8; 3:1, 7, 12, 14; 19:9; 21:5; et al. and constitutes a formula for such important messages.

---

[7]David Hill, *New Testament Prophecy* (Atlanta: John Knox, 1979), 75.

[8]Ibid., 85-86.

[9]Robert H. Mounce, *The Book of Revelation*, The New International Commentary on the New Testament (Grand Rapids: Eerdmans, 1977), 65.

2. ". . . the dead who die in the Lord. . . ." Some commentaries conclude that this beatitude is addressed expressly, even exclusively, to those who face martyrdom because they have rejected the claims of the apocalyptic monsters (14:9ff.). Nevertheless, here as elsewhere in Revelation, all consequences of a life of faith accrue to all steadfast Christians who die in the Lord, even if their obedience does not result in martyrdom.

3. ". . . rest from their labors, for their deeds follow them." The eschatological rest into which the faithful enter (cf. Heb 4:10) is eternal blessedness in the joyful service of God after the victory of God has been consummated and God's purpose for all creation has been realized. The labors of the faithful have involved rejection of the destructive and blasphemous machinations of the apocalyptic monsters, symbols of the anti-God powers. Further, since the beasts operate in every generation of the church to draw persons from God and appropriate ethical behavior, the labor of resistance is not only an end-time necessity; this labor is continually demanded. The works that accompany the faithful into the state of blessedness, while not grounds for meriting salvation, do function as confirmation that these persons are in Christ.

THE THIRD BEATITUDE

16:15 "Lo, I am coming like a thief! Blessed is he who is awake, keeping his garments that he may not go naked and be seen exposed!"

1. "Lo, I come as a thief! Blessed is he who stays awake. . . ." The speaker here is clearly Jesus Christ, the only time outside the letters when this is the case (with the likely exception of 22:14). The expression "come as a thief" speaks not of furtiveness or suddenness but particularly of unexpectedness. Vos concludes that here it presupposes an acquaintance with the parable of the faithful and unfaithful servants, which unmistakably conveys a concern for ethical practice. The call for watchfulness explicitly espoused in this beatitude implies an eschatological orientation similar to its parallels in the Synoptics.[10] Ladd observes, "In the present context, John assumes that the church has not lost its perspective and has not lost sight of the ultimate spiritual values in spite of the triumphant rule of the beast among the nations."[11]

2. ". . . keeping his garments that he may not go naked and be seen exposed." This garment symbolism is not identical to the white robes

---

[10]Cf. Louis Vos, *The Synoptic Traditions in the Apocalypse* (Kampen: Kok, 1965), 77.

[11]George Eldon Ladd, *A Commentary on the Book of Revelation* (Grand Rapids: Eerdmans, 1972), 216.

of justification in Rev 7:9; rather, here keeping one's garments points to perseverance, to purity and steadfastness (cf. 3:4, regarding the church at Sardis). Without such persistence, ethical integrity, and those good works that wrap one like a garment, a person is naked before God, and to one's shame it becomes evident that one is not "in Christ."

This beatitude clearly sounds a warning which at the same time presupposes the possibility of repentance and restoration in the face of constant seductive temptations.

THE FOURTH BEATITUDE

19:9 And the angel said to me, "Write this: Blessed are those who are invited to the marriage supper of the Lamb." And he said to me, "These are true words of God."

1. "And he said to me, 'Write. . . .'" John registers confusion in this confrontation with the agent of Revelation who delivers the fourth macarism. Prompted by respect or gratitude, he mistakes the speaker for the Lord and prostrates himself before that one, who pointedly reminds him of the inappropriateness of worshiping anyone but God. This figure is best identified with the angel interpreter previously introduced in 17:1. His command to write, reminiscent of parallels in 14:13 (cf. also 1:3), as well as in each of the letters to the seven churches, is significant as that term which certifies the authenticity of what follows.

2. "Blessed are those who are invited to the marriage supper of the Lamb." The image of the church as the bride of Christ has deep roots in the history of the people of God. The prophets frequently speak of Israel as God's wife, albeit a faithless wife who is called to repent from harlotry, i.e., faithlessness to the covenant relationship. "This dual concept of a covenant relationship rooted in history but to be perfected in the future is taken up in a fresh way in the New Testament and applied to Christ and the Church."[12] Paul especially utilizes the figure but chooses not to emphasize the faithlessness of the church; rather, he stresses the faithfulness and loving sacrifice of Christ, the Bridegroom, and the eschatological perfection of the church. Further, in Revelation the eschatological aspect is strengthened through its association with the universal feast, another symbol of the kingdom of God, and one that brings together a rich variety of salvation associations, including God's prior love for humans, the perfect nature of communion between God and his people, its joy and its happiness, and the work of Christ through the Holy Spirit by which the com-

---

[12]G. R. Beasley-Murray, *The Book of Revelation*, New Century Bible (Greenwood: Attic, 1974), 273.

munion is effectively established. The fact that John was likely acquainted with Synoptic tradition concerning the marriage feast (Mt 22:1-13; Lk 14:16-24) suggests that understanding of this literary connection may yield interpretative dividends.

For our concerns, it is especially helpful to note that the marriage feast metaphor in chapter 19, perhaps because of its very fluidity, speaks powerfully of the breadth and depth of the communion between Christ and his people. It is a passionate reminder of the necessity of faithfulness in the face of temptation and seduction, and stands as a strong condemnation of unfaithfulness; it emphasizes that God initiates and sustains this relationship in spite of the bride's shortcomings; it stresses an eschatological perfection for the bride; it serves well John's pastoral concern, not only sounding a warning but also instilling hope and encouragement in order to strengthen faith.

THE FIFTH BEATITUDE

20:6 Blessed and holy is he who shares in the first resurrection! Over such the second death has no power, but they shall be priests of God and of Christ, and they shall reign with him a thousand years.

1. "Blessed and holy is the one who shares in the first resurrection! Over such the second death has no power." This is the only beatitude that combines the term *blessed* with a second designation. Swete holds that the addition confers beatification, deserved because (1) such persons are not under the power of the second death; (2) rather, they will be God's priests; (3) they will reign with Christ. Following hard upon the recitation of the fate of those who persist in wickedness in league with the apocalyptic monsters, this beatitude speaks to the future of those who with God's help are faithful.

The term *first resurrection* has caused exegetes no end of difficulty, even while it has tempted them to irresponsible flights of fanciful interpretation. It is important, in my judgment, to see in 20:4-6 not an exclusive emphasis upon the special conditions and prerogatives of martyrs, but rather to recognize that they and all the other faithful, all those who have died in the Lord, will be granted participation in the first resurrection. They will join with the faithful who are alive at the Parousia and will rule with Christ. It is my conviction that none of the faithful need fear the application of God's ultimate punishment, which is the second death. The following observations are grounds for these conclusions:

(a) That the passage deals with more than the special class of martyrs can be seen from the author's characterization here of the rejection of the καραγμα as a decisive act required of *all* the faithful, an act which did not always result in death.

(b) The inclusion in the text of the generalizing word οἵτινες accompanied by καὶ signals the extension of the category beyond those "who have been beheaded for their testimony to Jesus and for the word of God." Charles, who opposes such an interpretation, not surprisingly terms this pronoun an editorial addition!

(c) Lastly, if the non-martyred faithful dead are not seen as sharing in the first resurrection but rather as being raised with the rest of the dead to be brought before God's throne (20:12ff.), we are faced with the nearly unbelievable situation that there is then no direct mention in this chapter of their future after the reporting of the judgment event. Following the latter, the emphasis is clearly upon the lot of those whose names were not in the book of life.[13]

2. ". . . but they shall be priests of God and shall reign with him a thousand years." We have already noted that those who are blessed shall reign with Christ. Again, this element may reflect the extension to the church of prerogatives formerly the inheritance of faithful Israel.

While our beatitude is in the pericope containing the premier text for discussion of millenarian views, we will not enter that fateful field of debate except to remark that our focus upon eschatology and ethics will necessarily require attention regardless of what millenarian view is espoused.

THE SIXTH BEATITUDE

22:7 "And behold, I am coming soon." Blessed is he who keeps the words of the prophecy of this book.

1. "And behold, I am coming soon." Kiddle terms the problem of identifying the speaker here a "superficial difficulty."[14] Indeed, whether v. 7 is spoken by the interpreting angel who communicates the material in v. 8 (and is the object of John's second misguided attempt to worship) or whether this statement comes directly from Jesus Christ is arguably of secondary importance, since the Lord stands behind the entire revelation.

The statement strengthens the resolve of all who struggle to endure and turns them to the One who can provide the needed resources. With respect to the problem of the delay in the fulfillment of Christ's promise,

it is best to take the utterance at face value and accept the difficulty of a foreshortened perspective on the time of the end rather than to

---

[13]Cruz, *The Mark of the Beast*, 129.

[14]Martin Kiddle, *The Revelation of St. John*, The Moffatt New Testament Commentary Series (New York: Harper, 1940), 447.

reinterpret it in the sense that Jesus "comes" in the crises of life and especially at the death of every [person]. Revelation has enough riddles without our adding more. Matthew 24:42-44 counsels every generation to be on the alert for the return of the Son of man. An infallible timetable would do away with that attitude of urgent expectation which has been the hallmark of the church through the centuries.[15]

2. "Blessed is he who keeps the words of the prophecy of this book." The sixth beatitude is in most respects a restatement of the initial one, calling attention to "the blessedness of those who maintain faith in Christ and loyalty to him at all costs,"[16] and emphasizing the imminent fulfillment of his promise to return. Repetition of these themes highlights their respective significance for the Christian community. In addition, since they are lifted up in both prologue and epilogue, they surely reflect central concerns of the author.

The high importance John attributes to this writing, reflected also in the warning of 22:18 against tampering with its contents, is in keeping with the responsible discharge of his office as agent of revelation along with Christ and the angels. Stress on imminence, while difficult to account for in all its implications, is understandable in light of his prophetic confidence that the foretold future will surely come to pass and that knowledge of that future and commitment to it will impact for good life in the present.[17]

THE SEVENTH BEATITUDE

22:14 Blessed are those who wash their robes, that they may have the right to the tree of life and that they may enter the city by the gates.

1. "Blessed are those who wash their robes. . . ." Again, the identity of the one declaring this final beatitude is not immediately clear; however, since it is surrounded by statements best attributed directly to Jesus Christ (vv. 12-13, 16), he is to be preferred over an interpreting angel as the one who pronounces v. 14. In the previous occurrence of this concept (7:14) the verb is found in the aorist tense, indicating once-for-all action; however, here the present tense is

---

[15]Mounce, *Revelation*, 391.

[16]Beasley-Murray, *Revelation*, 336.

[17]Notice this helpful statement from G. Caird: "Now we know that in calling his book a prophecy John is claiming more for it than that it foretells the future. The function of the prophet is to declare to God's people, and through them to the world, the whole counsel of God. John's book is a prophecy because it reveals the true nature of the conflict between the monster and the Lamb, between Babylon the great and the new Jerusalem, and summons men [and women] to the one victory that can overcome the world" (G. B. Caird, *A Commentary on the Revelation of St. John the Divine*, Harper's New Testament Commentaries [New York: Harper & Row, 1966], 283).

used, suggesting that a continual washing, i.e., a continual participation in Christ's redemption, is called for in face of the persistent onslaught of the beast whose mission is to introduce persons to all manner of evil.

2. ". . . that they may have the right to the tree of life and that they may enter the city by the gates." Simple logic would call for these two clauses to be reversed, so that entering into the city could be seen as gaining access to the tree located within. However, the author chooses to emphasize the source of blessing itself rather than the location of the tree of life (cf. also 22:1-2), which with its fruits represents the fullness of God's pervading presence in the new world, where evil no longer exists and where all hindrances to the activity of God have been removed. Entering into the city—confidently through the gates—symbolizes moving into eternal blessedness. Against Charles and others I would contend that this beatitude is not addressed exclusively to martyrs; rather, passage into the city and healing contact with the tree of life are among the prerogatives extended to all faithful Christians. The only division here (22:1ff.) is between the evildoers and the righteous.

The seventh beatitude sounds a fitting note with which to close the series. In essence, it represents a "declaration of acquittal in judgment."[18]

CONCLUDING OBSERVATIONS

Although the number seven functions in Revelation (as in all apocalyptic literature) as an extremely important image—seven churches, seven spirits, seven seals, seven angels with seven trumpets, seven thunders, etc.—it is not clear what symbolic meaning the number has in the context of the beatitudes. Further, there is no convincing explanation of the order and progression of the beatitudes. To be sure, Charles, after applying to this text the "ruthless surgery" he has frequently demonstrated elsewhere,[19] places the sixth beatitude (22:7) last, with the result that the series ends as it begins with a declaration of the "blessedness of those who have kept the words of the prophecy."[20] One suspects that Charles again is granting to his hypothesis sovereignty over the text rather than allowing the text to inform and discipline his hypothesis.

What is obvious is that certain themes are repeated within the series, i.e.:

---

[18]Beasley-Murray, *Revelation*, 339.

[19]Caird, *Revelation of St. John*, 187.

[20]R. H. Charles, *Revelation*, The International Critical Commentary, 2 vols. (Edinburgh: T. & T. Clark, 1959), 2:218.

1.   the emphasis on obeying these words of prophecy (1, 6);
2.   the rewards awaiting those who die in Christ (2, 5);
3.   the importance of possessing the garments, clean robes that identify those who are in Christ (3, 6);
4.   the emphasis on immanence of fulfillment of these promises (1, 6).

Noteworthy also is that in the immediate context of these seven beatitudes the elements most common are:

1.   warning concerning the evil beasts (2, 3, 4, 5);
2.   announcement of judgment (2, 3, 4, 5, 6, 7);
3.   Christ and his ministry (1, 2, 3 [in the beatitude itself], 4, 5, 6).

As this study has demonstrated, eschatology and ethics are continually in the forefront of the seven beatitudes. The Black church has long discerned this relationship. More recently, Allen Boesak, speaking from the South African context, has convincingly and dramatically stated the case. He contends that "in the Apocalypse of John, the suffering of churches as a result of political oppression is the explicit theme."[21] Further, "the church is now partisan of God in the struggle against the power of evil, for the sake of justice and for the sake of the new creation God has in mind."[22] In an especially helpful section on the Lamb of chapter 5, Revelation's favorite Christological symbol, Boesak encourages sorely tried Christians with the word that this powerful Lamb is fully able to do battle with the beast; furthermore, the wounded Lamb once slain for his people, bleeds still in identification with their present suffering. Boesak warns, even castigates, those churches that are guilty of collusion with the state in standing against, not for, the poor. "Christians who enjoy the fruits of injustice without a murmur, who remain silent as the defenseless are slaughtered, dare not become indignant when the suffering people of God echo the prayers of the Psalms and pray for deliverance and judgment."[23]

The true nature of Revelation as a hope-filled writing is highlighted in Boesak's book. He joins Rev 21, Is 65, and Ro 8 in a powerful combined witness to God's all-encompassing work of renewal and re-creation. In the resultant new heaven and new earth, men and women will experience the absence of all that oppresses, pollutes, and divides. God's presence will insure that peace, goodness, health, and joy flourish. This is God's will, and he will accomplish it.

---

[21]Allan Boesak, *Comfort and Protest: The Apocalypse from a South African Perspective* (Philadelphia: Westminster, 1987), 33.

[22]Ibid., 34.

[23]Ibid., 72.

Jack Sanders advances a quite different theory. He contends that it is because of its thoroughgoing immanent eschatology that "The Apocalypse has so little—nothing of lasting or fundamental value—to say about ethics."[24] In fact, "It is this retreat from the ethical dimension that is the basic evil of the Apocalypse."[25]

In my judgment, the book of Revelation and its seven beatitudes have a radically different thrust than that supposed by Sanders. His rejection of the Apocalypse betrays a basic misunderstanding of its nature and purpose. He apparently accepts as definitive a far-right interpretation of the meaning of the book, and it is on the basis of that assumption that he opposes its theology. That is, he assumes a reading that fails to discern Revelation's focus upon ongoing confrontation with evil as well as upon eschatological triumph; that appropriates for oppressors promises intended for lowly followers of the Lamb; that ignores the pervasive call for ethical obedience; and that is self-serving in seeking affirmation of the far right's own theology and ideology, while condemning those with opposing views. Such a reading must certainly be categorically rejected.

Boesak brings us back closer to the center as he reminds us that we must recognize the true nature of Revelation as a pastoral writing. For the mighty, exalted, and triumphant Lamb, the one who in God's name will be ruler of all that is, bears wounds that point both to his once-and-for-all sacrifice for humankind and to his continuing suffering with them. In the midst of their tribulation comes the promise that in spite of their weakness, through his strength, they will overcome. The true nature of Revelation as a revolutionary writing also is made clear by Boesak. He enables us to hear God's devastating judgment upon those who commit the sin of political and economic oppression of the poor and against those who fail to make the cause of the victims their own. The fate of Babylon and Rome awaits contemporary unjust governments; for Christ, the powerful Lamb, will again throw down the mighty from their thrones and exalt those of low degree; and the followers of the Lamb will participate in turning the world as we know it upside down. Boesak helps us discern the true nature of Revelation as an evangelistic writing. Warning and call to repentance are directed to those within as well as those outside the church. In Boesak's properly hard-hitting treatment we hear John say that judgment begins at the household of faith.[26]

---

[24]Jack T. Sanders, *Ethics in the New Testament* (Philadelphia: Fortress, 1975), 113.

[25]Ibid., 114.

[26]See Boesak, *Comfort and Protest*, passim.

The seven beatitudes of the Apocalypse constitute helpful and succinct statements concerning eschatology and ethics and the inter-relationships of these vital Christian motifs.

A Bibliography of Paul K. Jewett's Writings

I. Books

Systematic Theology. 3 vols. Grand Rapids: Eerdmans, forthcoming.

Election and Predestination. Foreword by Vernon Grounds. Grand Rapids: Eerdmans, 1985.

The Ordination of Women. Grand Rapids: Eerdmans, 1980.

Infant Baptism and the Covenant of Grace. Grand Rapids: Eerdmans, 1978.

The Lord's Day: A Theological Guide to the Christian Day of Worship. Grand Rapids: Eerdmans, 1977.

Man as Male and Female: A Study in Sexual Relationships from a Theological Point of View. Grand Rapids: Eerdmans, 1975.

El hombre como varon y hembra. Trans. Ernesto Subarez Vilela. Miami: Editorial Caribe, ca. 1975 [translation of *Man as Male and Female*].

Emil Brunner: An Introduction to the Man and His Thought. Chicago: Inter-Varsity Press, 1961.

Ecclesiology: Infant Baptism and Confirmation. Pasadena, Calif.: Fuller Theological Seminary, 1960.

Emil Brunner's Concept of Revelation. London: James Clarke, 1954.

II. Editions

The Baptist Catechism: Commonly Called Keach's Catechism, or, A Brief Instruction in the Principles of the Christian Religion, agreeable to the Confession of Faith, put forth by upwards of an hundred congregations in Great Britain, July 3, 1689, and adopted by the Philadelphia Baptist Association, September 22, 1742, being the edition published in London, in 1794 by John Rippon. Newly Revised by Paul King Jewett. Grand Rapids: Baker Book House, 1952.

III. Articles

"Sabbath Day's Journey," in *International Standard Bible Encyclopedia*, vol. 4 (Grand Rapids: Eerdmans, 1988).

"Sabbath, Second after the First," in ibid.

"Children of Grace." *Theology Today* 44 (1987): 170-78.

"Influences." *Theology, News and Notes* 34, no. 3 (November 1987): 17+.

"God Is Personal Being," in *Church, Word and Spirit*, ed. James E. Bradley and Richard A. Muller. Grand Rapids: Eerdmans, 1987.

"Lord's Day, part 1, Biblical," in *International Standard Bible Encyclopedia*, vol. 3 (Grand Rapids: Eerdmans, 1986).

"Reconciliation: A Theological Statement." *Theology, News and Notes* 32, no. 1 (March 1985): 18-20.

"Satisfaction," in *Evangelical Dictionary of Theology* (Grand Rapids: Baker Book House, 1984).

"Theological Issues in Domestic Violence." *Theology, News and Notes* 29, no. 2 (June 1982): 8-11.

"Vignettes of Seminary Life." *Christian Century* 99 (February 1982): 136-40.

"The Holy Spirit as Female (A Negative Response)," in *Women and the Ministries of Christ*, ed. Roberta Hestenes and Lois Curley. Pasadena, Calif.: Fuller Theological Seminary, 1979, 43-48.

"Man as Male and Female," cassette recording in the *Christian Life Commission Seminar Series*. Nashville: Broadman, 1978.

"Original Sin and the Fall of Man." *Southwestern Journal of Theology* 19 (Fall 1976): 18-30.

"Why I Favor the Ordination of Women." *Christianity Today* 19 (June 6, 1975): 7-10.

"Mary and the Male/Female Relationship." *The Christian Century* 90 (December 19, 1973): 1254-55.

"Concerning Christ, Christians, and Jews," in *Jerusalem and Athens: Critical Discussions on the Theology and Apologetics of Cornelius Van Til*, ed. E. R. Greehan. Nutley, N.J.: Presbyterian and Reformed, 1971.

"Relation of the Soul to the Fetus." *Christianity Today* 13 (November 8, 1968): 6-9.

With Ysbrugt Feenstra, "Baptism: the Baptist [and] Reformed View[s]," Wilmington: National Foundation for Christian Education, 1964.

"Adam," in *Baker's Dictionary of Theology* (Grand Rapids: Baker Book House, 1960).

"Neo-orthodoxy," in ibid.

"Satisfaction," in ibid.

"Wit and Humor of Life." *Christianity Today* 3 (June 8, 1959): 7-9.

"Emil Brunner and the Bible." *Christianity Today* 1 (January 21, 1957): 7-9.

"Majestic Music of the King James." *Christianity Today* 1 (November 26, 1956): 13-15.

"Concerning the Allegorical Interpretation of Scripture." *Westminster Theological Journal* 17 (1954): 1-20.

"Ebnerian Personalism and its Influence upon Brunner's Theology." *Westminster Theological Journal* 14 (1952): 113-47.

Scripture Index

Old Testament

Genesis

1	186
2	186, 187-89, 187n, 193
2:18	212
22:2	7
22:12	7
22:16	7

Exodus

3:13ff	25
17:7	226

Deuteronomy

6:4-5	28
6:14	35
6:16	226
8:3	221

2 Samuel

7:14	9

Psalms

2:7	7, 9, 21
82:6	31n
110:1	9, 10
147:3	135

Proverbs

8:22-31	24

Isaiah

6	237
9:1ff	83n
11:6-9	11
28:16	25
40:3	11
41:8	233
42:1	7, 11
45:22	25
45:23	25
52:7	11, 12
53	8n

61:1	7, 11, 12
61:2	11
64:1	11, 11n
65	281
65:17-25	11

Daniel

7:13	10

Joel

2:32	25

Zechariah

14:9	36

Malachi

2:10	36

Apocrypha and Pseudepigrapha

2 Baruch

29:3	6n
30:1	6n
40:1	6n
72:2-6	6n

1 Enoch

48:10	6n
52:4	6n

4 Ezra

7:28-34	6n
12:31-34	6n

Psalms of Solomon

17:35-36	6n

Sirach

24	24

Testament of Simeon

7:2	6n

Testament of Reuben

6:7-12	6n

Wisdom of Solomon

6-9	24

New Testament

Matthew

1:1	5n
1:18	5n
3:16	11n
4:1	215
4:1-11	211, 213
4:23	3n
5:28	199
22:1-13	277
24:42-44	279
28:20	240

Mark

1:1	4, 5, 5n, 6, 6n, 7, 9, 12, 13, 16, 17
1:1-2a	11, 16
1:2a	11, 13
1:2	6-7
1:3	7-9
1:4	9-11
1:4-8	11
1:4-15	11
1:4-16:8	4
1:9-11	7, 11
1:11	5, 5n, 6, 6n, 9, 10
1:12-13	11, 211
1:14-15	3n, 11, 13, 16, 17
1:14b-15	4
1:16-20	12
1:16-3:12	8, 12
1:16-8:26	13
1:16-8:28	16
1:16-16:8	12
1:21-22	12
1:23-28	12, 14
1:24	5, 6
1:24-25	9n, 14
1:29-34	12
1:32-34	15n
1:34	6, 9n, 10n, 12, 14, 15
1:40-44	15
1:40-45	12, 15n
1:41	12
1:44	10n, 15
1:44-45	15
1:45	15, 15n
2:1	11-12
2:1-12	12, 15n
2:1-3:6	5
2:2	12
2:3	12-13
2:4	13
2:6-10	8, 12, 13
2:7	8n
2:10	8, 9
2:13-14	12
2:15-17	12
2:18-20	12
2:20	13
2:28	8, 9
3:1	14
3:1-6	12, 15n
3:2	15
3:3	16
3:6	8n, 13
3:7-10	12
3:7-12	15n
3:11	5, 6, 6n, 7, 10
3:11-12	9n, 12, 14
3:12	10n
3:13-19	12
3:13-8:26	12
3:20-21	5
3:21	174
3:22-27	12
3:31-35	5
4:1-34	12, 17
4:35-41	12
4:40	5
5:1-20	12
5:7	5, 5n, 6, 6n, 7, 10, 14n
5:19-20	15n
5:21-24	12
5:24-35	12, 15n
5:25-34	12
5:35-43	12
5:40	15
5:41	12, 15
5:43	10n, 15, 15n
6:1	15
6:1-6	5
6:7-13	12
6:14	6
6:14-16	12
6:17-29	4, 4n, 13
6:32-44	12
6:45-52	12
6:51-52	5
6:53-56	15n
7:1-23	12
7:23-8:9	12
7:24-30	12
7:31-37	12, 15, 15n
7:34	15
7:36	10n, 15, 15n
8:1	15
8:1-9	12
8:11-12	5
8:14-21	5
8:22-26	12, 15, 15n
8:26	15
8:27	12, 15
8:27-33	5, 6
8:27-10:52	10, 13
8:27-13:37	12n
8:27-16:8	16
8:28	6, 12
8:29	3n, 5, 5n, 6, 6n, 13, 16
8:29-31	10
8:30	9n, 10, 13, 16
8:31	6, 8, 8n, 13, 13n
8:31-32	13
8:32	10
8:32-16:8	13
8:38	8, 9, 10, 10n, 17
9:1	7, 16, 17
9:2-9	17
9:5	6
9:7	5n, 6, 6n, 7
9:9	8n, 9n, 10n, 13n, 15, 16
9:12	8, 8n, 13, 13n
9:17-27	12n
9:25-26	14n
9:31	8, 8n, 10, 13n
9:41	5n
10:2-12	12
10:33	8, 8n, 10, 13

Mark (continued)

10:33-34	13n
10:37	6n
10:45	8n, 13, 13n, 247
10:46-52	12n
10:51	6
11:1-12:44	13
11:12-14	12n
11:15-17	12n
11:20-21	12n
11:21	6
12:1-12	6, 7, 9
12:13-44	5
12:29	28n
12:32	28n
12:35	5n, 6n, 7, 9
13:21	5n, 6n
13:21-22	6n
13:26	10, 10n
13:26-27	8
13:32	6, 7, 9
14:1-15:39	13
14:21	8, 8n, 10, 13
14:24	13, 247
14:36	7, 9
14:41	8, 8n, 10
14:45	6
14:60-64	5
14:61	5n, 6n, 7
14:61-62a	5, 9
14:61-62	6
14:62a	14
14:62	8, 10, 10n, 17
14:63-64	9
14:64	8n, 13
15:2-15	5
15:26	14
15:31	9
15:31-32	14
15:32	5, 5n, 6, 6n, 9, 14
15:33-39	7
15:39	5, 5n, 6, 6n, 9, 10

Luke

2:22ff	82n
2:40	69
2:52	69
3:21-22	11n

3:23-38	214
3:38	214
4:1-13	211
4:2	220
4:12	226
4:18-21	3n
14:16-24	277

John

1	110
1:1	31, 116n
1:1ff	83n
1:14	69, 89, 116n
1:17	5n
1:18	31, 89
2:15	133
3:16	94
5:18	31
5:23-24	31
5:36	31
5:37	31
5:44	31
6:38	31
6:38-39	31
7:16	31
8:28	31
8:41	31
8:46	200
10:30	31, 47
10:33ff	31n
10:37	31
12:28	274
12:45	31
12:49	31
14:8-9	90n
14:10	31
14:28	31
15:13	241
15:14	239
15:15	231, 239
17:3	5n, 31, 88n
20:21	31
20:28	31, 33n
20:30-31	3n
20:31	3n

Acts

2:36	21, 25
3:22-26	21
13:33	21
20	114

22:3	19

Romans

1:1	23
1:3	21
1:3-4	21
1:7	22
2:16	22
3:21-26	3n
3:22	30
3:23	197
3:24	22
3:24-25	21, 30
3:26	30
3:29	30
3:29-30	36
3:30	30
4	247
4:17	25
5	114
5:5	23
5:9-10	22
5:10	22, 94, 241
5:12-21	23
5:15	23
5:15-19	20
5:18	22
5:21	22
6:10f	247
6:23	21
8	281
8:3	21, 22, 24, 198n
8:9	23n
8:32	22
8:35	23
9:5	3n, 22, 27
10:9	25
10:11	25
10:13	25
13	261
14:9	25
15:8	19
15:16	23
15:19	23
16:16	23n
16:27	22, 30

1 Corinthians

1:3	22
1:9	29

1 Corinthians (continued)

1:17-25	3n
1:23-24	22
1:24	26
1:30	22
2	114
2:8	25, 26
3:10	23
3:23	30
4:5	22
8	29n
8:4	28, 29
8:4-6	28
8:6	22, 24, 28, 29n, 36
9:12	23
10:4	24
11:3	30
11:16	23n
11:32	22
12:3	25
12:4	28
12:4-6	29
12:31	133
15:1-5	3n
15:21	20
15:21-22	23
15:22	21, 22
15:28	29, 30
15:45	25
15:45-49	23
15:47	24, 24n
15:57	22
16:22	26
16:23	22

2 Corinthians

1:2	22
1:12	23
2:14	21
4:4	26
4:6	26
5:10	22
5:14	23, 247
5:18	21, 22
5:19	21
5:21	111, 200, 247
6:1	23
8:1	23
8:9	23
11:1-16	186n

12:8	26
12:9	217n
13:13	23
13:14	22

Galatians

1:3	22
1:7	23
3:1	3n
3:13	111, 112n, 247
3:20	29
4:4	21, 22, 24
4:4-5	87
6:18	22

Ephesians

1:2	22
1:10	53n
3:9	53n
3:19	23
4:32	21
6:8	22
6:23	22

Philippians

1:2	22
1:27	23
2	21, 21n
2:5	235
2:5ff	84
2:5-11	21, 24, 223
2:6a	24, 24n
2:6	26
2:6-11	26
2:7	20, 21, 67
2:7c	24
2:9	21
2:9-11	25
3:4-6	19
3:10	235
3:20	22
3:21	122
4:4	26
4:23	22

Colossians

1:3	22
1:13	23n
1:14	22

1:15	26
1:15-20	26
1:16	22, 24, 29
1:19	26
1:20	22
2:3	89
2:9	26, 89, 118
3:4	22
3:15-17	26
4:11	23n

Philemon

3	22

1 Thessalonians

1:1	22
1:10	22
2:2	23
2:8-9	23
2:14	23n
3:2	23
3:11	22, 26
4:14	22
4:15-17	22
5:9	22
5:28	22

2 Thessalonians

1:2	22
1:8	23
1:8-10	26n
1:9	26n
1:12	27
2:8	26n
2:16	22, 26

1 Timothy

1:17	30n
2:5f	247
6:15-16	30n
Titus	
2:13	27

Hebrews

1:3	89
2:10	199n
2:17-18	97
4:10	275
4:14-16	209

Hebrews (continued)

4:14ff	97
4:15	197-209
5:7	205
5:8	199n
5:9	199n
7:24-25	97
7:25	90n, 96n
7:26-27	200
10:19	97
10:22	97

James

1:13	197, 227
2:19	28n

1 Peter

2:21	137
2:22	200
4:15-16	204

1 John

2:16	211
3:5	200

Revelation

1:1a	273
1:1b	273
1:2b	273
1:3	269, 273-74, 276
1:5	264
1:5-9	270
1:11	274
1:12-17	236
1:19	274
2:1	274
2-3	270
2:8	274
3:1	274
3:4	276
3:7	274
3:12	274
3:14	274
5	281
7:9	276
7:14	279
12:4-5	271
12:9	271

12:17	271
13:11ff	270
14:9ff	275
14:13	269, 273, 274-75, 276
16	133
16:15	267, 275-76
17:1	276
19	277
19:9	269, 274, 276-77
20:4-6	277
20:6	269, 277-78
20:12ff	278
21	281
21:5	274
22:1-2	280
22:1ff	280
22:7	269, 273, 278-79, 280
22:8	278
22:12-13	279
22:14	269, 275, 279-80
22:16	279
22:18	279

Subject Index

A

Abba, 72
Abraham, 70, 214, 233
Adam, 23-24, 72, 84, 87, 92, 157, 190, 201n, 202, 212, 214, 216, 219-21, 227
Adler, Alfred, 177
Adonai, 26
Adoptionism, 21, 148, 155, 217n, 232
Advocate, Christ as, 57n, 96-97, 104, 172
Afterlife, 57n
Agent, Christ as, 20-25, 28-33, 36-37
Ahern, Barnabas, 45n
Ακούω, 273
Αμαρτία, 21, 202n
Ανθρώπων, 21
Αρπαγμο, 223
Ασθενεί, 217n
Alfaro, Juan, 45n
Allegro, J. M., 52n
Allen, Don Cameron, 219n, 225n
Ambrose, 81, 107n, 109, 112n, 153, 248
Amphilochius of Iconium, 109, 120, 123
Anabaptists, 257, 264, 265, 266, 267
Analogia fidei, 40
Anhypostasis, 151, 153
Anointed One, Christ as the, 3, 6n, 12, 16-17
Anselm, 74, 93, 148, 243, 248-51
Anthropology, theological, 45n, 49n, 56, 58, 65, 85, 180, 180n, 182n, 185-86
Apocrypha, 144
Apollinarianism, 85, 108,
150, 151, 152
Apollinaris, 81, 109, 112, 117, 148
Aquinas, Thomas, 231n
Aramaic, 8, 62n
Archetypal Man, Christ as the, 58, 155, 157-60, 190
Arevalo, Catalino, 45n
Arianism, 30, 81, 116, 148n, 152
Aristotelian, Aristotle, 223, 231n, 233-36, 240, 242
Arius, 81, 148
Arndt, Johann, 128, 138
Athanasian Creed, 80
Athanasius, 42n, 74, 81, 107-9, 112-13, 116-18, 148, 153, 248
Atheism, 63, 64n, 65, 73, 131
Atonement, 66n, 74, 84, 86-87, 91-94, 216, 245n, 246-47, 249-51
Atticus of Constantinople, 109
Attributes of Christ, 66n, 97, 99-100, 106, 112-13, 115-16, 118-19, 122, 148, 151, 197, 204, 223, 249-50, 279
Augsburg Confession, 30n, 54n, 71n, 80-81, 87, 90, 93, 96, 106n
Augustine, 42n, 94, 107-9, 112, 117-18, 136, 148n, 152-53

B

Babylon, 128, 272, 280n, 282
Bacht, Heinrich, 75n
Baillie, Donald, 198n
Balthasar, Hans Urs von, 45n, 66-67
Bammel, Ernst, 63n
Baptism, 5-7, 11, 173, 175, 213-14, 233
Baptist, John the, 4, 6, 11-13, 71, 272
Barth, Karl, 66-67, 68n, 84-85, 88, 100n, 141n, 156-57, 161n, 179-96, 197n, 198n, 201n
Barthélemy, Jean Dominique, 43n
Bartimaeus, 12n
Bartsch, Hans-Werner, 60n
Bauckham, Richard, 54n
Baur, F. C., 160-62
Baxter, Christina, 179n, 186n
Beasley-Murray, G. R., 61n, 276n, 280n
Beatification, 277
Beatitudes, 96, 269, 271-83
Beckwith, Isbon T., 269n, 271n
Becon, Thomas, 85, 86n, 89, 92-93, 96, 99
Beker, Johan C., 19n
Belgic Confession, 79-80, 85, 87, 88n, 89, 90n, 93, 95-96, 97n, 102-3
Belo, Fernando, 64
Bennett, John C., 181n
Benoit, Pierre, 43n, 44n
Bernard of Clairvaux, 118, 136
Bialowons, Hubert, 57n
Billerbeck, P., 52n
Binet-Sanglé, C., 172-73, 175
Binswanger, O., 171
Blessedness, 247, 275, 279-80

Blessing, 4n, 70, 130n, 131, 134, 280
Bliss, Kathleen, 181n
Bloch, Ernst, 64, 65n
Body of Christ, 22-23, 69, 82, 84, 87, 92-96, 101-3, 105, 110-11, 114, 117-24, 118n, 135, 248
Boesak, Allan, 281-82
Boff, Leonardo, 63, 64n
Bonhoeffer, Dietrich, 64n, 198n
Bonsirven, J., 52n
Borg, Marcus, 52n, 63n
Bornkamm, Günther, 61n
Bouillard, Henri, 66n
Bousset, Wilhelm, 37n
Bouyer, L., 68n
Bowman, John Wick, 165
Braaten, Carl, 54n, 61n, 68n, 142n
Bradshaw, Timothy, 54n
Brandon, S. G. F., 63
Brautmystik, 136
Brenz, Johannes, 106
Bromiley, Geoffrey W., 67n
Brown, Colin, 50n, 53n, 55n, 66n, 67n, 68n, 69n, 71n, 143n
Brown, Raymond E., 27n, 40n, 47n
Brunner, Emil, 141n, 203n 204n, 248, 251
Buber, Martin, 52-53
Bullinger, Heinrich, 83n, 95n, 98
Bultmann, Rudolf, 7n, 50n, 51, 60-62
Bundy, William E., 170n, 170-75
Burghardt, Walter, 45n
Burns, James MacGregor, 262-63
Busch, Eberhard, 67n

C

Caesarea, 5-6, 8, 109, 165
Caffarra, Carlo, 45n
Caird, G. B., 279n, 280-81
Calvin, John, 71n, 80-92, 93n, 94-96, 97n, 98-99,

101-3, 153n, 158, 215, 220, 228, 265
Calvinism, 99, 102, 153, 217n, 264, 265
Cameron, 54n, 219n
Campbell, Cynthia, 181n
Canon, 76, 211
Cantalamessa, Raniero, 45n
Cardedal, Olegario, 45n
Casamitjana, A., 44n
Cassian, John, 112n
Cazelles, Henri, 43n, 44n, 46n
Celsus, 221n
Chalcedon, 47-48, 74-75n, 80-82, 105, 107n, 108-9, 141-42, 148-49, 152, 154
Chardin, Teilhard de, 49, 56, 59, 64
Charles, R. H., 278, 280
Charlesworth, James H., 52n
Chemnitz, Martin, 105-9, 111-25
Church, 62, 65-66, 69, 72, 76, 93, 96, 119, 122, 134, 139, 145, 149, 156, 158, 159, 161, 162, 186, 195, 197, 223, 246, 251, 265, 270, 274, 276, 278, 279, 281, 282
Church, early, 3, 4, 21, 23, 25-27, 37, 61, 63n, 68n, 69n, 79-82, 111, 112, 118, 121, 141, 151-54, 169, 248, 249, 272
Church, Lutheran, 105-25, 128
Church, Reformed, 80-104
Church, Roman Catholic, 39-40, 42, 45, 49, 51n, 53, 57-58
Churchill, Winston, 238
Clayton, Philip, 54n, 68n
Cohumanity, 179-82, 185-87, 189-90, 194, 196
Collins, Anthony, 69n
Collins, Thomas Aquinas, 40n
Congar, Yves, 45n
Consensus Tigurinus, 102
Conzelmann, Hans, 61n

Covenant, 43n, 49n, 66n, 70, 180-81, 247, 276
Coverdale, Miles, 94, 95n, 101
Cox, Harvey, 64n
Creation, 11, 22, 24, 29, 39, 48n, 53, 66n, 69, 95, 106n, 141n, 144, 159, 166, 180n, 181-82, 185-87, 189, 203n, 204, 212, 214, 216-17, 222, 244, 251, 264-65, 275, 281
Cross, 3-4, 9, 11, 14, 16-17, 54n, 60, 61n, 62, 63n, 65n, 67, 83, 88, 93, 99, 134, 136, 151, 173
Cruz, Virgil, 272n, 279n
Cullmann, Oscar, 22n, 24n, 54, 54n

D

Damascenus, 107-8, 111
Damasus, of Rome, 109
Danielson, Dennis, 220n
David, 21, 71, 84, 214, 224, 233, 239
Davies, John H., 202n
Davies, W. D., 19n
Demythologization, 60, 61n
Descamps, Albert, 43n
Deutero-Pauline, 30
Devil, 92, 131, 133, 136-37, 198, 205, 208, 213-17, 214n, 220n, 222, 249, 271
Dickson, David, 201n
Dinkler, Erich, 61n
Disciples, 4n, 5, 9n, 10, 12-14, 16, 27, 52n, 62-63, 82, 84, 134, 159, 165, 231, 256, 266, 267
Divinity of Christ, 24-25n, 47, 68n, 85, 90-91, 110, 116n, 129, 137, 141-42, 146-49, 152-54, 157-60, 162, 201n, 226
Docetism, 81, 84, 94, 151
Dogma, 35, 48n, 57, 75n, 81, 141, 147
Dorner, Isaac August, 151
Dupont, Jacques, 43n, 44n

Duquoc, Chr., 68n
Díaz, José, 43n

E

Ebeling, Gerhard, 61
Ecclesiology, 70
Eckhart, 136
Eden, 24n, 216, 271
Edwards, Henry, 108n
Ego, 154, 170, 173, 200
Election, 191, 243, 267
Elijah, 6, 12-13, 221
Emesa, Eusebius of, 109
Enhypostasia, 49n
Epanalepsis, 225
Ephesus, 80, 108-9
Epiphanius, 107n
Ernst, Wilhelm, 45n
Eschatology, 4n, 6, 22, 54-
   55, 58, 60, 61n, 269-70,
   272, 274-76, 278, 281-83
Essence, divine in Christ,
   57n, 80, 84, 98, 101, 118-
   19, 122
Essenes, 71, 165-66
Estévez, Jorge Medina,
   45n
Eternity, 61n, 81, 94, 96,
   133, 146, 264
Ethics, 4n, 65, 144, 171,
   224, 231-42, 248, 251,
   253, 256, 259-65, 269,
   272-73, 275-76, 278,
   281-83
Eucharist, 101-3, 105, 120-
   21, 123
Eunomians, 81
Eunomius, 81
Euoptius, 108
Eusebius, 109, 221n
Eustachius, 109n
Eustathius, 109, 112, 113n,
   116, 120-21
Eutyches, 81, 98, 148
Eutychianism, 97-98, 102,
   105, 108-10, 112-13,
   150, 152
Evangelical, 4, 129, 165,
   197, 199, 204, 206, 249,
   252, 266
Evangelicalism, 138
Eve, 143, 211, 216, 219

Evil, 59, 74n, 136, 198,
   200-201, 204-6, 208,
   216, 270-72, 280-82
Exorcism, 12, 14-15
Extra Calvinisticum, 99-
   100, 153-54

F

Faith, 5, 25, 26n, 30, 38,
   40, 42, 53, 55, 56, 58, 60,
   62-63, 65, 68n, 69, 70,
   75-76, 79-81, 83, 88, 90,
   93, 129n, 133, 135, 170,
   172, 177, 198, 204, 209,
   219n, 220, 221, 233, 235,
   248, 257, 260
Fall, and its effects, 84,
   87, 91, 137-38, 190, 193,
   198, 201, 204, 216-17,
   219, 225
Faricy, R. L., 56n
Father, God as, 4n, 7, 25,
   28-29, 31, 36, 47, 49n,
   66-67, 72, 74n, 83, 87,
   88, 89, 92, 93, 94, 96, 97,
   99, 100, 101, 104, 111,
   116, 121, 130n, 159, 199,
   201n, 202, 206, 207, 216,
   217, 227, 231, 237, 241,
   247, 251
Ferm, Deane, 64n
Fideism, 51, 55n
Fiorenza, Elizabeth
   Schüssler, 272n
Fisher, James, 176-77
Fitzmyer, Joseph, 40n, 41,
   42n, 43, 44, 46, 46n, 47,
   47n, 48n, 49n, 50, 50n,
   51n, 52n, 53n, 54n, 56n,
   58n, 60n, 62n, 63n, 65n,
   67, 68n
Flannery, Austin, 43n
Flavianus, 109, 117
Flusser, David, 52
Fogarty, Gerald, 40n, 42n,
   69n
Fontenelle, Bernard, 221n
Formula of Concord, 80,
   81, 97, 98n, 99n, 100n,
   101n, 103, 105
Forsyth, P. T., 197-198n,
   206, 208n

Fraenkel, Peter, 106n
Franks, Robert S., 250n
Fraser, Elouise, 180n,
   181n, 187n, 193n, 194n,
   196n
Freud, Sigmund, 177
Fuchs, Ernst, 61n
Fuller, Reginald, 9n, 49n

G

Gadamer, Hans-Georg,
   51n
Gallican Confession, 79-
   81, 82n, 85, 87, 88n, 89-
   90, 93, 94n, 95-96, 95n,
   97n, 102
Galot, J., 47, 48n
Gehenna, 24n
Gelasius, 109
Genus Maiestaticum, 105,
   108, 115, 117-18, 125
Gerhardsson, B., 36
Gnosticism, 51, 157, 161
God-consciousness, 142,
   158-59, 161
Goetz, Ronald, 204
Goodman, Paul, 258
Goodwin, Doris, 238
Gorman, G. E., 76n
Gospel, 3-5, 8-9, 11-14, 16-
   17, 19, 21, 23, 31-33, 36,
   41, 43, 47n, 52-53, 55,
   60, 62n, 63, 64n, 69, 71-
   72, 83, 88, 104, 143, 151-
   52, 167, 169, 174-75,
   183, 190, 192n, 193, 213,
   219, 221n, 225, 265-67,
   274, 283
Gospels, 4, 5, 8, 25, 43, 49-
   50, 51-53, 64, 72, 76, 98,
   110, 152, 159, 161, 167-
   68, 170, 172-73, 176,
   178, 186, 211, 215, 219,
   224-25, 228
Grace, 22, 23, 83, 84, 91,
   96, 118, 139, 183, 184,
   190, 191, 200, 209, 240,
   241, 249n
Gradl, Felix, 65n
Grant, Robert, 221, 241
Green, Clifford, 181n
Green, Lowell, 128n

Gregg, Robert, 148n
Gregory of Nyssa, 107n,
    109, 111-12, 116, 120,
    123
Grelot, Pierre, 43n, 44n
Grenz, Stanley, 68n
Grillmeier, Aloys, 74n,
    109n, 154n
Groh, Dennis, 148n
Guelich, Robert, 4n, 8n,
    11n
Gutiérrez, Gustavo, 63

H

Hägglund, Bengt, 141
Hagner, Donald, 19n, 53n,
    203n
Hahn, Ferdinand, 54
Hamel, Eduard, 45n
Hamer, J., 66n
Hamerton-Kelly, Robert
    G., 23n
Hanson, John S., 6n, 13n,
    63n
Häring, Hermann, 57
Harnack, Adolf von, 4,
    23, 168, 250
Harris, Murray, 19n, 27n
Harrisville, Roy, 27n, 61n
Hawley, Lowell, 177n
Hayes, John H., 165, 166n
Hegel, G. F. W., 57n
Heick, Otto, 141n
Heidegger, Martin, 61,
    62n
Heim, Karl, 197n, 201n,
    207n
Héring, Jean, 202n
Hermeneutics, 62, 64, 143-
    44, 159n, 174, 186, 269
Herod, 63n
Herodians, 13
Heron, Alasdair, 141n
Hick, John, 37n
Higgins, Angus, 7n
Hilary of Poitiers, 81,
    107n, 109, 112n, 151,
    153-54
Hilkert, Mary, 58n
Hill, Christopher, 213n,
    215n, 217n

Hill, David, 274, 275n
Hippolytus, 109, 113, 116-
    17, 120
Hirsch, William, 172
Hitler, Adolf, 257
Hodgson, Peter, 160n
Hofmann, J. C. K. von, 53
Homoousios, 82, 148
Hooker, Morna, 7n
Hooper, John, 82, 92-93,
    96, 99, 101
Horsley, Richard, 6n,
    13n, 63n
Hudson, Wayne, 65n
Hughes, John Jay, 57n
Hultgren, Arland, 76
Hurtado, Larry, 26, 34, 37
Hutchinson, Roger, 84-87,
    89, 91-92
Hyman, Lawrence, 226
Hymns, 26-27, 37, 129
Hypostasis, 47, 85, 108,
    111, 114, 118, 150, 153,
    227

I

Ignatius, 45, 53, 67, 107,
    109
Illman, Karl-Johan, 34n
Image of God, 26, 44n, 56,
    58n, 72, 87, 90, 120, 137-
    38, 159, 166, 178, 179,
    181n, 182, 183-85, 193-
    94, 195, 227-28, 250,
    276, 280
Imhof, Paul, 57n
Imitation, 222, 261-62,
    266
Immortality, 30, 94-95,
    99, 102, 110, 121-22, 144
Immutability, 54, 87, 110,
    114, 123, 201
Impassibility, 54, 86, 91,
    110, 114-15, 119, 121
Incarnation, 20n, 24n, 34,
    37n, 47n, 48-49n, 56,
    56n, 57n, 66n, 68n, 74,
    80, 82, 83, 85-90, 92, 99-
    100, 100, 103-4, 105,
    111, 120, 143n, 148, 153,
    156, 160, 168, 198n, 207,
    212, 215, 223, 227-28,

236, 238, 242, 249,
    265-66
Incognito, 207
Inlender, Bouslaw, 45n
Inerrancy, 40, 116n
Infallibility, 41, 279
Innocence of Christ, 93,
    200, 205n
Inspiration, 39, 40, 49,
    50n, 90, 158, 167-68,
    261, 270, 271n
Intercession, 96-97, 104
Irenaeus, 53n, 89, 107n,
    109, 112-13, 115, 148n,
    157, 159
Irving, Edward, 198n
Isaiah, 8n, 11-13, 16, 41,
    53, 237
Israel, 3, 6n, 9, 14, 19, 28,
    31n, 35, 43n, 51, 70-71,
    219, 221, 224, 233, 276,
    278

J

Jacob, 88-89, 233
Jankowski, Augustyn, 43n,
    44n
Jerusalem, 21, 63n, 109,
    211, 270, 280n
Jewel, John, 82n
Jewett, Paul K., 24n, 38,
    165, 179, 179n, 181n,
    243, 246, 248n, 252, 269
Jewish-Christians, 21
Jews, 14, 25, 28, 30, 31n,
    35n, 52, 53n, 134
Judaism, 5-6, 8-9, 13, 19-
    20, 26-29, 31-38, 46, 52-
    53, 59, 63, 68n, 69, 73,
    214, 272, 274
Judgment, 22, 49n, 68n, 79,
    102, 115, 120, 171-72,
    176, 198, 203n, 217, 248,
    250-51, 277-78, 280-82
Jung, Carl, 177-78
Justes, Emma, 181n
Justification, 30, 66n, 90,
    93, 108n, 216, 233, 248,
    249n, 254, 276
Justin Martyr, 107, 116n,
    157
Jüngel, Eberhard, 67n

K

Kähler, Martin, 60, 61n
Kant, Immanuel, 147, 158
Käsemann, Ernst, 27n, 61n
Kasper, Walter, 68n, 74n
Keck, Leander, 19n, 142n, 158
Kegley, Charles, 61n
Kehl, Medard, 67n
Kelly, J. N. D., 154n, 157n
Kennedy, John F., 238-39
Kenosis, 67, 100, 151n, 223
Kern, Walter, 57n, 75n
Kiddle, Martin, 278, 279n
Kierkegaard, Søren, 204
Kim, Seyoon, 32n
Kingdom, 3-5, 4n, 11-13, 16-17, 23n, 32, 50n, 53, 54n, 56, 64n, 71, 96, 136, 169, 184, 206, 212n, 224, 259, 272, 276
Kingsbury, Jack D., 5n, 7n
Kingship, 7, 71n, 225, 265
Kirk, J. Andrew, 64n
Klausner, Joseph, 52
Kleinhans, Arduin, 42n
Kloppenburg, Bonaventura, 45n
Knight, G. A. F., 35n
Knox, John, 199n, 200
Koch, Dietrich, 14n
Kortholt, Christian, 128, 138
Kuhn, Karl, 201n
Kunkel, Fritz, 176
Kuschel, Karl-Joseph, 57n, 75n, 76
Kuyper, Abraham, 264-66
Kümmel, W. G., 75n, 76
Küng, Hans, 49n, 57n, 58n, 59n, 66n, 68n

I

Lacey, D. R. de, 26n, 29n
Lactantius, 221n
Ladd, George Eldon, 275, 276n
Lagrange, M. -J., 50
Lake, Frank, 176-77
Langford, Thomas, 226n
Lantero, E. H., 60n

Lapide, Pinchas, 35, 52n
Latimer, Hugh, 95n
Law, 12, 29, 31n, 62, 71, 92, 223, 243-45, 249, 251, 254, 265, 272
Leeuw, Gerardus van der, 156n
LeGuillou, Marie Joseph, 45n
Lehmann, Karl, 45n
Leo I, Pope, 107n, 149, 152
Leo XIII, Pope, 40
Léon-Dufour, Xavier, 51n
Lescrauwaet, Joseph, 45n
Lewalski, Barbara, 212, 217, 224, 226-27
Lewis, C. S., 244-46, 251
Leib, Michael, 226n
Lindars, Barnabas, 8n, 9n, 27n
Lindbeck, George, 143n
Lindeskog, Gösta, 34n
Logos, 49n, 110-11, 113-14, 118-19, 123, 148, 152-55, 157, 177
Logos asarkos, 153-54
Longenecker, Richard, 33n
Löser, Werner, 67n
Lubac, Henri de, 56n
Luke, 5n, 41, 63n, 143, 175, 211, 214-15, 228
Luther, Martin, 71n, 74, 82-83, 85-86, 88, 93, 94n, 105-7, 112n, 114, 118, 124, 128n, 136, 171
Lutheranism, 53, 71n, 97-103, 105-8, 114, 118, 118n, 124, 127-29, 134, 138, 267

M

Machiavelli, Nicolo, 259, 263
Machoveč, Milan, 64, 65n
Mackintosh, H. R., 198n, 201n
MacNamara, M., 52n
Macquarrie, John, 61n, 156n
Mahlmann, Theodor, 106n

Mahoney, John, 45n
Maimonides, Moses, 34n
Manchester, William, 238n
Manhood, Christ's, 93, 99, 110, 116, 199n, 228
Mani, 23, 70, 206
Mark, 3-17, 41, 63, 211
Marmorstein, Arthur, 28n, 34n
Marshall, I. H., 68n
Martelet, Gustave, 45n
Martin, Ralph, 24n
Martyrdom, 275, 277, 280
Marx, Karl, 63
Marxism, 64-65, 75n
Matthew, 5n, 36n, 41, 63n, 211, 213-15, 220, 228
Mauser, Ulrich, 36n
McDermott, Brian, 75n
McFague, Sallie, 237
McIntyre, John, 249n, 250n
McLean, Stuart, 182n
McNeill, Douglas, 208n
Mediation, 69-72, 86, 97, 155, 157-59, 247
Mediator, 22n, 29, 71-72, 82, 86-87, 91, 93, 96-97, 104, 148, 214n, 215, 248
Medina Estévez, Jorge, 45n
Meeks, M. Douglas, 65n
Meijering, E. P., 106n
Meilander, Gilbert, 232-33
Melanchthon, Philip, 105-7
Menninger, Karl, 243n
Mennonites, 266-67
Messiah, 3-7, 9-14, 15n, 16-17, 22, 24n, 46, 51, 63, 70, 71, 87, 118, 165-67, 170, 213, 219
Methodius, 109
Metz, Johannes, 65n
Metzger, Bruce, 27n
Michaelis, David, 239n
Miller, Athanasius, 42n
Ministry, 4n, 5-7, 9, 11-14, 16, 32, 58, 90, 96, 165,

174-76, 211, 215, 253, 255, 257, 260-61, 264-66, 281
Mishnah, 34n
Modernism, 39
Moffatt, James, 202n, 203n
Mohammed, 171
Moltmann, Jürgen, 35n, 54, 65n
Monism, 34
Monophysitism, 109, 152
Monotheism, 19-20, 26-29, 32-37, 38n, 272
Monothelitism, 108, 149-52
Montefiore, Hugh, 199n
Montefiore, J. C. G., 52
Mooney, C. F., 56n
Morris, Leon, 252n
Morrison, Douglas, 208n
Morrow, Lance, 244n, 246
Moses, 25, 29, 221, 226, 255
Mother, God as, 237
Moule, C. F. D., 23, 27n, 59, 63n, 68n, 205n
Mounce, Robert H., 274, 275n, 280n
Mulago, Vincent, 45n
Müller, Heinrich, 127-39
Muller, Richard A., 105-6, 124, 156n, 158n
Mustazza, Leornard, 220n

N

Narrative theology, 180, 183-84
Natures, 32, 56, 80-81, 85, 98-100, 107, 110-14, 117-19, 121-23, 141-42, 146-55, 217, 226
Nazianzus, Gregory of, 107n, 109, 112, 117, 122, 154, 198
Neo-Kantianism, 62n
Neo-orthodoxy, 156
Nestorius, 81, 97-98, 101, 107n, 108-9, 112-13, 114n, 148, 150, 152, 154, 155, 217n
Neufeld, Karl, 76n
Neusner, Jacob, 6n
Neve, J. L., 141n

Nicene Creed, Nicaea, 57, 80-81, 107, 109n, 148n
Niebuhr, Reinhold, 198n, 200
Niebuhr, Richard R., 155, 156
Niemöller, Martin, 177
Nouwen, Henri, 208n

O

O'Collins, Gerald, 45n, 58n
Oedipus, 218
Ogden, Schubert, 61n
Ogletree, Thomas, 192n
Olthuis, James, 236
Omnipotence, 101-2, 123
Omnipresence, 99, 101, 153
Ontology, 24-26, 28-30, 32, 34-35, 49, 54, 152-53
Orthodoxy, 47, 79-82, 106, 109-10, 117, 119-21, 127-29, 128n, 134, 136, 138, 142, 147, 149, 150-52, 155, 156n, 161-62, 167, 197-98, 227
Osiander, Adreas, 71n, 87

P

Paget, Nathan, 213
Pannenberg, Wolfhart, 54-55, 67n, 68, 71n
Paradise, 86, 211-13, 214n, 215-17, 218n, 219, 220n, 226n, 227
Parousia, 8, 277
Patristic theology, 47, 49n, 53, 72, 91-92, 106-7, 111, 112n, 123-24, 147-50, 152-57, 221
Paul of Samosata, 148
Pelikan, Jaroslav, 105, 108n, 148n, 166
Perkins, William, 128, 138, 213, 214n, 215, 219n, 222
Perrin, Norman, 9n
Person of Christ, Jesus', 15n, 22, 23, 24n, 32, 35, 47, 48, 49n, 55, 56, 65,

66-67n, 68n, 69, 71, 72, 74, 80-81, 85, 92, 94, 98-100, 103, 104, 112-13, 119, 122, 129, 137-38, 142, 144, 146-58, 161, 198, 216, 226-27, 250, 266-67
Peter Lombard, 115
Petersen, Norman, 17n
Pfammatter, Josef, 76n
Philippi, 5-6, 8, 165
Philippians, 21, 89n
Philo, 57n, 112, 116, 147, 161
Physeis, 47, 153-54
Pietism, 128-29, 131, 136, 138, 255
Pilate, 83, 188n
Pirot, Louis, 39n
Pistis, 157
Plato, 206, 232, 257
Platonism, 250
Plutarch, 221n
Politics, 4n, 53, 63, 65-66, 166, 219, 224, 243, 253-67, 281-82
Pollard, T. E., 47n
Praxis, 37n, 58n, 63-65, 266
Prayer, 25n, 26, 26n, 41, 96, 104, 129n, 137-138, 205, 235, 260, 281
Preaching, 3, 4n, 37n, 42-43, 129, 131, 136, 143, 155, 263, 272
Predestination, 94, 158n
Preexistence of Christ, 20n, 21n, 23-24, 69, 223
Proclamation, 4n, 11, 49n, 214, 272
Prophecy, 69n, 273-74, 275n, 278-81, 280n
Prophet, Christ as, 11-13, 53, 58, 60, 70-71, 171, 212, 271n, 273, 280n
Propitiation, 94, 96, 246-47
Protoevangelium, 214
Prudentius, 221n
Psalms, 41, 254, 281
Psyche, 165, 167, 176
Psychiatry, 172, 174-77, 245

Psychology, 165-70, 176-78
Ptolemais, 109
Puritans, 213, 219, 223

Q

Quasten, Johannes, 107n, 109n
Qumran, 52, 62n, 166

R

Radzinowicz, Mary Ann, 220n
Rahner, Karl, 49n, 56, 57n, 59, 65n
Räisänen, Heiko, 14n
Ranke, Leopold von, 50n
Ransom, 71, 247
Rasmussen, Emil, 171, 175
Ratschow, Carl Heinz, 65n
Ratzinger, Joseph, 45n, 64n
Recapitulation, 157, 211
Reconciliation, 21, 90-93, 97, 104, 148, 157, 159, 186-87, 248n, 252
Redeker, Martin, 141, 142n, 143n, 144-145
Redemption, 13-14, 22, 55n, 59, 65, 87-88, 92-93, 115, 127, 129n, 133-34, 141n, 143-47, 152, 155, 162, 215, 217, 227, 241-42, 247, 272, 280
Reformation, 84, 87-88, 99, 248
Reid, J. K. S., 204n
Reimarus, Hermann, 50n, 75n
Religion, 51-52, 63, 79, 156-57, 172-73, 194, 272
Renaissance, 259
Resurrection, 16, 21, 32, 54-56, 58, 61n, 62, 68n, 69, 83, 87, 94-95, 97, 104, 110, 119-20, 122, 165, 167-69, 277-78
Revelation, 11n, 43, 47-49, 58n, 66n, 67, 88-90, 97, 104, 145, 151, 226

Revelation, Book of, 72, 269-83
Rey, B., 68n
Richardson, Alan, 63n
Ridderbos, Herman, 23n
Ritschl, Albrecht, 250n
Roberts, Robert C., 207n
Robinson, Edward, 61n
Robinson, J. A. T., 197n, 206n
Robinson, James M., 50n, 61n, 62n
Romans, 14, 21, 30n, 37, 247
Roosevelt, Franklin, 238
Rosato, Philip J., 66n
Runia, Klaas, 57n, 58n

S

Sabellius, 81
Saber, Georges, 45n
Sabourin, Leopold, 54
Sacrifice, 38, 68, 87, 91-93, 226, 232, 240-41, 246, 276, 282
Sadler, William, 176
Safer, Elaine, 220n
Salvation and Salvation history, 12, 17, 32, 53-55, 58, 65, 67, 68n, 70-75, 86-87, 90, 92, 94-95, 104, 110, 114, 128, 130n, 134, 144, 145, 190-191, 193, 195, 217, 247, 249-50, 275-76
Samosatenes, 81
Sanders, E. P., 52n
Sanders, Jack, 282, 283n
Sandmel, Samuel, 52n, 53
Satisfaction, 86-87, 92-93, 130, 248-51
Sattler, Gary, 128n
Saul, 28
Schaefer, H., 174
Schaff, Philip, 79n, 94n
Schillebeeckx, Edward, 49n, 58-60, 65n
Schlatter, Adolf, 205n
Schleiermacher, Friedrich, 71n, 141-62, 197, 201n, 205n
Schmidt, K. L., 61

Schmithals, Walter, 61n
Schoeps, H.-J., 34n
Schönmetzer, A., 43n
Schoof, Ted, 58n
Schoonenberg, Piet, 48-49
Schreiter, Robert J., 58n
Schröder, Richard, 106n
Schultz, Howard, 212n
Schulz, Sigfried, 7n
Schürmann, Heinz, 45n
Schweitzer, Albert, 50n, 167, 175
Scots Confession, 79-81, 82n, 85, 87, 88n, 90, 92, 95, 96n, 102-3
Scotus, Duns, 151
Scriver, Christian, 128, 138
Secret, Messianic, 5, 9, 14-16, 71,
Segal, Alan, 24n
Segundo, Juan Luis, 64n
Self-consciousness, Jesus', 144-45, 159-60, 172
Semmelroth, Otto, 45n
Seraphim, 237
Servant, Jesus as, 7, 11, 53, 67n, 71-72, 90, 165, 166
Severianus, 109
Sharkey, Michael, 45n
Shawcross, John T., 212n
Siegman, E. F., 42n
Simmonds, James D., 220n
Simons, Menno, 83-84
Sin, Atonement for, 71, 74, 85, 87, 91-93, 95-96, 111, 115, 131, 144, 147, 191, 199, 204, 208-9, 218, 244, 248-52
Sinlessness, Jesus', 83, 85, 87, 93, 118, 155, 192n, 197-209
Sinai, 29, 265
Skinner, B. F., 259
Smalley, Stephen, 27-28n
Sobrino, Jon, 63, 64n
Solomon, 221
Spener, Philipp Jakob, 128, 138
Spicq, Ceslaus, 204n
Spinoza, Baruch, 50n
Spirit of God, 7, 11, 21, 23n, 25, 35n, 37n, 56, 58,

65, 66, 69, 71-72, 79, 85,
  87, 90, 99, 100, 102, 129,
  198n, 215, 233, 248, 274,
  276
Stancarus, Francis, 115
Steadman, John M., 217n
Stein, Arnold, 226n
Stendahl, Krister, 201n
Stoeffler, F. Ernest, 129
Strack, Hermann, 28n, 52n
Strauss, D. F., 69n, 142,
  158n, 160-62, 168
Strlè, Anton, 45n
Suffering of Christ, 7-10,
  13, 53, 54, 58n, 71-72,
  83, 85-87, 91-92, 98,
  110, 113-15, 124, 131,
  134-36, 165, 166, 202-8,
  218-19, 250
Suhard, Cardinal, 42n
Swete, H. B., 270n, 277
Swidler, Leonard, 57n
Sykes, S. W., 67n

T

Talmud, 28n
Tauler, Johann, 136
Taylor, Dick, 226n
Taylor, Jeremy, 231, 233
Taylor, Vincent, 5n, 24,
  25, 26, 54, 246-48
Temptation of Christ, 86,
  169, 197-209, 211-28
Tertullian, 107n, 154
Theissen, Gerhard, 15n,
  63n
Theodicy, 216, 227, 271
Theodore of Mopsuestia,
  152
Theodoret of Cyrus, 105-
  25
Theologia crucis, 47n, 114,
  124
Theosis, 108n
Theotokos, 109, 114n
Thielicke, Helmut, 197n,
  199-200, 201n, 206, 207n
Thoma, Clemens, 76n
Thompson, Francis, 241
Thompson, John, 67n,
  179n, 182n
Thuren, Jukka, 34n

Tillard, Jean-Marie, 45n
Tillesse, Georges, 14n
Tillich, Paul, 142, 155n,
  237, 254
Tödt, Heinz, 7n
Tolstoy, Leo, 207
Torah, 24n
Totalitarianism, 243, 246
Transgression, 96, 223
Trinity, 35, 38n, 47n, 48n,
  49n, 54n, 57n, 64n, 67,
  73n, 75, 79-81, 86, 100,
  103, 106n, 110, 136, 147,
  154n, 181-82, 181n,
Troeltsch, Ernst, 192n
Tuckett, Christopher, 8n,
  14n, 15n

U

Ubiquity, 101, 105-6, 117,
  123-24
Ullmann, Carl, 197n,
  203n, 206
Union, hypostatic, 81, 85,
  98-100, 108, 110-11,
  114-19, 122, 136-37,
  146, 150-54, 157, 227
Universalism, 66n
Urbild, 155, 157, 159

V

Vagaggini, Cipriano, 45n
Valentinus, 81
Vermes, Geza, 8n, 52, 53n
Vicarious sacrifice, 91,
  94, 104, 247
Vielhauer, Philipp, 9n
Vigilius, 114
Vorgrimler, Herbert, 57n

W

Wadell, Paul, 242n
Wainwright, Arthur, 35n
Waldrop, Charles, 67n
Walgrave, Jan, 45n
Wallmann, Johannes,
  128n
Weeden, Theodore, 7n
Weinsheimer, J. C., 51n
Weiss, Bernhard, 174

Weiss, Johannes, 4n
Westcott, Brooke Foss,
  201n, 202n, 203n, 208n
Whiteley, Denys, 26n,
  32n
Wiederkehr, Dietrich,
  75n
Wilckens, Ulrich, 27n
Williams, Stephen, 54n
Williamson, Ronald,
  197n, 199n
Williamson, George, 225n
Willis, Robert E., 181n
Wolff, Hannah, 166, 176,
  178

Y

Yadin, Y., 52n
Yahweh, 7, 25-26
Yoder, John H., 255-58,
  265
Young, Frances, 107n, 109n

Z

Zealots, 63
Zeitlin, Irving, 52n
Zwingli, Ulrich, 83, 85-
  86, 89, 91-92, 96, 98-99,
  101, 105